TO KEEP THE WATERS TROUBLED

TO KEEP THE WATERS TROUBLED

The Life of Ida B. Wells

Linda O. McMurry

OXFORD

UNIVERSITY PRESS

OXFORD

UNIVERSITY PRESS

Oxford New York
Athens Auckland Bangkok Bogotá Buenos Aires
Calcutta Cape Town Chennai Dar es Salaam
Delhi Florence Hong Kong Istanbul Karachi
Kuala Lumpur Madrid Melbourne Mexico City
Mumbai Nairobi Paris São Paulo Shanghai
Singapore Taipei Tokyo Toronto Warsaw

and associated companies in
Berlin Ibadan

mw

Copyright © 1998 by Linda O. McMurry

First published by Oxford University Press, Inc., 1998
198 Madison Avenue, New York, New York 10016

First issued as an Oxford University Press paperback, 2000

Oxford is a registered trademark of Oxford University Press

Library of Congress Cataloging-in-Publication Data
McMurry, Linda O.
To keep the waters troubled :
the life of Ida B. Wells/
by Linda O. McMurry.
p. cm. Includes bibliographical references and index.
ISBN 0-19-508812-3 (Cloth)
ISBN 0-19-513927-5 (Pbk.)
1. Wells-Barnett, Ida B., 1862–1931.
2. Afro-American women civil rights workers—Biography.
3. Civil rights workers—United States—Biography.
4. Journalists—United States—Biography.
5. United States—Race relations. I. Title.
E185.97.W55M38 1998 323?092—dc21
[B] 98-6068

1 3 5 7 9 10 8 6 4 2

Printed in the United States of America
on acid-free paper

To Allen W. Jones,
who made a historian out of a housewife,
and to
John A. Edwards,
who has brought that historian much happiness

⸻⸙⸻

CONTENTS

PREFACE

W hen I began this study, I had no idea how much I would discover. Very few events of any significance to African Americans happened between the 1890s and 1930 without the involvement of this remarkable woman. Among the most difficult tasks has been deciding how to capture the complexity of Ida B. Wells and the times in which she lived in less than a five-volume work. One decision I made was to give relatively more attention to the first half of her adult life. My major reason was the emphasis that she gave to her later life in her autobiography. I decided to summarize and evaluate incidents that she discussed fully—including her second British tour. Events to which she devoted entire chapters I sought to place into context and examine other participants' accounts. Also, I became convinced that Wells's personality and career were rooted in the environment and experiences of her young adulthood, so I tried to recapture those formative years in much greater detail.

I would like also to note that although I believe such terms as race, white, and black are biological nonsense, I have used those terms in the only way they make sense: as socially defined categories, flawed by prejudice.

Every scholar owes many people for direct and indirect help. Any accounting of my debts will be incomplete for reasons of limited space and memory. One category of aid has come from the many people over the

years who have studied and written about Ida B. Wells. The greatest debt is
to those who have made her words available and easily accessible. These
include her daughter Alfreda Duster, who edited and struggled for years to
have her mother's autobiography published, and Miriam DeCosta-Willis,
who did the same for Wells's diaries. DeCosta-Willis provided invaluable
service with her tedious work in identifying the many people mentioned
only by initials in Wells's diary of the 1880s. At the Memphis Public Library, I found a very useful bibliography compiled by Albert Lee Kreiling.
Numerous scholars have examined Wells-Barnett from various perspectives. I found all useful; but after skimming each, I put them aside and
wrote directly from my own research notes to prevent being overly influenced by any. Thus, my debts to many are not adequately reflected in
my footnotes, and I have appended a bibliography of the works on Wells-
Barnett that I found most useful.

Because Wells-Barnett participated in so many major events and was
involved with so many issues, I am also grateful for the research of others
regarding the historical context of the times in which she lived. I have tried
to list the most helpful sources in my notes (without making the notes
longer than the text). Ironically, my most serious sins of omission will probably be of those works that became such a major influence on my understanding of the era that it is almost impossible to separate their ideas from
my own. That group includes, but is certainly not limited to, the writings
of John Hope Franklin, Louis Harlan, David Levering Lewis, August
Meier, Elliott Rudwick, Paula Giddings, Howard Rabinowitz, Darlene
Clark Hine, George Frederickson, and C. Vann Woodward.

Although many people have noted the relative neglect of Wells-
Barnett by scholars, there has been a virtual explosion of scholarship in recent years. The variety of perspectives and interpretations is a testament to
both her complexity and importance. I am convinced that as scholars continue to study her, people will realize that it may be more appropriate to
compare such recognized titans as Booker T. Washington and W. E. B. Du
Bois to her, rather than the other way around. Since these major male
African American leaders have been the subject of several extensive bi-
ographies, I hope and expect the same for Wells-Barnett. The extent and
power of her words are staggering—and open to multiple interpretations.
Thus, I decided to expose readers to as many of those words as feasible
through extensive quotations. I hope her words will inspire others to explore some of her many writings, which are now widely reprinted.

There have been so many who have provided direct assistance over so long a period—many whose names I never learned—that I am afraid of forgetting someone. In some archives as many as a dozen staff members provided help. Rather than risk leaving names out, I choose to thank the entire archival or museum staffs of the following: National Archives, Library of Congress, University of Chicago, Chicago Historical Society, Illinois State Archives, Tennessee State Library and Archives, Marshall County Historical Museum, Memphis Public Library, University of Memphis, Rust College, Howard University, Wilberforce University, and Duke University. I am also grateful for the published and microform editions of the papers of such individuals and groups as Booker T. Washington, the NAACP, Albion Tourgee, W. E. B. Du Bois, the American Temperance Movement, and Marcus Garvey as well as numerous newspapers. This acknowledgment brings me to the two agencies that undoubtedly provided the greatest assistance: the Interlibrary Loan Department at North Carolina State University and the Microforms Collections Department at the University of North Carolina at Chapel Hill. The individuals to whom I owe the most are my research assistants over the years—Ellen Turco, Janine Cairo, Shana Hutchins, Seulky Shin, Joanna Grant, and Parie Hines. I would also like to acknowlege the help of my colleagues, especially John David Smith and William C. Harris at North Carolina State University and James Hunt at Shaw University; Peter Ginna, Allison Arieff, Isabella Robertson, and Kim Torre-Tasso at Oxford University Press; and on a more personal level, all the friends and family who have formed my cheering section in times of discouragement—especially my husband John, whose moral support and patience through repeated delays for the Bahamas baptism of our new boat is truly appreciated.

INTRODUCTION

⸻ ⚭ ⸻

A fter the Civil War, many extraordinary African Americans rapidly rose from obscurity and bondage to incredible positions of fame and autonomy. Outstanding ability often overcomes adversity, but rarely have so many climbed so far so quickly with so little help. Among the numerous stories of personal courage and fortitude, few are more heroic than that of Ida B. Wells. Born into slavery and orphaned as a teenager, Wells took charge of herself and her younger siblings, supporting them by teaching. In an age when women were often considered dependent on male protectors, both the insecurity and the liberation of relative independence profoundly shaped Wells as she sought to balance her desires and multiple duties. She felt a keen sense of responsibility to a number of people and causes. Often she was asked to chose between competing ideals: support of black "manhood" and the need for strong black women; race unity and belief in the oneness of humanity; political realities and personal integrity; racial uplift and class identity; tolerance and high moral standards; integration and black autonomy; nurturing her family and crusading for justice. Wells supported many reform movements only to discover that white leaders of such causes as woman suffrage and temperance expected her to put their movements' interests ahead of the struggle for black rights. This she refused to do. For almost half her life she remained single and struggled with the social expectations of womanhood, while emerging as an activist more militant than most of her male colleagues.

Wells was barely twenty years old when she sued a railroad company in 1883 for expelling her from a first-class coach. Her account of the case launched her into a part-time career in journalism, which became her full-time vocation when the white school board in Memphis dismissed her for publicly criticizing its actions. As editor of the Memphis *Free Speech*, Wells began a crusade against lynching. Her editorials infuriated local whites, who eventually closed down her newspaper and forced her exile. Moving to New York, she immersed herself in the antilynching cause, which included two British lecture tours.

For several years in the 1890s, no African American, except for Frederick Douglass, received more press attention than Ida B. Wells. She played a role similar to the aging abolitionist, arousing British public opinion against the new evil of lynching as Douglass had against the old evil of slavery. Both were entertained by royalty and other prominent people and launched British movements that brought unwanted attention to America's racial problems. When Douglass died in 1895, Wells was his logical heir apparent; they had closely collaborated on several projects. She was better known than W. E. B. Du Bois and more ideologically compatible with Douglass than Booker T. Washington—the two men who eventually became the main contenders to fill Douglass's shoes. However, Wells had a major problem: She was a woman.

In post-Reconstruction America, black women faced a serious dilemma. White southerners were attempting to repeal the advances made by African Americans by stripping black men of not only their power but also their pride. Southern white men defined manhood partly as the ability to protect their "helpless" women. To deny black manhood, they forbade any sexual contact between black men and white women, while claiming for themselves the right of sexual access to black women. Lynching was a major tool for the emasculation of black men. To support their men and to counteract the challenges to black manhood, black women usually assumed some of the roles played by white women in this patriarchal society. They, too, were expected to be submissive and to lend support rather than to provide leadership. For a woman to be spokesperson and leader for African Americans belittled black "manhood."

The first step by Wells into the role of spokesperson grew out of her rage over the lynching of a close friend in 1892. The horror of that event focussed Wells's attention and anger on the evil of mob violence. She correctly diagnosed the major purpose of lynching in the 1890s as an antidote to black success rather than the result of black degradation, a form of racial terrorism. Few African Americans were lynched prior to the Civil War because of slaves' monetary value as well as slavery's effectiveness as a system of racial control and domination. After emancipation, white southerners increasingly used lynching to intimidate black men. The practice reached its peak in the 1890s, the same time whites were forging a new system of racial subordination based on segregation and disfranchisement. That decade also witnessed the growing use of rape charges as the justification for lynching.

Wells's attack on the lynch law focused on refuting the prevailing notion that lynching was needed to defend white women from the lust of black men. She was not the first to attack the rape myth, but she became the loudest and most persistent voice for truth. Thus while white men proclaimed themselves protectors of their women's purity, a woman emerged as the defender of black men's honor and lives. This role reversal caused controversy, and Wells provoked animosity as well as admiration. Further undermining her ability to follow expected gender roles was her assertiveness. Her uncompromising militancy made most male leaders look timid. Although many African Americans supported Wells's efforts, from the beginning of her career some black men challenged her femininity. Their attacks sometimes took the form of vocalizing doubts about her purity and propriety, both of which were crucial to her ability to support herself as well as to advance the cause of her people. Wells, therefore, struggled to balance her need to be perceived as a "lady" with her natural militancy.

Although Wells chafed under the restrictions resulting from her gender, she consistently placed race interests above gender issues. Feeling a divided duty to the fight for equal rights by women and by African Americans, she participated in both movements. Black women of her era typically saw racism as a greater evil than sexism, and Wells was not an exception. More than most women of either race, however, she was ambivalent about her gender identification. Her actions challenged gender roles largely because she identified with men rather than women. Wells often seemed to view other women as if she were an outsider who found most women to be weak, shallow, and petty. As a result she got along better with men, who elected her to offices in national organizations while women's groups did not. Nevertheless, she encountered male resentment of her leadership roles and, consequently, felt alienated somewhat from both sexes. Being a black woman activist required a delicate balancing act, and Wells could not walk the tightrope as deftly as some other women.

Her militancy also placed Wells out of sync with the growing moderation of black leaders. After causing her exile from Memphis, Tennessee, her temper led her tongue to alienate even those who were ideologically compatible. Wells was a person, however, who could not be ignored. Very little happened in the struggles for black and women's rights without her participation from the 1890s to her death in 1931. She was active in the founding of numerous organizations, such as the NAACP, and collaborated with many leaders, including Du Bois, William Monroe Trotter, Henry McNeal Turner, and Marcus Garvey. At the same time, she worked with such white women activists as Susan B. Anthony and Jane Addams. In the end she chastised most coworkers for compromising and founded her own groups in her new hometown of Chicago. Her inability to work successfully with most people meant that she became alienated from movements and failed to get appropriate credit for her work both during her life and for a long time afterward. Nevertheless, she played a very important role in history by being, in her own words, the "disturbing element which kept the waters troubled."

Her personal life was almost as frustrating as her public one. Wells sought to play numerous roles simultaneously and was often torn between her desires and her responsibilities. Forced at sixteen to become the head of the household, she became accustomed to a degree of independence that would have been threatened by marriage. Her relationships with men were problematic personally as well as professionally. For almost half her life she remained single, unable to find a man she could respect who did not threaten her independence. When she finally found a man with whom she was compatible, Wells was in her thirties and at the peak of her career. Marriage and motherhood limited—but did not stop—her activism. Soon after her first child was born, her suffragist friend Susan B. Anthony complained that Wells "had a special call for special work" and that motherhood gave her "a divided duty." She fought until her death to fulfill her duties as woman, African American, and activist.

TO KEEP THE WATERS TROUBLED

1

Childhood and Early Adulthood

"A *happy, light-hearted schoolgirl*"

The remarkable journey of Ida Wells began during the Civil War in the northern Mississippi town of Holly Springs. It was not the most auspicious place for an African American to be born, for Mississippi has been the site of horrific incidents of white racism and violence. In the antebellum period, slaves from other states feared being "sold down to Mississippi"; later, some of the bloodiest chapters of the civil rights movement would be written there. Nevertheless, Ida B. Wells was born at a time and place in Mississippi that offered African Americans cause for hope as well as discouragement. Her parents also emerged from slavery with more opportunity than many.

Although slavery was hardly a benevolent institution, as white southerners sought to paint it, some slaves were more privileged than others. Sources of privilege included kinship with the master, acquisition of valuable skills, and the opportunity to be "hired out" in cities. Ida's father, James Wells, apparently benefited from all three. His master/father owned a plantation in Tippah County and had no children by his white wife, "Miss Polly." Like many slave owners, he had a black "family" with a slave—Peggy. Born in 1840, James Wells was their first child and was cherished by his father, who was relatively old when James was born. Such liaisons were deeply resented by most slave owners' white wives, who felt the bitterness of betrayal and the humiliation of seeing tangible, public proof of their husbands' infidelity in the skin color of the children. These wives' wrath was sometimes unleashed on the slave women who shared their husband's attention, whether or not the bondswomen were willing participants in the relationships. James Wells recalled how Miss Polly had gotten someone to strip and whip Peggy the day after her husband died.[1]

Before his death, James's father had taken him to Holly Springs, in northern Mississippi, to be apprenticed to a carpenter. Thus at age eighteen, James Wells gained a valuable skill and a measure of independence as a hired-out slave living in town. Masters hired out their slaves to other people for a variety of reasons—usually for compensation or for their slaves to acquire certain skills. Hired-out slaves enjoyed a wide range of freedom, and some received very little. Life in cities and towns, however, gave many hired-out slaves some freedom from supervision, and most found more autonomy than the slaves on their masters' plantations.[2]

In Holly Springs, Wells learned carpentry and acquired a mate at the residence of a contractor and builder named Bolling. He fell in love with Elizabeth Warrenton, the cook in the Bolling household. As slaves they could not legally marry, but they lived as man and wife and legalized their vows after emancipation—as many slaves did. Unlike James, Elizabeth (born in 1844) had not been sheltered from bondage's worst abuses. One of ten children born to slaves in Virginia, she vividly recalled receiving beatings from her masters. She also suffered one of the worst abuses of slavery: She and two of her sisters were sold and separated from their family. Such separations were painful reminders of slaves' vulnerability and cut them off from the very people who provided comfort and support to cope with the harsh realities of slavery. Like so many others, Elizabeth sent inquiries back to Virginia after emancipation in a vain attempt to find her lost family.[3]

Ida Bell Wells was the first child born to the couple. Her birth on 16 July 1862 was in the midst of the Civil War. At first the Union and the Confederacy carefully tried to separate the issue of slavery from their war aims, but the process of the war ultimately destroyed the system of human bondage. When Union troops arrived nearby, many slaves sought to liberate themselves by fleeing behind Union lines. After a period of confusion over the status of these fugitives (at first, slaves were often returned to their Confederate masters), the U.S. Congress directed that escaped slaves of rebel masters could be considered contraband of war and proclaimed free. Nevertheless, when Union troops moved out of a region, some of the newly freed slaves found themselves recaptured in the web of slavery. For many southerners of all shades, the transition from slavery to freedom was chaotic and confusing. Ida Wells's birthplace was the scene of more-than-average confusion.[4]

Holly Springs was captured and recaptured by the two armies, changing hands at least fifty-nine times during the war. Its geography and its history made the city's experiences of the war and Reconstruction both typical and atypical of most of the state. When Ida was born, Holly Springs had existed for only a few decades. In 1832 the Chickasaw ceded the region, known as the Chickasaw Cession, to the federal government. Four years later the territory was divided into counties—the largest of which was Marshall County with Holly Springs as its seat. While still carving the city from the wilderness, its settlers sought to make it a cultural center. Even before the town was incorporated, residents voted in a town meeting to establish the Holly Springs Female Institute, the first of a number of educational institutions. By 1850 the county was spending more on higher education than all the rest of the state, excluding the budget of the University of Mississippi.[5] A history of the state noted that in 1891 Holly Springs, called the "City of Flowers," was "widely known for the hospitality and culture of its people."[6]

One reason for the culture and prosperity in Holly Springs was the arrival of successful cotton planters, who had moved west for more fertile soil, as well as many others who grew cotton on a smaller scale. "King Cotton" demanded slaves; the 1840 county population of 17,536 included 8,260 slaves and 8 free blacks. As a new town with many land claim cases, the city also was the home to numerous lawyers. Both lawyers and planters tended to join the Whig party, which dominated the town's early politics—until the rise of the slavery issue in national debate. The controversy destroyed the party there as elsewhere and "no compromise" Democrats rose in power.[7]

By 1860 the county's population had grown to almost 29,000, including 1,295 slave owners and 17,439 slaves; the free black population remained at 8.[8] Now a minority, whites became even more determined to retain slavery as a source of control and power, and Marshall County played an integral role in Mississippi's march toward secession. One of its residents was coauthor of the state's ordinance of secession, and when it was signed on 9 January 1861, the county provided five signatories—more than any other county.[9] Thus a year and a half before Ida Wells's birthday, her parents and the rest of Holly Springs probably waited anxiously for the outcome of the bold move toward disunion.

Downtown Holly Springs at the time of Ida B. Wells's birth (courtesy of Marshall County Historical Museum).

Because whites were outnumbered, a constant fear of racial revolt lingered in many minds. Such fear was intensified by the uncertainties of war. Early in the hostilities planters summoned home some of their hired-out slaves. The state legislature also moved to control slaves by penalizing masters who granted their bondsmen and bondswomen too much freedom. Even so, rumors spread like epidemics, fanning the fever of fear with lurid descriptions of insurrection plots. Hysteria required no tangible evidence. The month Ida was born, the provost marshal of Natchez reported the hanging of forty African Americans during the preceding year, foreshadowing the postwar terror and murder of black men to retain white control.[10] By the end of the century only the dominant excuse had changed— from insurrection to rape.

At first Holly Springs seemed to have been spared the worst of the hysteria and war. Not until about two weeks before Ida's birth in July 1862 did the first significant Civil War skirmish occur near Holly Springs. A considerable number of Confederate troops remained in the area until later that fall when Union General Ulysses S. Grant began moving troops into northern Mississippi in preparation for the Vicksburg campaign. Before his army reached Holly Springs, Confederate forces partially dismantled the local foundry and retreated to a more defensible position. Grant proceeded to establish a large supply depot in the city. Weapons, ammunition, food, and other materials filled every public building as well as churches, the Masonic Temple, and even a few private homes. While he briefly made his headquarters there, the city's black population celebrated a rare degree of freedom.[11]

As Grant's army moved deeper into slave territory, slaves began coming in larger numbers to the Union camps. To handle the hordes, Grant asked Chaplain John Eaton to establish a camp for the "contrabands." Eaton chose Grand Junction, Tennessee, as the camp's location—just across the state line from Holly Springs. Eaton later described the scene of slaves "coming garbed in rags or silks, with feet shod or bleeding, individually or in families and larger groups,—an army of slaves and fugitives, pushing its way irresistibly toward an army of fighting men."[12] Although the Wells family and many other slaves chose to remain in Holly Springs, the camp's nearby location had an ameliorating impact on slavery in that city.

Late in the fall of 1862, Grant's army moved south, leaving only twenty-five hundred troops in Holly Springs. Until that time Holly Springs had suffered little damage, although the town and the surrounding countryside had changed hands frequently. On a plantation near Holly Springs, eighteen-year-old Cordelia Scales wrote letters describing the changing parade of Union and Confederate troops that camped in her yard. Both seem to have foraged—but not unduly.[13] Some outlying plantations suf-

Rebel Armory at Holly Springs during the Civil War (courtesy of Marshall County Historical Museum).

fered more than others, but major destruction of the town began with the raid by Confederate General Earl Van Dorn on 20 December 1862. Van Dorn's men quickly routed the outnumbered and unsuspecting federal troops in Holly Springs. Knowing they had little time, Confederate soldiers rapidly looted the easily transportable federal supplies. Then, from early morning until 4:00 P.M., they set fire to the many buildings housing the remaining stores. Exploding ammunition caused further destruction and some deaths. J. G. Deupree, a participant, described the scene as

> wild and exciting: Federals running; Confederates yelling and pursuing; tents and houses burning; torches flaming; guns popping; sabres clanking; negroes and abolitionists begging for mercy; women, *in dreaming robes* and with disheveled hair floating in the morning breeze, shouting encouragement to the raiders; a mass of frantic, frightened human beings.[14]

Of all the "frantic, frightened human beings" few were more scared than the "negroes and abolitionists begging for mercy." James and Elizabeth Wells may well have feared for their six-month-old infant.

The destruction was not yet complete. Two days later federal troops returned. One Iowa soldier watched sadly as every "portion of the *fated* city seemed given over to *pillage* and destruction and no hand was raised to save anything from the general *sack and ruin*." He was especially disturbed by the sacrileges committed in a church and the "women and children standing in their homes wailing with the most piteous cries."[15] Before Confederate forces in Mississippi surrendered on 4 May 1865, Holly Springs had witnessed more than a dozen major skirmishes. After so much chaos and confusion, the county's slaves must have wondered if freedom had actually come to stay, while whites worried about what would replace slavery. Former masters and former slaves warily sought to redefine their new relationships.

After the war was over, James Wells accepted Bolling's invitation to continue working for him. Like most freed people, Wells sought to test and taste the varied fruits of freedom. He first exercised those rights that white southerners had grudgingly conceded—legalizing his marriage and seeking education for his family. The Wells family continued to grow in the years following the war, and eventually Ida had four brothers and three sisters. Both parents were eager for their children to go to school. Former slaves realized that education had been forbidden because it was a key to freedom and a source of white power. Most slave children had worked at an early age; their freed fathers wanted them to have childhoods more like those of their former masters' children. Ida Wells later recalled, "Our job was to go to school and learn all we could."[16]

She began school at such an early age that she could not remember when or where she started. Her earliest recollections were of reading the newspaper to her father and his friends and of her mother going to school with the children until she was able to read the Bible. Students of all ages clustering around a limited number of books in small schools was a common sight to the newly freed slaves during Reconstruction. Whether Ida's father learned to read is unclear. Her reading the newspaper to him and his friends could have represented a father's desire to show off the accomplishments of his offspring or his inability to read for himself. Like many freed heads of households, James Wells was undoubtedly busy and apparently did not attend school with his family. However, he may have learned to read and write from his father or as an apprentice. Regardless, Wells was deeply involved in education because he was one of the trustees of Shaw University, the school Ida attended in Holly Springs.

In addition to exercising their rights to marriage and education, freedmen eagerly embraced the right to vote. For the entire Republican Reconstruction period in Mississippi (1867–1875), African Americans comprised a majority of the county's population and overwhelmingly supported Republicans despite white Democrats' efforts to win their votes. The Democrats used both carrots and sticks to woo black voters. Many used economic intimidation to persuade African Americans to vote for Democrats. James Wells was one victim of such tactics. When Bolling found out that Wells had not voted Democratic, he locked Wells out of his shop. Wells, however, was not easily intimidated. Without saying a word to anyone, he bought his own tools, rented a house, and moved his family out of the dwelling owned by Bolling.[17]

Some African Americans followed the path of James Wells, but black voters responded in a variety of ways. Like Wells, a number openly demonstrated their independence—a few attended Democratic barbecues and picnics adorned in caps with the Republican insignia. Others dissembled. One man, threatened with eviction by his white landlord if he voted Republican, won a reprieve with the explanation that he had been forced to vote for Republicans by black threats to run him out of town. Many accepted Democratic gifts and then voted Republican anyway. A few did become Democrats either out of loyalty to former masters or employers or because of economic threats and incentives. The leader of a black Democratic club was rewarded with the gift of a small house by his white fellow Democrats.[18]

Although a numerical minority in Marshall County, Democrats were able to get most of their candidates elected as late as the election of 1871. To do so, they utilized both intimidation and fraud. Tactics included counterfeiting Republican ballots, attempting to confuse voters by using African Americans to distribute Democratic tickets, hiding in the building to stuff ballot boxes while the election clerks were eating supper, and requiring black voters to present written proof of their age. As a result of reported electoral fraud, the state legislature refused to seat two Marshall County Democrats elected in 1871. In the next election, the Republicans swept all the county's offices. One African American served as state senator and three as representatives. However, two years later in 1875, the Democrats returned to power—permanently.[19] Black Mississippi politician John Roy Lynch later noted, "The new order of things was then set aside and the abandoned methods of a few years back were reviewed, reinaugurated, and readopted."[20]

Ida recalled that her father was interested in politics and remembered the "anxious way my mother walked the floor at night when my father was out to a political meeting."[21] Her mother had good reason to be concerned. Whites resented all black political participation but especially loathed the Loyal League, a black political organization founded and often controlled by white Republicans across the South. The Holly Springs branch of the League was established by A. C. McDonald of Shaw University and Nelson Gill of the Freedmen's Bureau. It usually met in Gill's home or in the black Baptist church. During one meeting, members of the local Ku Klux Klan hid under Gill's house listening to the proceedings and waiting for J. L. Holland, who had been chosen among them by lot, to shoot Gill. When Holland finally decided it was time and aimed his pistol, another Klansman had second thoughts and knocked the gun out of Holland's hand just as he fired it. No one was hurt, but all were scared. Afterward, pickets were posted outside during Loyal League meetings.[22]

Heated campaigns led to physical assaults and fights—apparently instigated by Democrats. Republican speakers were pelted with sticks and brickbats, had their coattails ripped, were "buggy-whipped," and had their legs broken.[23] The most serious incident of violence was the fatal shooting of Tyler Williamson, an African American who was called "a very turbulent leader and exceedingly impudent to the white people."[24] Despite that incident, Holly Springs remained more peaceful than many towns and cities during Reconstruction. Ida Wells noted in her autobiography that she could not remember any riots in the city, "although there were plenty in other parts of the state."[25]

Political violence and Klan activities frightened Elizabeth Wells and others, but Reconstruction also brought new hope and opportunity to Mississippi's black population. Although brief, the period of Republican ascendancy in Holly Springs had to be a source of great pride to the Wells's and other black families. Most whites, although they resented black political power, agreed that the city had been blessed with extraordinarily capable and honest black officeholders. Two were singled out for praise: James Hill, who rose from the state legislature to become Mississippi's secretary of state from 1874 to 1878, and Hiram Rhodes Revels, who moved to Holly Springs in the mid-1870s, and became the first African American U.S. senator. Both won white respect by their conciliatory attitudes. But whites also noted that although State Senator George Allbright was a "willing and eager tool in the hands of Gill," he was "a negro who was above average in intelligence."[26] At the height of black political power in Holly Springs, Ida Wells was a child of about ten. The events she witnessed may have whetted her interest in politics, which remained strong her entire life.

Although James Wells was known as a "race man" who was intensely interested in politics, he apparently never held office but stayed busy running a business and taking care of his growing family. As in many households, however, Ida's mother played the biggest role in the day-to-day affairs of the children. A very religious woman, Elizabeth Wells made sure that her children attended church regularly. The Wells family likely belonged to Asbury Methodist Church, where Shaw University classes were first held. Ida was baptized in that faith at the age of twelve. Ida recalled that her mother "won the prize for regular attendance at Sunday school, taking the whole brood of six to nine o'clock Sunday school the year before she died." Elizabeth Wells was a strict disciplinarian who kept close watch over her children. She regularly went to their school to check on their progress, taught them how to do household chores, and assigned each tasks around the home. Ida proudly asserted that her mother "brought us up with a strict discipline that many mothers who have had educational advantages have not exceeded."[27]

Like many African American families, the Wells family was part of a network of kinship. Although Elizabeth Wells had been unable to locate her parents and other siblings, her sister Belle, who had also been sold to Mississippi owners, lived out in the country near Holly Springs. James

Rust College Administration Building (courtesy of Rust College).

Wells's mother, Peggy, married a black man (probably named Butler) after emancipation and also lived nearby. They apparently lived as man and wife during slavery and had a daughter named Margaret and at least one other son. The Butlers tilled a number of acres and brought their corn and cotton to sell in Holly Springs each fall. Utilizing that trip for a family visit, they usually brought gifts, some of which Ida called "souvenirs from hog-killing time." On one such visit, Ida recalled her father angrily refusing his mother's request to go see his father's widow, "Miss Polly," reminding his mother of how Miss Polly had her whipped and saying, "I am never going to see her. I guess it is all right for you to take care of her and forgive her for what she did to you, but she could have starved to death if I'd had my say-so. She certainly would have, if it hadn't been for you." In addition to those visits, Ida sometimes went to stay with her grandmother and aunt and uncle, who helped Peggy and her husband on the farm. Apparently, another uncle and his wife, Fannie Butler, had three children and lived in Memphis, Tennessee.[28]

When Ida reached her teens, she enrolled at Shaw University (informally called Rust College until 1890, when the name change became official), where she was greatly influenced by the missionary spirit of the school. Under the jurisdiction of the Methodist Episcopal Church, North, Rust was "strongly tinged with evangelical Christianity." Students were required to attend daily chapel, weekly prayer meetings, and church on Sunday. W. W. Hooper, who became president of Rust while Ida was a student, was remembered as a religious man who "prayed in chapel with his eyes open and would call your name when he got through if you didn't behave."[29] Such an environment reinforced the religious training Ida received at home.

Rust's curriculum spanned from elementary education to normal school training for teachers—a four-year high school level program. A. C. McDonald founded the school to make former slaves and their children useful, independent citizens. In 1875 he wrote the following:

> It is our aim to do no hot-house work, seeking to hurry students through a college curriculum . . . sending them into the battle of life only to disgrace themselves and bring reproach upon the cause of education at large, but to take the far more difficult and tedious plan of trying to lay well a foundation for a broad, thorough and practical education.[30]

As in many schools for African Americans of that era, Rust's faculty was predominately white. Most of the teachers were northerners who saw themselves as missionaries. The white women teachers influenced Ida's concept of ideal womanhood and her acceptance of Victorian codes of propriety. At the same time, she may have been inspired by the example of black faculty member Ophelia Smith who wrote, "I love my race."[31]

While a student at Rust, Ida encountered the joys and sorrows of puberty. She experienced her "first love" and its painful demise. James B. Combs was a Rust student from Georgia, who boarded with a local family. Described in the 1880 U.S. census as "mulatto," Combs was about five years older than Wells and apparently was the one to end the relationship. He married someone else and remained in Holly Springs for at least ten years—his presence reminding Wells of the impermanence of love. Throughout her twenties Ida remained skittish of committing herself to just one man.[32]

Other relationships caused difficulties for Wells at Rust. In late 1885, she referred to her tenure at Rust as "my darkest days." Ida's fiery temper often got her in trouble, and a confrontation with President Hooper apparently led to her dismissal sometime in 1880 or 1881.[33] For years she resented him tremendously for her expulsion, but in June 1886 she admitted to herself that her own "tempestuous, rebellious, hard headed wilfulness" was to blame. She rued her "disposition to question his authority" and asserted, "I no longer cherish feelings of resentment, nor blame him that my scholastic career was cut short."[34]

In 1878 Ida B. Wells encountered the next painful chapter of her life while on a visit to her grandmother. That year witnessed a devastating yellow fever epidemic in the Mississippi Valley. The region had undergone previous epidemics of yellow fever, but none was as extensive or deadly as the 1878 outbreak. An unusually mild winter, an early spring, and a blistering hot summer had allowed the mosquitoes, which served as the fever's agent of transmission, to breed prolifically and over a wide range of territory. Thus the fever spread to areas that had never experienced an epidemic; therefore, most residents of those regions had no acquired immunities to yellow fever. Compounding these factors, the strain of virus that year was particularly deadly, which caused higher mortality rates even in areas previously infected. In some regions the mortality rates exceeded 50 percent.[35]

Lacking a good understanding of how the fever was spread, most Holly Springs residents believed their town to be immune, so the city opened its doors to people from other infested cities. The first "refugees" were housed in a small brick building that had served as the original land office. Within a week one of the refugees had died, which was only the beginning of the terrible toll the fever would exact in Holly Springs. On 4 September 1878, the New Orleans *Picayune* reported fifty cases of yellow fever in Holly Springs and two deaths; an epidemic was declared and panic began, causing "a frenzied effort at flight from the unseen terror" so that streets "were jammed with every conceivable type of vehicle loaded with baggage and human beings." By the next day a different scene was described: "The hurry and confusion of panic is gone. No hurried footsteps sound along the forsaken streets unless they seek help or a doctor. Hollow echoes mock their passing." The mass exodus reduced the town's population from about thirty-five hundred to fifteen hundred, comprised of three hundred whites and twelve hundred African Americans. One who remained telegraphed on 5 September, "The stores are all closed. . . . Physicians are broken down. . . . Many cases will die today. . . . Gloom, despair, and death rule the hour, and the situation is simply appalling." Only a few dozen of those who stayed escaped the fever; by the end of the epidemic, 215 whites and 89 African Americans had died.[36]

While Holly Springs was reeling from yellow fever, Ida was safe at her grandmother's house and presumed that the rest of the family had evacuated the city and gone to stay with her mother's sister Belle. When no word came from them, she assumed delivery of the mail had been disrupted. Then three men from Holly Springs brought her a letter, which she scanned until, as she later recalled, four sentences caught her eye: "Jim and Lizzie Wells have both died of the fever. They died within twenty-four hours of each other. The children are all at home and the Howard Association has put a woman there to take care of them. Send word to Ida." She immediately fainted and came to in a "house of mourning" surrounded by her grandmother, aunt, and uncle. Her father had died on 26 September and her mother the next day.[37]

Wells was concerned about her younger siblings in Holly Springs. Two years earlier the next oldest child, Eugenia, had developed severe scoliosis that had bent her spinal column until she became paralyzed below the waist. Next in order of birth were her brothers James, age eleven, and George, age nine. Her two youngest sisters were five-year-old Annie, and Lily, about two. The youngest sibling was a nine-month-old baby named Stanley. Another brother, Eddie, had died a number of years earlier of spinal meningitis. Wells wanted to go to the children immediately, but her relatives would not allow her to leave until they received a letter from a doctor saying that she should come.[38]

When Ida arrived at the house, she found out that all the children except Eugenia had been stricken with the fever. Although most had slight cases, the baby had died on 3 October, and two still remained in bed. Eugenia told her what had happened since the fever struck, recounting their father's contribution to the emergency. To protect his family while he built coffins and comforted the sick, James Wells left home but came daily as far as the gate to bring food and to check on them. Elizabeth, however, was the first of the family to be stricken. An Irish woman was sent to nurse her, and James came home to help—only to come down with the fever himself.[39]

James Wells had been a master Mason, which in the black community often operated as a safety net for its members and their families. Thus once the epidemic had passed, a group of Masons gathered at the Wells home to discuss what was to become of the children. After many hours of discussion, they had come to an agreement on the arrangements. They decided that Ida was old enough to take care of herself, but the others would have to be parceled out. Two of the Masons' wives each agreed to take one of the younger girls, Annie and Lily. The two boys were to be apprenticed to two different men—one of whom was a local white who was familiar with their father's work and hoped his son shared Wells's carpentry skills. The big problem was Eugenia. Because of her paralysis, no one wanted the responsibility of caring for her, so she was to be sent to a poorhouse.

While the men were divvying up the children, Ida had sat quietly. When they finished, however, she calmly announced that her parents would "turn over in their graves to know their children had been scattered like that" and she did not intend to let it happen. She would care for them if the Masons would help her find work. Although they initially scoffed at the idea, Ida was adamant and they relented—probably relieved to be rid of the responsibility. Wells later subtly altered the past and her experiences at Rust University by recollecting, "After being a happy, light-hearted schoolgirl I suddenly found myself at the head of a family."[40] Actually, her days there were less than idyllic, and she continued to attend Rust between school terms until her expulsion some two years later.

At age sixteen, Ida B. Wells was able to keep her family together because her father had been industrious and frugal. He had left them a house free of debt and accumulated savings of at least three hundred dollars. That met their needs for awhile, but Ida needed to find work. On the suggestion of the Masons, she sought a teaching job in a country school. She successfully passed the examination and was assigned to a school six miles outside of Holly Springs with a salary of twenty-five dollars a month. While she waited for school to open, Wells lengthened all her skirts for the transition from schoolgirl to schoolmarm.

Until that time, Wells had been sheltered by her parents, who were very protective. She had not been allowed to be in the presence of men unchaperoned, and her contacts with boys had been limited to what she called "children's parties." She was naive and society was suspicious of women living without the protection of a father, husband, or male relative. The result was a pattern of rumors that would plague her until she married. After she insisted on staying in the family home with her siblings, the word spread that Wells wanted the house for illicit assignations with a white man. She was dimly aware that such arrangements existed, but she was deeply shocked and hurt that people believed her capable of such action.[41]

Although Wells was listed as the head of the household in the 1880 U.S. census, she received help in meeting her responsibilities from her extended family and friends. Mr. and Mrs. James Hall, family friends who were in their early thirties, served as guardians. After fallacious rumors that

Wells was having an affair with a white doctor, her grandmother, Peggy, came from the country to stay with them. Although she was in her seventies, she tried to help out by working during the day. However, one night Peggy collapsed with a paralytic stroke, and her daughter took her back to the country to care for her until she died.[42]

Once Wells started to work at the country school, she needed someone to watch the children during the week. An old friend of her mother's (probably Rachel Rather) agreed to do so. Rather was from Virginia, twenty-four years older than Elizabeth, and may have served as a surrogate mother to her. She took care of the children until Ida would come home every Friday, "riding the six miles on the back of a big mule." Before she returned on Sunday afternoon, Wells did all the laundry and housecleaning for the week. She also cooked for the children, often using eggs and butter that people near her school had given her. Fortunately, she did not have to keep up this frantic pace for too long. Gradually, she was relieved of the responsibility for some of the children. By 1880, her brother James, who the family called Jim, had left home and had become apprenticed to a carpenter. Although he was no longer under her direct supervision, Wells still worried about Jim. She later called him her problem child because he was constantly getting into minor difficulties, especially with women. He would then go to Ida, who would help him out of the trouble. George was quieter and also became a carpenter's apprentice, eventually moving to Kansas.[43]

Wells taught for three years in Marshall County and Tate County schools and for six months in a school in Cleveland County, Arkansas. In 1881 Wells accepted the invitation of her aunt, Fannie Wells, to come to Memphis. Fannie lived there with her three small children, having been widowed by the yellow fever epidemic. Wells brought her two youngest sisters with her to Memphis, while Eugenia went to live with their Aunt Belle on her farm. After she arrived in the city at the age of nineteen, Wells continued to teach—first in the nearby town of Woodstock, and after 1884 in the city schools of Memphis.[44]

Forced into an early adulthood by her parents' deaths, in Memphis Wells began to feel the pull of conflicting duties and desires that marked her entire life. As she struggled to balance her responsibilities to her family and her race, Wells also sought to fulfill her personal needs for independence and security. Her quest for self-identity was complicated by a temperament that made it difficult for her accept the gender and racial roles expected of her. After much seeking and struggling, Wells became both a woman and an activist in Memphis.

2

Memphis and the Railroad Suits

"I had hoped such great things"

M emphis provided an interesting backdrop for Ida B. Wells's coming of age. The city contained an arresting amalgam of opportunity and discrimination for African Americans. Its contrasts are evident in the lives of two of its leading citizens: Nathan Bedford Forrest and Robert R. Church. Forrest made his fortune as a Memphis slave trader, led a massacre of black troops as a Confederate general, and reentered civilian life as a founder of the Ku Klux Klan. Church became one of the first African American millionaires by acquiring Memphis real estate during the yellow fever epidemic of 1878, helped to save the city by buying its compromised bonds in 1881, and was respected by white Memphians because of his generous support of worthy causes. Both men were part of the paradox of Memphis in the late nineteenth century.

During the Civil War, the city's character was profoundly influenced by its Union occupation from June 1862 to war's end. Memphis served as a magnet for escaping slaves, and its black population grew to over sixteen thousand by 1865. This represented a 450 percent increase from the 1860 slave population of thirty-five hundred and free black population of two hundred. The increasing black population and the protection it received from federal troops galled many of the city's white residents. A local paper decried the "thousands of lazy Negro men and women," who were "spending most of their time sunning themselves by day and stealing at night."

The real source of white hostility, however, was the Negroes' new status. A later account deplored "the elevation of their race to the rights of franchise which was denied to white men, whose birthright it was" and charged African Americans with being "very impudent and self-assertive." Another white recalled black soldiers not yielding the sidewalks to white women and complained, "Any stranger seeing those Negroes would have supposed the blacks not whites were masters in the South."[1]

Most of the black newcomers were former slaves from plantations in the surrounding rural areas of Tennessee, Mississippi, and Arkansas. Similar to Irish immigrants, they were poor country people. Their influx brought them into direct competition with the Irish for low-cost housing and low-skilled jobs. The city's link with cotton provided the former slaves with opportunities for which they were experienced and better equipped than the Irish. They eagerly sought work, and their success created a bitter rivalry that culminated in the Memphis riot of 1866. It gave the freed persons a violent baptism into the world of freedom.[2]

Growing tension between the city's Irish and African American residents was especially apparent in the interactions of black soldiers stationed at nearby Fort Pickering and the Memphis police force comprised of 180 men, 167 of whom were Irish. A white army officer noted that the police force "is far from being composed of the best class of residents here, and composed principally of Irishmen, who consider the negro as his competitor and natural enemy."[3] The soldiers were incensed by the rough treat-

Memphis during the riots of 1866 (from Harper's Weekly *[May 1866]).*

ment fellow African Americans often received at the hands of the police. As the black soldiers were mustered out, competition for work and housing increased. On 1 May 1866 a few former soldiers tried to stop several Irish police officers from arresting a black man in South Memphis. As in many later riots, that spark ignited a fire fueled by white racism. Over the next three days the police were joined by firemen and other whites in a brutal assault on the black community in South Memphis. Once the smoke cleared, forty-six African Americans and two whites lay dead. In addition to the loss of life, the community lost over ninety houses, four churches, and twelve schools.[4]

The hardships and hostility encountered by the former slaves paradoxically helped to create community institutions that made Memphis a desirable location for African Americans. Many southern whites predicted the former slaves' demise without the "paternal" hand of their masters to guide them. In August 1865 Tennessee Governor William G. Brownlow echoed the chorus of doomsayers:

> The negroes, like the Indian tribes will gradually become extinct, having no owners to care for them, . . . they will cease to increase in number—cease to be looked after and cultivated—while *educated labor* will take the place of slave labor. Idleness, starvation, and disease will remove the majority in this generation.[5]

The former slaves, however, displayed a resourcefulness that contradicted all the dire predictions. They refused to be run out by the Irish and avoided the morass of dependency and crime expected of them. Indeed, at the height of Freedmen's Bureau relief efforts—from May to December of 1865—only about 3 percent of African Americans living in Memphis received public assistance. Earlier that same year, arrest records reveal that while black residents comprised 40 percent of the population, they accounted for only 27 percent of the arrests.[6]

Several factors account for African Americans' success at making the dual transition from slavery to freedom and from rural to urban living in Memphis. The city's location and history helped. Memphis was still a rather young, small city sitting in the middle of rich lands, which made growing gardens and obtaining food easier. More important, however, to the freed people's success were the coping strategies adopted under slavery—especially communal self-help networks. On many plantations and farms, the slave community functioned as an extended family. In freedom those informal support networks became structurally organized as church groups or benevolent organizations that provided aid to families in crisis. A good example was the delegation of Masons who stepped in after Ida's parents died to see that the children were cared for. Memphis was rich with such institutions.[7]

Those survival tactics helped African American Memphians during the yellow fever epidemic in 1878. As it had in Holly Springs, the epidemic devastated the city. In four days some twenty-five thousand fled the city to escape the pestilence, leaving about twenty thousand residents. Approximately fourteen thousand of those remaining were African Americans, and the vast majority of the rest were poor Irish. For two months the fever raged, infecting some 17,000 residents and leaving 946 African Americans and 4,204 whites dead. White witnesses noted that during the crisis the city's black citizens had been trustworthy and helpful; one asserted that "No race of people on earth were ever truer."[8]

The epidemic obviously caused demographic changes. While the black population grew in relation to whites, the epidemic decimated the Irish population and scattered the old planter elite. Over the next two decades, the city grew rapidly, and most of the newcomers were rural folk from the surrounding countryside. Industrialization began, and Memphis pursued the widely held dream of becoming a New South city. Government was reorganized and modern sewage and public health measures were undertaken. The resultant culture was a sometimes raucous blend of rural and urban. As the city was "reborn" following the epidemic, it retained a rough, frontier quality as a riverboat town that offered sinful pleasures to the weary traveler. As late as 1903, the city had over 500 saloons, while Atlanta had fewer than 100 and Birmingham had 125. Two additional characteristics were an inordinately high homicide rate and the presence of more churches per capita than other cities its size.[9]

One scholar has referred to this period in Memphis history as the "era of the redneck, of the overgrown country town, of the 'hick town' on the lower bluff."[10] Certainly the influx of rural white southerners profoundly influenced the city's culture. Another scholar noted, "From every man was demanded allegiance to four conventional ideals: to an unadulterated Protestant fundamentalism; to a fantastic entity called the Old South; to the principle of white supremacy; and, rather paradoxically, to the Constitution of the United States."[11] Added to the list could be a chivalric code of honor, which included carrying a pistol and a belief that the "seduction" of a wife or daughter justified murder. A propensity toward violence combined with ardent faith in white supremacy made many Memphis whites perpetual threats to the black community.

On the other hand, "redneck" culture and its threats coexisted with black culture and its opportunities. Economic opportunity drew black rural migrants. Then, as the black population increased, social and cultural networks also grew. During Ida B. Wells's sojourn in Memphis, the city was a mecca for African Americans of the region. Black institutions arose for all segments of the population. The vibrancy and diversity of culture was found on Beale Street, called the Main Street of Negro America and the Birthplace of the Blues. The mile-long strip became best known for its middle blocks—the so-called black magic district populated by gamblers, prostitutes, voodoo doctors, and saloons. The first three blocks, however, represented a different black culture—that of the elite and respectable middle class. Here were found the offices of black professionals, the headquarters of such black business leaders as Robert R. Church, and important cultural institutions, such as Beale Street Baptist Church.[12]

Memphis was an exciting city in transition when Wells arrived. In 1881 only three years had passed since the yellow fever epidemic, and Wells was only nineteen years old. In some ways the city and the woman grew up together. For the first few years Wells was teaching ten miles outside the city in Shelby County at Woodstock. She was busy preparing herself for classes, studying for the examination required of potential teachers in the city schools, and commuting back and forth to Memphis to be with her siblings. Except for her participation in church activities, she likely had little involvement in the activities of the city's black community. She later recalled, "As a green girl in my teens, I was of no help to the people outside of the schoolroom, and at first, I fear, I was little help in it, since I had no normal [teachers'] training."[13]

Teaching was demanding and offered few emotional rewards for Ida B. Wells. She never liked being in the classroom and later admitted, "I never cared for teaching, but I had always been very conscientious in trying to do my work honestly." At the time her options seemed limited to her. "There seemed nothing else to do for a living but menial work, and I could not have made a living at that," she wrote.[14] This frustrated Wells, who recognized her duty to her siblings but had her own dreams for the future. Several years later a colleague noted her desire to become "a full fledged journalist, a physician, or an actress."[15] Seeking a different life for herself, Wells continuously pushed herself to work at self-education and improvement while teaching.

In her early teaching at country schools, both in Mississippi and Shelby County, Wells faced and shared the hardships of her students. Often there was no oil for lamps or spare candles. Frustrated by her limited formal education, Ida continued to be a voracious reader. Before leaving Holly Springs, she read the entire Bible as a result of her religious mother's persuasion and coercion. No other book could be read on Sundays. Her other early reading included all the fiction in the Sunday school and Rust College libraries. To expand her mind and fill empty hours during her years teaching at Holly Springs and Woodstock, Wells escaped into books. She overcame the lack of oil lamps and candles, she noted, by sitting beside "the blazing wood fire with a book in my lap during the long winter evenings and read[ing] by firelight."[16]

The books Wells read in her late teens and early twenties helped shape her emerging ideals and vision of the world. Late in life, she wrote, "I had formed my ideals on the best of Dickens' stories, Louisa May Alcott's, Mrs. A. D. T. Whitney's, and Charlotte Brontë's books, and Oliver Optic's stories for boys."[17] She also noted that she had read all of Shakespeare's works. In diary entries from 1885 to 1887, Wells commented on six books: Sir Walter Scott's *Ivanhoe*, Augusta Jane Evans Wilson's *Vashti or Until Death Do Us Part*, Albion Tourgee's *Bricks Without Straw*, Edward Bulwer Lytton's *Rienzi: The Last of the Roman Tribunes*, Henry Rider Haggard's *She: A History of Adventure*, and Victor Hugo's *Les Miserables*.[18]

Her reading list is filled with larger-than-life heroic figures, outcasts, orphans, and underdogs. It is a cast to whom she could easily relate as an orphan who undertook the heroic task of keeping her family together while enduring scurrilous gossip about herself. Most of the books are grandly romantic and deal with honor, justice, and virtue. Many of the characters stand tall in the face of adversity, and their example undoubtedly gave her courage and hope to confront segregation. Throughout her life, Wells expected herself and others to battle injustice and refuse to compromise. Interestingly, the heroes of her early reading were all white. Before going to Memphis, Wells could not recall reading anything by or about African Americans. The only book mentioned in her diary that dealt with the black experience at all was *Bricks Without Straw*, an account of Reconstruction written by the white liberal author, Albion Tourgee, who Wells noted "is actuated by a noble purpose and tells some startling truth." Tourgee would later become one of her many white allies. Her reading may have enabled Wells to see whites as potential allies as well as enemies.[19]

Literature also influenced Wells's self-image as well as her ideas about womanhood. She wrote that Wilson's creations displayed "inflexible sterness, haughtiness, independence, unyielding pride, indomitable steadfastness of purpose throughout all trials, sacrifice of self." All those qualities would be noted in Wells by those who worked with her throughout her career. Her reaction to female characters reflects an ambivalence about the proper roles for women that continued until her death. Wells remarked that in Wilson's books "the women have an exorbitant ambition that they feed, & trample every thing & every body under their feet—to accomplish." Although this description was unflattering, Wells was even more contemptuous of passive women, depicting the heroine in Les Miserables as "sweet, lovely and all that, but utterly without depth—fit only for love, sunshine & flowers."[20]

Wells later wrote, "My only diversion was reading and I could forget my troubles in no other way," but she also sought relief and comfort in churches. Winning perfect attendance awards for Sunday school in Holly Springs, her mother had trained her well. Ida usually attended church services at least once on Sundays and often taught Sunday school. Like much in her life, however, she felt dissatisfaction with the churches of her girlhood. She later noted, "I had already found out in the country that the churches had preachers who were not educated men, that the people needed guidance in everyday life and that the leaders, the preachers, were not giving them this help."[21]

For a spirited young woman, the daily ritual of performing work you did not like, living in isolation from friends and family for much of the week, and then commuting by train for brief weekend visits undoubtedly grew monotonous. The year 1883 brought Ida B. Wells much needed excitement and change. One Saturday evening in September Wells boarded the train in Memphis to return to her school in Woodstock. As she was accustomed to doing, she purchased a first-class ticket and took a seat in the "ladies' car." Although she most likely expected to ride in peace that day, she must have been aware that she could be challenged and asked to move to the "smoking car." Debate over the issue of segregation on Tennessee railroads had been raging since Reconstruction but had escalated still further in the early 1880s. Local white opinion and tolerance usually determined whether African Americans had access to public accommodations.[22]

African Americans increasingly found themselves forced into segregated coaches or shunted to smoking cars on railroads. Black women were particularly distressed by their treatment in public transportation. Segregation in inferior seating was a very public humiliation. Other public facilities could be avoided, but many black women such as Ida B. Wells were dependent on public transportation. They or their mothers had experienced the degradation of slavery when they had been denied the protections granted to white women in the antebellum South. In bondage many women were worked like men and bred like animals. As property, they could be sexually exploited without recourse, displayed naked at slave auctions, and separated from their children by sale. To meet the human need for peace of mind and soul, masters both dehumanized and defeminized bondswomen. African American women realized that until they could command respect as women, neither they nor their men were really free. The significance of calling first-class coaches "ladies' cars" was obvious; the inability to sit in first class labeled one as not a lady. Fighting public humiliation on public transportation, therefore, became a high priority for some black women activists.[23]

Often African American women would do as Wells had done—board a first-class car not knowing for sure how they would be treated. Before the 1890s they frequently would be allowed to ride in peace in some parts of the South. Other times—even on the same railroad—they would be asked to leave the "ladies' car." If refused first-class service, many quietly left; causing a commotion was considered "unladylike." Black women were thus placed in a no-win situation: Both submission and defiance relegated them to "non-lady" status. To avoid having to make such a humiliating decision, some lighter-skinned women, such as Fannie Barrier Williams, "passed" as white on trains. Others sought to make themselves acceptable. Mary Church Terrell recalled her mother's meticulous attention to attire and behavior in hopes of avoiding ejection from the ladies' car.[24] The dilemma of black women on railroads was poignantly detailed in *A Voice From the South* by Anna Julia Cooper. She described the "feeling of slighted womanhood" as "holier than that of jealousy, deeper than indignation, tenderer than rage" and noted: "Its first impulse of wrathful protest and proud self vindication is checked and shamed by the consciousness that self assertion would outrage still further the same delicate instinct."[25]

In September 1883, Ida B. Wells refused to allow "delicate instinct" to stop the "proud self vindication" of her "slighted womanhood." When a conductor on the Memphis to Woodstock line of the Chesapeake, Ohio &

Southwestern Railroad came to collect Wells's first-class ticket, he told her to move to a second-class car. At first Wells ignored the conductor and continued reading. After he collected the other tickets, however, he removed her baggage and umbrella, telling Wells that he would treat her "like a lady," but that she would have to go to the other car. Wells replied that if he "wished to treat me like a lady, he would leave me alone."[26]

When Wells refused to surrender her ticket or seat, the conductor grabbed her by the arm to remove her forcibly. Instead of meekly submitting, Wells held on to the back of her seat, braced her feet on the seat in front of her, and sank her teeth into his hand. Some passengers came to the aid of the bleeding conductor by moving the seat on which Wells was bracing herself and helping to carry her out of the car. Rather than sit in the smoky second-class car, Wells left the train at its next stop. Disheveled, with the sleeve of her duster torn, she was further humiliated by the loud cheers of white passengers as she stepped off the train. She still, however, refused to bear the indignities with ladylike silence and sued the railroad.

Wells drew inspiration from a number of other African-American Tennessee women who, when refused service from public accommodations, had previously challenged their treatment in the courts. In 1879 Mr. and Mrs. Richard Robinson unsuccessfully filed suit after Mrs. Richardson and her nephew were denied access to the first-class car on the Memphis and Charleston Railroad. Although they lost their case, the next year a federal judge ruled against the railroad, awarding Jane Brown damages of three thousand dollars for her ouster from a ladies' car. Then, in March 1881, Julia Hooks took a seat in the section of the local theater reserved for whites, was asked to move, and refused. Two police officers arrested and charged her with disorderly conduct, for which she received a five dollar fine.[27]

To the impressionable young Ida Wells, Hooks must have seemed heroic in her resistance, which included unsuccessfully filing assault charges against the arresting officers. A well-respected member of the Memphis black community, Hooks was a teacher in the local schools and an accomplished pianist. To the newcomer Wells, she would have seemed a perfect role model. The incident was also a lesson in the lack of respect black women received from white society. Despite her obvious refinement and social standing, the local paper called Hooks "a cheeky wench," described her as "decorated in her best store clothes" and "perfumed to the highest essence," and claimed that in her excitement she "became black from coffee-colored."[28]

That same year other events also brought the issue of segregation to the forefront. In fact 1881 seems to have been a pivotal year in Tennessee race relations. The four African Americans serving in the state legislature lobbied for a new law prohibiting discrimination on Tennessee railroads. However, over their objections, the legislature instead passed a law stipulating that the railroads provide "separate but equal" facilities for African Americans.[29] That October African Americans in Nashville attempted for three successive days to board ladies' cars in an attempt to challenge the new law. The railroads' response was described as "a curious game of musical chairs." Conductors shuffled white passengers into and out of first- and second-class cars ahead of or behind the entrance of black passengers. The attempt to get the cases heard in federal courts was rejected in mid-October.[30]

Such was the climate the year Wells first arrived in Memphis. All of these occurrences must have helped her to decide to seek legal redress two years later. She may have also been inspired by a $750 settlement the Louisville and Nashville Railroad had given Ada Buck just the year before "for ejecting her from the ladies car, although she had a first class ticket."[31] Wells hired Thomas F. Cassells, an African American lawyer and legislator, who solicited the help of a white attorney, James M. Greer. The two men pursued the case, and in May 1884 Memphis Circuit Court Judge James O. Pierce found for Wells and awarded her two hundred dollars in damages.[32] When the railroad appealed, however, Cassells did not seem eager to continue the suit. After months of delay, Wells became convinced that he had been bought off by the railroad.[33] Her decision to replace Cassells as lead attorney with Greer turned Cassells into her lifelong enemy.[34]

By this time Wells had been hired to teach in the Memphis schools and was no longer riding the train regularly. Nevertheless, that same month she was once again denied first-class service despite the assurances the railroad had given Cassells that Wells "would not be disturbed any more." On her way back to Memphis after visiting in Woodstock, she was barred from entering the ladies' car by the conductor, who "put his hands upon her to push her back and did do so."[35] When Wells refused to surrender her ticket, he stopped the train. This time she agreed to leave, and a black porter assisted her off the train.

Wells immediately had Greer file another suit against the railroad for assault and discrimination. In November 1884 the case was heard before the same judge, James Pierce, a Union veteran from Minnesota. He dismissed the assault charges but agreed to hear arguments regarding the charges of discrimination. The railroad's lawyer, Holman Cummins, painted Wells as a deliberate troublemaker who held a grudge because of her previous ejection from the ladies' car.[36] Judge Pierce rejected those arguments, found once again for Wells, and awarded her five hundred dollars in damages. Pierce ruled that the railroad had violated the 1881 "separate but equal" law by failing to provide Wells with first-class service for her ticket. According to that law, separate first-class accommodations had to be "kept in good repair, and with the same conveniences and subject to the same rules governing other first-class cars, preventing smoking and obscene language."[37] Thus the ruling was not a victory for integration; however, it would have made segregation more expensive, while also providing better service to black customers.

The previous May only African American newspapers had noted the damage award to Wells. The Memphis *Living Way* ran an account by Wells of the incident, which was remarked upon by the *New York Globe*.[38] In December, however, white papers covered the verdict. The 25 December 1884 headline of the *Memphis Daily Appeal* read: "A Darky Damsel Obtains a Verdict for Damages against the Chesapeake & Ohio Railroad— What It Cost to Put a Colored School Teacher in a Smoking Car—Verdict for $500." At the same time a black paper exultantly reported that the case proved that whenever a person was denied first-class service, "if the party aggrieved will only institute suit under the common law and maintain his cause he will always receive damages. This is as it should be."[39]

That optimism proved to be premature. Wells continued to have problems on trains. In her diary she noted that on a trip to Holly Springs in June 1886, "we had the usual trouble about the first-class coach but we conquered." Later that month Wells objected to the decision of her fellow teachers to ride on the Chesapeake, Ohio and Southwestern Railroad to a National Education Association convention in Topeka, Kansas. On that trip, Wells complained that in St. Louis "they put us in a dingy old car that was very unpleasant, but thanks to Dr. Burchett we at last secured a very pleasant place in a chair car."[40]

To avoid the precedent of paying damages and admitting guilt, the Chesapeake, Ohio and Southwestern Railroad sought to persuade Wells to settle out of court. She later recalled that "the railroad's lawyer had tried every means to get me to compromise the case, but I indignantly refused."[41] The railroad then filed an appeal, which finally reached the state supreme court in the spring of 1887. Before then, the railroad began a smear campaign against Wells. In April 1886 Wells wrote obliquely in her diary of a "conspiracy . . . that is one foot to quash the case." She further lamented, "It is a painful fact that white men choose men of the race to accomplish the ruin of any young girl."[42] Black males, however, also came to her defense. Several men served as surrogate fathers to Wells in Memphis. In May, Wells noted that one of them, Alfred Froman, "told me of the dirty method Mr. Cummins is attempting to quash my case. He told him to stop it." In December the black-owned *Cleveland Gazette* wrote of the case: "The most ridiculous and despicable part known in the proceedings is the attempt to put up a blackmailing job and attempt to tarnish the character of the fair prosecutrix."[43]

When the case reached the state supreme court, Wells learned what many others who followed in her footsteps would—that state courts in the South were not as supportive of black rights as the federal courts. The Tennessee Supreme Court justices accepted the premise of the 1881 Tennessee law that accommodations could be "separate but equal." Indeed, so did Wells's lawyers, who simply argued that the accommodations offered to Wells were not equal in quality to those denied her. They argued, "We had might as well say that the colored man should not be allowed to buy the best article of groceries, though he pays in full for such and we pretend to sell him only the best."[44]

The railroad's attorneys, on the other hand, denied that the car Wells rejected was filled with smoke, despite evidence to the contrary. In addition, they characterized her as a troublemaker. In the end the justices agreed that the accommodations offered "were alike in every respect as to comfort, convenience, and safety." They ruled that Wells's purpose "was to harass with a view to this suit" and held her liable for court costs, which she later recalled as "over two hundred dollars."[45]

Like the heroes she read about, Wells saw herself standing tall and heroically facing the unjust assault on her character and her limited finances. During a period of great discouragement before the decision, she wrote, "I will wait and watch and fear not."[46] The final outcome was devastating. In her diary she recounted Greer telling her that four justices "cast their personal prejudices in the scale of justice & decided in face of all the evidence to the contrary." Wells's diary reflected a despair that assailed her faith both in human law and divine justice.

> I felt so disappointed, because I had hoped such great things from
> the suit for my people generally. I have firmly believed all along that
> the law was on our side and would, when we appealed to it, give us
> justice. I feel shorn of that belief and utterly discouraged, and just

now if it were possible would gather my race in my arms and fly far
away with them. O God is there no redress, no peace, no justice in
this land for us? Thou hast always fought the battles of the weak and
oppressed. Come to my aid at this moment & teach me what to do,
for I am sorely, bitterly disappointed. Show us the way, even as Thou
led the children of Israel out of bondage into the promised land.[47]

Her lawsuits cost her dearly. The least of her losses was still significant;
her lawyers' fees and court fines added to Wells's continuing battle to pay
her bills. More importantly, the suits planted seeds of bitterness and a sense
of betrayal that grew larger over the years, convincing Wells that other
African Americans often abandoned her to fight alone. In the autobiography she wrote late in life, Wells used words to describe the cases that
echoed throughout the remainder of the book: "None of my people had
ever seemed to feel that it was a race matter and that they should help me
with the fight. So I trod the winepress alone."[48]

The railroad's smear campaign and Wells's own defiantly physical behavior also undermined her claims to respectability. Rumors of her immorality haunted her entire single life. Her youth, lack of an older male
relative, and newness in the city made her vulnerable to attacks for the
same actions others could do without criticism. Most "southern ladies" of
the black community who fought against segregation withdrew gracefully
from the disputed facility and filed suit—often with their husbands. Julia
Hooks physically resisted but did not bite anyone, and she was ten years
older than Wells, married, and an entrenched member of the local black
aristocracy. While many in the community intellectually supported Wells's
actions, a number may have had an uneasy feeling that her actions were inappropriate for a woman.

The apparent gains were few. The ruling hammered another nail in
the edifice of segregation being built upon the foundation of "separate but
equal." In 1896 the U.S. Supreme Court placed the roof on the "House of
Jim Crow" with its *Plessy v. Ferguson* ruling that upheld the constitutionality of separate accommodations for African Americans so long as facilities
were substantially equal in quality. Almost a decade before *Plessy*, the
Wells's case had shown how flimsy the legal guarantees of equality would
prove to be. Legalized segregation inevitably led to inferior funding for
schools, health care, housing, and all that brings equality of opportunity.

The two major gains from the cases were instead personal ones for Ida
B. Wells. Her account of the incident for the local paper started her on the
path toward journalism, which spurred her life of activism, and equally im-

portant, she began to find her true self. Coming-of-age is almost always a confusing and painful journey of self-doubt and uncertainty. Wells faced larger than usual obstacles in discovering who she was and how she fit into her universe. Much of what she felt and wanted contradicted society's expectations of her—and even sometimes her own expectations. She battled class, gender, race, and religious conventions that sought to define her. Unlike the court cases, these battles were often fought within the black community.

3

Social Activities of the Black Elite

"It was a breath of life to me"

B ecoming a teacher in the public schools of Memphis immediately
catapulted Ida B. Wells into the ranks of the black elite of that city.
Wells was dazzled by the cornucopia of cultural and social activities. No
longer could she claim that reading was her "only diversion" as she reveled
in such newly found diversions as the theater, parties, concerts, and
lyceums. Exhilaration, however, was tempered with frustration. Because of
various financial obligations, she did not have economic resources equal to
her social status and discovered that membership in the elite brought burdens as well as blessings. Proscribed roles for a "lady" often conflicted with
her temperament and talents, making the struggles to define herself a con-
test of conflicting desires and duties. During her decade in Memphis,
Wells experienced both joyous excitement and self-doubting despair on
the road to womanhood.

While reporting on the wedding of Robert R. Church to his second
wife in 1885, a white-owned Memphis newspaper described the society
into which Wells moved:

There is as much distinction in the society of colored people of the
South as there is among the whites. In every community, town and
city the blacks are divided into classes governed by education, intel-

ligence, morality, wealth and respectability. This distinction is scrupulously observed here in Memphis by the colored people. The educated and intelligent who, by honest industry, have accumulated a competency and who live exemplary lives create a fashionable social circle of their own.[1]

Another white-owned newspaper described the bride, Anna Wright, as "a belle in colored society" and declared she was "in every way worthy to reign as the mistress of the beautiful home to which she has been transplanted."[2] An agricultural journal later described that home: "It is a three-story frame, and was the first Queen Anne style of architecture erected in this city. It has fourteen rooms, besides cellar, butler's pantry, bath room and store rooms. The mural decorations and frescoing were done by a celebrated Italian artist."[3]

While Church's wealth far exceeded that of most residents, Memphis had a sizable and prosperous black middle-class community, which was chronicled and celebrated by correspondents to black-owned newspapers. A column (possibly written by Wells) in January 1884 extolled the opportunities in Memphis, declaring that African Americans' "relations with whites here are as amicable and their wants as few as might be found to exist in any city of the whole country." The account further noted their freedom from intimidation and mob rule as well as their ability to vote. On an imaginary stroll through the city, the correspondent described entering the post office and seeing white and black clerks working "side by side." At the post office the writer found "seven or eight railway postal clerks of the despised race" and learned that seven of the thirteen letter carriers were black. Down the street the journalist questioned a policeman whose "color was easily distinguishable" and was told that eight of the city's twenty-five police officers were colored. Other positions held by African Americans included a street commissioner, the collector of revenue, carpenters, bricklayers, and foremen. The column ended, however, lamenting that opportunity had not led to property ownership or educational levels equal to that of whites.[4]

The city's black middle class was large and rich enough to support African American professionals. A 1885 column on Memphis in the black-owned *Cleveland Gazette* asserted, "Our colored lawyers and doctors are doing well and still there is room for more." Praising the available opportunities, it stated that African Americans could do "better here in augmenting their means than in many a northern city where competition is slow and business crowded out."[5] The presence of so many successful black Memphians provided rich social and cultural experiences for those included in their circle.

Ida B. Wells became a recognized member of the middle class by virtue of her late father's success and reputation in Holly Springs as well as by her status as a public school teacher in Memphis. Among the Memphis elite were quite a few former Holly Springs residents, including businessmen Robert R. Church, M. W. Dogan, and Alfred Froman; attorney Benjamin F. Booth; and teacher Green P. Hamilton.[6] Especially important to Wells's future was her relationship with Froman, who functioned as her primary father figure after her father's death. Owner of a saddle shop and former printer of the *Memphis Weekly Planet*, Froman was appointed to the Memphis school board in 1883.[7] As the only black member, he may have used his influence to secure the teaching position for Wells even though she had not graduated from Rust College. Of course, at that time many black schoolteachers had somewhat limited educations. Because most southern states outlawed teaching slaves to read and write, only a few African Americans were literate at the time of emancipation. During and immediately after the Civil War, northern white teachers, employed by such organizations as the American Missionary Association (AMA), opened most schools for the freed slaves (as in Holly Springs). In the decades that followed, however, black teachers began to replace the white missionaries as public schools replaced private ones.

Although teaching was often burdensome to Wells, she thoroughly enjoyed the status it brought her. About the same time that she started teaching in Memphis, a literary group began meeting at Vance Street Christian Church on Friday evenings. Named the Memphis Lyceum, its members were mostly teachers, but other members of the black elite also participated. According to Wells, its programs "consisted of recitations, essays, and debates interspersed with music." She became a regular participant, calling it "a breath of life to me."[8] Taking an active role by reciting, planning programs, and raising money, she was also more diligent than many in her attendance. On several occasions, she remarked in her diary that attendance was low; once she reported that she "went to the L[yceum] last Friday evening but no meeting."[9]

Wells especially enjoyed participating in dramatic recitations. On one occasion she and fellow teacher Virginia Broughton donned costumes and presented a scene between Mary Stuart and Queen Elizabeth, which a newspaper called the "crowning literary effort of the evening." Wells also presented an essay that evening, and two of her closest teacher friends, Fannie J. Bradshaw and Fannie J. Thompson, read as well. The Lyceum ended as it usually did with the reading of the *Evening Star* by its editor, Virginia Broughton. Published by the Lyceum, the *Evening Star* was later described by Wells as a "spicy journal" that included "news items, literary notes, criticisms of previous offerings on the program, a 'They Say' column of pleasant personalities—and always some choice poetry."[10]

Another reason the Lyceum appealed to Wells was because of her desire to improve herself and expand her knowledge. Acutely aware of her limited education, Wells found the Lyceum meetings helpful. Programs provided opportunities to be exposed to a variety of viewpoints and experiences. At one meeting the white pastor of the Linden Street Christian church lectured on "The World's Hidden Force." Wells herself solicited a lecture by P. B. S. Pinchback, who had served as lieutenant governor and acting governor of Louisiana during Reconstruction, making him one of the highest elected officials among African Americans of that era.[11] Composing and listening to original essays also stimulated Wells to think and to write effectively.

Later in her career, Wells's oratorical skills became as important as her writing ability. She honed those skills through participation in dramatic recitations and plays at both the Lyceum and the LeMoyne Literary Society, located at the LeMoyne Normal Institute, which had close ties to black Memphis teachers. Discovering a taste and a talent for drama, late in 1885 Wells began taking elocution and dramatic lessons from a local woman. Considering Wells's persistent financial problems, her determination is reflected in her willingness to pay 50 cents a lesson— 10 cents more than she paid daily for her board. The priority she gave to the lessons is also indicated by a diary entry in mid-February: "Did not get any money as I expected yesterday and went nowhere—*not even to take a lesson* (emphasis added)."[12]

After a year of sporadic readings and parts, Wells wanted a more regular outlet for her talents and organized a dramatic club. The first meeting, held in April 1887, was attended by "a score of young ladies & gentlemen," who selected Wells to chair a committee "to draft [a] plan for permanent organization." Although the club met at least one more time in May, it apparently did not get well established before school ended on the last day of the month.[13] During that month, however, Wells participated in a fundraising concert, which she described in her journal in early May as a "grand success." She further noted:

Our program was good . . . & they sold out nearly everything. I recited "Le Marriage de Convenience" for the first time here and every one admired it. Indeed Judge Latham paid me a very high compliment when he said it was the most artistic piece of elocution he had ever heard. I felt greatly flattered. Jimmie W—Mr. Carr—& Mr. Froman were my especial helpers. The last named gave me a basket of flowers costing $1.10. Taken all together it was a big success, for I learn we made clear nearly $60. Thank the Lord for His blessing![14]

Wells truly loved the theater—watching it as well as performing. She frequently attended both amateur and professional productions. In her diary, which she sporadically kept from late December 1885 to September 1887, Wells remarked on ten plays she attended, ranging from light comedies to Shakespeare. She went to most with female friends or in mixed groups. Only twice did she mention going to a play alone with a man. She went to see *Monte Cristo* with an unidentified "Mr. A" in January 1887, and with a "Mr. G" she saw *The Burning of Moscow* the following September. After *Monte Cristo*, Wells wrote in her diary that she "felt like a guilty thing" for going and noted, "Already I've had it thrown at me for so doing, & I regret having yielded."[15] It is unclear, however, whether she regretted the company or the activity.

Some of the black middle-class community did view the theater as a source of corruption and criticized Wells for her attendance. Men of all ages gave Wells advice and guidance, apparently because she had no older male relative to do so. George Dardis, Jr., at whose concert Wells gave a dramatic recitation in May 1886, nevertheless disapproved of her going to see a professional play performed. Walking her home from Sunday school, he gave her "a severe lecture on going to the theatre." After naming several male leaders who also disapproved of the theater, Dardis told Wells that she was "one who failed to practice as I preached," setting a bad example for the young. Wells noted in her diary:

I regretted it more than I can say all along, but not so keenly did I see the wrong, or think of the influence my example would exert until then. I had not placed so high an estimate on myself. He certainly gave me food for thought and here after when I grow weary or despondent & think my life useless & unprofitable, may I remember this episode, and may it strengthen me to the performance of my duty, for I would not willingly be the cause of one soul's being led astray.[16]

Setting a good example was one of the many duties of teaching, but Wells was too vital and lively to fit comfortably into the moral straitjacket worn by some middle-class African Americans. Although she attended church several times a week, she also played hard. Her diary is filled with accounts of visiting and receiving visitors. On these occasions such games as checkers, "logamachy," and Parcheesi were sometimes played. Wells also went on numerous picnics and frequent horseback rides—once suffering a "terrible fall" when riding a strange horse that was afraid of streetcars. At the first car the horse encountered, "he ran up on the mules & began rearing and plunging." Her fall left Wells "swollen & painful" as well as grateful. "I think of my escape with a solemn thankfulness," she wrote.[17] On another occasion Wells went to a professional baseball game, where she confessed to losing her temper and acting "in an unladylike way toward those in whose company I was."[18]

Wells attended and gave frequent parties as well. In October 1885 she "entertained quite a number of ladies and gentlemen," and in February 1887 she gave a "storm party" for her fellow teachers. Group parties were common in Memphis, and Wells participated with others in giving several. In January 1885 Wells delivered the toast at a large reception given for a group of visiting teachers from Kansas City. Held at the U. B. F. Hall, the entertainment was sponsored by many of the city's elite. Among the honorees was the editor of the *Gate City Press*, J. D. Bowser, who was apparently impressed with Wells's oratorical skills and recruited her to write letters for his newspaper.[19]

By this time Wells was freed from most of her parental duties, since the boys were grown and her Aunt Fannie had taken Annie and Lily to California. To help support her sisters, Wells promised to send ten dollars a month but was frequently torn between duty and desire. While preparing for one party, she worried about doing her aunt "an injustice to spend money in frolic when she is bearing all the load." Nevertheless, she borrowed someone's imitation diamonds, wore her black silk dress, and enjoyed herself "hugely." At the party Wells received a love poem from one young man and rebuffed an "attempted familiarity" from another. Apparently anxious about engaging in her first group dance, Wells noted in her diary, "Was on the floor in a set for the first time in my life and got through better than I expected."[20]

The irrepressible Miss Wells also enjoyed numerous trips. She occasionally visited old friends in Holly Springs as well as people she met while teaching in Woodstock. Trips to Holly Springs were often bittersweet; some memories were so painful that Wells did not return to her birthplace until four years after she had left in 1881. In December 1885 she toured the campus at Rust College on her first trip home, and then she "went out for a walk; strolled around town, meeting many I knew in the days of 'auld lang syne,' greeting some pleasantly, passing others indifferently, unconcernedly." During the rest of the day, Wells visited her parents' graves and attended a social. The trip elicited a burst of emotions and introspection recorded in her diary.

> The day has been a trying one for me; seeing old enemies, visiting old scenes, recalling the most painful memories of my life, talking them over with those who were prominent actors during my darkest days. They counsel me to forget, to cast the dark shadows out and exorcise the spirit that haunts me, but I—forgetting the vows that I had taken on myself to forget, and the assurances I have made that I was glad because my Father saw fit to send these trials & to fit me for His kingdom—clenched my hands darkly and proudly declared I would never forget![21]

After another trip to Holly Springs in June 1886, Wells noted she "spent a very pleasant time at home, better than ever before." Yet that trip also aroused painful emotions and introspection as well. The first came while Wells attended Rust's commencement exercises.

> As I witnessed the triumph of the graduates and thought of my lost opportunity a great sob arose in my throat and I yearned with unutterable longing for the "might have been." When Will said to me afterward: "Ida, you ought to come back here and graduate," I could not restrain my tears at the sense of injustice I felt, and begged him not to ask me why I said "I could not." I quickly conquered that feeling and as heartily wished the graduates joy as no bitterness had mingled with my pleasure.[22]

Another incident upset Wells on that trip; her old beau James B. Combs, who had married, was sent to pick up Wells and the other female visitors for a party. Wells declared herself "speechless with surprise when he presented himself with all his old sang froid [sic] and announced that he was our escort." She went to the party but kept Combs "at a respectful distance," going with his wife to see their babies.[23]

Wells also went on several excursions—short trips that were a very popular form of diversion at the end of the century. One of her favorite destinations was Raleigh, a small town and health resort eleven miles from Memphis. Wells relished "the quiet of the place," which was known for the scenic beauty of its laurel bushes, rustic bridges, and fountains. Visitors enjoyed touring an old cemetery, visiting spas and natural springs, and exploring Tapp's Hole Cave. For a period of time Raleigh became a resort of the rich, who flocked to the Raleigh Inn built by members of the Duke family, who had made their fortune in tobacco. After Wells's first visit in May 1887, she declared, "It all had the beauty of novelty to me." A few weeks later she returned on Sunday with an "omnibus full of us."[24]

Traveling seemed like tonic to Wells, and as a young single woman, she wandered often and far. She visited acquaintances in numerous such cities as Nashville, Tennessee; Lexington, Kentucky; and Detroit, Michigan. In Michigan she attended a five-course luncheon "in honor of a number of visiting friends," at which the "floral decoration was a garland of pond lilies tied with pale blue ribbon."[25] Wells also traveled to various conventions, including those of the National Educational Association in Topeka, Kansas, during July 1886 and the National Press Association in Louisville, Kentucky, during August 1887. On such trips Wells attended the sessions but also played the role of tourist. In Topeka she visited the Capitol Building, calling on Edwin P. McCabe, an African American who had been elected state auditor. In Louisville she "went over the river to Indiana" with another young woman and two men. They "took in the town & returned on the daisy line." In both cities Wells attended various receptions and dinners and visited in the homes of prominent black citizens.[26] Those activities reflect the national network of a small black aristocracy whose members were aware of their counterparts in other cities through kinship and friendship ties as well as extensive coverage of their activities in black newspapers with wide circulations. Such papers as the *Cleveland Gazette*, Indianapolis *Freeman*, and *New York Age* regularly published correspondents' reports from towns and cities in both the North and South.

Racial prejudice in the white world influenced class relations in the black world, especially among the black elite. In the late nineteenth century, many African American aristocrats owed their economic and educational advantages to kinship with whites. In some places, such as New Orleans, white leaders deliberately cultivated relations with the free black population. They solicited black aid to maintain power by treating free blacks as superior to slaves—and indeed, sometimes superior to poor whites.

The antebellum white elite sought to manipulate both class and racial consciousness in the much poorer, and often dependent, black elite. Their success, however, was limited by a number of factors. From many of their mulatto offspring, masters could expect no more than divided loyalties— their children had black families as well. In addition, powerful whites often attempted simultaneously to keep poor whites in line by assuring them of their superiority to all African Americans, regardless of legal or economic status. After emancipation white leaders fluctuated wildly between both tactics, depending on political circumstances. Sometimes they played the race card, other times the class card.

As intelligent, self-interested beings, successful African Americans had difficulty deciding how to navigate such a minefield to protect their own personal interests. That task was complicated further by moral issues. Because whites often judged all African Americans by the actions of the most degraded, black elites believed it important to demonstrate the possibilities of the race by setting themselves apart from the struggling masses. At the same time, however, upper-class African Americans' own advancement depended on alleviating the poverty and ignorance of lower-class African Americans. Not only would those conditions continue to be used to justify discrimination toward all blacks, but black professionals also depended upon black patronage. They needed people who could afford their services. As victims of oppression themselves, successful African Americans usually felt a moral obligation to those on the bottom of society as well. In addition, after the debasement of slavery, racial pride was seen as essential to advancement, and unity was crucial to success. This was made more difficult by the actions of whites, who perpetuated the advantages given to the children of masters by favoring lighter-skinned blacks in employment and other areas. Color thereby became one determinant of status both without and within the black community.[27]

All middle- and upper-class African Americans had some degree of ambivalence regarding the relative importance of race and class. Ida B. Wells, however, was probably more ambivalent than most. Her father was the privileged son of his white master—one entrée to the black aristocracy. Becoming a teacher provided her with another key to acceptance. On the other hand, she was darker skinned than the Churches, Settles, and other members of the Memphis elite. Some African Americans openly expressed a preference for light skin. Many who intellectually rejected the importance of skin color were, nonetheless, still influenced unconsciously by it to some extent. Wells, decidedly mulatto, could never have "passed" for white like so many aristocrats of color. As a result, she seemed less influ-

House in which Wells boarded from March 1886 to September 1887 (from G. P. Hamilton, The Bright Side of Memphis [1908]).

enced by color prejudice than many contemporaries. Her color, however, may have enhanced her feelings of being an outsider in the society she inhabited.

Limited financial resources created another obstacle to Wells's attempts to fit into Memphis's black elite. As a teacher in the city's public schools, Wells received a salary of sixty dollars a month. By the era's standards this was a relatively generous salary. However, she only received a salary while teaching; if she did not secure a teaching position during the summer, she was paid no wages for those months. She also could not rely on getting paid regularly. The city's precarious financial condition led to late payments to teachers. The school board also sometimes made only partial payments.[28]

Though her salary fluctuated, Wells had regular fixed expenses. She had promised to send her aunt ten dollars a month to help support her sisters. Like most single women of her age and status who could no longer live with their parents, she boarded with various older women or families. In order to obtain a room from "respectable" people and to be close to where she worked, Wells paid from ten to fifteen dollars a month. Finding suitable accommodations was yet another constant problem. One landlady could not make ends meet—partly because Wells was sometimes unable to pay rent on time—and gave up her home to hire herself out as a domestic servant. Her next landlady moved far from where Wells worked. From

March 1886 to September 1887, Wells lived with Mr. and Mrs. Josiah T. Settle, who were influential members of the city's black aristocracy. Becoming friendly with Theresa Settle, Wells was very content living in the big house on Lauderdale Street until she became annoyed with the "parsimony" of the Settles. Wells believed she was being overcharged at times and decided to move out when the wealthy Settles apparently wanted money for a pair of used shoes for Lily. She hoped at that time to fulfill her dream of setting up an independent household by buying her aunt's Memphis house. However, Wells could not borrow the money and was forced to find new quarters, lamenting, "I am sick & tired begging people to take me to board."[29]

Participation in the social activities of the black aristocrats of Memphis required more money than Wells could comfortably afford. The women dressed regally for the lavish affairs given by the various exclusive social clubs of the city. One such event, sponsored by the Live Oak Club, was described by the Memphis *Watchman* in February 1889.

> The reception began at 8 P M, dancing at 9, and refreshments were served at 11 P M. Elegant cards of invitation tied in satin ribbon were issued, and the menu consisted of turkey, ham, oysters, salads, ice cream, fruits and wines. The exercises at the banquet were carried out with imposing ceremonies. . . .The lovely ladies who graced the occasion with their presence wore exquisite and tasteful costumes.

The article then described some of the women's attire. The dresses were constructed of silk, brocade, satin, velvet, moire, and tulle; the accessories included diamonds, pearls, and fresh flowers. Miss Ida B. Wells was listed as wearing a "blue surrah lace overdress."[30]

Wells wanted to fit into the social circles of the black elite, but she agonized over the amount of money spent on clothing. Constantly getting in debt and juggling her payments to various creditors to keep them at bay, Wells often chastised herself for extravagant clothing purchases. In December 1885 she declared, "I am very sorry I did not resist the impulse to buy that cloak; I would have been $15 richer." The next month she fretted, "I am so sorry I bought that sacque when I could have done without it." Over a year later Wells noted, "Bought a hat costing $3.50 that I am sorry for now." To cut expenses she often remade dresses or added lace or other trimmings to her existing wardrobe. Clothing was not her only extravagance. One social custom was the exchange of photographs, and Wells spent money to get new pictures made frequently, perhaps because she was rarely pleased with the results. In August 1887 she noted, "Paid $1.25 for my pictures & am afraid for that reason I shall not be satisfied with them; they are too cheap."[31]

Despite her precarious position in the black elite, Wells enjoyed her hectic social life. Memphis provided her an abundance of social and cultural opportunities. She was therefore alarmed when duty threatened to take her away from it all in the summer of 1886. Her life increasingly became a frustrated attempt to live up to the world's expectations of her as a woman. The summer offered excitement but ended with an agonizing struggle by Wells to meet both her duties and desires. Her Topeka trip was actually the start of a much longer journey that took Wells to California — not entirely of her own free will. Although Wells enjoyed the trek across the continent, she was not excited about the destination. As mentioned earlier, her Aunt Fannie (who had first invited Wells to come to Memphis with her sisters) moved to Visalia, California, a few years later, taking Annie and Lily as well as her own children with her. Because of the drains on her financial resources and the school board's habit of not paying salaries on time, Wells was late with some of her promised support payments. Knowing that she

Memphis shopping district 1888, including Menken's Department Store, to which Wells was frequently in debt (courtesy Memphis/Shelby County Public Library & Information Center).

sometimes splurged on luxuries, she felt guilty about making her aunt carry most of the load. It was hard to resist Fannie's pleas to come to California, but Wells was extremely reluctant to leave her life in Memphis.

Fannie's lobbying campaign began in early 1886, when a friend of hers wrote to Wells, enclosing an application for a teaching position in Visalia. Wells resisted. She answered the letter without returning the application. In her diary Wells confessed that "[I] never thought of sending in my application for the school, until I received aunt F's letter the same day I mailed it—when I answered aunt F's tho' I sent the application thro' her." When Wells learned in April that the examination for new teachers would be held on 15 June in California, she seemed relieved to not be able to get there in time. A month later, however, after Fannie wired Wells to come immediately for the exam, Wells despaired, "I don't know what to do, my business is not arranged to leave on such short notice."[32]

Wells postponed making a decision—perhaps hoping that her aunt would rescind her demands or events would make it impossible to go. Her aunt chastised her for her indecision, saying that Wells "ought to be sure of something." On 28 June Wells noted in her diary, "Received a letter from aunt F who is very angry and disappointed because I did not come to California. Answered and tried to pacify her as much as I could." On 4 July Wells departed on an excursion for the West, still undecided about whether she would merely visit her aunt or stay and work in California.[33]

Wells left on the 4:00 P.M. train with a group of Memphians to attend the National Teachers Association meeting in Topeka, Kansas. The group included two of Wells's female teacher friends, Fannie J. Thompson and Fannie J. Bradshaw; B. K. Sampson, the principal of Kortrecht school; Sidney Burchett, a physician; and I. J. Graham, a fellow teacher and suitor, among others. After riding for almost five hundred miles, they arrived in Kansas City, where Wells found herself caught up in confusion and controversy. She had been corresponding with two young men from the city, who volunteered to find her housing. Without a mother to guide her, she naively accepted their offer. Other women questioned both the reliability and the propriety of the arrangements, and events soon proved their wisdom. Wells had never met one of them, Paul Jones, but eagerly looked forward to doing so. When he failed to meet the train, Wells learned that Jones drank, and she rebuffed an invitation to go carriage riding. She was especially disturbed by a note from Jones in which he claimed to "have heard bad things" about Wells. "I was so angry," she declared, "I foamed at the mouth, bit my lips & then realizing my impotence—ended in a fit of crying." The encounter reminded Wells of the power men had to influence her life and began a running feud between her and the two young men.[34]

Even though things did not turn out as Wells anticipated, her stop in Kansas City was filled with a hectic schedule of socializing typical of the black middle class. J. D. Bowser, editor of the city's *Gate City Press* for which Wells now occasionally wrote, invited her to dinner. She attended a reception, was introduced to "hundreds of folks," and met two male teachers—a Mr. Yates and R. T. Coles—who "made themselves very agreeable." In addition to numerous parties, her week of "excitement and dissipation" included sight-seeing and shopping, which she described in her diary.

> Mr. Towsen took us for the first ride thro' the city in a carriage, we also visited the cable line, engine house & the Coates Hotel that day besides a ride on the cable. Next day we went shopping & had our pictures taken. Thursday evening we went to Mrs. Andrews' to an entertainment, Mr. Coles accompanying me and we had a royal time.[35]

Leaving Kansas City on 13 July, Wells continued to Topeka for the convention. The National Education Association was a biracial organization, which had been founded as the National Teachers Association in 1857. At the 1886 meeting several thousand teachers attended. Only about thirty were African American. "I never saw so many teachers in my life," Wells exclaimed, "but none that I knew." Aside from a session on "The Bible in Public Schools," she seemed mostly unimpressed, declaring "we went out to the meetings at the opera house and the Methodist Church where we heard considerable spouting." Wells turned twenty-four in Topeka and went sight-seeing with Granville Marcus, Jr., a fellow teacher from Memphis. She noted in her diary that "Mr. Marcus took us driving through town Friday morning before we left; as that was my 24th birthday & the first time he had so honored me I took it as a birthday gift."[36]

Wells left Topeka at one o'clock that afternoon and rode all night to Pueblo, Colorado, arriving at nine o'clock the next morning and leaving at six o'clock that evening for Colorado Springs. There she got her "first glimpse of the mountains," visited Manitou Springs, "spent the day in the mountains drinking of the different springs," but did not "undertake the ascent of the Peak" as she did not have adequate shoes or warm clothing. The next morning Wells left for Denver, where she found the scenery "beautiful in the extreme," noting "there was something awful, majestic in the height of the mountains & solitary grandeur of the peaks." She visited some "fine public buildings," including "the finest and most complete opera-house" she had ever seen and "a magnificent courthouse."[37]

In an area where the young men outnumbered the women, Wells made quite an impression. One new acquaintance, Wells declared, "was ready to propose on the spot almost." She was especially enchanted with Edwin Hackley, a newspaper man who became a candidate for the Colorado State Legislature. Following a three-hour buggy ride to view the city, Wells gushed, "I like him, better than any one I've known so short awhile." Before Wells left Denver, Hackley told her that he hated to see her leave. "I can easily believe him, for I know I have never hated so badly to bid a stranger goodby."[38]

Next, Wells traveled forty-one hours to Salt Lake City. Arriving at midnight, she went to a hotel and "spent a fitful remainder of the night on a cot, without covering, in a sitting room of the place." After a quick visit to the Mormon Tabernacle, where Wells "listened to a harangue from one of themselves," she left at four o'clock that afternoon and rode straight through to San Francisco. She stayed in that city for about five days, and visited the office of the *Elevator*, a militant local black paper and had "quite a talk with the editor," L. H. Douglass. Wells took advantage of the opportunities to expand her contacts in the newspaper world, but also did the usual sight-seeing, circulating "around the city looking at the shops and public buildings and going thro' Chinatown with its thousands of 'Heathen Chinee' in all branches of industry." Of her other activities, Wells wrote:

> Visited the Palace Hotel, said to be the largest in the world and has 1780 rooms. Went to the Cliff House and had a magnificent view of the ocean and sat for hours gazing out on the billows that "break, break, break, on the cold gray stones," and being fascinated with the white foam that looked like milk. The rocks in front of the house were lined with seals that looked like so many brown bags as they lay basking in the sunlight. Golden Gate Park, of more than a thousand acres, took up a considerable share of our time—with its broad smooth walks, beautiful parterres of flowers and conservatory with all manner of plants & flowers.[39]

Along the route of her trip, Wells's excitement and pleasure at traveling were interrupted from time to time by reminders of duties calling her from the life she loved. In Topeka three forwarded letters from her aunt arrived, urging her to come to Visalia. In San Francisco, Wells was dismayed to talk to a man who, she noted, "paints Visalia and the colored inhabitants thereof in anything but glowing colors and makes me almost afraid to go there." She despaired that she had sold her return ticket for fifteen dollars. "My heart is indeed heavy," Wells lamented, "and I know not what to do." After praying to God for mercy and guidance, Wells wondered why her aunt would want to stay in Visalia. "Poor Aunt F," Wells wrote on 29 July, "she has had a burden to bear that was very heavy. I will not run and leave her alone. As I am anxious to see her I will leave tomorrow for there."[40]

Traveling all night, Wells arrived at Visalia about daybreak on 1 August 1886. She found everyone well but was startled to see how much the girls had grown. Her cousin and namesake Ida as well as her sister Annie were now as tall as Wells and "look[ed] very much like women." Annie was just entering her teens, and Wells declared, "I look at them in amazement and find the little sisters of whom I spoke, shooting up into my own world and ripening for similar experiences as my own." Wells must have seen in them how swiftly youth departs. Her life was in such flux, she may have felt overwhelmed by the swiftness with which her own adulthood called for choices she was not ready to make. She was a teacher but was being drawn increasingly toward journalism and drama. Many of Wells's friends were getting married, and she could not even decide if she ever wanted to marry.[41]

The stay in California provided Wells with a break from the hectic pace of Memphis to sort out her life, but she was eager to be living, not thinking. Visalia seemed to her more of a dead end than a crossroads. Founded by a Kentuckian in 1852, Visalia was largely settled by Confederate sympathizers. Most of the few African American residents had come from the South as servants to former slaveowner migrants after the war. The gregarious Miss Wells could not understand her aunt's desire to stay. She later wrote of the town, "Not a dozen colored families lived there, and although there was plenty of work, it was very dull and lonely for my aunt and the five youngsters in the family." Wells tried to convince her aunt that "it was even worse for me, a young woman, to have nothing to look forward to, as I was just beginning to live and had all my life before me."[42]

Fannie was not easily convinced to give up her help and companionship. From the beginning of August until mid-September, Wells kept changing and rechanging her mind. On 2 August, Wells determinedly declared:

> Poor aunt F! she wants me to stay the year with her anyhow, whether
> I get any work to do or not & I, seeing how careworn she is with hard
> work and solicitude for the children—know she is right & I should

help her share the responsibility and God helping me I will! It is not enough to take them and go right away if I could, but I will stay with her a year.[43]

Two days later, however, Wells received a letter from R. T. Coles, the teacher she had met in Kansas City, with an application for a teaching job there. Wells filled it out and returned it the same day. She also wrote Alfred Froman, asking her "Dad" for advice about staying.[44]

By August 9, Wells was obviously miserable. She complained of working very hard, bemoaning "the usual swelling of the hands & feet that always attended me after a hard day's manual labor." The climate was distastefully "hot & dusty" and Wells suffered "drooping spirits." She lamented, "I begin to feel lonely so far away from everything & everybody." Recalling that the Memphis school board was to elect teachers on that day, Wells once again made an unequivocal declaration: "if I am reelected will return & take Annie, if not both of the children with me; for I've no books, no companionship & even an embargo is laid upon my riding out with the only one who can take me."[45]

Wells seems to have battled recurring bouts of depression and indecision, and Visalia was pulling her down into a pit of despair. Used to a large amount of freedom for someone her age and sex, Wells chafed under the guiding hand of her aunt. She missed the intellectual and social activities that she called "a breath of life for me." In late August Froman urged Wells to return until her railroad suit was settled; he gave Wells a "duty" to return—offsetting her duty to stay. If she had possessed the money needed to return that day, she probably would have. To raise the funds she wrote R. R. Church requesting a loan of one hundred dollars. She then threw herself into making dresses for her aunt, perhaps in penance for her plans to leave.[46]

For the remainder of the summer, Wells continued having difficulty making up her mind. After she received a job offer in Visalia, she talked herself into remaining in California and prepared to "send the letters announcing my determination." Reflecting on her divided duties, she wrote:

I know Mr. F will be disappointed but I can't help that. I feel more & more that my first duty is to my sisters & my aunt who has helped me when I had no other helpers. And I will stay this year if it were ten times more unpromising than it is and at whatever personal cost to myself. Once I've made up my mind, I will have little difficulty in adhering to my fiat. I will begin school tomorrow and not be so ungrateful for the blessings that come to me on every hand.[47]

Wells persevered for four days in the "makeshift one-room building" that served as school for the eighteen African American school-age children. On Tuesday she received two letters. One was from Froman informing her that R. R. Church would lend her $100 to pay her way home. The other was from the Bowsers, who joined in the chorus of requests for Wells to teach in Kansas City. She went home determined to resign her Visalia position. Her aunt's friend sought to dissuade her, telling Wells "to do the duty that lies nearest." Fannie insisted that Wells should go but "then turned about and cried half the night & all the morning." On Thursday Wells resigned and made plans to go to Kansas City to teach, or to Memphis if the Kansas City position was no longer available. To justify her decision to herself, Wells declared, "I know I owe [Fannie] a debt of gratitude but she makes it so burdensome for me as to make it very distasteful. Forced acts of gratitude are not very sincere I should say."[48]

Wells left California with her younger sister Lily, who was about ten. Annie wanted to stay with her cousin Ida, who was her own age, and Aunt Fannie wanted Annie to stay for the same reason. Wells was relieved, realizing that "it would be much easier for me to manage with one instead of two half-grown girls on my hands."[49] She first stopped in Kansas City with the intention of teaching there. However, arriving in Kansas City on 21 September 1886, Wells again found herself in the center of controversy. Learning that some teachers resented the "employment of 'imported teachers' to the exclusion of home talent," she taught one day before resigning. Afterwards she declared, "I breathed freer after it was all over & I turned my face to the only home I know."[50]

4

✼

Coping with Gender Roles and Spirituality

"An anomaly to myself as well as to others"

✼

I n her writings and diaries, Ida B. Wells left many tantalizing hints of her emotional journey to womanhood. Moving into adulthood is often painful and difficult. Wells had to accomplish the passage rapidly and without the aid of her mother or father, who had provided her with a sheltered existence until their early deaths. Wells lengthened her dresses in preparation for her first teaching job—the physical transformation to adulthood required merely a needle and thread. However, Wells began to look and act like an adult long before she felt like one. The difficulties of this emotional transformation were heightened by the race and gender conventions of the age, which jarringly contradicted Wells's temperament and talents. Unsurprisingly, she often felt almost like a creature on a strange planet. As a woman, she tended to feel that she, not the planet, was alien.

Wells arrived in Memphis at 4:00 P.M. from California and was at the teachers' meeting the next morning to get her assignment—a class of seventy children at the Clay Street school. After the meeting, she learned from fellow teacher and suitor I. J. Graham that they had been linked in a salacious rumor. She soon learned another rumor was circulating in Kansas City that Lily was her daughter, rather than her sister. Wells "could not help getting furiously angry."[1]

Because of her status and temperament, Wells found herself the target of slander on a fairly regular basis. Such rumors posed a grave threat. Charges of immorality seriously jeopardized both her social standing and ability to earn a living. When confronting one of her accusers, Wells remembered, "I told him that my good name was all that I had in the world, that I was bound to protect it from attack by those who felt that they could do so with impunity because I had no brother or father to protect it for me."[2] Certainly part of the problem was a lack of elder male kinfolk. However, she did not lack male guidance; a number of older men assumed the role of surrogate father. At times it seemed as if the lack of a father encouraged almost every black man in Memphis to offer advice. Instead of having to appease one father, Wells had to cope with dozens.

But three older men played especially important roles. Foremost was Alfred Froman, whom Wells referred to as "Pap" and "Dad." Froman was a forceful, politically oriented, and fiercely independent man who may have helped shape her vision of ideal manhood. He was born into slavery but moved north as a free man before the Civil War. During the war, he distinguished himself for meritorious service while serving with the Fifty-fifth Massachusetts Regiment in the Union army. Described as a "self-made man," Froman edited the Memphis *Planet* in the 1870s before opening a saddle and harness shop. After the election of Rutherford B. Hayes and the defeat of the federal Force bill to guarantee free elections, Froman became disgusted with the Republican party. He joined an influential group of African American Democrats in Memphis and, in the words of a Republican newspaper, became "a straightout Democrat, yet, as he claims, subordinating everything to the good of his people." Even his political enemies recognized that Froman "has the very genius of hard, practical common sense, speaks fluently, forcibly and pointedly, giving evidence of an inexhaustible store of knowledge from general reading."[3]

Wells was most likely to seek advice from Froman. She consulted him about such concerns as her railroad suit, problems with her younger brothers, financial worries, her career, and the question of whether to remain in California. He lent her money as well as advice and sometimes accompanied her to concerts and plays. From her diary, however, it does not seem as if she consulted him on more personal matters. Froman appears to have been her political mentor—a fact that made her sympathetic to black Democratic editors, who were often charged with bolting the "party of Lincoln" for political self-advancement. Although Wells usually supported Re-

Josiah T. Settle, Wells's
landlord and one of her
surrogate fathers (from G. P.
Hamilton, The Bright Side of
Memphis *[1908]).*

publicans, she adhered to Froman's dictate that race interests must come before party interests.[4]

While Alfred Froman played the role of political mentor, Theodore W. Lott was an intellectual mentor. Lott, a teacher in the Memphis public schools, was described by a fellow teacher as "brilliant, ambitious, irrepressible, and inimitable." Wells looked to Lott for guidance in her quest for self-improvement, even paying him for elocution lessons. She borrowed books and magazines from Lott, gave him money to purchase a philosophy book for her, and enjoyed sparring with him intellectually. In January 1886 Wells noted in her diary, "He is very fond of teasing and as he firmly believes that he is teasing me I let him delude himself with the idea as he seems to take so much pleasure in it." Later that month, Wells called on his wife "expecting some fun from her mischievous spouse but he was not present." Although Mrs. Lott was described as "a St. Louis belle, of rare beauty" at the time of their marriage a year before, Wells depicted her in bland terms as "an easy sweet tempered, sweet minded mortal." Wells obviously preferred the "irrepressible" Mr. Lott, but he overstepped the boundaries of his role when he criticized Wells for her treatment of the young men of Memphis. After a lesson on 28 April, Wells wrote, "Mr. Lott made me very angry by declaring I only was amiable to men in order to repulse them and attributing every thing to me that is associated with a heartless flirt." Apparently that lesson was the last Wells took from him.[5]

A third father figure was Josiah T. Settle. Wells boarded with him and his wife from March 1886 to September 1887 on Lauderdale Street. Settle and his wife Theresa moved to Memphis in 1885 and quickly became leading citizens. Born in 1850, J. T. Settle was only thirteen years older than Wells, but his record of achievement earned Wells's respect. He graduated from both Oberlin and Howard, became a lawyer, and served in the Mississippi legislature before moving to Memphis. In 1885 a newspaper noted, "He possesses rare attainments as a scholar. He is modest, affable, generous and brave, and is bound to succeed."[6] Unlike her response to Lott, Wells listened to Settle when he tried to guide her behavior. Settle had watched the numerous suitors come and go while Wells boarded there. She seemed to encourage them all. At the breakfast table one morning, he cautioned her, saying "you are playing with edged tools." Wells pondered his statement and wrote in her diary, "I feel that I have degraded myself in that I had not the courage to repulse the one or the other."[7]

Part of Wells's problem with men was that she could neither comfortably accept nor reject the gender roles of her era. When Wells was born, the cultural elite of the nation, especially in the South, espoused the "cult of true womanhood" and the notion of a "proper sphere" for women. Nineteenth-century American society had become increasingly patriarchal. In the South, patriarchy assumed exaggerated forms in the defense of slavery as a "positive good" for the "childlike" slaves, who supposedly needed the guiding hand of a "father." Politically and economically dominant, white males had the power to define both African Americans and women in order to maintain dominance. Both were "put in their place" by southern white men. For African Americans of both sexes that place was in slavery; for southern white women that place was on a pedestal—each severely circumscribed behavior and required submissiveness.

In the cult of true womanhood, the ideal woman was seen not only as submissive but also gentle, innocent, pure, modest, and pious. Her proper sphere was the home, and her life was to revolve around her husband. Women were to honor and defer to men and yet provide a moral influence. Avoiding nagging or any overt criticism, a woman was to use her "wiles" and tact to gently guide the robust, active man to cultural refinement and moral rectitude. A "lady" did not enjoy sex but reveled in the opportunity to bear children. She was expected to profess ignorance of the "coarser things of life," including politics as well as nonmarital sex. She should be cultured but not intellectual.[8]

Although the role of "true womanhood" could only be played effectively by middle- and upper-class women, all women could aspire to it. Slave women, however, received most of the burdens of womanhood and few of the blessings. Not only were they worked like men, their womanhood was debased. Slave women's sexuality became a commodity and was discussed like that of an animal. Because being a "good breeder" increased a slave's value, the intimate details of her reproductive system were openly advertised. Rape was only one of the humiliations slave women endured. Rape also helped strip male slaves of the trappings of "manhood." In the Victorian model "real men" were in control—of their lives and their wives. Slave men, however, could not even control much of their own lives, much less protect their women.[9]

The potency of masters dramatically influenced gender relationships in the black community both before and after emancipation. Black women felt the need to bolster the ravaged egos of their men by allowing them as much opportunity as possible to be "real men." African Americans recognized that one way whites demonstrated their power was to deny slaves the power to emulate the white definitions of true manhood and womanhood. Therefore, after emancipation, most former slaves had come to see that power as a key element of freedom and sought to replicate white gender roles. For example, many black males were willing to sacrifice economic returns for emotional returns to keep their wives and children out of the fields. Among upper- and middle-class African Americans, the result was emulating the cult of true womanhood.[10]

Wells was not immune to these pressures, which were reinforced by black male journalists, who often tried to steer their readers toward behavior consistent with white gender roles. One article declared, "Would to God that an age of chivalry might dawn upon the Afro-American." It criticized "men who are eternally spread-eagling over 'protection to our women' and who will wax eloquent in wrath upon the white man 'that insults our ladies'" for not practicing what they preached. Another newspaper warned men, "Upon the choice of a wife depends both success in business and happiness in life." George Knox, editor of the Indianapolis *Freeman*, described women's special sphere as dramatically as any white man had.

Know that good women make good men, bad women can destroy nations. . . . All women may not shine before the world, yet they can be glorious sun beams in that heaven on earth, the home. But if they are not just right, that home will not be what God intended it to be. Every young woman's ambition is to have a home of her own some day, and just let me tell you, that it makes no difference how much wealth, how much beauty you may possess, your brilliant talents, if you are void of the purity of purpose, nobleness of soul, you are not what God intended.[11]

In the middle- and upper-class black community of the late nineteenth century, the enthronement of the cult of true womanhood sought to empower African Americans as a whole by imposing a patriarchal dominance over black women.

Unfortunately for Ida B. Wells, this arrangement required characteristics foreign to her temperament. As the first-born child, Wells acquired a sense of "specialness" common to that status. She also seemed especially close to her father, whose early death not only allowed her more independence but also enabled her to romanticize his memory. What she remembered of her father late in life is significant. Those memories highlighted her father's independence and pride. She recalled his being unintimidated by his white employer and unwilling to pay deference to "Miss Polly," his former owner. He also fearlessly entered politics, defying the possibility of Ku Klux Klan violence. Finally, he was an upright man, who sought to protect his family from yellow fever while risking his life to help others suffering from the illness. Not only was that image hard for her suitors to replicate, but when Ida Wells assumed Jim Wells's role as head of the household, she may have assumed his characteristics as her role model.

As a woman Wells's keen intellect and quick temper were burdens as well as blessings. The qualities that made Wells an effective activist also made her an unconventional nineteenth-century woman. The African American middle class usually allowed more display of independence and intellect by women than the white elite did, but because black women had been subjected to sexual degradation, higher levels of respectability were expected of them. Wells often pushed and occasionally exceeded the limits of gender roles.

As an ardent supporter of black rights, Wells often found herself in a dilemma. At the turn of the century, the definition of those rights was usually couched in the rhetoric of "manhood rights." Wells wanted black men to have and to exercise those rights—as her father had tried to do. Upholding the gender roles that made her so uncomfortable became a duty to her race. Her diary indicates that she had internalized the current definitions of manhood and womanhood. In 1888 Wells penned a portrait of the "Model Woman" for the *New York Freeman*. She wrote that a "typical girl's only wealth, in most cases, is her character," which was to be hoarded and guarded as a miser does his gold. Wells argued that there was "no sacrifice too great for the preservation of honor." Because African Americans were charged with "immorality and vice," Wells declared, "it depends largely on the woman of to-day to refute such charges by her stainless life." She also defined the characteristics of a model woman as follows:

> In the typical girl this jewel of character is enriched and beautified by the setting of womanly modesty, dignity of deportment, and refinement of manners; and the whole enveloped in a casket of sweetness of disposition, and the amiability of temper that makes it a pleasure to be near her. She is like the girl of fairy tales, who was said to drop pearls from her mouth as she talked, for her language is elegant from its simplicity and chastity, even though not always in accordance with rules of syntax, is beautiful because of the absence of slang.[12]

Interestingly, Wells refers to the "casket" of sweet disposition and amiable temperament. Her beliefs conflicted with her desires and temperament. While accepting much of the cult of true womanhood intellectually, emotionally the ideals felt like a straitjacket or "casket" to her. She wanted a "real man" who took charge, but at the same time she did not want to cede control. Any man who met her expectations also threatened her independence. A man she could dominate, however, lost her respect. She preferred the company of men to that of women and needed their approval more, but she had difficulty defining the terms of her relationships with them. In her diary Wells admits, "I am an anomaly to my self as well as to others. I do not wish to be married but I do wish for the society of gentlemen."[13]

Wells had no trouble attracting the attention of men. One newspaper account in 1885 described her as "about four and a half feet high, tolerably well proportioned, and of ready address." In 1893, at age thirty-one, Wells was called "young and comely." After she became well known among male journalists, they debated the extent of her beauty. Her eyes were considered her most attractive feature. Dark and soulful, they were said to "snap when she speaks of the wrong her race is suffering." More important than any physical features was a fiery spirit that drew men to her like moths to a flame. Most of the men Wells attracted, however, wanted her exclusive attention and a romantic relationship. At one point, Wells lamented, "It seems I can establish no middle ground between me and my visitors—it is either love or nothing."[14]

For Wells courtship held the key to male companionship. Yet because of her unwillingness to surrender her independence, courtship became more like war. Her romantic relationships were power struggles marked by series of skirmishes that sometimes escalated to total warfare. In her diary, Wells plotted strategy like a general preparing for battle. She was aware of both the power of her sexual attractiveness and her tendency to alienate her suitors. In June 1886, while pondering her dilemma of wanting male companionship but not marriage, Wells declared:

> With me, my affairs are always at one extreme or the other. I either have an abundance of company or none at all. Just now there are three in this city who, with the least encouragement, would make love to me; I have two correspondents in the same predicament—but past experience will serve to keep me from driving them from me.[15]

Men resented Wells's sexual power over them—and her knowledge of that power. One of her persistent suitors, I. J. Graham, informed Wells that someone had reported her as saying that "any young man I went out with ought to feel honored because of the 'privilege' & that whenever any one was with me all the young men in town knew it & said of him that he was highly honored." Wells was furious with Graham and wrote:

> When I think of how I could & can fool him and of his weak imaginings to the contrary, petty evidences of spite work, that he has been safe hitherto because I would not stoop to deceit—I grow wild almost & determine to pay him back. But I cannot do that; . . . I have never stooped to underhand measures to accomplish my end and I will not begin at this late date by doing what my soul abhors; sugaring men, weak, deceitful creatures, with flattery to retain them as escorts or to gratify a revenge. . . .[16]

During her Memphis years, Wells engaged in power struggles that posed for courtship with numerous young men—often simultaneously. Each new suitor seemed at first to be the right one but ultimately disappointed Wells. From most she expected total surrender before she would make a commitment. Her suitors, on the other hand, knew that they were one of many and were reluctant to propose, perhaps fearing rejection. To their circumspect and guarded declarations of love, Wells countered with increased demands coupled with enough reassurance to keep their hope alive. Terrified of being without male companionship, she held on to suitors like prisoners of war. Eventually some sought revenge—others merely sought release.

I. J. Graham was a fellow teacher who began teaching in the Memphis schools a year after Wells did. He was a graduate of Atlanta University and evidently from a privileged background. A fellow teacher called Graham "the wealthiest school teacher in the state of Tennessee." He eventually became principal of the Virginia Avenue School. For over a year Graham alternately courted and argued with Wells. Knowing she was seeing several other men, he was reluctant to propose marriage without assurances from Wells. She complained, "He seems to think I ought to encourage him to speak by speaking first—but that I'll never do. It's conceding *too* much and I don't think I need to buy any man's love." What really bothered Wells was that she had earlier made a tactical mistake by dropping her guard and allowing a little more intimacy than the current rules of black middle-class courtship allowed. She confessed, "I blush to think I allowed him to caress me, that he would dare take such liberties and yet not make a declaration."[17]

Wells kept Graham teetering on an emotional seesaw. At a party in May 1886, Graham handed Wells a note, which she characterized as "a verse declaring he knew I loved him & he longed to sip the nectar from my curling lip." Wells then noted, "I received it in silence, but intend keeping it." A few days later, Graham asked for a kiss, but Wells "gently but firmly refused." She wondered why he did not take the opportunity for "springing the question that evidently seems uppermost in his mind." Early in June, Graham did declare his love, but received less than an impassioned response. "I told him," Wells recorded, "I was not conscious of an absorbing feeling for him but I thought it would grow."[18]

That feeling seemed to grow little. Wells soon referred to him as "very thin, poor fellow." She continued to receive other male callers, but was angry when Graham did not come to see her when she expected. "I am too proud to beg," Wells declared, "but I must be loved with more warmth than that." Wells declined to admit to another suitor that she was "pledged to any one" and rationalized, "For with all the encouragement I've given G he has not sought to bind me to him & seems so utterly indifferent that I don't and can't feel that I belong to him." Wells then left for her summer trip to California, where she received a letter from Graham. Writing in her diary, she lamented, "I don't know what to think of him. He says he always feels as if in a tight jacket when in my presence and wishes to know if I love him and will live with him. I fear I don't but then I also fear I shall never love anybody."[19] Graham finally found release and shocked everyone by marrying someone else less than a month after Wells's return from California.[20]

Apparently Graham believed that Wells had "lost her heart" to Edwin Hackley while she was in Denver. When Wells was in California, she "eagerly devoured" the contents of one of his letters. She noted, "He writes in the easy, natural manner that he speaks." Wells answered "right away" and "told him many things." Soon, however, their correspondence became a long-distance power struggle. Less than a month later, she lamented not receiving a letter from Hackley and noted, "I would write again but it would have the appearance of eagerness." The next day she received a newspaper from Hackley containing an account of his nomination by the Republicans for the Colorado legislature. Wells exclaimed, "Hurrah for Edwin! but as he has not answered my letter yet I don't know that I shall write to congratulate him."[21]

After finally receiving a letter, Wells then plotted to wait for his next letter "ere I answer this & then very coolly."[22] They continued to correspond that fall, but Wells did not appear to rank him any higher than other suitors. Others seemed to think otherwise. In December, the regular column about Memphis in the *Cleveland Gazette* made a cryptic reference that also reflects how Wells was perceived:

> Wedding bells will soon be heard round about Clay street school building, if Dame Rumor puts it right. But we think not yet, for the one who is said to have left her heart in the wilds of the West, certainly *could not* have done so. Now who said that "Iola" [Wells's pen name] ever had a heart? And who would dare to mention the name in conjunction with that of a candidate for the matrimonial state, the Legislature, or any other office?[23]

Regardless of the rumors, Wells and Hackley corresponded regularly until March 1887, after which their correspondence tapered off, and in August Wells referred to Hackley as "my Denver one-time-friend."[24]

Wells had another long-distance suitor—Charles S. Morris, a journalist from Louisville, Kentucky, who began studying at Howard in 1886. Her relationship with him illustrates her acceptance of the idea that men should be the dominant partner in a relationship as well as her reluctance to accept a subordinate role. They started corresponding in late 1885, before they had ever met face-to-face. When Wells received a picture, she noted, "I told him I liked the face but it is the face of a mere boy; whereas I had been led, from his writings to suppose him a man." She feared he was younger than she and decided to withhold her age until she knew his, declaring, "I wish to make the unpleasant discovery that I am his senior—first."[25] Morris turned out to be two years younger than Wells—a fact she found upsetting because in other ways he seemed to be what she was looking for in a man. She tried to sort out her tangled emotions in her diary.

> He speaks so authoritatively about things and I could accept his calm reproof, superior criticism & logic if he were not my junior; he is what I have long wished for in a correspondent, an interested, intellectual being who could lead & direct my wavering footsteps in intellectual paths. His youth, tho, prevents my asking & seeking information of him as I would one who was my superior in age as well as intellectuality. I may overcome the feeling tho' as there is not any pleasure without its alloy. . . . He writes a good letter & I feel my sceptre departing from me, before him as before no other & it is somewhat humiliating.[26]

Wells was certainly ambivalent. She wanted a man who could "lead & direct [her] wavering footsteps" but also found her strong feelings for him "humiliating."

Morris remained Wells's favorite correspondent for some time. She answered his letters before all others and relished his, which "instructed entertained and amused" her. Wells thought she had found a soul mate, writing:

> He understands & sympathizes with my position of almost complete isolation from my fellow being[s] on account of lack of congeniality—and I think he does so the more fully because his *own* experience coincides with mine. His fine humor & sarcasm are very refreshing & I believe I can say at last I have found a thoroughly congenial correspondent, and I sincerely hope it (the correspondence) may not die the death of the others but may be the foundation of a lasting friendship increasing with the years, such as I read about, often, see very rarely and have experienced—never![27]

Nevertheless, Wells was soon plotting strategy with him as well—as apparently he, too, was doing. The ardor cooled and they began a verbal sparring match by mail in which both accused the other of being slack in their correspondence.

Of all her courtships, perhaps the relationship between Wells and Louis M. Brown was the most stormy—and passionate. Brown had been living in Memphis when Wells began teaching. He was a journalist, writing for the *Living Way* when Wells also wrote for it. Brown became the paper's Washington correspondent but left the *Living Way* in January 1885 to assume the city editorship of the *Washington Bee*, a spicy journal edited by W. Calvin Chase.[28] The nature of their relationship is evident in Wells's diary, where she described him as "a petty warrior," lamented "his petty mode of warfare," and noted that he "as usual is on the warpath."[29]

Neither of them wanted to care too deeply for the other. One time when Brown admitted loving Wells, she noted that he told her "he'd carefully guarded against such as I was the kind of girl of whom he would become infatuated." Wells seemed strongly drawn to Brown, referring one time to the "glamour of his presence," even though she could not respect him because he seemed to be "still hunting for his place." Her diary is filled with disparaging remarks, but it also recounts an incident in which "he kissed me—twice—& it seems even now as if they blistered my lips. I feel so humiliated in my own estimation at the thought that I cannot look any one in the face. I feel somehow as if I were defrauded of something since then."[30]

Wells found herself in a dilemma of Victorian womanhood. As a woman, she was not expected to have strong sexual feelings.[31] Doubly difficult was the fact that Wells felt them for a man she otherwise found lacking. Most of the important suitors in her life were already, or were in the process of becoming, successful. They also were what was then called "race men," that is, active in the cause of black rights.[32] Brown, on the other hand, seemed to bounce around from job to job. It is hardly a wonder that Wells agonized over his power to "steal" kisses from her.

For a period of time, Wells attempted a feat tried by women in every era; she sought to "redeem" Brown through his love for her. When he sought a commitment from her, she "commended his determination and told him to do something that called forth admiration and respect and the rest would be easy." In September Wells was pleased with Brown's progress, noting, "He is developing symptoms more to my ideas of what becomes an earnest man and I told him so, as well as that if he succeeded in his new venture & winning my love in the meantime, I would help him prove to the world what love in its purity can accomplish."[33] Brown could not live up to her expectations, however, and later accused her of turning her back on a friend who was "down in the world." Wells replied, telling him to "be a man, a strong liberal minded man, or be none at all."[34]

Wells's difficult relationships with men sometimes interfered with her career. Using the pen name Elembee, Brown battled with her in the pages of the *Washington Bee*. In his "They Say" column he labeled "Iola" a "liberal creature with criticisms," whose "young days must have been devoid of that essential attribute to quiet maidenhood—love." Wells apparently retaliated, claiming Brown's attack was a personal vendetta because she rejected his overtures, that he was not respectful to black women, and that he stole the idea of the "They Say" column from her. Brown fired back with both barrels, saying among other things, "That she is evidently at sea when she supposes our offer of assistance a proposition to extract her from the mice of old maidenhood, as we are bountifully supplied—at present."[35] Such sniping diminished Wells's image at the very time she was beginning to fight for recognition as a legitimate journalist.

As difficult as they were, Wells considered her relationships with men more important than those with women. Both her diaries and her autobiography focus more on men than women. In her twenties she apparently wished to have more women friends but had difficulty in establishing and sustaining meaningful female relationships. She socialized with some of her fellow women teachers, yet in her diary she seldom more than briefly noted these activities. Even when Wells had misunderstandings with such close women friends as Fannie J. Thompson and Fannie J. Bradshaw, she did not seem to agonize over the problems as she did with disagreements with her suitors. In one diary entry, Wells noted that Fannie Thompson "has been singularly uncommunicative this week & I have not sought to woo her from her silence." The next month Wells wrote that Fannie J. Bradshaw "was here when I came from school but as she came ostensibly to see Mrs. Hill I made no effort to deprive her of the visit."[36] Neither woman seemed the type to overshadow Wells. Bradshaw was described at different times as "sedate and erudite," "admired for her quiet and graceful manner," and "sweet, tender-hearted." Thompson was labeled "level-headed and efficient."[37] On some occasions, Wells appeared to resent women as sexual rivals for the favors of men. After serving as a chaperon for one young couple, she commented on the news that the young man was leaving by writing, "I am not sorry, for I got tired playing second fiddle & running around with them."[38]

In both her private and public writings, Wells was generally critical of women. In her diary she criticized one woman for being "very quarrelsome & picayunish" and another for failing to show appropriate gratitude for a letter of recommendation from Wells. Another entry noted "the complicated labyrinth of woman's various moods & petty fancies." In her only published short story, "Two Christmas Days: A Holiday Story," Wells ignored or belittled women, with the exception of the heroine and one older woman. "The other girls," Wells wrote, "are so taken up flirting with their partners they neither know nor care when their turn comes to play [croquet]."[39]

On the validity of the Victorian cult of true womanhood, the dissonance between Wells's intellect and emotions is palpable. In her public writings (and even overtly in her diary), Wells rarely challenged the desirable characteristics of an "ideal woman" as being submissive, genteel, and soft of heart and voice. Yet her praises of such women often seemed to dismiss them as insignificant. She described one as "the sweetest, quietest and most lady like little creature it has been my good fortune to meet" and another as "good & kind and soft as a mouse."[40] Obviously, "little creatures" and "mice" do not have the power to command respect.

Sometimes Wells seemed to wish that she valued more highly the qualities considered to be feminine. When learning of the death of a suitor named Harry, she recalled how he had defended her against slander. She regretted sending him a "cruel letter in answer to his last declaration of love for me!" Wells labeled him "gentle, kind and tender as a woman," but those very qualities appear to have led her to also consider him "weak and irresolute" as well as "not of a decided character."[41] Wells apparently equated gentleness with weakness.

In her diary, Wells penned her most effusive praise for the cult of true womanhood in her description of a music teacher at Rust who embodied the virtues of an "ideal woman." After a trip to Holly Springs, Wells wrote:

> Was introduced to Miss Atkinson the music teacher, who seemed so fair and pure, so divinely good, whose motions were grace & poetry personified—she seemed to me, one of the few women that I have met who come near justifying the ravings of poets and proving their metaphors not inspired alone by the imagination. She seems so thoroughly pleasant, so bubbling over with the effervescence of youth, health, high spirits, cheerfulness and withal such an exuberance of vitality in every look or motion that everyone is charmed without knowing why.

Wells seemed to relish the combination of "vitality" and "grace." Nevertheless, she was not entirely sure that the two could coexist successfully. Wells further noted, "She is quite young—just from college and when she is toned down somewhat, will be a truly noble-minded woman."[42]

Though Wells did not seem terribly concerned about her relationships with docile women, strong, ambitious women evoked a different response from Wells. She plotted strategies for winning their friendship much like she did with male suitors. Virginia Broughton, a Memphis teacher demoted for her outspokenness, was aloof with Wells. Wells sought to discover why and finally decided:

> I have discovered the keynote of her actions, I think. That she would
> have, is most desirous of, she labors to appear indifferent to but her
> real aim is to secure her ends without seeming to put forth effort. Her
> studied indifference to "me royal Highness" has piqued me & I am
> determined that she shall not succeed in making me show interest in
> her without a corresponding show on her side.[43]

Broughton and most of the women Wells respected were older than her. With one woman her age, however, Wells thought she had found a soul mate. Mary (Mollie) Church was the daughter of millionaire Robert R. Church and his first wife. When Mollie Church came to visit her father in the summer of 1887, she and Wells met and felt an instant affinity. Writing of their acquaintance, Wells broke with her pattern and called Church by her first name immediately after meeting her. She wrote:

> Miss Mollie was down Friday evening to call and said she wished to
> have a talk with me. Her ambitions seem so in consonance with
> mine that I offered to come up the next morning. I did go and I came
> away after about a two hours chat—very much enthused with her.
> She is the first woman of my age I've met who is similarly inspired
> with the same desires hopes & ambitions.[44]

When Wells first met Mary Church, she felt a little less like an alien. Church, however, did not stay in Memphis. Her father would not let her work outside the home, telling her that she "would be taking the bread and butter out of the mouth of some girl who needed it."[45] Instead, she toured Europe and then taught at Wilberforce University in Ohio and later in the public schools of Washington, D.C., where she met and married Robert Terrell, a lawyer who became a judge. Her friendship with Wells apparently did not survive the separation. Both became well known for their activism, but their similarities seemed to drive them apart instead of together. Later in life their rivalry caused more friction than friendship.

By the time Wells met Mollie in 1887, she had realized that she did not really wish to be married, even though she preferred the company of men. Nevertheless, in 1886 and early 1887, Wells was constantly invited to weddings and noted in February 1887 that she was "the only lady teacher left in the building who is unmarried." Feeling "singularly lonely & despondent," Wells wrote former suitor B. F. Poole "on the spur of the moment" and implied that if he came back to Memphis, she would marry him. She later regretted the impulse and asked him to return the letter.[46] Instead, she consoled herself with an article in the *Cleveland Gazette*, which described the weddings in Memphis as "epidemic" and noted two exceptions:

> A flourishing literary circle furnishes rare entertainment, greatly to the delight of admiring audiences. Of these, most prominent are Miss Fanny J. Thompson and Miss Ida B. Wells. These ladies, though they have a host of loving admirers, keep so busy that they have not time to devote in emulation of those who woo and win.[47]

Although Wells may have felt left out and different as wedding after wedding took place, she shied away from commitments that could lead to marriage. She seemed to prefer the abstraction of holy matrimony to the reality of wedded life. She did not envy most married women—especially those with children. She noted one acquaintance was "rather pretty" but had been more so before she married. "The inevitable baby is there," Wells declared, "with the habits peculiar to all babyhood."[48]

Perhaps Wells was wary of motherhood because of the frustrations she felt in the role of mother to her siblings. After her aunt moved to California and took Annie and Lily with her, Wells no longer had any day-to-day responsibilities of surrogate parenthood—at least until she brought Lily home with her. Her brothers were old enough to be on their own, but Wells still fretted over their decisions and behavior. Jim especially was troubling. He had a weakness for gambling and never seemed to visit except when he was in trouble and needed help. In January 1886 he came to school to see his sister because he needed money. Wells wrote, "He has gotten into trouble & can't go back where he was." She had no money to lend him and referred him to Alfred Froman, who sent him to another friend for help. He was supposed to let her know what happened but did not.[49]

Almost a year later Jim showed up again. He freely admitted that he had been roaming around "following a passion for gaming." Wells pleaded with him to quit, warning him of the "depths to which he would sink." He assured her that "the passion would never get such a mastery of him," and she could not convince him "to quit & let the adherence or the struggle be the test of the power it had already acquired over him." Wells considered trying to get Jim to stay and operate a chicken farm with her. Once again he left with promises to return that he did not keep. Wells prayed, "O God, hear my prayer & help my wandering boy to come back to the innocence of his childhood! Let me be a feeble instrument in Thy Hands to reclaim him!"[50] She was relieved when Jim decided to make a crop with his brother George. In a letter signed "your wild & reckless brother," Jim professed that "it takes time to break up a habit that has been forming for years." In times of trouble he continued to turn to Wells, who went immediately to him in the summer of 1887, after he sent a postal telling her that he was sick and asking her to come to Millington, Tennessee.[51]

Wells was in much more constant contact with George. While they both lived in Memphis, her diary reflects that he visited her several times each month. Not nearly as "wild & reckless" as Jim, George still was a source of concern for Wells. She especially worried about his inability to manage money and sought to help him by holding money for him. She also came to his aid in March 1886, getting him work with her friend Louis Payne in Woodstock when George could not find a job in Memphis. That May he brought her $1.15 to go with the $1.70 she already had. Wells exulted, "His pile grows slowly." Nevertheless, she was disgusted the next month when he went to Holly Springs with her and neglected to bring any money for the return trip. The next fall Wells worried that George was about to marry unwisely. She sought to dissuade him by talks, letters, and even enlisting the help of Jim, who assured her that "there is nothing of George's marrying."[52]

Wells seemed closest to George—he was the only sibling she mentioned exchanging presents with at Christmas in 1886. Nevertheless, they often had disagreements. In February 1886, Wells noted that George "hardly spoke to me & refused to tell me goodby. I think he is carrying his 'miff' to a great extent." Later that year she noted he "seemed somewhat constrained in his manner."[53] Wells's difficulties with her brothers bothered her. After having success with a Sunday school class of young men she had organized, she lamented: "But I seem to be a failure so far as my own brother is concerned for I speak harshly or indifferently & repulsively to him before I think of the consequences. I can get along well enough with other boys but am too hasty & impatient with my own."[54]

After she brought Lily back from California in 1886, Wells had to deal with the ten-year-old girl on a day-to-day basis. Other than the rumor that Lily was her own daughter, Wells seemed to have little difficulty at first. From their arrival at Memphis in September until after Christmas, Wells made no mention of Lily in her diary. The lack of entries indicates not only a lack of trouble but also perhaps a devaluation of Lily in comparison to the male siblings whose activities were regularly noted. By January 1887, the reality of full-time responsibility for a child began to plague Wells. When invited to spend the coming summer with an older woman, Wells lamented, "alas, I cannot on Lily's account. I like not the idea of sending her away from me & to strangers at that."[55]

Problems with Lily began to arise in the spring of 1887. She did not get along well with Wells's landlord and turned rebellious. In May Wells declared, "Lily & I had a pitched battle this morning for some of her felonious practices." The next month she lamented, "Had to whip Lily severely this morning for her second peculation." By the next fall, Lily was staying with a woman who was to teach her to cook.[56] Wells had learned further of the difficulties of single motherhood. Without the help of her extended family—especially Aunt Fannie—Wells could not have managed full-time teaching, part-time journalism, and a hectic social life.

Extended families are often systems of support for people with limited resources. In slavery and freedom, many African Americans living in marginal conditions relied on both kinship and friendship networks. The communal qualities of such networks, and indeed most closely knit families, require some degree of submission of the individual to the group interest. As a young woman, Ida B. Wells had difficulty enduring such restraints. A sense of duty required her to assume some degree of responsibility for her younger siblings but the role was not comfortable for her. Despite being outwardly gregarious, Wells was an emotional loner. Thus her ties to extended family members other than Fannie and one cousin were not as strong as might have been expected. Her aunt was helping her with the children, and her cousin, Stella Butler, moved in the same social circles as Wells. Even so, although Wells was maid of honor for Stella Butler's marriage to I. F. Norris, Wells seldom mentioned her in her diary. She completely lost contact with other key family members. When notified by her Aunt Margaret that her Grandmother Peggy had died in March 1887, Wells expressed shock "to know she had been alive all this time & I never knew it or where she lived."[57]

In addition to familial duties, money problems plagued Wells, who was constantly in debt. In June 1887, frustration led Wells to lament, "I wish I could feel that my money was not so persistently sought after. I wonder if I shall ever reach satisfaction in this world."[58] Satisfaction seemed to elude Wells in practically every aspect of life during her mid-twenties. Dissatisfaction sometimes gave way to despair. In January 1886, Wells wrote of her "winter of discontent." Wells was more than merely discontented, however; she seems to have suffered bad bouts of depression. Her diary is filled with references to days during which she can only summon the energy to get out of bed after sleeping long hours. In two March 1886 entries, she noted that she found it "hard to rouse my sluggish nature" and that on one Saturday "the biggest job undertaken & finished was—a bath."[59] Her social life sustained her, while probably simultaneously depleting her energy. In April she wrote:

> Had no visitors today. I am in as correspondingly low spirits tonight as I was cheerful this morning. I don't know what's the matter with me, I feel so dissatisfied with my life, so isolated from all my kind. I cannot or do not make friends & these fits of loneliness will come & I tire of everything. My life seems awry, the machinery out of gear & I feel there is something wrong.[60]

About a year later she declared, "I am not happy & nothing seems to make me so. I wonder what kind of creature I will eventually become." Six months later Wells admitted, "I've had no heart to write any one else, I've been in a state of such depression."[61]

Depression frequently results from anger not directed at its source but instead turned against oneself. That Wells continually found fault with herself is hardly surprising given the environment in which she lived. Victorian culture made impossible demands of women. They were expected to be strong enough to mold men and weak enough to submit to their control. At the same time women were held to unrealistically high standards of purity and self-sacrifice. African American women found the burdens even heavier. They were held largely responsible for the advancement of the race, while constantly being debased by the white media. They suffered a double dose of powerlessness because of their sex and race. Feelings of inadequacy and failure were hard to avoid for many black women, but they were even more difficult for Ida B. Wells.

Wells was aware of the personality traits that caused her problems in conforming to her assigned roles but seemed powerless to modify them. Throughout her diary, she beseeched God for help to control her temper and her tongue. In one entry she pleaded, "O My Father, forgive me, forgive me & take away the remembrance of those hateful words, uttered for the satisfaction of self. Humble the pride exhibited and make me Thy child." Other entreaties include "O help me to better control my temper!" and "O guard my tongue from evil" as well as "Father help me, I pray be more thoughtful & considerate in speech."[62]

Wells sought divine help to curb her rebelliousness and impatience while embarking on self-improvement projects as well. To make up for her limited formal education, she supplemented the lessons she took from Mr. Lott with independent studies and reading but encountered difficulties. "I don't know what books to read that will do the most good," she complained, "& know not where I am to obtain the knowledge."[63] Wells also found it hard to exercise the self-discipline needed for self-directed learning. Her failures led to further feelings of inadequacy. In March 1886, Wells chastised herself once again: "I now think of the golden moments wasted, the precious hours I should have treasured and used to store up knowledge for future use. It seems so hard to get at it (study) and I've made so many resolutions I am ashamed to make any more."[64]

Although Wells used her diary to castigate herself, she also utilized her pen to provide relief from despair. Her diary provided an emotional catharsis for disappointment, fear, and pain. After a particularly trying day, Wells wrote in her journal, "Came home feeling very, very badly but at this writing am some better." Few people put anything in writing without at least unconsciously considering how the words would sound to someone else. Wells may have done some self-censoring, but she clearly intended her diary to be a private place to express freely things she never would have discussed with others. She kept it locked in her writing desk and hid the key.[65]

For Wells religion played a large role as both a source of guilt and relief. It also helped her to define herself. At the same time, attendance at church was a vital part of her social life. Vance Street Christian Church became her spiritual home for several reasons.[66] The church seemed to be especially active in the community, hosting not only the Memphis Lyceum but also meetings about segregated schools. Theologically, the Christian Church (also called the Church of Christ and the Disciples of Christ) was also compatible with Wells's independent spirit. An American creation, the church drew from disaffected Presbyterians, Baptists, and Methodists and held its first national convention in 1849 at Cincinnati.[67]

The church's central tenet was freedom of religious thought. Attempting to "restore" the original church founded by the disciples of Jesus, it rejected the theological debates that divide Christians and proclaimed, "We have no creed but Christ." Christians were defined as anyone who can answer affirmatively to the question: "Do you believe that Jesus is the Christ, the Son of the Living God, and your Savior?" Disciples believed that the Bible contains all that is needed to be known about God and that this knowledge can be understood and interpreted by each individual. Faith, not specific beliefs or practices, was required of Disciples. The decision to follow Christ begins a personal journey during which believers are bound to slip and fall. Nevertheless, true repentance—a sincere desire to change—always leads to God's forgiveness. Such freedom of thought and action must have had a powerful appeal to Wells's independent personality. At the same time, the Christian Church's emphasis on Christian unity allowed her the freedom to attend numerous churches.

Her diary shows that Wells regularly went to services at other churches. Raised in the Methodist church, she was most active in Avery Chapel—the largest African Methodist Episcopal (A.M.E.) Church in the city. The A.M.E. denomination had its roots in the segregationist actions of a Philadelphia Methodist church one Sunday morning in 1787. When Richard Allen was asked to leave the "white" section of his own church, he left permanently and formed the A.M.E. church. Its membership grew steadily in the North and at the end of the war expanded rapidly among southern black Methodists seeking religious independence from the white Methodists. An African American missionary sent from the North to Memphis organized Avery Chapel A.M.E. Church, and it became a large success. Its members originally met in the basement of a white Methodist church, but they were thrown out when they refused to affiliate with the Methodist Episcopal Church, South. They then erected a three thousand dollar church, which was destroyed in the riot of 1866. In 1867 the congregation built a ten thousand dollar edifice on the corner of Desoto and Hernando streets.[68]

Wells not only attended church at Avery Chapel, she also organized a Sunday school class there in January 1887. The class was for "young men or rather youths, just merging into manhood" (another indication of her preference for the company of men). Wells decided to teach the class during her New Year's reflections, after having taken communion. She admitted, "I reviewed my past year of existence & I am so overwhelmed with the little I have done for one who has done so much for me." She resolved to lead a class and declared, "I shall begin this year with that determination, so that another year may find me with more to offer the master in the way of good works."[69]

Wells also attended a number of other churches less regularly for a variety of reasons. She went to the Beale Street Baptist Church for political reasons. The Second Congregational Church appealed to her because its pastor, Benjamin A. Imes, combined advanced education with religious fervor. She seems to have attended two other churches because of her ties to the black elite. Most of the upper class attended either Emmanuel Episcopal Church or Collins Chapel Colored Methodist Episcopal (C.M.E.) Church. Such black aristocrats as Anna Wright Church, Dr. A. J. Burchett, and the J. T. Settles went to Emmanuel. When Wells moved in with the Settles, she acquired another entrée to the upper class. Her diary first mentions attending Emmanuel the month after she moved in. A number of times she refers to the church only as Theresa Settle's church. Emmanuel was called "ver[y] imposing in its appearance" from the outside, but it never acquired one hundred members until the 1890s. The congregation must not have considered black autonomy very important for the church remained under white supervision long after the lower-class, more nationalist churches had declared their religious independence.[70]

Wells seems to have attended the Episcopal church because many of her friends did. Her social relationships may have also induced her to attend the other church, which was popularly known as "high-tone." She became good friends with Dr. and Mrs. C. H. Phillips soon after he assumed the pastorship of Collins Chapel in 1885. Whereas the A.M.E. Church sprang from the antebellum free black population of the North, the C.M.E. Church was rooted in the southern slave experience. It originated from the Methodist Episcopal Church, South, which was formed when the issue of slavery caused a split in the national Methodist Episcopal Church. After emancipation that church wanted to hold on to its 207,000 African American members, who were moving to the A.M.E. Church in droves. The white Methodists wanted black Methodists under their denominational umbrella but not their church roofs. When the denomination tried to establish segregated conferences, the pastors of its remaining forty thousand black members did not demand their independence but rather respectively petitioned to be allowed to form a new denomination in 1870.

Black Methodists who stayed in the Methodist Episcopal Church, South, until 1870 tended to have close ties with whites. The 1870 petition declared, "You were our masters, you were kind, conscientious, and exhibited the deepest anxiety for our welfare."[71] Many had been members of the slave aristocracy as a result of their kinship with white masters. Thus the denomination was known for the light skin of its leaders. One black newspaper noted, "On the bench of bishops there is now but one of the dark hue, all the others being mulattos, quadroons or octoroons."[72] C. H. Phillips, however, was an exception as a darker-skinned pastor. Collins Chapel was not as elitist as Emmanuel and drew many more members. In 1908 Collins had 1,200 members and Emmanuel only 125. Collins Chapel became known as the "most refined and quiet large congregation in the city."[73] Wells's church in Holly Springs had been affiliated with the northern branch of Methodists rather than the southern. She was not as ideologically compatible with the C.M.E. Church and visited Collins Chapel only infrequently, despite her friendship with its minister.

Scholars have debated whether religion provided African Americans with an opiate for their ills or with a revolutionary vision. In most cases it did both and much more. Wells found comfort in her faith, felt guilt for her spiritual shortcomings, and was incensed by racism in the white church. When worried about her aunt, she asked for the prayers of church members. On her twenty-fifth birthday, Wells described her heart as "overflowing with thankfulness to My Heavenly Father for His wonderful love & kindness." That same day she asserted that her greatest regret was that "I am not so good a Christian as the goodness of my father demands." Wells constantly felt as if she was lacking as a Christian. The previous Easter season she was moved by a sermon in which Imes "preached about our religion costing us something" and lamented that "my thoughts had strayed away from the true significance of the time to less important matters of dress; that I have made no preparation for an Easter offering." She then promised to do so and "instead of spending my holiday in fun & pleasure for myself will fast for my many sins of dereliction & remain home to work, watch and pray." Seldom could she live up to such resolutions, however. On Easter day Wells went to church, to a friend's house for dinner, and then home to read the novel *She*.[74]

Like many African Americans, Wells viewed God as the advocate of the persecuted. "Thou hast always fought the battles of the weak & oppressed," she wrote of God in her diary. She believed in divine justice and was sometimes distressed and confused when evil seemed to triumph. When she lost her railroad suit on appeal, Wells asked, "O God is there no redress, no peace, no justice in this land for us?" She believed God had the power to right wrongs and relied on that faith for courage. "Yet I do not fear," Wells wrote in her diary, "God is over all & He will, so long as I am in the right, fight my battles, and give me what is my right." Her theology was influenced by the black church's emphasis on the God of Moses. She appealed to God, "Show us the way, even as Thou led the children of Israel out of bondage into the promised land."[75] This faith at times made the black church a revolutionary force for change. It helped create both Martin Luther King, Jr., and Ida B. Wells.[76]

Wells sometimes visited white churches as well as black ones. Asbury Methodist Church in Holly Springs had been founded by a white northern missionary and local blacks. Rust College grew out of it, and the school's white faculty may well have gone to Asbury. Ties also existed between the black Vance Street Christian Church and the white Linden Street Christian Church. Although the black congregation at Vance had hooted and stamped their feet at a sermon by the Linden Street minister in 1876, by the 1880s relations seemed to have improved. In March 1885 Linden Street's pastor lectured at the Lyceum. On several occasions, Wells referred in her diary to the Christian church, once remarking that she visited it. She most likely meant Linden Street. Her casual mention of the visit may mean that she worshiped there without incidence.[77]

Sometimes her experiences in white churches angered Wells. On Thanksgiving in 1886, she attended the Stranger's Church on Union Avenue. Its white congregation did not eject her, but its members made their displeasure obvious. Wells described the incident in her diary: "Thanksgiving also went to the Strangers Church & heard a good sermon & witnessed practical evidence of 'white folks' christianity,' in the haste with which they passed us by when choosing a seat."[78]

On another occasion, Wells visited a white church to hear Dwight L. Moody, one of the foremost evangelists of the age who was immensely popular at home and abroad. Headquartered in Chicago, Moody usually followed local custom on the matter of segregation. In the North seating was open to all, but in the South he accommodated white prejudice by allowing separate seating by race. During his 1886 southern tour, Moody spoke at both Avery Chapel and the white Cumberland Presbyterian Church in Memphis. Wells attended both meetings and was glad she had gone to Avery, because she found it hard to hear from the area set aside for black worshipers at Cumberland. Like many who heard Moody preach, Wells was mesmerized by his preaching. Her comments not only describe Moody's style but also illumine Wells's own religious orientation.

His style is so simple, plain and natural. He told the old, old story in an easy conversational way that charms the listener ere he is aware and the secret, I think—that he does not preach a far-away God—a hard to be reconciled Savior but uses a natural easy tone and tells in a natural way without any long drawn doctrine or finely spun theology or rhetoric the simple truth that Christ Jesus came on earth to seek & save that which was lost.[79]

Her praises for Moody, however, were tempered by deep disappointment that such a Christian leader condoned the degradation of fellow Christians through Jim Crow sanctuaries. Wells was distraught that Moody left town before she could confront him on the issue. She lamented:

I intended writing Mr. Moody a letter asking him why ministers never touched upon that phase of sin—caste distinction—practised even in the churches and among christianity (?) but rather, tacitly conniving at it by assenting to their caste arrangements, and accepting it as a matter of course, instead of rectifying it—but I had no chance, & he left the city yesterday; so I know not where to address him.[80]

Later in life Wells publicly aired her disappointment with Moody's failure to combat forcefully the sins of bigotry and lynching.[81] At the time she obviously felt a religious superiority to the practitioners of "christianity (?)" who distorted the precepts of Jesus to maintain their own positions of power. One function of religion both under slavery and after emancipation was to allow African Americans to see themselves not only as slaves but also as children of God, while viewing whites as both pitiful sinners and powerful masters. Her religion undoubtedly had a great impact on Wells as she was coming-of-age and seeking to define herself.

As Wells struggled in her mid-twenties to reconcile her duties and her dreams, she became increasingly aware of injustice. Memphis was her testing grounds, the site of great pain as well as joy. On her twenty-fifth birthday, Wells looked back on her life:

As this day's arrival enables me to count the twenty fifth milestone, I go back over them in memory and review my life. The first ten are so far away, in the distance as to make those at the beginning indistinct; the next 5 are remembered as a kind of butterfly existence at school, and household duties at home; within the last ten I have suffered more, learned more, lost more than I ever expect to, again. In the last decade, I've only begun to live—to know life as a whole with its joys and sorrows.[82]

Her experiences provided the cocoon from which Wells emerged as a journalist and activist. Although she did not realize it in 1887, the next ten years of her life would prove to be even more tumultuous as she moved from teaching into journalism.

5

Moving from Teaching to Journalism

"An outlet through which to express the real 'me'"

The transformation of Miss Wells the teacher into Iola the journalist was so gradual that she was largely unaware of where her choices were leading. Expected to play uncomfortable roles in an era belittling to both her race and sex, Wells was dissatisfied and angry. Her hectic social life brought some joy and excitement but seemed often to leave her feeling lonely and isolated. Religion brought comfort but was heavily laced with guilt. Wells tried hard to fulfill many expectations that were unnatural for her, all the while wondering "what kind of creature I will eventually become?" Journalism helped her find a way out of this confusion. She later wrote that "newspaper work gave me an outlet through which to express the real 'me.'"[1] One could argue that it also provided the means to determine just who that person was. She came to Memphis a teacher confused as to who she was; she left as a strong, competent woman who would rock the English-speaking world.

When social relationships failed to satisfy her yearnings, Ida B. Wells turned to her work and political activities for sustenance. At first her job provided little relief because she disliked teaching. Nevertheless, working in the public schools during a period of increased politicization of the system exposed her to the racial politics of Memphis, which stimulated her newspaper career. Dissatisfaction with teaching also pushed Wells toward journalism as an alternative vocation. Increasing political militancy came to provide a focus for the anger that poisoned her relationships with others and also with herself. The injustices she witnessed both fueled and caused her to act out her personal anger.

Although Wells found little satisfaction in her role as teacher, teaching provided an income and an entrée into the ranks of the privileged. She recognized that she was fortunate to have the job, but it drained rather than fulfilled her. In her diary, Wells never wrote anything positive about her job or about individual students. Instead, it was filled with a litany of complaints that helps shed light on her personality. The anger and impatience that fueled her activism made her temperamentally unsuited for teaching. "Was to school this morning by 8:00 and felt peculiarly pleasant and—good," Wells wrote, but continued, "A day's worry with these children has brought my temper to the surface." Sometimes a sense of powerlessness seemed to be at the root of her problem. The rambunctious children were not always easy to control. She felt unable to reach them, once complaining, "Friday was a trying day at school. I know not what method to use to get my children to become more interested in their lessons."[2]

Many black women saw teaching as their contribution to the advancement of African Americans. Wells was eager to play a role in racial uplift, but she hated teaching and thought of it as a way to earn a paycheck rather than a calling. At the close of the 1887 school term, Wells admitted, "School is out tomorrow. I cannot say I'm sorry." Yet she also realized, "I don't feel glad. Expenses go on just the same and I don't wish to leave town yet. I wish to get a school this summer if possible."[3] In the 1880s, Wells could not imagine making a decent income as a full-time journalist. The pittances she received for various articles could never have supported her. Fewer journalistic opportunities existed for women than men, and most male journalists held down other jobs while writing or editing newspapers. Some were also teachers; others preached, practiced law, or held government positions. Thus, Wells was anxious to keep her disagreeable job—and teach in summer school—to make ends meet. When time came for the renewal of contracts, she worried until she learned for sure that she had been reappointed. Preparing for her trip in the summer of 1886, Wells fretted, "Am assured that I will be re-elected to my position but am afraid to leave until I know it as a certainty."[4]

Wells realized that, if forced to teach, she was fortunate to do so in the Memphis public schools. The working conditions were superior to those found in most black public schools of the era. This was particularly true regarding salaries. In 1874, when state salaries averaged $33.03, Memphis paid its teachers an average of $80.33 monthly.[5] Unlike many other municipalities, the city paid the same salaries to black and white teachers. Women were also paid equally with men after 1878. The principal reason for equalization was to reduce costs, so average salaries began to decrease, causing many male teachers to leave.[6] Even so, Wells's salary of sixty dollars remained generous compared to other school systems.

Another desirable feature of teaching in Memphis was the unusual degree of respect awarded to black teachers by the white community in the early 1880s. Stores, such as Menken's, freely granted credit exceeding her monthly salary to Wells. White newspapers accorded African American schools' activities extensive coverage with articles about graduating classes on the front page. The editors also referred to the teachers with the prefixes of Mr., Mrs., and Miss—a designation not awarded to others in the black community by the white press. In some ways black teachers were treated the same as white ones. They took the same employment examinations and taught using the same curriculum and textbooks.[7]

Nevertheless, teaching in Memphis remained a difficult challenge even for those who loved the profession, and it was especially hard for African American teachers. In 1881 the city had eleven public schools, many of which were substandard and overcrowded. Only one of the four black schools was close to adequate. An attractive, two-story brick building constructed in 1873, the Clay Street colored school (which was renamed Kortrecht and later Booker T. Washington) was the most desirable. It had eight rooms as well as water and sewer connections. The other black schools were two-room frame structures, which were poorly ventilated, shabby firetraps. The school superintendent frequently noted black schools' "poor sanitary condition." In 1885 disaster was averted when Julia Hooks acted to prevent panic when one school caught fire due to a defective flue.[8] Wells taught in several schools, including Saffarans and Grant. She was undoubtedly excited to learn in October 1886 of her assignment to the Clay Street school. Excitement turned to disappointment later that month when Wells was reassigned to a different school in South Memphis. Following the switch, she complained, "I've had a tough time with tough pupils ever since."[9]

Overcrowding was a problem in all the schools, including Clay Street. For the brief time in 1886 that Wells taught there, she had seventy students. Some other schools were even more crowded. African Americans may have had salaries equal to their white counterparts, but they worked harder for the money. In 1883, when the student-teacher ratio for all schools averaged forty-seven, black teachers were struggling with as many as eighty-four students. A less-expensive alternative to additional school construction became split sessions—especially for black schools. In 1883 almost one-third of black classrooms had split sessions—compared to 4.6 percent for white classrooms.[10]

Although dissatisfied, Wells felt a duty to do her best and later professed to have tried to do her work conscientiously. Not only does her continued reappointment give credence to her claims to conscientious effort, but her participation in self-improvement activities for teachers also reflects her desire to be a better teacher. In 1886 Wells attended the National Teachers' Association meeting in Topeka. While motivated partly by the social activities the trip entailed, she reported going to hear "the different papers on different subjects." Wells also joined an educational society known as the Chatauqua, which published a journal and provided textbooks for an independent study course.[11] Wells participated in teachers' institutes held during summer breaks to improve the effectiveness of her teaching.[12] In addition to the institute at LeMoyne, she probably also went to the one at Fisk University. A number of biographical sketches refer to Wells having attended Fisk in the summers, but most likely it was the teachers' institute. Such attendance may have been the source of numerous social relationships she had with teachers and others from Nashville.[13]

Another reason to improve her teaching credentials was a desire for promotion to a less challenging and more personally satisfying job. One way to improve her situation would have been to teach older students at higher academic levels. Wells later remarked, "I was never promoted above the fourth grade in all my years as a teacher. The confinement and monotony of the primary work began to grow distasteful." However, Memphis teachers at advanced levels had more formal education than Wells. In November 1887 another possible solution arose. After she was reassigned and removed from the Clay Street school, Wells met with school superintendent Charles H. Collier. The next day she wrote in her diary that "he advised me to study up & get a principal's certificate & he would give me a school." Although proclaiming, "I believe its worth the trial," and vowing to begin "studying in real earnest," Wells appears to have put her energy and time increasingly into furthering her journalistic career, instead.[14]

Nevertheless, her tenure as a teacher taught Wells a lot about racial politics. The Memphis school system was enmeshed in the political struggles of the larger community. Few things were more important to African Americans than access to adequate education. As one key to economic independence, black education became a major issue in the relationships among white southerners, black southerners, and white northerners. Indeed, education became a blackboard upon which was written many of the major questions of the day: integration, black autonomy, party alliances, class divisions, racial violence, and suffrage. Nowhere was this more true than in Memphis, Tennessee. To be a public school teacher in the 1880s meant one was automatically in the middle of a political maelstrom.

In Memphis the political roots of black education went back to the first year following the Union occupation of the city in June 1862. White Memphians publicly opposed educating African Americans, and in February 1863 burned down a church that housed a private school for blacks. The extent of opposition was made blindingly clear in the flames of the race riot of 1866, during which whites torched every African American school and church. Before "congressional reconstruction" brought Republicans into office, the city continued to exclude all blacks from public schools. The void was filled by private schools operated by white northern missionaries, the Freedmen's Bureau, and educated African Americans. In 1866 twelve black schools employed twenty-two teachers: nineteen white northerners and three African Americans, all three of whom had been educated at Oberlin College.[15]

Major changes in public education occurred after African American men received the right to vote in February 1867. The next month a Republican-sponsored law provided for publicly funded black education — in separate schools. White Tennesseans had made clear their willingness to abandon all public education rather than to support integrated schools. In Memphis the white conservative leaders on the school board responded to the school law of 1867 by officially incorporating the black schools that were run by northern white missionaries but not those headed by African Americans. Perhaps because it was less expensive to do so, the board allowed northerners to continue to run the schools. One of them, J. H. Barnam, became superintendent of the colored schools. After that office was abolished, Barnam was principal at the only school offering secondary education, the Clay Street school, when it opened in 1874. Native whites and those from the North agreed on one thing: African Americans were not capable of running their own schools.

The paternalism of the white northerners, who also controlled the state's Republican party, was demonstrated by Barnam. He was reluctant to hire black teachers, believing them to be less competent than white northerners. Those he did hire were usually light-skinned members of the wealthy black elite—a group that tended to favor integration and often wanted white teachers for their own children. Such educators could not understand the desire for autonomy among the hordes of recent rural black migrants, who joined the Educational Association of Memphis (EAM) and lobbied for schools to elevate all the race, "not the few at the expense of the many."[16] In July 1873 the group held a mass meeting and petitioned the school board for only black teachers in the black schools. They argued that whites' "educational training is calculated to render them unfit for positions in our schools" and resolved "that in view of the fact that we are prescribed by law to separate schools for our children upon the assumption of 'inferiority,' we respectfully ask that we have the benefit in full, and that every teacher from principal on down be elected from the prescribed class."[17]

The issue of black school control climaxed in January 1875 when black teacher Mrs. S. H. Thompson filed formal charges against Barnam. She had been unhappy at the Clay Street school because Principal Barnum seemed to favor the school's four white teachers. He assigned the split sessions and weaker students to the black teachers, who were then unfairly evaluated on the basis of their students' performance. Barnam countered with charges against Thompson. The conflict actually reflected two larger questions: Would there be black or white control in black schools?, and Who were the best political allies for African Americans, southern white Democrats or northern white Republicans?

Not surprisingly, black support for Thompson largely divided along the chasm of class. The old wealthy elite tended to support Barnam; Thompson's backers came from the constituency of the EAM and from black politicians disenchanted with Republican paternalism and duplicity. White support, on the other hand, divided according to political affiliation, which was closely tied to sectional origins. By the mid-1870s, southern Democrats were most interested in wresting political power from northern Republicans and sought to woo African Americans as political allies. Because white southerners ultimately controlled all public education through the power of the purse, they were willing to cede the day-to-day administration of the schools to African Americans to rid the schools of northern, usually Republican, influence.[18] The coalition of white Democrats, disaffected black Republicans, and black advocates of autonomy won a major victory when Benjamin K. Sampson was hired to replace Barnam in

1875 and the faculties of black schools were all African Americans. In the 1876 election, the Democrats reaped their harvest when many blacks switched parties.

The fact that black votes often affected the balance of power in Memphis allowed African Americans opportunities to form coalitions to promote their interests. Even after Tennessee was "redeemed" from Republican rule in 1870, the party continued to be viable in Memphis. Conservative Democrats faced not only Republican competition but also competition for control of their own party. Black Memphians took advantage of white divisions to elect African Americans: Two served on the city council in 1872 and four in 1873. In 1874 six African American candidates were part of an ethnic coalition with Irish and Italians that wrested control of city hall from the Anglo-Southerners, and African Americans also served on the police force and on grand juries.[19]

The scramble for votes frightened the city's small economic elite. In 1879 they convinced the state legislature that the city had been misruled and run into debt by the ethnic coaliton—even though most of the city's problems resulted instead from the rule of yellow fever. As a result, the legislature revoked the city's charter and Memphis became a taxing district under the nominal control of the state and actual control of the white economic elite. Although the revocation eliminated ethnic control of the city council, Anglo-Southerners continued to have trouble controlling the school board. The ward system of voting meant ethnic neighborhoods could elect their own members to represent them, and the black majority in Ward Five elected Edward Shaw in 1880. Shaw had become estranged from the Republicans for their failure to support his political ambitions and thus was not too objectionable to the conservative Democrats. However, further expansion of black power was not deemed desirable. When two seats on the school board in black-majority wards became available in 1881, ballot boxes were closed to prevent the election of two additional black members. Even more disturbing to the conservatives was the continued power of Irish immigrants, which led to school reorganization in 1883. The ward system with twenty school board members was changed to a commission with five members elected at large—effectively diminishing the political power of ethnic neighborhoods.[20]

Although some black Memphians, such as Fred Savage, remained diehard Republicans because of loyalty or ideology, others joined any alliance to further the interests of African Americans. Apparently Wells sided with the latter. Like many people, however, she seemed to be influenced by people—especially Alfred Froman—as well as principles. After school reorganization in 1883, the newly elected Democratic governor appointed five members to serve on the board until elections were held. One of these was Froman, who with other black "fusionists," such as Shaw, joined one faction of a badly split Democratic party.[21] Froman argued that Republicans were not worthy of unqualified support and asserted

> Long ago the Republican party surrendered its principles, withdrew its protection from the Negro, and left him to shift for himself. What was the use of the whole race, shivering and helpless, clinging to an organization which could not, dared not, succor us from the dangers surrounding us.[22]

His lament would later be echoed by Wells, but she was independent enough not to blindly follow anyone's lead, even Froman's. She also had other political mentors. In spring 1885 a woman Wells admired became the center of another controversy in the Memphis public schools. The first black woman to graduate from college in Tennessee, Virginia Broughton was considered one of the city's "oldest and best" teachers. She protested when Principal B. K. Sampson gave a coveted position to Green P. Hamilton, who was only eighteen years old and had been teaching for just a year. As usual, the battle had political overtones. The white school superintendent, Charles Collier, saw Broughton's actions as a challenge not only to his power but to white Democratic control of black schools. Fred Savage, who had won Alfred Froman's seat in the January 1884 school board elections, supported Broughton's challenge as well as black autonomy. Wells admired Virginia Broughton and possibly resented the implicit sexism in the choice of Hamilton for head teacher. She also respected Savage for successfully standing up to the white school superintendent and forcing the replacement of Hamilton with Broughton. Thus Wells apparently did not follow the lead of Froman in this case and instead supported the Republicans. Nevertheless, although Collier lost the first round, he eventually won the power struggle and demoted both Broughton and Julia Hooks—who had openly supported Broughton—for the 1886–87 school term.[23]

The controversy had a number of effects on Wells. First, her relationship with Broughton provided her with a role model for rebellion. Wells obviously looked up to Broughton. On 28 June 1886 Wells noted in her diary that she and "Mrs. B" had "a long confab & came nearer being acquainted than ever before." When Broughton left Memphis in December 1886, Wells collected money from Lyceum members for a farewell gift, which they presented to Broughton at a testimonial dinner. Able to raise only $4.25, Wells contributed a generous seventy-five cents to purchase a five dollar pen. Her admiration for Broughton undoubtedly inspired Wells to make her own challenge to the school board, which would result in her dismissal in 1891.[24] Broughton's departure also meant that the Lyceum lost its *Evening Star* editor. Wells's election to the editorship marked another step away from teaching toward journalism.[25]

The incident provided Wells with a lesson on the link between internal school politics and the larger political scene. It was Savage's failure to be reelected to the school board in January 1886 that allowed Collier and Sampson to reverse the school board's decision and demote Broughton and Hooks. Even before her friend's demotion, Wells had been upset by the defeat of Savage. Following the election, Wells wrote in her dairy, "Thursday was city election day; I was not interested in anything but the School Board & both colored men were beaten; we now have an entirely white Board." The other candidate had been Taylor Nightingale, the pastor of Beale Street Baptist Church. Wells did not have much confidence in Nightingale at the time, writing

> As Mr. S could not be elected I was heartily glad the other one could not be, for I believe him to be a toady and could unknowingly be used by the white men. Then he boasted so and conducted himself generally in such an obnoxious manner that it completely disgusted me with him.[26]

Much later, however, Nightingale would win Wells's support when he was attacked by the white press for being too radical.

The next year Wells was once again caught up in school politics. Shortly before school started in September 1887, she wrote in her diary, "Everything and every body is stirred up over the school matters. Mr. W had a fine article on the question in Sunday's Avalanche that is stirring up a lot of sand. I hope it will be successful."[27] (Mr. W was the Reverend D. R. Wilkins, pastor of Vance Street Christian Church, and his letter was a caustic critique of the black schools and Principal Sampson.) The letter is especially interesting because of the relationship between Wells and Wilkins. He was not only the minister of Wells's church but also a suitor. Wilkins had just moved to Memphis the previous March. Immediately, Wilkins took an especial interest in Wells.[28] She admired his strength and tact, writing in her diary in April 1886:

> I want here to speak a word of delight in our preacher. He is the most energetic man I know. He has made the waste places blossom as a rose and the church is beginning to look up. He is also a hard student and good preacher. The way he handles belligerents is admirable, for they are becoming as quiet as lambs, and yet they all stick to him and respond when he calls on them. They yet remain his friends. He is certainly a splendid judge of human nature. Mr. W.[29]

Although Wells respected Wilkins as a minister, she eventually decided he was not much of a suitor.[30]

Since Wilkins was a newcomer to Memphis and was spending a lot of time with Wells, his letter to the editor criticizing Sampson may very well have derived from Wells's complaints of the school situation. The letter appeared three days after the "pro-fusion" Democratic *Appeal* had published an article praising the school system and noting that a former "Clay Street School pupil led her class at Roger Williams College." Wilkins's letter appeared in the rival Democratic newspaper, the *Avalanche*. White Democrats were divided over the school issue largely based on the stands taken by their different black political allies. The *Avalanche* probably welcomed a chance to trash fusionist Sampson.[31]

Wilkins was critical of the level of preparation black students received in the public schools and accused Sampson of hiring incompetent teachers for personal reasons. Wilkins further charged that Sampson had examination papers prepared for teachers who could not pass on their own, and that Sampson's main interest was collecting his "fat salary." Instead of being guided by the interests of the race, Sampson took directions from a "dirty ring composed of a few would-be leaders" in the black community.[32]

Sampson denied the allegations and hurled counter-charges at Wilkins in a reply printed in the *Avalanche* three weeks later. He explained Wilkins's attack in two ways. First, he claimed that soon after moving to Memphis Wilkins had sought to increase his political influence in the community by calling a meeting at his church to discuss possible demands for integrated education. According to Sampson, Wilkins had announced that the principal would be the keynote speaker without consulting him. Sampson refused to be a party to demands so "obnoxious" to white Memphians and rebuffed Wilkins, who was now getting his revenge. Second,

Sampson hinted that Wilkins was serving "unnamed" people who had personal agendas. He claimed that objections to a specific teacher (probably Hamilton) were the result of professional rivalry for the best classroom assignments.[33]

The white school board was drawn into the controversy; at the next meeting they voted to establish a high school for African Americans with Sampson as principal. City politics were likely the cause of the decision. With this move, fusionist Democrats could publicly reward Sampson's loyalty and woo black votes for the upcoming city election. The other Democratic faction was attempting to overthrow the taxing district administration that was headed by fusionist David "Pap" Hadden. To defeat the challenge, the fusionists made an additional overture to black voters by placing a black candidate on their slate for the school board. The tactics worked, the black-owned paper, the *Watchman*, endorsed the fusionists, and every fusionist except one—the black candidate—won election. The black community also lost. No African American would sit on the school board for forty years. The 1888 election marked a turning point for Memphis blacks, who were soon effectively disfranchised and stripped of political power. Coalition had brought short-term gains at a large cost.[34]

The political turmoil during Wells's tenure as teacher whetted her appetite for activism. Increasingly, journalism became the outlet for that activism. Many of her early articles reflect her struggle for identity, focusing on issues that she was grappling with personally, such as the role of women, race and class identity, and her disillusionment with both political parties and with black leadership. Her pen became her tool for confronting much of what angered her. It helped her as she "exorcised the demons of unrest and dissatisfaction."[35] Journalism was also the medium through which she eventually defined herself.

In the aftermath of emancipation, journalism served as a means of self-definition for the black community. African Americans had long been defined by white society, which justified the owning of other human beings by characterizing slaves as either childish or bestial or some combination of the two. The ability to define their slaves also gave masters another way to keep them "in their place." Masters knew the power of the written word. Their fear of it found expression in legal bans on teaching slaves to read and write. Keeping slaves illiterate protected the right of masters to define African Americans both in the outside world and in the slaves' quarters.

Even with their control of the law and the press in the South, whites had failed to convince most African Americans that their natural state was slavery. Nevertheless, the continuous assault on their character had its psychological impact on black men and women. After emancipation many white newspapers highlighted black crime and irresponsibility to justify exploitation, exclusion, and segregation. White popular culture and scholarship trumpeted "white supremacy." In a quest for spiritual as well as physical freedom after emancipation, African Americans rapidly established newspapers and journals as instruments of self-definition. Indeed, one issue the black press debated was what label to give the race: colored, Negro, or Afro-American.

Hundreds of black newspapers were founded; a few flourished, but most failed. In his book, *The Afro-American Press and Its Editors* (1891), I. Garland Penn claimed that 154 black newspapers existed in 1890. Because many had short life spans, that number reflects only a fraction of those founded and most likely underestimates the existing papers considerably. Penn listed Tennessee as having only nine papers, yet Memphis at that time had at least three active papers, not including those published at LeMoyne and Howe Institutes. Even towns with much smaller black populations hosted one or more black newspapers. Starting a newspaper required little capital, but keeping one running was a challenge. Black newspapers rarely had the circulation or the advertising income to make them profitable. The swift rise and demise of weeklies made counting them difficult.[36]

African American papers proliferated because they met many needs. They provided news of the activities within a town's black community. They highlighted individuals and institutions, giving them new legitimacy and importance. Through columns with such titles as "Race Gleanings," they linked numerous black communities into a national network of mutual interest and support. They exhorted and educated their readership. Editors with political ambitions utilized their newspapers as platforms to enunciate philosophies and programs—as well as to curry favor and win appointments from victorious candidates at all levels of government. The press also furnished income for journalists and a medium for advertisers. While African American newspapers shared many of these functions with white ones, race journals additionally provided a voice for the voiceless.

In the worsening racial climate of the late nineteenth century, the voice was usually one of protest, and in the Deep South it often arose from the church. In the 1880s all three major black papers in Memphis were founded by clergymen. For Ida B. Wells the religious connections of Memphis papers provided an aura of respectability from which to articulate her protest. Her first newspaper contribution appeared in the *Living Way*, a journal run by two Baptist ministers: R. N. Countee and William A. Binkley. With her original subject being the court case against the railroad, Wells avoided a trap that ensnared many women journalists. She never became identified as a writer for female audiences on "women's topics." About half of the women listed in Penn's book wrote for women's papers, such as *Our Women and Children*, or wrote women's columns in male-edited papers. Wells followed this pattern to a degree in her early journalism career by writing articles, such as "Woman's Mission," "A Story of 1900," "Our Women," "The Model Woman: A Pen Picture of the Typical Southern Girl," and even later in her career with "Two Christmas Days: A Holiday Story."

Women journalists were aware that they were entering a profession dominated by men, although it became increasingly less so in the last decades of the nineteenth century. With the spread of coeducation and of higher education for women, many began to redefine womanhood. Black journalist Mrs. N. F. (Gertrude) Mossell declared it the "Women's Century" and marveled at the "yielding of the barriers that surround her life." Like many of her sister journalists, Mossell believed that journalism offered greater opportunities to women than many other fields. Much of the work could be done at home and "fit in" around other chores. She also noted that "sex and race are no bar, often they need not be known."[37]

Others argued women's suitability for newspaper work even more assertively. In the article "Women in Journalism" Carrie Langston noted, "ever since the existence of man he has, in some mysterious way, held a superior place, not only in the political world but in the field of letters." Although men had long intimated that "woman was created for either a houseplant or a domestic drudge," Langston asserted change was coming and claimed:

> . . . the time is not far distant when the intellect of woman shall cope
> with that of man's, and woman shall wield her scepter over man, as
> a philosopher, scientist and journalist. As woman sways her pen in
> writing, men see words fall from that delicate touch that conveys [sic]
> meanings that he is powerless to express, and when the earnest heart
> of true womanhood is beating with ambition to do something good
> or be something great, . . . she decides that she can accomplish more
> good and win laurels and conquests by her work in journalism.[38]

African American women journalists often believed they received less resistance from their male cohorts than did white women. Mossell explained, "Our men are too much hampered by their contentions with their white brothers to afford to stop and fight their black sisters, so we slip in and glide quietly along." Lucy Wilmot Smith's explanation was more charitable to black men.

> The educated negro woman occupies vantage ground over the Caucasian woman of America, in that the former has had to contest with her brother every inch of the ground for recognition; the negro man, having had his sister by his side on plantations and in rice swamps, keeps her there, now that he moves in other spheres. As she wins laurels, he accords her the royal crown. This is especially true of journalism.[39]

A number of black male editors were supportive of women journalists, giving them both jobs and praise. Editor T. Thomas Fortune in 1888 declared, "I think our women are going to stretch our men in the variety of their information, the purity of their expression and in having the courage of their convictions, without which these are but pearls cast before swine."[40]

African American women, however, realized that they faced certain challenges in dealing with black male journalists. In an article for women on how to get started in journalism, Mossell advised a woman to "learn to control her emotions and put pride in her pocket." If one would "ignore what is unpleasant at first," her male coworkers would come to "regard her with a feeling of brave comradeship and as a good fellow." Then the men would "help instead of hindering" and soon the "disagreeable things will cease of themselves." Mossell recommended a woman give up "all thoughts of matrimony until her success is made." At first, she cautioned, "It is best not to expect any pay for [your articles]." After one's work had appeared "a good number of times," Mossell declared, "the gifted writer might modestly hint that if the able editor cared further for her contributions perhaps he would not mind putting a proper price on them."[41]

Although not always able "to control her emotions and put pride in her pocket," Wells had much in common with other black women journalists. Nineteen women were profiled in Penn's book. Although different data were given for each, some patterns can be found. Most entered journalism at a young age—Wells was twenty-one. Many seem to have deferred marriage: In 1891 the majority were unmarried, including at least five who were in their thirties. Of the nineteen, at least twelve had been born in the South. Wells and eight others were known to have first published in church-related papers. Most had at least some high school education or normal school training; about half were college-trained. The family backgrounds of fourteen of these women are given; they are especially interesting. Of the five known to be raised by both parents, at least three came from prominent families. Nine had lost one or more of their parents while young: Three had lost their fathers to death; three, their mothers; and three, including Wells, both parents. Adversity seems to have been an advantage for black women journalists.[42]

The career of Ida B. Wells followed the same course of many black women journalists. Beginning by contributing to a newspaper run by ministers, Wells received little or no pay for her articles in the *Living Way*. Nevertheless, those articles launched her literary career. Because many newspapers exchanged copy, an article written for a local paper could be reprinted or noted in papers nationwide. In May 1884 the *New York Globe* commented on one of Wells's *Living Way* articles about her lawsuit. The *Globe*, whose name was changed to *Freeman* and then *Age*, was edited by T. Thomas Fortune. He was among the best-known African American editors at the time; his paper was one of several that had subscribers from all across the United States.[43] Wells likely knew of Fortune even before her entrance into journalism. In fall 1882, Fortune had begun to write letters to the *Memphis Weekly Appeal*, in which he supported more friendly relations between Democrats and African Americans. As noted earlier, Wells's mentor, Alfred Froman, had allied with a faction of the Memphis Democrats that year.[44]

In January 1885 Fortune's *Freeman* ran another Wells story on the railroad suits. (Wells had most likely heard of the paper's interest and had written to Fortune.) Throughout her career, she initiated correspondence with numerous leaders and journalists. In 1885 Wells was sympathetic with Fortune's call for more political independence by African Americans. Many black editors had lambasted Fortune for his stand, usually charging that he was seeking political appointments from the Democrats. Wells came to his defense and won a powerful ally. In February Fortune reprinted an article from the *Living Way* with the byline Iola titled "A Word Concerning Southern Editors." In it Wells declared that of the one hundred black papers there were "none more fearless, outspoken" and "none more worthy of support" than the *Freeman*. She found it puzzling that the paper had enemies "who claim it has been disloyal to the Republican party." Of its editor, Wells wrote, "Mr. Fortune has always claimed to be working in the interests of the race, which he holds to be superior to those of any party, and not for party favors or interests; and his position is the right, the true one."[45] Fortune began regularly printing her articles and served as her champion many times in the future.

Her article also reflects what Wells considered to be an important role for the press. Referring to the election of Grover Cleveland as the first Democratic president since the war, Wells wrote, "One good result of the late political revolution is already apparent; it has aroused the mass of colored people as never before since the war. Every paper contains a protest, a gem of its kind." Wells urged black papers to continue to voice "the sentiment of a long-suffering people" until "every wrong is righted."[46] She viewed race newspapers as both a voice of protest and a force for change.

During 1885 papers began to note the voice of Iola. The *Freeman* reprinted an article by Wells from the *Living Way* in September. Titled "Functions of Leadership," it was her analysis of upper-class black leaders and their failure to use their resources to create jobs for other African Americans. Wells scolded others frequently, and almost from the beginning, her career was marked by controversy. Soon after Iola's *Living Way* articles appeared in black papers with national audiences, Wells criticized fellow journalists—for their criticisms of each other. Even though she was practicing what she was preaching against, Wells made a legitimate point. African American editors too often viciously attacked one another; one editor lamented the "low bickerings" of his colleagues. Another referred to a fellow editor as "the lank, lean and unterrified sinner who shovels wind for the *Globe*."[47] One of the most vitriolic editors was W. Calvin Chase of the *Washington Bee*, which had the motto "Honey for friends—stings for enemies." Chase especially liked to sting Fortune, whom he called "crank of the colored press." After the two male editors had exchanged barbs regarding their stances on Cleveland's election, Wells waded into the fray. She praised the new president for his early stands and actions regarding African Americans and then noted Chase's "chagrin at finding his eloquence nipped in the bud by being confronted with some of his own eloquences against Mr. Cleveland before he was president." Wells asserted Chase should have "acknowledged his fault and begged forgiveness, and subsided at once."

Fortune also received a tongue-lashing from Wells for his words against Chase. After claiming that Chase's change of heart had resulted from his desire to hold onto his appointment in the government printing office, Fortune had urged Cleveland to punish Chase. Wells chided Fortune for his hypocrisy and for attempting to "dictate to Mr. Cleveland" how to treat Chase. She further stated, "Nor do I think it becoming Mr. Fortune's dignity to speak so disrespectfully of a brother editor." She closed by asking, "How can the people follow your teachings, Brother Fortune, about pulling together, aiding each other and all that if you, who do the preaching, practice the contrary?"[48]

An indication of their respect for Wells as a journalist, and perhaps deference to her as a woman, was the manner by which both men defended themselves. Each printed her comments before responding. Both men replied with criticisms of each other rather than of Wells. By the end of the year, both had sung her praises. Fortune referred to Wells as "one of the brainiest of our female writers" before reprinting a long tribute from the *Washington Bee*. The *Bee* article called Wells "the remarkable and talented young school marm from Memphis." Noting that for a long time her "writings were confined to the *Living Way*," the writer declared that "like a person of her ambitious nature she found other channels through which to express herself." The *Bee* further stated, "From a mere, insignificant country-bred lass she has developed into one of the foremost among the female thinkers of the race."[49]

By that time Wells was writing regularly for the Kansas City *Gate City Press*, edited by J. D. Bowser. As Mossell suggested, she apparently did not ask for pay at first. By the end of January 1886, Wells had gained enough confidence to approach Bowser. In her diary she noted a letter from "Mr. Bowser who is evidently disposed to favorably regard my asking for pay & asks me to state my price—which is an embarrassing thing to do." Her confidence in herself was still limited. She worried, "I have no idea of its worth & shall tell him so when I answer."[50]

Wells also wrote unsolicited letters to the New York *Freeman* before Fortune solicited an original article from her. Even then he did not pay her a fee. For her article, "Woman's Mission," which appeared in December 1885,[51] Fortune sent Wells ten copies of the paper. Her compensation came from selling those copies. About the same time, the manager of the *Little Rock Sun* approached Wells with a scheme to have Wells edit a local version of his paper. After noting with disgust that he called her a "powfull writer," Wells concluded, "Shall not accept as I could not make it pay."[52]

By the end of 1885, Wells saw her articles and letters widely published and praised. She began to think of herself as a professional journalist and desired to be paid for her efforts. Remuneration would both ease her financial bind and give "Iola" increased legitimacy. In a series of articles for the *Living Way*, Wells apparently discussed the state of black journalism and rebuked editors for not paying writers for their essays. Something she wrote angered Chase, who delivered to Iola her first public thrashing. The *Bee's* sting was long and caustic. Calling her the "star-eyed goddess," Chase asserted that the paper for which Iola "wields her trenchant pen, is the most conspicuous for grammatical and typographical errors."[53]

Chase maintained that magazines were the appropriate places to submit essays for paid publication and that "should 'Iola' *really write* anything worthy of public interest the A.M.E. Review, will, no doubt publish it, and allow her something by way of compensation." Chase charged, "The fact that her communications to the *Way* are so numerous, gives rise to the suspicion that if they are paid for, which we very much doubt, there cannot be much left in its treasury and 'Iola's' pockets wear a 'silver lining.'" In closing he remarked, "Regard for the financial condition of the *Way* and the *Gate City Press* and the interests of colored journalism . . . require the temporary, if not permanent retirement of 'Iola' from literary effort."[54]

Such words were a jolting change from the choruses of praise Wells had been receiving. When her letter, "Freedom of Political Action," was published in the *New York Freeman*, Fortune had noted the "very clear and forcible article on the present state of parties" from "a lady in Memphis." He continued, "The lady in question has gained very much merited praise for the very sensible and polished articles she has contributed to the Memphis *Living Way* under the pseudonym of 'Iola.'"[55] After such acclaim, Wells was shocked to learn of Chase's brutal attack when Louis Brown, who was now working for Chase, sent her a copy of the paper.

Not yet confident enough to publicly duel Chase with her pen, Wells instead fumed in her diary about the "article from the pen of his [Brown's] very incapable editor." After quoting a few of Chase's barbs, she called him "contemptible & juvenile in the extreme." Wells vowed to herself, "I would not write for him for great pay & I will write something some day that will make him wince." She finally relented somewhat and admitted, "I think he has good ideas about most things but he has no tact or ingenuity about *how* to express them in a way to gain attention or give weight to his words; he is either a fanatic or talks like one."[56] Similar charges would later be leveled at Wells.

In late 1885 and early 1886, Wells entered a fight that would make her enemies in her own city of Memphis. A long-standing rivalry existed between the city's clergy and secret societies for the support of the people—financially and otherwise. Even before the Civil War, the free black community had established the Social and Benevolent Society (1854). While Memphis was under federal occupation during the Civil War, such fraternal organizations as the Masons, Sons of Ham, Daughters of Zion, and Odd Fellows multiplied rapidly. These societies served many functions, especially for the rural black migrants flooding into the city. They combined the communal support system of the slave community with the functions of insurance companies, supplying funds for medical and funeral expenses from membership dues. The strength of these organizations is one reason Memphis preachers played a somewhat less active role in politics than in other locations.[57]

Many ministers were critical of the societies for several reasons. Membership dues depleted the meager resources of their congregations—diminishing the amount of contributions the churches received. Pastors suspected that the societies' officers were using some of the funds for personal purposes. The societies also sponsored numerous social events where alcohol, dancing, and various forms of revelry were abundant. The ritualistic features of the groups worried pastors as well. A black Memphis resident recalled that "a great deal of stress was put upon fantastic grips, mysterious handshakes and incomprehensible passwords."[58]

In July 1885 the Memphis Lyceum debated the role of the secret societies. Following that meeting, R. N. Countee, pastor of Tabernacle Baptist Church and comanager of the *Living Way*, renounced from the pulpit his membership in all societies and beseeched his congregation to do likewise. At the next meeting of the Lyceum, the debate continued; the Congregational minister, B. A. Imes, infuriated some listeners by revealing Masonic secrets. A few men forcefully grabbed Imes's manuscript and accused ex-Mason Countee as being the source of the information. Anger erupted into the threat of violence after the *Living Way* published a letter by Imes that revealed more secrets. Early in August, a mob surrounded Countee's home at a little before three o'clock in the morning. The minister, in his nightshirt, ran out the back door of his house to safety. Even after Countee insisted that he had not been the source of Imes's information, local law enforcement officials had to post a guard at his house for sixty days.[59]

The mob did not intimidate Countee permanently. In September the *Living Way* published an article by Iola highly critical of secret societies. Despite her father's membership in the Masons and their efforts to help the family after her parents' deaths, Wells agreed with Countee on the influence of such groups. The *Freeman* reprinted a paragraph which noted:

> To the history of an enormous amount paid into their treasuries with nothing to show for it in the way of real estate, parks, or even a multitude of widows and orphans cared for, [as well as] the promiscuous conglomeration of all classes and influences, let us add the union of the mob and we have the history of what societies have done for the elevation of society in general, complete up to to-day.[60]

That fall the *Cleveland Gazette* carried items about the controversy. One Memphis defender of the secret societies charged that the *Gate City Press* and other supporters of Countee "know nothing of the facts and do gross injustice to the secret orders of our city." While denouncing the attack on Countee, the defender asserted that the crusade was based on the editor's desire to establish a benevolent order "under his own control in his church." The writer claimed another fraternal critic was upset because he had been kicked out of a society for failing to repay a loan from the group. Finally, the defender asserted that the societies were "not doing the mischief charged to them" and that "some of the best men in Memphis" belonged to such orders.[61]

Wells was probably the author of the *Gate City Press* articles referred to in the *Cleveland Gazette*. In an article quoted from the *Gate City Press* in the Washington *Bee*, Iola wrote:

> Our city has been very much aroused over the fact that societies have not been exempt for the past five months from the general discussion, and men in the heat of bigotry and fidelity to obligations, have forgotten that this is an age of free speech, and have attempted summary vengeance on those who exercise this God-given prerogative, when it touched societies and their doings.[62]

The article apparently won Wells some important enemies in Memphis. In March she noted in her dairy that Louis Brown "tried to show me the folly of fighting against the tide & told me what I already know of the enmity of the men in the societies against me for expressing my honest convictions." Ten days later she referred to the comfort she received from the indignation expressed by Charles S. Morris "about the persecution I am undergoing concerning societies."[63]

In the midst of the controversy, Wells's diary reflected the religious

faith that inspired her uncompromising militancy then and later. She proclaimed, "Yet I do not fear; God is over all & He will, so long as I am in the
right, fight my battles, and give me what is my right." She also asked for further courage and direction and implored, "God help me to be on the watch
and to do the right; to harm no man but do my duty ever." Wells firmly believed that divine authority superseded any human law or action and that
her duty was to renounce anything that contradicted God's will.[64]

By mid-March 1886, Wells had further expanded her journalistic network. The *Little Rock Sun* accepted her proposal that she represent it at the
National Press Association convention in Washington, D.C. Wells also received a letter from the Detroit *Plaindealer* asking her how much she
would charge for writing two letters a month for that paper. Nevertheless,
Wells still had trouble getting sufficient pay for her work. Wells noted,
"The Sun unhesitatingly accepts my offer . . . but remains pointedly
mum about the money question." She was also disgusted that Fortune had
requested her to renew her subscription to the *Freeman* and exclaimed,
"Mr. F might afford to send me his paper, I think as I've sent him several
subscribers." Wells suggested two dollars an article to the *Plaindealer*, but
was disappointed a week later to learn that the paper was "not able to come
up to my figures, so they say."[65]

Even as the demands for articles by Iola increased, the remuneration
remained low. In the next year and a half, Wells was asked to become a con-
tributor to such newspapers and periodicals, as the *A.M.E. Church Review*,
the *Indianapolis World*, the *American Baptist*, the *Kansas City Dispatch*,
and the *Chicago Conservator*. The *American Baptist* became a regular outlet for her articles. It was edited by William J. Simmons, who was president
of a Baptist-supported normal and theological school in Louisville. Simmons played an important role in the development of female journalists.
He was the first to publish articles by four of those mentioned in Penn's
book and in 1888 founded *Our Women and Children*, which provided a
platform for women writers. Simmons met Wells on a trip to Memphis in
October 1886 and engaged her as a regular correspondent, paying her one
dollar each for weekly articles to appear in the "Woman's Column" of the
American Baptist. He also agreed to pay her way to the press convention in
Louisville in 1887 in return for a signed contract calling for Wells to write
two articles a month on an exclusive basis for six months.[66]

Late in her life Wells credited Simmons as being her mentor. "In every
way he could," Wells wrote, "Dr. Simmons encouraged me to be a newspaper woman, and whatever fame I achieved in that line I owe in large

measure to his influence and encouragement." Although Fortune and others also played major roles, Simmons was the first to treat Wells as a true professional by offering a contract and compensation. Countee had been the first to publish her articles, but he informed her in August 1886 that "they are unable to employ me regularly as a correspondent." The *Indianapolis World* rewarded Wells with a two-year subscription to the paper, an act Wells characterized as "Cheeky."[67]

Regardless of the subject, in 1886 and 1887 Wells was widely quoted and praised. She wrote letters to such white-owned newspapers as the *Memphis Scimitar* as well as numerous race journals. She networked and cultivated contacts with male editors. She was well on her way to becoming hailed as the "Princess of the Press." Yet Wells still questioned her own talent and training. Praise did not entirely convince her of her merit. After receiving a letter from the editor of the *A.M.E. Church Review*, Wells noted he was "asking an article from my brilliant (?) pen." She worried about making "little progress" when writing and, after she signed a contract to produce regular articles for the *American Baptist*, fretted that she was "running out of subjects." Never having finished at Rust, Wells believed her education was inadequate. Sometimes she became so discouraged, she wondered why she kept writing.[68] No other critic was as harsh as Wells herself when she evaluated her work.

> Finished & at last mailed to the A.M.E. Church Review . . . my article on "Our Young Men" not because I was satisfied with it or thought it worthy of publication by reason of the lucid exposition and connected arrangement, but as a trial to get the opinion of others. . . . I think sometimes I can write a readable article and then again I wonder how I could have been so mistaken in myself. A glance at all my "brilliant?" productions pall on my understanding; they all savor of dreary sameness, however varied the subject, and the style is monotonous. I find a paucity of ideas that makes it a labor to write freely and yet—what is it that keeps urging me to write notwithstanding all?[69]

Wells worked to expand her store of knowledge by reading, taking lessons from a variety of people, and attending educational events. She experimented with various types of writing and sought to write a novel with Charles Morris in 1886. After attending a lecture by an African named T. L. Johnson, she considered coauthoring a book with him. Wells also tried her hand at writing a short story in the fall of 1886. Noting that she had begun her first attempt at story-writing, Wells wrote in her diary, "I know not where or when the ending will be. I can see and portray in my mind all the elements of a good story but when I attempt to put it on paper my thoughts dissolve into nothingness."[70]

By the next summer Wells had not given up on her dream to write a novel. She sometimes jotted down material she thought she could use — such as a case where a white man who could not get a license to marry an African America woman cut her finger and sucked her blood so he could say he "had Negro blood in his veins." One newspaper reported that she was going to spend the summer of 1887 at Woodstock and "devote her time and talents to writing a novel." Eventually she succeeded in writing at least one short story for publication, but a novel had not materialized before she turned her energy to writing of the evils of lynching.[71]

Her diary sometimes served as a writing lab. Often Wells seems to have just jotted down whatever was on her mind, without regard to writing style. Other times, however, she appears to have worked on the art of expression, especially in writing descriptive paragraphs. In February 1886 Wells described the aftermath of a snowstorm.

> The weather has moderated and the snow is — under the very warm rays of the Sun god — melting fast away. He has unlocked Jack Frost's fingers & loosened old Jack's grasp on the face of mother Earth; for which kindness she is now weeping tears of joy as she smiles and basks in the warmth of his presence. That which Old Boreas used to harden and freeze her with — The Sun God turns to tears of joy at her release and eventually will dry *them* all away.

Wells was skeptical of such flowery language. At the end of this passage she wrote, "But it's *awfully* muddy & sloppy for all that."[72]

Hard work helped Wells to become an extraordinarily powerful writer. She honed her skills while her experiences fueled her anger. That anger was combined with an uncompromising passion for justice fanned by her taste for grandly romantic literary heroes. Wells could articulate the disillusionment and frustrations of African Americans in a hostile world. At the same time, her keen intellect and independence of spirit and thought forced them to examine disconcerting issues. Those abilities made her a growing force in black newspapers.

During the summer of 1887, Wells took a large step down the road to her career in journalism by attending her first National Colored Press Association meeting. Simmons paid her way to the meeting in Louisville,

Kentucky, in return for some articles from her. His motive may not have been entirely journalistic or altruistic. Wells attended as a representative of the *Little Rock Sun* with its proxy to vote in association elections. The *New York Freedman* claimed that Simmons had appointed ten proxies so that they would "cast their votes in favor of his re-election" as president of the group. Indeed, the meeting was criticized by a number of journalists. The *Cleveland Gazette* proclaimed it "not a success" and claimed the "strongest and best papers" had ignored it. One participant declared, "The majority of the delegates impressed me as being more anxious to appear big guns, than be of real service to the cause of progress."[73]

Wells was disappointed that the "convention was but poorly represented north of Mason's and Dixie's [sic] line." Nevertheless, she was glad to have attended and met so many fellow journalists, many of whom paid calls to her while she was still in Louisville. She presented a paper on "How I would edit a paper" at an early Wednesday evening session and seemed content with her performance. Wells did regret that when she had been "called on to respond to 'Women in Journalism' at the banquet Wednesday night [I] was so surprised that I omitted to say many things I should have said." She rued not mentioning "on behalf of my sex" gratitude to the male editors for the "flattering encomiums" and "hearty welcome" given to the women. She also deplored not having used the opportunity "to urge the young women to study & think with a view to taking places in the world of thought & action."[74]

However flawed, the convention helped Wells to find a place "in the world of thought & action." She was a smash hit at this and all later conventions she attended. Even those who were already impressed with her writing seemed to be totally captivated by her charisma when they met her in person. Although disappointed with the 1887 convention in general, the correspondent of the *New Orleans Weekly Pelican* was pleased by a few of those he met—and Wells was on the top of that list. He called her the "brilliant and earnest" Iola and continued, "She is the pleasant-faced, modest Miss Ida Wells." Calling her "the most prominent correspondent at present connected with the Negro press," he declared, "If she does not suffer her head to become unduly inflated, there is a brilliant and useful future opening before her."[75]

Wells later recalled "being tickled pink over the attention I received from those veterans of the press." She speculated it was because she "was their first woman representative." The convention was apparently the first to include women journalists, but Wells was not the only woman in attendance. One action William J. Simmons had taken as president was to open the all-male domain to women. He sponsored not only Wells but also two other women: Mary V. Cook (Grace Ermine) and Lucy Wilmot Smith. Cook read a paper, "Is juvenile literature demanded on the part of colored children?" Wells, however, seems to have made the greater impression and became the first woman to hold an office in the organization when she was elected first assistant secretary the next year.[76]

Her relationships with Simmons's other two protégées is interesting. Smith, whose style was described as "grave, quiet and dignified," seems to have willingly ceded first place among women journalists to Wells. In an 1889 article on "Woman as Journalists" Smith wrote,

> Miss Ida B. Wells, "Iola," has been called the "Princess of the Press," and she has well earned the title. No writer, the male fraternity not excepted, has been more extensively quoted; none struck harder blows at the wrongs and weaknesses of the race.
>
> Miss Wells' readers are equally divided between the sexes. She reaches the men by dealing with the political aspect of the race question, and the women she meets around the fireside.[77]

Smith clearly saw Wells as spanning the distance between men and women journalists and helping to expand the topics on which women could legitimately write and gain male acceptance.

On the other hand, "Grace Ermine" seemed to be more in direct competition with "Iola." She succeeded Wells as writer of the "Woman's Column" at the *American Baptist* in 1888 and seems to have been similar to Wells in writing styles. Her writing was described as being "argumentative, pointed, terse."[78] She and Wells wielded their powerful pens in a journalistic duel, which was noted in February 1888 by the *New York Age*:

> That newspaper rows are not confined to the sterner sex is proved by the tilt of the types between "Grace Ermine," . . . and her talented predecessor "Iola." There is too much vinegar in the decoctions which these charming creatures weekly present to each other, and we feel called upon to quote the late reverend Dr. Watts to the effect that
>
> > Children, you should never let
> > Your angry passions rise;
> > Your little hands were never made
> > To scratch each other's eyes.[79]

Obviously, even two very strong female writers were not immune to condescension from their male cohorts. Both were deemed "masculine" from time to time. Cook was said to have "left the well-beaten tracks of most of the lady speakers, and dealt entirely with facts." Wells was labeled as "one of the few of our women who handle a goose-quill, with diamond point, as easily as any man in the newspaper work." Nevertheless, the precious title "Princess of the Press" implied a separate category for female journalists. From 1888 to 1892, Wells would be a full-time journalist and work hard for the right to be taken seriously.

6

Editorship of the *Free Speech*

"A woman editor and correspondent was a novelty"

B y 1889 Ida B. Wells was widely known as Iola, the "Princess of the Press." Black newspapers around the nation printed and reprinted her columns, which reflected her experiences in Memphis. Wells sought enlightenment and consolation in both her private musings and her public writings. She used the public forum to explore issues important to her, to sound out her ideas, to clarify her thoughts, and to resolve internal conflicts. Given her ambivalence and confusion about the status of women, it is hardly surprising that many of her early newspaper and periodical articles probed the proper roles for women. Several of her writings eulogized the ideal woman as depicted in the cult of true womanhood, claiming such status for black women as for white. Like many African Americans of that era, Wells felt the need to combat the racist rantings that had become so common in both white popular culture and academic literature. Some white writers actually asserted that Negroes were a different species suited only to do manual labor for "true human beings." African Americans spent thousands of hours trying to prove what should have been taken for granted—that they also were human and capable of all the achievements of other races.

White men justified sexual exploitation of black women by asserting they were depraved and promiscuous with an animal-like sensuality. For example, in historian Philip A. Bruce's, *The Plantation Negro as Freeman*

(1889), he asserted, "Chastity is a virtue which parents do not seem anxious to foster and guard in their daughters." He further declared, "A plantation negress may have sunk to a low point in the scale of sensual indulgence, yet her position does not seem to be substantially affected even in the estimation of the women of her own race." Declaring that under slavery some black women "copied the manner and morals of the mistress they served," Bruce believed that forces for morality ended with slavery. To him the black woman in freedom imitated only the worst qualities of the white woman. "She copies her extravagance in tawdry finery that is a grotesque exaggeration of fashion," he wrote, "she copies her independence in utter abandon of all restraints, she copies her vices and adds to them frills of her own."[1]

Such assaults against black women's dignity and morality stung bitterly. Wells used her pen to decry "the wholesale contemptuous defamation of their women" in her newspaper columns. She accused white critics of forgetting that "our enslavement with all the evils attendant thereon was involuntary and that enforced poverty, ignorance and immorality was our only dower at its close." Referring to the hostile criticism of African Americans by whites, Wells declared:

> While all these accusations, allowed as we usually are, no opportunity to refute them, are hurtful to and resented by us, none sting so deeply and keenly as the taunt of immorality; the jest and sneer with which our women are spoken of, and the utter incapacity or refusal to believe there are among us mothers, wives and maidens who have attained a true, noble, and refining womanhood.[2]

Black middle- and upper-class women naturally sought to change their image in the public's mind. To do so they tried to educate all black women how to behave "properly," that is, to model themselves after the Victorian image of true womanhood. Wells's efforts can be seen in several of her articles written between 1885 and 1888. In "Woman's Mission," which appeared in the *New York Age* in 1885, she described a "womanly woman" as "upholding the banner and striving for the goal of pure, bright womanhood through all vicissitudes and temptations."[3]

In 1888 Wells wrote her greatest paean to the Victorian image of the ideal woman. It also appeared in the *Age* and was titled "The Model Woman: A Pen Picture of the Typical Southern Girl." Her ideal woman was "not without refinement" and was "not coarse or rude in her manners,

nor loud and fast in her deportment." Wells explained the great need for
black women to conduct themselves carefully:

> For the sake of the noble womanhood to which she aspires, and the
> race whose name bears the stigma of immorality—her soul scorns
> each temptation to sin and guilt. She counts no sacrifice too great for
> the preservation of honor. She knows that our people, as a whole, are
> charged with immorality and vice; that it depends largely on the
> woman of to-day to refute such charges by her stainless life.[4]

Such beliefs must have made the recurring charges of immorality
against Wells especially painful. Perhaps the need to assert her own respectability partly prompted her to champion the cause of purity so frequently in the press. She was defending her personal honor as well as that
of other black women. At the same time, Wells's personality was more
suited for bold action than quiet refinement. The need to reconcile her
temperament with her ideology may have influenced her to assert that
more than gentility was expected of African American women. Her writings also praise women of action and strength. Asking "What is, or should
be a woman?", Wells answered:

> Not merely a bundle of flesh and bones, nor a fashion plate, a frivo-
> lous inanity, a soulless doll, a heartless coquette—but a strong, bright
> presence, thoroughly imbued with a sense of her mission on earth
> and a desire to fill it; an earnest, soulful being, laboring to fit herself
> for life's duties and burdens, and bearing them faithfully when they
> do come.[5]

In the same article, Wells asserted that in "all histories, biblical and political, ancient and modern" there were women "who have won laurels for
themselves as philanthropists, statesmen, leaders of armies, rulers of em-
pires." She noted that woman has risen where "men have become more enlightened" and in the nineteenth century there "are few positions she may
not aspire to."[6] To her the duties of womanhood were both extensive and
contradictory.

Wells was ambivalent about class issues as well as gender issues. In
"Functions of Leadership," she chided black male leaders for ignoring the
problems of their people because their own wealth shielded them from
many of the indignities of discrimination. "The ambition," she wrote,
"seems to be to get all they can for themselves, and the rest may shift for
themselves; some of them do not wish, after getting wealth for themselves,

to be longer identified with the people to whom they owe their political preferment; if no more."[7] It was the first of several articles in which Wells contemplated class and race issues—a subject that seemed to haunt her, perhaps because of her perilous position in the Memphis black elite.

Her writings reflect an ambivalence born from what Wells saw as two duties of the upper class. While its members were supposed to advance racial unity, they were expected also to break down white stereotypes, which could only be accomplished by differentiating between themselves and lower-class African Americans. Wells urged black leaders to be "identified with the people," yet on several occasions Wells criticized middle-class black Memphians for mingling too freely with the "masses." In 1885 she railed against the "promiscuous conglomeration of all classes" and was upset by those who participated in such lower-class diversions as dances in public parks and excursions (even though she enjoyed "higher-class" versions of the popular activity). In one newspaper column, she lambasted a minister for preaching against such activities and then participating in a "big procession" of thirty-five hacks where "some of the people were gorgeously and some hideously dressed."[8] She wrote directly to the point in another column.

> I stood and looked on the conglomerate mass at Festival Park last night and heaved a sigh. We kick about all being made to go to one place in the theater; here nobody forces, yet school teachers, sporting women, saloon toughs, honored wives and mothers, and black legs, all dancing together on the floor and many times in the same set. Who can blame white men for thinking we are all of one kind? If we do not draw the line between the respectable and the scum of the city, can we wonder that white people don't do it? Yet some of our best society girls think it awful if they cannot get out to this place.[9]

Nevertheless, in an 1887 article in the *American Baptist*, Wells attacked black business owners for separating themselves from the lower classes and refusing to serve other African Americans. "The feeling that prompts colored barbers, hotel keepers and the like to refuse accommodations to their own color," Wells wrote, "is the momentum that sends a Negro right about when he presents himself at any similar first-class establishment run by white men."[10] With a strong sense of duty, she was torn between the contradictory duties of the elite.

Like many African American women of her era, Wells believed the privileged had a duty to uplift the masses. In "A Story of 1900," written for the *Fisk Herald* (April 1886), she penned a portrait of a young woman teacher "who went from one of the many colleges of our Southland to teach among her people." After the teacher "awakened to a true sense of her mission," she visited homes "where squalor and moral uncleannes [sic] walked hand in hand with poverty" to teach parents how "to be self-respecting so they might be respected." Wells ended the story by urging teachers "not to be content simply to earn a salary" but also to "use their opportunity and influence."[11] Wells obviously wrestled with the disparity between her idealized vision of the teaching profession and the reality of its drudgery for her.

While this article sought to inspire educated African Americans to use their knowledge to help the less fortunate, more frequently Wells openly scolded the black elite for their leadership failures. Despite ambiguity and ambivalence, the preponderance of her writing makes clear that she considered race more important than class and believed black leaders should do so also. In the 1880s and 1890s, the black press often discussed what qualities were needed for leadership. The discussion mainly arose because of the aging of Frederick Douglass. Famous for his abolitionist activities and widely recognized as the foremost black leader and spokesperson, Douglass was sixty-seven years old in 1885 — an old man by the day's standards. Speculation about who might fill his shoes was intensified as many black leaders began jockeying to place themselves in position to assume the mantle of race leadership.

One letter writer to the Detroit *Plaindealer* proffered a list of possible candidates to which Wells responded. Acknowledging that the listed men had acquired "fame and wealth" and "are now declaring themselves devoted to the interest of the people," Wells asked how many were "exerting their talents and wealth for the benefit or amelioration of the condition of the masses." She wrote she knew of none who invested capital in enterprises to create jobs for other African Americans and claimed that their "ambition seemed to be to get all they can for their own use." To her they were wrong to seek to be "no longer identified" with poorer members of their race from whom they often derived their power and wealth.

> They are able to pay for berths and seats in Pullman cars, and consequently can report that—"railroad officials don't bother me, in traveling," and give entertainments that have but a single representative of their own race present, can see and hear of the indignities and insults offered our people [and] . . . can look and listen unmoved saying, "if it were my wife or daughter or relative I would do so and so," so what real benefit are they to their race any way?

Wells rejected the assertion that they benefited the race by "inspiring others to follow in their footsteps with a hope of similar success." She declared, "True, I had almost forgotten that; example is a great thing, but all of us can not be millionaires, orators, lawyers, doctors." She then asked, "What then must become of the mediocrity, the middle and lower classes that are found in all races?" and closed with the question, "What material benefit is a 'leader' if he does not, to some extent, devote his time, talent and wealth to the alleviation of the poverty and misery, and elevation of his people?"[12]

Wells also believed that racial allegiance was more important than political loyalty. In "Freedom of Political Action," she expressed her political disillusionment and reproached African Americans for being too inflexible in their attitudes toward political parties.

> According to their logic the side they espouse is all good, the opposite—all bad; the one, the Republican party, can do no wrong—however they use colored men for tools; the other, the Democratic side, can do no good—whatever the profession—because of past history. More could not be expected of ignorant, unthinking men than to be incapable of giving one credit for honest difference of opinion. It is considered a sign of [a] narrow, bigoted mind to be unable to listen to a diverse argument without intolerance and passion, yet how few among so-called "leaders," editors (moulders of public opinion) but are guilty of this same fault, are ready to cry "stop thief" to those who dare to step out of the beaten political track and maintain honest opinions and independent convictions of their own.[13]

Although Wells championed freedom of thought here, later in her career she was sometimes guilty of thinking all truth was on her side. In 1885 her stance as a political independent won her supporters from both sides of the political fence. Who could not find something to agree with in her discussion of the two parties?

> I am not a Democrat, because the Democrats considered me chattel and possibly might have always considered me, because their record from the beginning has been inimical to my interests; because they have become notorious in their hatred of the Negro as a man, have refused him the ballot; have murdered, beaten and outraged him and refused him his rights. I am not a Republican, because, after they—as a party measure and an inevitable result of the war—had "given the Negro his freedom" and the ballot box following, all through their reign—while advocating the doctrine of the Federal

Government's right of protecting her citizens—they suffered the crimes against the Negro, that have made the South notorious, to go unpunished and almost unnoticed, and turned them over to the tender mercies of the South entirely, as a matter of barter in '76, to secure the Presidency.[14]

It was a subtle and perceptive view of events that was upheld much later by historians. The letter also reflects Wells's greatest talent as a writer and speaker—the ability to articulate outrage. Her call to put race interests ahead of all others was a constant theme in her writing and foreshadowed Marcus Garvey's cry of "Race First" and Stokely Carmichael's "Black Power."

Independence of thought seems to have been a frequent topic for Iola, perhaps reflecting the teachings of the Church of Christ. In "Broken Idols," Wells urged African Americans to stop accepting without investigation the words of their religious, political, and social leaders. Instead they should question the status quo and examine all actions to see "if existing methods further the object to be desired of all others—the well-being of the Negro as a race, morally, socially, intellectually." In politics such an examination had caused African Americans to break from "the fallacious theory and practice of servile obedience." In religion, Wells wrote, "Men have come to think it is not indispensible [sic] to salvation to be either a Baptist or Methodist."[15]

Wells drew material for her articles from events in Memphis as well as news from other papers. She attended a great many local political and educational meetings. For example, in December 1886 Wells went to a Knights of Labor meeting at which white suffragist Lide Meriweather spoke. Unlike the American Federation of Labor that was formed later, this labor organization and reform group truly sought to overcome color barriers in the South as well as the North. Wells was impressed by Meriweather and marveled at the absence of discrimination and wrote a letter to the *Memphis Watchman* describing the meeting. She noted that black women were "seated with the courtesy usually extended to white ladies alone in this town." Wells asserted that it was the "first assembly of this sort in this town where color was not the criterion to recognition as ladies and gentlemen." To someone who had been ejected from the "ladies' car," this was very significant.[16]

The experience of seemingly genuine integration provoked other thoughts from Wells that she shared in an article for the *American Baptist*. In that article she waded into the controversy over the merits and costs of integration. It was a long and complicated debate. Some African Americans favored self-imposed segregation for a variety of reasons. Separate churches gave them the freedom to worship as they pleased and also to believe in God as the advocate of the oppressed rather than the supporter of the status quo. Many parents, especially working-class ones, preferred their children to be taught by black teachers who would respect them than by white teachers who would treat them as inferior. Segregation was viewed by some as the price of black autonomy. They preferred becoming officers in their own organizations to receiving second-class status in white-controlled groups. Others materially benefited from segregation by eliminating white competition for black patronage. Without coining the term "Black Power," some race thinkers anticipated its tenets, including the idea that it was suicidal to try to practice color blindness in a nation obsessed with race consciousness. In an 1889 article urging support for black newspapers, Josephine Turpin Washington declared, "But why speak of our drawing the color-line? It is drawn and most persistently by the whites. For us to attempt to ignore the fact would be like trying to walk through a stone wall by simply making up your mind it is not there. The wall stands and you have only a broken head for your pains."[17]

Unlike in the late 1960s when black nationalism and separatism were the credos of militancy, at the turn of the century most militants argued for integration. The great abolitionist, Frederick Douglass, remained consistently and militantly integrationist in ideology until his death. Although Wells argued for racial unity and placing black interests first, she also believed leaders who truly wanted what was best for African Americans should fight for inclusion into mainstream society. In the *American Baptist* she criticized African Americans who sought separate Knights of Labor assemblies and those who provided separate seating for "white friends" when they attended "our concerts, exhibitions, etc." Wells argued, "Consciously and unconsciously we do as much to widen the breach already existing and to keep prejudice alive as the other race." Drawing on her experiences the previous summer, Wells noted that no separate school existed in California "until the colored people asked for it." She believed, "To say we wish to be to ourselves is tacit acknowledgment of the inferiority that [whites] take for granted anyway." She could forgive "the ignorant man" for being "short-sighted" but condemned "the man or men who deliberately yield or barter the birthright of the race for money, position, [or] self-aggrandizement in any form."[18]

Wells was influenced by what she read as well as the activities in which she participated. Her role as a journalist, underpaid or not, required Wells to read many of the weeklies on a regular basis. Doing so exposed her increasingly to the injustices faced by African Americans far from her home city. What she learned began to both fuel and focus her anger. It also caused her to question God for answers to the evil of the world. In March 1886, she mourned the death of "thirteen colored men . . . shot down in cold blood" in Mississippi and implored, "O, God when will these massacres cease—it was only because they had attempted to assassinate a white man (and for just cause I suppose). Colored men rarely attempt to wreak vengance [sic] on a white one unless he has provoked it unduly."[19]

The impact lynching had on Wells, even before she made it her crusade, is seen in her response to that Mississippi incident and a later one in Jackson, Tennessee, which she described in a diary entry, writing that a "colored woman accused of poisoning a white one was taken from the county jail and stripped naked and hung up in the courthouse yard and her body riddled with bullets and her body left exposed to view!" Once again Wells demanded, "O my God! can such things be and no justice for it?" She considered the evidence against the victim flimsy and in a "pitch of indignation" over the "great outrage" she wrote a "dynamitic [sic] article . . . almost advising murder!" She worried, "It may be unwise to express myself so strongly but I cannot help it & I know not if capital may not be made of it against me but I trust in God."[20] Her faith continued to propel her to protest injustice in powerful language, which brought her increasing fame.

That fame paved the way for her election as the first woman officer of the National Colored Press Association in 1888, which provided new status and legitimacy in the eyes of fellow journalists. Her election as first assistant secretary of the National Colored Press Association was followed by her election as secretary in 1889, a job she held until 1891.[21] The group had been organized about 1880 by John W. Cromwell, editor of the Washington *People's Advocate*. Reflecting the debate over race labels, the group underwent name changes from "Colored" to "Afro-American" to "Negro." Its primary function was to hold yearly conventions at which journalists could meet each other, exchange ideas, and pass resolutions—in keeping with the tradition of the black convention movement dating back to 1830. Each time the organization met in Washington, it was granted an audience with the president—Chester Arthur and William McKinley. Although its prestige rose and fell over the years, most major journalists held office at some time. The election of Wells in 1889 was especially significant—she defeated founder Cromwell for the job.[22]

Wells apparently enjoyed conventions and conferences. She attended teachers' meetings, church gatherings, and political assemblies all over the nation. In July 1888 she went to Indianapolis to attend a highly controversial meeting of black Democrats and independents. W. Calvin Chase of the *Washington Bee* and other avid Republicans tagged the gathering as the "Boodle Conference," implying the chief purpose was obtaining political appointments (boodles) for its participants from Democratic elected officials. Although labeled as nonpartisan, the group was accused of being financed by President Grover Cleveland and the Democratic party. Chase huffed, "We could have bought a majority of the gathering for $500." The proceedings became quite heated; one participant actually pulled a revolver at one point. The *Bee* reported, "Several ladies who were present, Miss Ida B. Wells, the talented journalist, being one, rushed for the door, men of all sizes did likewise until the would be assassin could be unarmed."[23]

Wells not only witnessed that dangerous incident but also made valuable contacts. One of the key participants was T. Thomas Fortune. Although he and Wells had corresponded for quite some time, they had never met face-to-face. When Wells had first seen his picture, she had been disappointed. "With his long hair, curling about his forehead and his spectacles," she wrote, "he looks more like the dude of the period than the strong, sensible, brainy man I have pictured him." Whether seeing him in person altered her first impression is unknown, but he was certainly impressed by both her mind and her body. Directly after the meeting he noted her ability to "handle a goose-quill pen, with diamond point, as easily as any man." He also wrote, "If Iola were a man, she would be a humming independent in politics. She has plenty of nerve, and is as sharp as a steel trap, and she has no sympathy with humbug." His sketch included a physical description: "She is rather girlish looking in physique, with sharp regular features, penetrating eyes, firm set thin lips and a sweet voice." He seemed intrigued at how Wells could be "manly" in her writing style and political interests and at the same time be "girlish" and "sweet" in her physical attributes.[24]

In his comments about Wells over the years, Fortune attempted to reconcile the dual existence of attributes then defined as masculine and feminine. This was especially true in an article he wrote for L. A. Scruggs's book, *Women of Distinction,* in 1893.

She handles her subjects more as a man than as a woman; indeed, she has so long had the management of a large home and business

interests that the sharpness of wit and self-possession which charac-
terize men of affairs are hers in a large measure.

Few women have a higher conception of the responsibilities and
the possibilities of her sex than Miss Wells. She has all of a woman's
tenderness in all that affects our common humanity, but she has also
the courage of the great women of the past who believed that they
could still be womanly while being more than ciphers in "the world's
broad field of battle."[25]

Beginning with the Louisville Press Association convention, Wells met
and impressed many male and female journalists during the next few years.
Before that time most, if not all, of her contacts had been with male journalists. While in Kentucky for the convention, Wells encountered and befriended female journalist Mary E. Britton. Known as Meb, she edited the
women's column for the *Lexington Herald*. Calling her "a sensible pleasant girl," Wells enjoyed spending time with Britton in Lexington and continued to correspond with her after returning to Memphis. At some point
Wells also met Meta E. Pelham, who wrote for the *Detroit Plaindealer*, and
visited her in Detroit in the summer of 1890.[26]

Although Wells sparred with Mary Cook (Grace Ermine) in 1888, she
seems to have gotten along better with other women journalists. In 1889
Wells received glowing reviews not only from Lucy Wilmot Smith but also
Gertrude Mossell. Like Wells, Mossell contributed to a wide variety of
newspapers. In January 1889 she wrote "Our Women of Letters" for the Indianapolis *Freeman,* in which she recalled becoming aware of Wells's talents when reading her article in the December 1886 *New York Freeman.*
Mossell then gushed,

> Miss Wells has already made her non-de-plume Iola a power, and
> her articles are much sought after. She writes with a vim and sparkle
> that holds the attention. One always reads her articles to the end and
> never casts aside the humblest publication after seeing her signature,
> until one finds what she has to say.[27]

The next month Mossell wrote an article "To Make Our Papers Pay,"
proposing a payment system that would have helped female correspondents. She closed by asking all women journalists to write her with further
ideas, singling out Iola to "say a word" because Mossell had "great confidence in her judgment."[28]

At the time, Wells was using her judgment to determine her permanent journalistic home. Countee had been unwilling to make her a regular paid correspondent for the *Living Way* in August 1886. The other major black newspaper in the city then was the *Memphis Watchman*, which had originated as the *Mississippi Baptist* in 1872 and changed owners and names in 1883. The two papers were apparently rather bitter rivals. In March 1886 the *Washington Bee* had quoted the *Watchman* as declaring, "The most senseless, idiotic and brainless 'thing' in the land is that abortion in the shape of a newspaper, the *Living Way*." Soon after Countee's rebuff Wells had begun contributing more regularly to the *Watchman* than to the *Living Way*.[29]

Within the next year a new newspaper arrived in Memphis. Called the *Free Speech*, it was edited by the Reverend Taylor Nightingale and was headquartered in his church, Beale Street Baptist. In 1888 Nightingale joined forces with J. L. Fleming to form the *Free Speech and Headlight*. Until July 1888 Fleming edited the *Marion Headlight* in Marion, Arkansas—about ten miles from Memphis. At that time, however, whites in Marion decided to no longer tolerate African Americans' holding office in their town. Under the pretext of a "suspicious charge" made in anonymous letters, over one hundred white men carrying Winchester rifles ran all black officeholders as well as two pastors and Fleming out of town.[30]

Wells had written for the *Marion Headlight* since at least August 1887. After Fleming joined Nightingale, they naturally approached Wells about writing for the new *Free Speech and Headlight*. For a long time, she had dreamed of becoming a newspaper owner and editor. As she later recalled, "Since the appetite grows for what it feeds on, the desire came to own a paper." Wells had gained self-assurance by then and refused to join Nightingale and Fleming "except as equal with themselves." Buying a one-third interest, she eventually became the editor; Fleming acted mainly as business manager and Nightingale as sales manager. Fleming was able to sell about two hundred dollars worth of advertising a month—mainly to white Memphis businessmen. As pastor of the largest church in Memphis, Nightingale sold at least five hundred copies every Sunday to his congregation. They made the paper financially viable, and Wells brought it stature in the journalistic community as the outlet for her powerful and popular writings.[31]

In late June 1889, black newspapers around the country announced Wells's affiliation with the *Free Speech and Headlight*. The next month both the Indianapolis *Freeman* and the *Cleveland Gazette* carried identical biographical sketches of Wells. Calling her "one of the brightest geniuses

*Picture that Wells disliked in
the Indianapolis* Freeman,
25 November 1893.

of the rising generation of women," the articles discussed her railroad suit, her journalistic career, her purchase of an interest in the *Free Speech and Headlight*, and her election as secretary of the National Colored Press Association. Once again she was compared to her male colleagues: "She is a terse and forcible writer, and plunges into politics and other matters of national importance with the vivacity of a full-fledged journalist of the masculine gender."[32] Male and full-fledged were presented as almost synonymous.

Both papers included drawings of Wells; neither was flattering, but the one in the *Gazette* was especially dismal. To the disgust of some, Wells rejected the role of honorary male and reacted like "a typical woman." The *Free Speech and Headlight* took note of the complimentary articles but quoted "a young unmarried man" as saying Iola "will never get a husband in the world as long as she lets these editors make her so hideous." "I used to see 'em before I knew her," the quote continued, "and my mental conclusion was: well, that woman certainly can write, but if she looks like that, good Lord deliver us!"[33]

Wells and her male partners may have meant the editorial as a light-hearted jest, but both the *Gazette* and the *Freeman* responded savagely. The *Gazette* claimed the quote came from "one of the mouthy youths of Memphis who is 'mashed' on Miss Wells" and asserted that she was not "any better or worse looking" than the picture. The *Freeman* was even more brutal:

> Iola makes the mistake of trying to be pretty as well as smart. She should remember that beauty and brains are not always companions. George Eliot, George Sand, Harriet Beecher Stowe and many other bright minds of that sex were not paragons by any means. The picture which the Cleveland Gazette published flattered her. Remember Cromwell's injunction to the artist, Iola. "Paint me as I am."[34]

After these exchanges, Wells's relationship with both editors remained rocky. She sometimes agreed with one or the other on specific issues, but an undercurrent of antagonism lingered. As her reputation grew, so did the attacks upon her. Given the venomous verbal assaults male journalists exchanged, turning their poisoned pens on Wells was actually recognition of her being accepted as part of the "fraternity." At the same time, however, many couched their criticisms of Wells in sexist terms that belittled her. By sometimes framing her response in the language of wounded womanhood, Wells contributed to her failure at times to be taken seriously—until her increasing militancy collided with racial violence in Memphis to propel her into the ranks of race leadership.

Most verbal warfare between male editors revolved around political affiliations or personal rivalries for political appointments. The battles between male editors and Wells were sometimes over issues but seemed mainly to grow out of personal antipathies. Most of her conflicts occurred with Edward E. Cooper of the *Freeman*, who was a political independent, and H. C. Smith of the *Gazette* and William Calvin Chase of the *Washington Bee*, both of whom were avid Republicans. At the same time she apparently had good relationships with the four male owners of the Detroit *Plaindealer*, who were Republicans; C. H. J. Taylor of the Kansas City *American Citizen*, who was a Democrat; and T. Thomas Fortune of the *New York Age*, who was an independent. Personalities seemed to play a greater role than politics in determining Wells's relationships in the newspaper world.

Wells had received her first drubbing from Chase in 1886. Not surprisingly, the sniping continued. Indeed, the *Washington Bee* seemed to treat Wells with more contempt than either the *Freeman* or the *Gazette*. When she joined the *Free Speech and Headlight*, the *Bee* noted, "Miss Iola has now got both paws in the soup." Afterward, the paper routinely referred to Wells as "our little sweetness" or "Sweet Iola." When she disagreed with a *Bee* editorial, Chase remarked, "Dear Ida you are a little too fresh." After she defended C. H. J. Taylor from a *Bee's* attack, Chase retorted, "Now, Iola, you are a dear sweet little girl and a pet with the gang, but, has it ever occurred to you that Taylor was a crank?" Another time when they disagreed over an issue, Chase sarcastically noted, "We regret that our idol should allow such things to mar her sweet temper."[35]

In 1890 one of the largest controversies regarding Wells's status in the journalistic world centered on a cartoon published in the *Freeman* titled "Fortune and His Echo." In it two little dogs identified as Fortune and Iola were yipping at a much larger dog, the *Freeman*. They were labeled "a species of canine" with a "propensity to bark." While insulting, that part of the cartoon was not sexist. Yet in the left-hand corner was a smaller picture of a woman dressed like a man with the words "I would I were a man." Although the phrase likely referred to Iola's writing style and political interests, which were deemed not womanly, some male editors appear to have read sexual innuendo into it. One called it "a cartoon too foul in suggestiveness to be described" and implied that Cooper should not get "within shooting range." Even the *Gazette* came to the defense of Wells—in a paternalistic assurance that she was a "lady" who had "as protectors every gentleman journalist of color in this country."[36]

The *Freeman* published a rather long response to the criticism of both Wells and her "protectors." Cooper claimed that he "in various ways have assisted her over rugged places in a road strange to feminine feet" and complained that "much of this has been repaid in abuse and captious criticism." The cartoon "contained no ulterior suggestion, and those who represent it so simply reveal the foulness and corruption of their own imaginations." Cooper's most telling blow was aimed at Iola's trying to have it both ways by asking to be treated like a man when it served her purpose, but then evoking protection as a woman when things got rough. "Iola," he wrote, "however deserving she may be, has been petted and spoiled by a very generous press, and forgets that in a journalistic sense she must sometimes take a man's fare."[37] Although there was a grain of truth in this assertion, men sometimes found her playing the role of a "full-fledged journalist of the masculine gender" offensive. Since Wells was penalized for being a woman, why should she not demand some of the privileges of woman-hood?

The *Freeman's* treatment of Wells and other articles appearing in the paper indicate that some black men still wholeheartedly ascribed to the cult of true womanhood. But although her femininity was patronized and ridiculed, Wells was fast becoming a major figure in black journalism. She was also emerging as an heroic figure among women. In September 1889 African Americans in Indianapolis established the Iola Literary Club in her honor. Her influence increased as she traveled and participated in meetings in various locations, such as a teachers' convention in St. Paul, Minnesota.[38]

In the summer of 1891, Wells headed south for an extended visit at the invitation of Isaiah Montgomery. Montgomery was a remarkable man, who as a slave had run his master's plantation in Mississippi. After emancipation Montgomery became a very successful planter, helped other African Americans to purchase land, and in 1887 established an all-black town named Mound Bayou. A prominent politician, Montgomery became the only black delegate elected to the Mississippi constitutional conven-

Controversial cartoon from the Indianapolis Freeman, *19 April 1890.*

tion of 1890, where the state's constitution was rewritten to virtually exclude African Americans from voting.

The new Mississippi constitution was the first to include provisions to circumvent the Fifteenth Amendment, which barred states from denying suffrage on the basis of race, color, or previous condition of servitude. Its poll tax and literacy test were upheld by the United States Supreme Court and became widely copied throughout the South during the next decade and a half. (Of course, those and other methods were already being used on a limited basis in localities around the South. In the early 1880s, Memphis had switched to at-large elections and failed to provide ballot boxes in predominantly black areas to curb black political influence. The *Free Speech* [which had shortened its name in October 1889] reported that in the city's fall elections of 1890 black voting was further minimized by a poll tax requirement and a confusing ballot box system.) Nevertheless, by writing disfranchisement into a state constitution, Mississippi provided the means to destroy any meaningful black political power over wide areas of the South.[39]

Because of its significance, many African Americans had been horrified to learn that Montgomery had voted to accept the 1890 constitution. After the *Free Speech* attacked his action, Montgomery came to its office to explain his vote. Wells later noted that "although we never agreed that his course had been the right one, we became the best of friends." He suggested a southern tour might increase her paper's circulation and invited her to visit Mound Bayou. Leaving in June 1891, Wells "went to most of the large towns throughout the Delta, across the Mississippi into Arkansas, and back to Tennessee."[40]

Going "wherever there was a gathering of the people," Wells sought new subscribers and correspondents for her paper. At the same time she wrote letters about her trip and the happenings in various towns for publication in the *Free Speech*. Pleased with her reception, she noted, "A woman editor and correspondent was a novelty; besides, Mississippi was my native state." At a meeting of African American lawyers in Greenville, Wells "came out with the subscription of every man present." In Water Valley, Mississippi, a Masonic lodge suspended its session for a thirty-minute appeal by Wells, after which she "was weighted down with silver dollars and had to go straight to the bank." Her success prompted her to take other such trips; she visited Helena, Arkansas, in November 1891 and Natchez, Mississippi, in March 1892.[41]

Increasing circulation became critical to Wells in the fall of 1891 when she lost her teaching job. In an article critical of the conditions within the city's black schools, Wells attacked not only inadequate school buildings but also the training and character of some of the newer teachers.[42] According to Wells, some had "little to recommend them save an illicit friendship with members of the school board." Fearing the charges could lead to her termination, she had asked co-owner Nightingale to sign the article after it was already set in type. After he refused, Wells claimed it was "too late to substitute something else, as the forms were locked up ready to go to press."[43]

When the time came for renewal of teachers' contracts, Wells's was not renewed. The school board did not notify her of its decision until time for school to start, leaving her no time to find another job. She sent a lawyer to the board to find out the reason for her dismissal. He was told that there were no complaints about Wells's work or character. Instead the board showed him a copy of the *Free Speech* article and said they "didn't care to employ a teacher who had done this." According to her later recollections, the worst part of the experience "was the lack of appreciation shown by the parents," who could not understand why she did something that would get her fired. She was also criticized by the Memphis correspondent to the *Freeman*, who claimed Wells "seems anxious for a sensation." "But I thought it was right to strike a blow against a glaring evil," Wells exclaimed, "and I did not regret it."[44]

At the time she was fired, the *Free Speech* was not making enough money to pay Wells a decent salary. She threw herself into increasing circulation with phenomenal success. "I felt I had at last found my real vocation," Wells later declared. She claimed that in less than a year she had increased the number of subscribers from fifteen hundred to four thousand, making it possible for her to earn within ten dollars of her teacher's salary.[45] Freedom from teaching allowed Wells to become more deeply involved in various organizational efforts that predated her becoming a full-time editor. Her roles in the Southern Afro-American Press Association and the National Afro-American League expanded her impact as a racial advocate.

Holding its first meeting in the offices of the *Free Speech*, the Southern Afro-American Press Association resulted from the discontent of southern and western editors with the eastern press's attempts to dominate black journalism. In May 1891 Edwin Hackley, editor of the *Denver Statesman* and former suitor of Wells, lamented, "An honest criticism from the West or South is sure to bring a flood of conceited and abusive lambaste from the black Czars of the North and East, who, it seems, would reserve the right to doctor everything to suit themselves."[46]

The principal organizer of the Southern Afro-American Press Association was Jesse C. Duke, editor of the *Pine Bluff Weekly Echo*. Born a slave in Alabama, Duke had been the editor of the *Montgomery Herald* and president of Alabama's black press association until he published an editorial against lynching, which commented upon "the partiality of white Juliets for colored Romeos." Montgomery whites soon drove Duke out of town. He maintained that the "howling, bloodthirsty mob" used the article as a pretext to terrorize all the city's educated African Americans—primarily because of opposition to locating a black state university there. Many black editors criticized Duke's action, but his ideology undoubtedly planted a seed for Wells's later editorial that would bring her the same consequences.[47]

Wells and Duke were both praised and criticized for their roles in forming the Southern Afro-American Press Association. The *Topeka Times-Observer* asserted that the move was politically motivated, and the Detroit *Plaindealer* charged that the group "was promoted with the full knowledge that its ultimate success would cripple the National association." Commenting on Wells's support of the group, the *Plaindealer* asked, "Was not the fair sex always the bulwark of the rebel cause?" On the other hand, the Indianapolis *Freeman* wished the group well, noting that "we of the cold and frigid North, are dependent upon the southern Negro press for much of the reliable information touching matters and questions affecting the surroundings of our people in the race's fatherland." The *Cleveland Gazette* speculated that the association "will work in harmony with the national organization and be of additional service, not only to the profession, but also to the race."[48]

As it turned out, the new group had little impact either positively or negatively. In her account of the first meeting, Wells declared, "Editor Duke has no cause to feel ashamed." She blamed the low attendance on "bad weather and late trains." Only seven people attended the January 1892 meeting, including two from Memphis; a dozen more sent letters and telegrams of support. They agreed to meet again in June "to complete permanent organization." Wells then read a paper by Hackley, who could not attend. After a discussion of the paper, the group adjourned at 8:00 P.M. and went to Smith's Restaurant, where "the visiting delegates were entertained by Miss I. B. Wells at dinner."[49]

The National Afro-American League, in which Wells also played a role, had little early success either. Many had espoused the need for an organization of black unity when, in May 1887, T. Thomas Fortune issued a call: "Let the thousand and one organizations we now have unite into one grand body for the uplifting and upbuilding of the fortunes and rights of the race." Significantly, the appeal opened with, "There should be some way to suppress mob law in the South." After a discussion of the failure of the white press and politicians to seek resolution of the evil of lynching, Fortune proclaimed, "There is no dodging the issue; we have got to take hold of this problem ourselves, and make so much noise that all the world shall know the wrongs we suffer and our determination to right those wrongs."[50]

The words resonated with Wells, and she became one of the League's earliest and most adamant supporters. In the *American Baptist* she joined her voice with Fortune's to challenge African Americans to action:

> We have reached a stage in the world's history where we can no longer be passive onlookers, but must join in the fray for our recognition, or be stigmatized forever as a race of cowards.
>
> The first step, then, is organization. No more pitiable spectacle can be realized than a disorganized mass of intellect and power, swayed by every wind that blows or used as a tool by any designing body. We have been asleep long enough, let us awake, march to the front and do noble battle for the establishment of the Afro-American League.[51]

Her appeals to courage and battle reflect Wells's heroic image of manhood. On this and other issues, she challenged black men to live up to her idealized vision of manliness—usually to be bitterly disappointed by their powerlessness.

Sometimes Fortune also couched his arguments in language that appealed to Wells's religious faith. Over the next two years, Fortune sought to inspire African Americans by drawing on their faith in a just God who sided with the oppressed. In 1887 he declared, "Almighty God never intended great evils to rule unchallenged among men." Two and a half years later, at the meeting to perfect organization, Fortune exclaimed, "The great moving and compelling influence in the history of the world is agitation, and the greatest of agitators was He, the despised Nazarene, whose doctrines revolutionized the thought of the ages."[52] Likewise, Wells reminded African Americans not to place their faith in white action but in God. She declared, "Congress seems powerless to help us, the State executive machinery is unwilling to do so and we are at last beginning to see that 'God helps those who help themselves.'"[53] She called for a kind of holy war, urging action on the League: "Do not let it die! Agitate and act until *something* is done. While we are resting on our oars, seemingly content with expressing our indignation by resolutions at the outrages that daily occur, others are presuming upon this inaction and encroaching more and more upon our rights—nay upon life itself."[54]

Fortune urged the establishment of state Leagues in 1887 as the first step toward a national organization. He envisioned a kind of central federation of groups that elected delegates to the national body according to the number of members each had. The central body would remain totally nonpartisan, but local chapters could do as they wished about endorsing candidates. In November 1889 Fortune issued a call for a national meeting to be held at Nashville in January 1890. Later that month the *Free Speech* proposed the organization in Memphis of a group "to merge . . . into a league such as indicated by Mr. T. Thos. Fortune." Criticizing one opponent of the League, Wells also noted that "all thinkers of the race who have given an opinion unite in declaring the league's the thing, save Mr. J. D. Bowser." However, the site of the national meeting was changed to Chicago, and Wells did not attend. She apparently was not elected to the Memphis delegation of twenty-five, which was headed by B. K. Sampson. Most leading editors attended, adopted a constitution, and agreed to meet the next year in Knoxville—perhaps because there had been proportionately few southerners at the northern meeting.[55]

Apparently few women attended the first meeting, even though Fortune had declared that unless "the women of the race take hold of the Afro-American League it will never be the power it should be." Like Frederick Douglass, Fortune seems to have advocated the acceptance of women as organizational equals. He believed, "As the women of the race are, so will be the men." The next year Fortune took special pains to include women. In the *Age* he answered the question "What is the status of women in the Afro-American League?" with "There is no difference. In the League a woman is just as good as a man. Out of it she is usually much better." He also invited Wells to be on the program.[56]

More women and southerners attended the Knoxville meeting in July 1891, but few northerners or westerners showed up. Fortune blamed their absence on "the new separate car law of Tennessee, . . . which is as villainous a thing as ever provoked a pious man to profanity." Some papers were critical of the meeting; the *American Citizen* called it "a coming together of disgruntled black office seekers." Nevertheless, most agreed on one thing: Ida B. Wells and her speech were among the highlights. One participant remembered her as "bright and witty whether in conversation or on the platform." The *Knoxville Daily Journal* remarked upon her "elegant language" when discussing women's role in the League. Describing the speeches, the *Plaindealer* mused that "the best of all was that of Miss Well [sic], who starting out by declaring she couldn't make a speech, captured the house by her apt and clear illustrations of the points in her address."[57] The longest evaluation came from Fortune in his notes over the meeting:

> The women were not silent. At the mass meeting Miss Ida B. Wells . . . delivered an address which kept the audience in a bubble of excitement. She is eloquent, logical, and dead in earnest. . . . She should use the gift of speech God has given her to arouse the women of the race to a full sense of duty in the work of the Afro-American League. Every woman of the race should rally around such a woman and hold up her hands.[58]

In Knoxville the League passed numerous resolutions, including one calling segregated transportation "a gratuitous indignity—an insult to our manhood" and another declaring that "lynch law is one of the greatest evils which we are called upon to endure."[59] Wells wanted the League to attempt more concrete methods of change and urged such actions as a boycott of the railroads. She was bitterly disappointed with the male leaders of the League, especially its president, J. C. Price of North Carolina. In the *Free Speech* Wells lashed out at the group's inaction:

> A handful of men, with no report of work accomplished, no one in the field to spread it, no plan of work laid out—no intelligent direction—meet and by their child's play illustrate in their own doings the truth of the saying that Negroes have no capacity for organization. Meanwhile a whole race is lynched, proscribed, intimidated, deprived of its political and civil rights, herded into boxes (by courtesy called separate cars) which bring the blush of humiliation to every self-respecting man's cheek—and we sit tamely by without using the only means—that of thorough organization and earnest work to prevent it. No wonder the world at large spits upon us with impunity.[60]

Wells's analysis of the group's weakness was widely applauded and proved accurate. Within two years Fortune was forced to declare the League defunct. It would remain so until 1898, when Wells and Fortune would play roles in its revival.[61]

Although the organizations Wells supported were not succeeding, her newspaper was. When Wells became the full-time editor of the *Free Speech*, she began printing it on pink paper to make it distinct. Fortune noted that "the *Free Speech* has adopted a pink dress with a black overskirt, and looks real fetching."[62] The distinctive look served another purpose. According to Wells, some newspaper "butchers" had been substituting other papers for the *Free Speech* among illiterate black customers. Those not able to read for themselves could ask for the "pink paper." They did so in increasing numbers "all up and down the Delta spur of the Illinois Central Railroad," following Wells's trips into the region.[63]

The main reason for the *Free Speech*'s popularity was the lively writing style of Iola. After Wells joined the paper, its editorial pages joined the discussion of all major issues confronting African Americans. Many other papers quoted and commented upon Iola and the *Free Speech*. Even if politics were considered a male domain, Wells did not hesitate to wade into the middle of any controversy. One of the era's most heated debates was the question of party affiliation. Although practically all black voters religiously voted Republican throughout Reconstruction, by the 1880s many were disillusioned with the party. With radical Republicans retiring or dying, the party appeared to have sold its antislavery soul in the interest of big business. Some African Americans switched parties, but most argued that Republicans, with all their sins, were still better than Democrats, many of whom openly proclaimed white supremacy. Local political situations as well as personal political ambitions helped determine allegiance.[64]

Wells joined Fortune and others in proclaiming a third option: independence. They advocated voting by candidate and issue rather than being such reliable party supporters that they need not be courted. Iola naturally fit into this group. Although she generally favored the Republicans, Wells believed everything was secondary to race advancement. "I am a Republican," she wrote in 1892, "but I was an Afro-American before I was a Republican."[65] Her personality made Wells most effective as a critic who exposed evil to the scrutiny of society. Her residual anger found release in denunciation. By remaining independent, Iola remained free to castigate everyone.

In 1890 two pieces of proposed legislation became litmus tests for white Republicans—and most flunked. The first was the Lodge Election bill, allowing the use of federal power to ensure integrity of voter registration and elections in the South. With the rising tide of disfranchisement throughout the South, a meaningful law would have had dramatic impact on the region's future. "That one of some kind is needed," Iola wrote, "goes without saying." In June 1890 Wells proclaimed, "If the Republican party lets this opportunity go by, without doing something in the interest of honest elections, it deserves to be defeated for years to come." In the end Republicans bartered away the Lodge bill for support of a higher tariff.[66]

The "opportunity" to which Wells referred was Republican control of both houses of Congress and the presidency—a very rare occurrence in the decades following Reconstruction. Republicans had previously proposed the Blair Education bill to provide federal funding for underfunded public schools, and blamed Democrats for blocking its passage. In 1890 Republicans not only had control of Congress but also a treasury surplus that they wanted to spend to prevent a bid for lower tariffs. Nevertheless, they let the Blair bill die. In response the *Free Speech* made a plea for self-help: "Now that the Blair bill is dead after eight years, it behooves us to bestir ourselves to greater efforts for the education of our children. Make better use of the opportunities we have and save money for greater. The road to our success lies through the door of moral, intellectual and financial education."[67]

The editorial expressed a self-help ethic much like that of Tuskegee Institute's president, Booker T. Washington, whose views became controversial later in the decade. The Alabama educator tied self-help ideology with an acceptance of segregation, urging black southerners to place economic and educational advancement above political rights. On the other hand, the *Free Speech* did not seem to grieve over the Blair bill unduly because of its seeming endorsement of segregated education. Wells had often denounced black acceptance of segregation. Other southerners, such as J. C. Price of North Carolina, disagreed and argued that the people of the South were "crying for education" and did not care "what manner the money for education came to them, if only it came."[68]

In addition to support for self-help, Wells shared another sentiment with Booker T. Washington in 1890—criticism of corrupt and ignorant clergy. Washington became a focus of controversy when he publicly denounced and ridiculed many of the nation's black pastors. Some felt he had been too harsh; others were upset at the manner of his censure. In a climate reeking of white supremacy, many argued that African Americans gave whites more ammunition by airing their criticisms of one another in public forums. Others asserted that black public officials and leaders were not held "to strict enough account" because of "a sickly sentimentality and super-sensitiveness about us that we were better off without."[69]

Wells never hesitated to criticize *anyone* she thought deserved it, especially the clergy. She wholeheartedly agreed with Washington's criticisms, writing to him, "I read your manly criticism of our corrupt and ignorant clergy." In her letter Wells enclosed some clippings of her own articles on the clergy and closed by saying, "To a man whose conscience is his guide, words of encouragement and sustenance are not necessary, yet I cannot refrain from adding my mite to the approbation your utterances and work have received from the rank & file of our people."[70]

Wells likely had a wide selection of articles to enclose. Indeed, one time she so enraged the black Memphis ministry that the "preachers' alliance" voted to boycott the *Free Speech*. The precipitating incident was Wells's "caustic comments" about a minister caught in bed with a parishioner by her husband. After the ministers informed Wells of the battle they proposed to wage against her paper from their pulpits, she later asserted,

> We answered this threat by publishing the names of every minister who belonged to the alliance in the next issue of the *Free Speech*, and told the community that these men upheld the immoral conduct of one of their number and asked if they were willing to support preachers who would sneak into their homes when their backs were turned and debauch their wives. Needless to say we never heard any more about the boycott, and the *Free Speech* flourished like a green bay tree.[71]

The denunciation of immorality reflected her mother's guidance and the impact of the missionary teachers at Rust; Wells often looked at the world through Puritan eyes. In 1891 she chastised the clergy for participating in "excursions," because of "the money wasted for hacks and clothes, the time taken from work, the beer and whiskey guggled." When Wells criticized the intermingling of "teachers, sporting women, saloon toughs, honored wives and mothers, and black legs" at a local park, her main concern was their immoral behavior. In her diary she often judged herself by harsh standards; in her articles she did the same for everyone else.[72]

Her prudery sometimes won Wells rebukes from fellow journalists. For example, when George Washington Williams—the author of *A History of the Negro Race from 1619 to 1880*—died in 1891, Wells was very critical of the deceased. Williams was indeed controversial and had been accused of selling out his race and deserting his wife for other women. His public actions were considered legitimate topics of journalism, but Wells apparently discussed his personal failings and mentioned his father's desertion of his mother. The *American Citizen* declared, "The *Free Speech* especially is very harsh and condemnatory and even refers to his parents with a sneer as though he were responsible for his birth." The paper also asked, "why pull aside the curtain and hold up to public scorn his private life, that does not belong to the public, no one is benefited, no wrong is righted, no skeleton is clothed anew." The Indianapolis *Freeman* censured *Free Speech* for the "flippancy and ease with which reputations are made and unmade."[73] Given the assaults against her own reputation, Wells seems to have been too willing to do the same to others.

Wells aimed most of her criticism, however, at perceived failures of leadership. She believed a handful of Reconstruction leaders had predominated too long and become more interested in rotating the juiciest plums of patronage than in protecting black rights. Some seemed to remain loyal to the Republican party primarily for the federal offices they received. In 1889 the *Free Speech* declared, "Give the young Republicans a chance and relegate some of these chronic office holders to the rear. Some of the old people will die pretty soon and who are to save the country then." Two years later Wells published a letter that declared, "A man, in a fat office . . . to which he has been appointed by a white official, does not and can not safely fulfill the requirements of leadership for the colored race." According to Wells, this lack of independence was found on the local level as well. In December 1891 she declared that "in every community there are Negroes who persecute and betray their race of their own accord to curry favor with white people and win the title of 'good nigger.'" Another complaint by Wells was self-proclaimed male leaders' substitution of talk for action. In spring 1890 she noted plans for the third convention of colored men to be held within six months. She moaned, "If it keeps on at this rate, the Negro and his grievances, which some of the would be leaders seem to think can be talked down, will become ridiculous as well as monotonous."[74]

Although few men lived up to the heroism she attributed to her father, Wells especially targeted one man for her scorn. Blanche K. Bruce was a fellow Mississippean, who after serving as that state's senator, continued to be appointed to various federal offices. He was very wealthy and conservative on racial issues—the kind of man the white power structure could and did co-opt. Wells insisted, "What can history say of our Senator Bruce, save that he held the chair of a Senator for six years, drew his salary and left others to champion the Negro's cause in the Senate Chamber?" She further noted that Bruce "had controlled men as pieces on a checker board, and made them stepping stones to his ambition" and that he "would have a more enduring name in history if he possessed more love for his people."[75] Later Bruce would return her rebuke.

As much as Wells faulted black leadership, she directed her harshest criticisms at whites. When the *New York Age* asked whether the white

South was civilized, Wells answered, "We are constrained to say not, when we observe their brutal treatment toward us the weaker race. We believe it is only savages who impose upon those inferior to themselves." Even before the brutal Memphis lynching of 1892, Wells was especially disgusted with white justice, often noting the disparities in the sentencing of black and white criminals. "Negroes are sent to the work house, jail and penitentiary for stealing five cents worth of bread or meat, but whites are made honored citizens, when they steal thousands." She wryly noted that the Negro "Is imitating the white man too much with different results. If a white man steals he often times goes to the legislature or congress, and the Negro goes to jail or the penitentiary." To illustrate her point Wells compared a white city official who stole six thousand dollars of taxpayers' money with a black man who stole "a box of cigars, four bottles of whiskey and two steaks, worth about $7.00." The white man was pardoned by the governor after serving only fifteen months, while the black one was sentenced to eight years, "or one year for every eighty-seven and one-half cents he stole."[76]

The *Free Speech* not only revealed injustice and discrimination but also sought remedies. In February 1891 the paper launched a boycott of one of the city's white newspapers, whose editor seemed "to never lose an opportunity to abuse the race." The white editors of Memphis criticized the militancy of the *Free Speech* on various occasions, sometimes reprinting editorials they found offensive. In 1889, for example, the *Avalanche* quoted the *Free Speech* statement, "The dailies of our city say that the whites must rule this country. But that is an expression without a thought. It must be borne in mind that the Lord is going to have something to say about this and all other government." The offending article also claimed, "The old Southern voice that was once heard and made the Negroes jump and run like rats to their holes is 'shut up' . . . for the Negro of today is not the same as Negroes were thirty years ago."[77]

White Memphis citizens were especially outraged in September 1891 by a fiery *Free Speech* editorial on a lynching in Georgetown, Kentucky. They were shocked at the angry words:

> Those Georgetown, Ky., Negroes who set fire to the town last week because a Negro named Dudley had been lynched, show some of the true spark of manhood by their resentment. We had begun to think the Negroes . . . where lynching of Negroes has become the sport and pastime of unknown (?) white citizens, hadn't manhood enough in them to wriggle and crawl out of the way, much less protect and defend themselves. Of one thing we may be assured, so long as we

permit ourselves to be trampled upon, so long we will have to endure it. Not until the Negro rises in his might and takes a hand resenting such cold-blooded murders, if he has to burn up whole towns, will a halt be called in wholesale lynching.[78]

Although its style makes it likely Wells wrote it, whites blamed Taylor Nightingale for the inflammatory article. They could not conceive that it might be written by a woman. Nightingale was known as a militant minister, and rumors began circulating that he preached hatred from his pulpit. He was said to have required his congregation to buy Winchester rifles for upcoming racial warfare and to have advised a nurse to grab the white infant for which she cared and burst "its brains out against the sidewalk."[79]

White fear and anger were rampant in the fall of 1891. African American resistance to the rapid increase of segregation that year alarmed many whites, and Nightingale became a lightning rod for white hostility. At the same time Nightingale became vulnerable to white action because of dissension in his congregation at Beale Street Baptist Church. Against the advice of Wells and Fleming, Nightingale had been writing articles in the *Free Speech* to discredit his opponents, who were led by Thomas F. Cassells, the black lawyer who had first handled Wells's railroad suit. A showdown occurred at the church and Nightingale had the dissenters forcibly removed from the sanctuary.

Assault charges were filed by both sides in the argument. The white press painted Nightingale as irresponsible and unpopular in biased accounts of the incident. The *Appeal-Avalanche* even printed a letter supposedly written by the preacher in his own defense. Filled with misspellings and grammatical mistakes, the letter could hardly have been the work of an educated minister and editor. Even though legally represented by former judge James M. Greer, who had taken over Wells's railroad suit from Cassells, Nightingale was easily convicted of assault and sentenced to eighty days in the Shelby County workhouse. Rather than serve the sentence, he sold out his interest in the *Free Speech* and fled to Oklahoma—the outcome for which the white citizens had probably hoped.[80]

Wells thus became half-owner of the *Free Speech*. In one of the articles in the black press announcing the change, the *Age* noted, "The *Free Speech* is a mighty bright newspaper, and Miss Wells furnishes the light of it."[81] Less than a year later the light provided to Memphis by the *Free Speech* was extinguished, following another editorial on lynching.

7

The Memphis Lynchings

"Neither character nor standing avails the Negro"

E vents that drastically changed the shape of Wells's future began in the "Curve" in Memphis. Located where the streetcar line sharply curved at the corner of Walker Avenue and Mississippi Boulevard, the area was populated by both African Americans and whites. For awhile it was served exclusively by a white-owned grocery store operated by W. H. Barrett. Like many white store owners in mixed neighborhoods, Barrett had become accustomed to having no competition. Following the demise of Reconstruction, however, black economic nationalism became one means of racial advancement, and African Americans undertook cooperative business ventures to raise the necessary capital. In 1889 a number of prominent black residents established a joint stock grocery store—the People's Grocery Company—in direct competition with the existing store. Thomas Moss, a close friend of Ida Wells, was the president of the corporation.[1]

Losing his monopoly, Barrett was hostile to the operation from the beginning. Most black residents of the Curve were members of either Moss's lodge or church, giving him a competitive advantage. Even some white residents began patronizing the People's Grocery. Barrett sought a solution for his diminishing business; a few instances of violence provided a way to destroy his competitor. According to Wells, the problems began with a game of marbles. A disagreement over the game led to a fight between a group of white boys and a group of black boys. When the white boys got the

130

worst end of the fight, Cornelius Hurst, a father of one of them, became enraged and personally whipped one of the black victors on Wednesday, 2 March 1892. The dispute snowballed as some angry black fathers gathered in the vicinity of Hurst's home, which was very close to the People's Grocery. Labeling the group a mob, white residents called the police. Twice officers went to the Curve and found absolutely nothing happening.[2]

What occurred next was disputed by the participants. Barrett claimed that he came to the aid of Hurst and was assaulted with a pistol and a mallet. "My head was badly bruised and my face covered in blood," he stated.[3] Calvin McDowell, clerk at People's Grocery, said that Barrett entered the store, accused him of hiding a black participant of the fray, and struck him with a pistol. "Being the stronger, I got the best of that scrimmage," McDowell reportedly explained.[4] Barrett quickly exploited the dispute for his own purposes. He and Hurst went to Judge Julius J. DuBose of the Shelby County criminal court. DuBose issued a bench warrant for McDowell, who was arrested on Thursday, posted bond, and was released.

The proprietors of the People's Grocery had been drawn into the fray, and Barrett got a Shelby County grand jury to indict the grocers for maintaining a public nuisance. Before those charges were dismissed with nominal fines, a meeting occurred in the black community. At that gathering, a few participants let anger color their rhetoric, suggesting dynamite as a remedy for the "damned white trash." The threat was not serious, but after hearing rumors of it, Barrett persuaded Judge DuBose that a conspiracy against whites existed. DuBose issued arrest warrants for two of the inflammatory speakers, who were believed to congregate at the People's Grocery on Saturday nights.

Knowing that officers would be going to the People's Grocery to arrest the men, Barrett spread a rumor that a white mob intended to raid the store. To prepare for the anticipated raid, the store's owners consulted an attorney, who informed them that they were justified in defending themselves because they were outside of the city limits and, consequently, also outside the police protection of the city. Therefore, they stationed armed guards to protect the store from the expected Saturday night assault. At about ten o'clock that night, clerk Calvin McDowell was waiting on a few final customers when shots rang out in the back room. The guards had fired on nine armed white men, dressed in civilian clothes, who were approaching the store.

Three deputies were wounded during the brief shoot-out before most of the black patrons and guards fled. The remaining deputies sounded the alarm, gathered more troops, and returned to the store, where they arrested about a dozen men, including Calvin McDowell and Will Stewart, a stockholder in People's Grocery. Prisoners seemed to have been rounded up at random; only four admitted even being at the store. Thomas Moss, president of the company, was not among those arrested and was not mentioned in the early accounts. Soon, however, he was described as the ringleader and the one who shot the most seriously wounded deputy—even though another man had first been named and Moss and his wife insisted he had been at home during the incident.

Memphis whites immediately magnified the incident. Headlines screamed "A Bloody Riot." People rapidly spread frightening rumors of a massive black uprising. The Sunday paper described the People's Grocery as "nest of turbulent and unruly negroes."[5] A day later the *Appeal-Avalanche* described the deputies as "being led into an ambush and subjected to the murderous fire of a band of negroes who were without grievance, and were actuated solely by race prejudice and a vicious and venomous rancor."[6] Many white men and boys were deputized, and most whites armed themselves for the coming "war." A few participated in looting the People's Grocery and were reported as taking some eighteen hundred dollars worth of goods. By the time the frenzy was finished, white "deputies" had broken into over a hundred black homes and arrested thirty more so-called conspirators, including Thomas Moss. The accused men were held without bond and not allowed any visitors. Some were beaten; one required crutches for a long time afterward.

On Sunday and Monday nights the jail was guarded by the Tennessee Rifles, an African American state militia, of which Calvin McDowell was a member. Indeed McDowell was wearing his militia fatigues when arrested. Eventually, Judge DuBose issued an order to disarm all the city's black citizens—including the Tennessee Rifles. Gun shop owners were forbidden to sell guns to African Americans. Whites forcibly entered the black militia armory, taking the confiscated rifles to the sheriff's office. The black militia officers protested to both city authorities and the state militia commander. After their protests fell on deaf ears, some of the men issued a statement to the press expressing their bitterness. They noted, "To wear the livery of a commonwealth that regards us with distrust and suspicion, a commonwealth that extracts an oath from us to defend its laws and then fails to protect us in the rights it guarantees, is an insult to our intelligence and manhood."[7] Refusing to drill with wooden sticks for rifles, the men of the Tennessee Rifles disbanded, never to meet again.

White fear remained unrelieved and white anger unsatiated. Sensational press accounts inflamed passions. Four days after the shoot-out at the People's Grocery, a group of whites entered the jail and seized three prisoners: Thomas Moss, Calvin McDowell, and Will Stewart. Significantly, the three had no prior criminal records and claimed not to have fired any shots. All were prominent and respected citizens of the black community. Moss was employed by the federal government as a mail carrier and taught Sunday school at Avery Chapel A.M.E. Church. (When arrested on Sunday afternoon, he still had Sunday school literature in his pocket.) The major "crime" seems to have been the three men's prominent positions in the ownership and operation of the People's Grocery. The black community insisted all three were model citizens; on the other hand, even white neighbors denounced Barrett's store as "a crap den and gambling hell."[8]

The three prisoners were seized around three o'clock in the morning and carried about a mile north of town. Moss reportedly begged for his life for the sake of "his wife and child and his unborn baby" and, when asked if he had any last words, replied "tell my people to go West—there is no justice for them here." He was then fatally shot. Calvin McDowell was reported to have gotten hold of one lyncher's gun and refused to release it until a bullet shattered his fist. Both he and Stewart were also fatally shot, and McDowell's eyes were gouged out. Their bodies were discovered at dawn laying stretched out and partly covered with brush.[9]

The first articles about the lynching in white newspapers reported the jailer's account of a lynch mob of seventy-five masked men wresting away his prisoners. The *New York Times* carried a particularly vivid account of this version. The jailer described how he was chatting with a friend when the bell rang. He asked "Who's there?" and someone claimed to be delivering a prisoner. The jailer unlatched the gate and two or three men shoved through so rapidly that the jailer claimed he did not realize that they were masked until after he "had been trapped." The jailer's account continued to detail his being searched for the cell keys and tied around the hands. The mob then supposedly searched the cells, terrorizing the twenty-seven black inmates until Moss, McDowell, and Stewart were found and gagged. The account was so vivid that it seemed to provide credible reasons for the jailer's failure to identify any of the mob members. The only problem is that it was riddled with falsehoods. By the end of March, all accounts agreed that no more than ten men had participated in the brutal murders.

The first white newspaper account of the lynching is both telling and chilling in its description of the methodical actions of the mob:

> The affair was one of the more orderly of its kind ever conducted, judging from the accounts. There was no whooping, not even loud talking, no cursing, in fact nothing boisterous. Everything was done decently and in order.
>
> The vengeance was sharp, swift and sure, but administered with due regard to the fact that people were asleep all around the jail, and that it is not good form to arouse people from their slumbers at 3 o'clock in the morning.[10]

African Americans in Memphis were certain that the responsible parties were known to law enforcement officials. One newspaper carried detailed accounts of the lynching that could only be known to a participant or witness. Nevertheless, the inquest held on the day the bodies were found issued the verdict: "We find that the deceased were taken from the Shelby County Jail by a masked mob of men, the men overpowered, and taken to

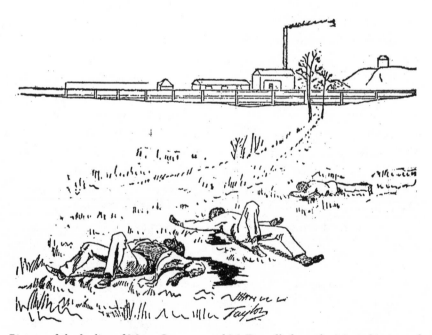

Picture of the bodies of Moss, Stewart, and McDowell, from the Memphis Appeal-Avalanche, *10 March 1892.*

an old field and shot to death by parties unknown by the jury." The attorney general proclaimed that the lynchers would be tried and convicted. He requested the governor to provide a five hundred dollar reward for the arrest and conviction of each participant. The grand jury met in several sessions to hear the testimony of many witnesses, all of whom claimed not to be able to identify any of the lynchers. After almost two weeks of hearings, the grand jury failed to indict anyone, and no one was ever tried for the crimes.

The black community in Memphis was outraged by the murders. When the bodies were taken to Walsh's undertaking establishment on 9 March, a crowd of about two hundred African Americans surrounded the building, muttering and cursing. That crowd and another that began gathering at the Curve were dispersed by about 150 armed whites sent by Judge DuBose to "preserve order." Before too long, almost everyone except the armed deputies were off the streets. Both white and black citizens waited anxiously in their homes, fearing further escalation of the hostilities.

The following afternoon the funerals of the three victims were held simultaneously at Avery Chapel on Desoto Street. A large crowd filed past the three coffins in front of the altar. Many had skipped work to be there. A number visibly reacted with either grief or anger—especially when they saw the mutilated face of Calvin McDowell. They also frequently interrupted the funeral address with sobs and shouts. Although the address was emotional and forceful, a witness noted that the minister "said nothing calculated to incite his hearers to deeds of violence."[11] After the service, the bodies were taken to the Mount Zion Cemetery for interment. The crowds' emotions were unabated; Tom Moss's widow fainted at the graveside of her husband.

Ida Wells was in Natchez during the entire episode and did not get back to Memphis in time for the funeral, but she was among those mourning Moss. She called Tom and Betty Moss "the best friends I had in town" and served as the godmother of their daughter Maurine. Wells admired Thomas Moss for his willingness "to defend the cause of right and fight wrong." She lamented, "He was well liked, a favorite with everyone; yet he was murdered with no more consideration than if he had been a dog."[12] She expressed her anger in an editorial that week.

The city of Memphis has demonstrated that neither character nor standing avails the Negro if he dares to protect himself against the white man or become his rival. There is nothing we can do about the

lynching now, as we are out-numbered and without arms. The white
mob could help itself to ammunition without pay, but the order was
rigidly enforced against the selling of guns to Negroes. There is
therefore only one thing left that we can do; save our money and
leave a town which will neither protect our lives and property, nor
give us a fair trial in the courts, but takes us out and murders us in
cold blood when accused by white persons.[13]

Others agreed with Wells about the hopelessness of the situation. A little less than two weeks after the lynching, African Americans in Memphis
organized an evening protest meeting. More than a thousand people attended. Former city council member Lymus Wallace served as the chair,
and the Reverends W. A. Binkley and B. A. Imes gave talks. Before adjourning at 11:00 P.M., the crowd approved a set of resolutions that condemned the lynchings and urged the prosecution of the offenders. They
also exhorted thousands of black citizens to leave the city and "seek among
strangers the protection of just laws, impartially enforced, which is denied
them here." The group denounced the white press for "magnifying street-
corner brawls into a race riot" and for asserting the victims "belonged to the
tough, desperate element of the colored community [which] is shamefully
false."[14]

Despite giving biased accounts of the triple murder, at first the white
newspapers had proclaimed, "The lynching can be defended on no possible ground." One editorial declared that "the community has been
wronged, and public sentiment outraged." After the protest meeting, however, the paper "deplored" the meeting as premature and urged black citizens not to leave until after the grand jury had acted. One prominent white
citizen urged a biracial mass meeting to raise funds to bring the lynchers to
justice "in view of the fact that much valuable labor is leaving our city."[15]
Over time, however, many white Memphians became defensive about the
lynching after the city was roundly denounced in black and white papers
nationwide.

Lynching was on the rise throughout the South, and black papers deplored its rise and condemned its participants. The Memphis lynchings
seemed to crystallize all the feelings of rage and bewilderment. The Detroit *Plaindealer* described that reaction:

The events of the past few weeks are enough to set the blood rushing
with fire and indignation in the youth and to create a fever in the
blood of age. All over this country the people should be aroused,

Wells (at left) with Betty Moss, the widow of Tom Moss and his children (courtesy of the University of Chicago Library).

meetings held, organizations formed, and offers of assistance in a substantial way be made to bring these murderers to justice.[16]

The Kansas City *American Citizen* was more outspoken, claiming that the lynching "seems to us to call for something more than patient endurance—It calls for dynamite and blood-shed." The *Langston City Herald* echoed those sentiments, asking "What race or class of people on God's footstool would tolerate the continual slaughter of its own without a re-volt."[17] The Coffeyville, Kansas, *Afro-American Advocate* deplored the "in-appeasable [sic] appetites of those Southern bloodsuckers" and declared, "Something must be done before it is too late." The desire of many to do *something* led African Americans to organize a national day of fasting to de-nounce murderous mobs and to hold protest meetings in cities across the nation. In Chicago a thousand people assembled at Bethel A.M.E. Church and heard *Chicago Conservator* editor Ferdinand Barnett and others ex-press their anger.[18]

The white Memphis press took note of the Chicago meeting and de-plored the damning editorials in northern white newspapers. Within a few months, Memphis whites began to explain and defend lynching. The *Scimitar* did not mince words and proclaimed, "Whenever it comes to a conflict between the races the Scimitar is for the grand old Anglo-Saxon every time no matter what the original cause. To preserve the purity and su-periority of the white race is a duty we owe to God and civilization." The *Appeal-Avalanche* continued to state its opposition to lynching, but began to blame the victims. In replies to editorials in white Boston and Chicago papers, it raised the issue of rape, although rape had nothing at all to do with this particular lynching. Asserting in one day's paper that when "an unprotected woman is assaulted . . . chivalrous men in the neighborhood forget there are such things as courts," the *Appeal-Avalanche* the next day declared, "There is strong sentiment in the South against lynch law, but the negro himself can stop it more effectually than anybody else. Let him call a halt on surreptitious crimes on white people and the lynchings will stop." The *Weekly Commercial* deplored the fact that even lynching did not seem to deter rape. Citing two rapes that followed a widely publicized lynching, it lamented the "uncontrollable viciousness of the negro and the increasing difficulty of restraining his brutal passions by punishment, how-ever prompt and extreme."[19]

The *Free Speech* was also filled with news of the lynching and its after-math. The black press widely reprinted its articles and editorials. The *Topeka Times-Observer* noted Wells's "flattering tribute" to the lynching victims and proclaimed, "Her editorials on it, are vigerous [sic] and to the point." The Detroit *Plaindealer* carried her accounts of such events as the disbanding of the Tennessee Rifles and the sheriff's sale of the People's Grocery. The *American Citizen* reprinted a *Free Speech* editorial that re-counted the contributions of African Americans to the city and the aid they provided during the yellow fever epidemic before demanding the lynchers be brought to justice in "the name of God and in the name of the law we have always obeyed." The *Afro-American Advocate* quoted Wells's comments on the death of Judge DuBose's fourteen-year-old son, "They say the Judge's grief over his loss was terrible. So was that of the families of the murdered men to whom Judge DuBose refused bond, and left an easy prey to the mob." She described how they were "dragged away and murdered [by] what seems the connivance of the strong arm of the law."[20]

Wells was convinced the lynchers were known and abetted by DuBose and others. She was furious with white Memphis officials, but she was also deeply disturbed by the failure of black leadership and God to protect her people. Her vision of manhood called for heroic action; her vision of God called for justice. The wanton murder of her close friend gave reality to the bleak statistics on lynching. Struggling to understand how it could have happened, she came to believe neither the federal government nor African Americans had done enough to prevent the slaughter of innocent people. She felt black leaders had become too self-serving to be able to wrest protection from the government. She voiced her frustrations and rage in one editorial:

> Where are our "leaders" when the race is being burnt, shot and hanged? Holding good fat offices and saying not a word — just as they were when the Civil Rights bill was repealed and the Blair Educational and Federal Election bills were defeated. They tell us this great government can protect its citizens on foreign soil, but is helpless when it comes to protecting them at home, and hence however much the Negro is abused and outraged — "our leaders" make no demands on the country to protect us, nor come forward with any practical plan for changing the condition of affairs. A few big offices and the control of a little Federal patronage [are] not sufficient recompense for the lives lost, the blood shed and the rights denied the race.[21]

Her words foreshadowed the 1960s Black Power advocates' ideology of co-opted leadership and their assertion that black visibility is not the same as black power.

African Americans' sense of powerlessness escalated as they increasingly were denied both suffrage and the equal protection of the laws in the late nineteenth century. With the collapse of Reconstruction came mounting hostility from white southerners and waning support from white northerners. Emigration schemes flourish in times of disillusionment, and black

Memphians had grown more and more disillusioned following the 1886 city election. Like black southerners everywhere, some began to believe their only effective defense was flight. Like white southerners everywhere, white Memphians debated the desirability of black emigration. Even before the 1892 lynching, African Americans had begun to leave Memphis while competing white choruses sang "good riddance" and "stay, we need your labor." Some whites sought to drive black citizens out of the city; others tried to intimidate emigration agents with violence. In 1889 the *Free Speech* wryly noted, "The Negroes in this part of the world are between two hot fires. The *Avalanche* will not let the colored brother remain in the South in peace and the *Appeal* will not let the sons of Africa get away in safety. What must they do?"[22]

White and black leaders were divided over the issue of black emigration. At the end of the century two major sites were proclaimed as the promised land for African Americans: Liberia and the American West. Generally, exodus was more favored by the black working class than the elite, who had financial ties to their southern homes. Wells was ambivalent toward emigration. Respecting the great militant A.M.E. Bishop Henry McNeal Turner, she supported his idea of turning Liberia into an African homeland and power base for African Americans—at least for those who desired to go. For most Memphians, however, Oklahoma seemed a more likely location for resettlement—an idea promoted by E. P. McCabe, the former African American state auditor of Kansas. The federal government was opening more land for settlement in Oklahoma as the result of the cession of Cherokee lands. With the hope of making Oklahoma into a predominantly black state, McCabe founded Langston City, Oklahoma, in late 1890 and urged African American settlement in the territory. In January and February 1892, debates raged in both the black and white communities of Memphis over the desirability of black emigration to Oklahoma. Wells's cousin's husband, I. F. Norris, was an emigration agent. Others in Memphis, however, formed an Anti-Oklahoma Society. Until the lynching, Wells was apparently skeptical of Oklahoma as a land of opportunity.[23]

After the lynching, Wells joined others in urging African Americans to leave Memphis. In April she noted, "Many of our exchanges have been calling Memphis hell, without stopping to think they were doing the real hell an injustice. Hell proper is a place of punishment for the wicked— Memphis is a place of punishment for the good, brave and enterprising." Many quoted the purported last words of Thomas Moss urging his people to go West. Western newspapers used the lynching to solicit immigrants.

After declaring that "Memphis would be a good place for the colored people to leave," the *Langston City Herald* stressed its city's black control and described conditions there. "Here your life is safe. Here your liberty is unquestioned. Here your rights are granted freely because they belong to you. Here you can develop whatever manhood or womanhood you possess. Here you can be all that God intended you to be."[24]

Migration had begun in earnest months before the lynching and rapidly accelerated after it. White and black papers all over the country commented on the exodus. In Memphis some of the white papers sought to discourage emigration by painting dismal pictures of life in Oklahoma. I. F. Norris convinced Wells that she should investigate the conditions there and report back to the *Free Speech* so that the people could know the truth.[25]

Railroads serving the West were major propagandists for western settlement in order to increase traffic and to sell the land granted them to finance construction. They gave passes to individuals who they thought would lend support. Wells recalled that when she approached the general passenger agent in Kansas City for a pass, he informed her that "We have two men, one of whom is a preacher, getting facts." According to Wells, she told him, "Yes, but the folks say these men are in the employ of your road and are being paid to travel over that road." When he asked, "Wouldn't they say the same thing about you?", she replied, "No sir, they would believe whatever I told them." She got her pass.[26]

In early April 1892, Wells spent about three weeks in Oklahoma visiting a number of cities. Accompanied by an attorney, W. R. Berry, she called on the governor and state offices before dropping by the desks of the daily papers in Guthrie. Her next stop was the United States Land Office. She then visited the *Langston City Herald*, which reported her visit and her later trips in its columns. As usual she made quite an impact on those she met. The *Herald* gushed over her "real interest in the race" and the courage with which she "boarded the train at her home alone, unattended." The paper described Wells as "rather prepossessing in her personal appearance" and "an easy agreeable conversationalist."[27]

After she left Langston City, Wells journeyed to Oklahoma City and left there to visit Kingfisher, which was to be the site of a race for new lands. Potential settlers were to gather there to await the official opening of area for settlement, at which time they would rush across the starting line to stake their claims. According to the *Langston City Herald*, Wells did "not take kindly to Oklahoma." The paper suggested that she expected "too much of those who inhabit the 'wild and woolly west.'" Although the *Herald* agreed with Wells that there was "no ready employment" to support "an indiscriminate exodist [sic] of our people," it charged that Wells erred when she asserted she could not find "any inducements for men of money to come."[28]

If Wells had reservations about Oklahoma, it did not stop her from continuing to support emigration from Memphis. She was especially pleased to see the impact such emigration had on white Memphians. The Memphis business community was feeling the economic impact of the flight of its black citizens. About six weeks after the lynching, officers of the City Railway Company came to the offices of the *Free Speech*. Distressed by the declining black patronage of their streetcars, they believed that African Americans feared electricity and asked the paper to reassure its black readers. Wells pointed out that the cars had been run by electricity for six months but the patronage had declined only in the previous six weeks—since the lynchings. After they left, Wells reported the interview in the *Free Speech* and "told the people to keep up the good work."[29]

Many took the advice of Wells and others and left to try their fate elsewhere. Newspapers all over the nation reported groups of hundreds leaving Memphis. Two Baptist ministers, R. N. Countee and W. A. Binkley, went West with a large portion of their congregations. After the lynchings, both the *Living Way* and the *Free Speech* vigorously supported colonization, much to the disgust of another of the city's black newspapers. The *Memphis Reflector* declared, "It is easy enough to cry go! go! go! but it takes a little longer to figure the cost."[30] Most African American newspapers, however, supported the flight from Memphis and reveled in the economic distress of the city's white population. Sensing black economic clout was a potent tool against lynching, the Detroit *Plaindealer* tried to organize a fund-raising effort to provide loans to the citizens who wished to join the exodusters.[31]

The lynchings rocked Memphis and the nation; they also shook the very foundations of Wells's personal world. She had been angered for a long time by the humiliating expansion of segregation and had been disturbed by the declining political power of African Americans. These were the focus of her concern as a member of the black middle class. Although Wells had considered it deplorable, lynching was distant from her personal concerns. It was unfair, unjust, and happened to other people. In her world, innocent persons were lynched—but not respectable ones. She later recalled:

> Like many another person who had read of lynching in the South, I
> had accepted the idea meant to be conveyed—that although lynch-
> ing was irregular and contrary to law and order, unreasoning anger
> over the terrible crime of rape led to the lynching; that perhaps the
> brute deserved to die anyhow and the mob was justified in taking
> his life.
>
> But Thomas Moss, Calvin McDowell, and Lee Stewart had
> been lynched . . . with just as much brutality as other victims of the
> mob; and they had committed no crime against white women. This
> is what opened my eyes to what lynching really was. An excuse to get
> rid of Negroes who were acquiring wealth and property and thus
> keep the race terrorized and "keep the nigger down."[32]

With the lynching of a friend, her eyes were opened and her spirit enraged.
Even more than segregation and disfranchisement, lynching inspired a
fury that forced Wells to act.

Wells filled the columns of the *Free Speech* with antilynching tirades.
She also began to study white and black newspapers for the alleged causes
of various lynchings, quickly discovering that rape was not even *charged* in
at least two-thirds of the cases she examined. Of those charged with rape,
the guilt of many was doubtful. Sometimes merely looking at a white
woman in the "wrong way" was called rape. Other times the cry of rape
arose when clandestine, voluntary sexual liaisons between white women
and black men were exposed. In whites' minds such relationships were as
bad as, if not worse, than rape. They were in some ways even more of an af-
front to the cult of true womanhood—at whose shrine so many southern
white males worshiped.

Wells correctly diagnosed the major purpose of lynching in the 1890s
as racial terrorism. At that time rape was only beginning to be used as the
primary excuse for lynching. Few African Americans had been lynched
prior to the Civil War. Not only did slaves have a monetary value but slavery itself also served as a sufficient system of racial control and domination.
Immediately after emancipation, white southerners greatly feared the unknown consequences of slavery's end. One wellspring of that fear was the
specter of black revenge. Although slaveowners had fervently wished to believe that their slaves were happy and content, they knew that potential Nat
Turners lurked behind the masks of deference worn by even their most
trusted slaves. Emancipation exacerbated that terror, and whites began to
imagine signs of coming insurrection. Lynching black suspects exorcised
the demons of white hysteria.

As Wells soon learned, the horror of insurrection began to subside in white minds as more and more of the so-called plots turned out to be the figments of overwrought imaginations. A genuine threat to white domination existed, however, in African American political power after black franchisement during Reconstruction. "Black rule" became an apparition almost as terrifying as black insurrection. Firmly believing in black inferiority, white southerners recoiled from the idea of African Americans controlling their lives. Demonized black politicians were painted as ignorant, corrupt, and incompetent. Lynching became a way of intimidating black voters and was justified as necessary to prevent the destruction of white civilization by black barbarism.

In the 1890s, however, the threat of black political power waned with the imposition of "legal" means of disfranchisement. Across the South, poll taxes, literacy tests, and residency requirements reduced the numbers of black registered voters—often by arbitrary and unfair enforcement of the provisions. Nevertheless, African Americans would not move submissively into "their place." Black advancement threatened the ideological and social underpinnings of the South. As W. E. B. Du Bois noted, "There is one thing that the white South feared more than negro dishonesty, ignorance, and incompetency, and that was negro honesty, knowledge, and efficiency." Black success did not generate respect but revulsion and fear. White store owners like Barrett did not want to have to compete with black businessmen like Moss—they might lose. The elevation of educated African Americans meant the degradation of poor, ignorant whites. If African Americans would not stay in their place at the bottom of society, some whites might be forced to occupy that place. That would be a blow to poor whites' psyches and would jeopardize elite whites' ability to use race to control the poor white voter.[33]

Legalized segregation provided tangible and continual reminders of "black inferiority" to all whites as well as African Americans. Segregation was never really about separation but degradation. Interracial contact and indeed intimacy continued to be allowed—provided those contacts did not in any way imply equality. White babies nursing at black breasts was legal; interracial checker playing was not. Sexual liaisons between white men and black women were tolerated; physical intimacy between white women and black men was the strongest of all the emerging taboos associated with Jim Crow. In a patriarchal society dominated by the cult of true womanhood, women were presumed not to enjoy sex, so all sexual relations represented male "conquest." Thus white men could have sexual intercourse with black women without any suggestion of equality; indeed, the prevalence of white men raping black women after emancipation was a continued assertion of sexual power.[34] However, white women who submitted—either willingly or not—to sexual acts with black men forfeited power and therefore status to the "inferior race."

Rape became a metaphor in the white mind for any assault on white supremacy. It also became a convenient excuse for lynching, when "black rule" lost its credibility. Although motivations for lynching varied in different regions and different time periods, in the South of the 1890s lynchings usually were assertions of white supremacy and black powerlessness. During that decade, they grew to average more than two a week precisely because African Americans were resisting segregation and disfranchisement. Lynching was necessary to force acceptance of Jim Crow and to limit black advancement. Nevertheless, executing people for excelling hardly seemed honorable or civilized; protection of the purity of womankind was a more appealing rationale.

Honor, chivalry, and violent retaliation as the bases of "manliness" lingered longer in the South than in the North for various reasons. The presence of slavery had become intertwined with a code of honor in which a person's good reputation was the most valuable asset to possess. Honorable men were expected to respond immediately to any slight of them or their families—especially their women—with physical force. The power of such ideals in early America is seen in the widespread practices of dueling and gunslinging. The code of honor had always been strongest in the South. By the late nineteenth century such modernizing forces as industrialization and urbanization had weakened the code's hold in the North, and restraint and discipline began to replace the violent defense of one's honor as the qualities of "true men."[35]

At the same time, military defeat and the economic dependency of the South challenged southern whites' manhood. Not able to excel in the postwar economic and social climate, Dixie's men refused to accept new definitions of manliness and clung stubbornly to old concepts of honor. African Americans' reluctance to play the deferential roles of slaves became especially galling as southerners sought to recreate the past in which the South had wealth and power. Lynching was often a lesson in role-playing made heroic by dubbing it a chivalrous defense of womanhood. Even white racial "liberals" in both the North and South accepted the lie and moderated their attacks on lynching. The horror of lynching was tempered by the atrocity of rape.[36]

Rape as a new rationale required some historical distortions to be creditable. How did one explain why rape had only recently required lynching as a remedy? The only plausible answer was that black rapists had just become a problem. Why had black men not raped white women in the past and why had they suddenly become a race of rapists? The solution to that riddle became the proclaimed ability of slavery to restrain the "bestial tendencies" of African Americans. White southerners argued that a new generation of Negroes was emerging—one that had never experienced the guiding hand of masters. Without such tutelage the children and grandchildren of slaves reverted to their savage natures. Ironically, both the defenders and attackers of lynching accepted the myth that black men had not raped white women before or during the Civil War. Records show otherwise. Both during and after slavery black men did rape white women, though not nearly as often as white men raped black women. The antebellum cases did not, however, provoke the same level of fear and rage among whites. Some black men were actually acquitted of charges if there was evidence of the white woman's consent, especially if the woman was from the lower classes.[37] Rape in the 1890s came to have a new symbolic power as a dramatic display of black insubordination. It also provided a convenient excuse for lynching after earlier ones were discredited.

Ida B. Wells's anger grew as she began to grasp the true meaning of lynching in the 1890s. She was not the first to expose rape as a mythical cause of mob action, but she soon became the loudest and most persistent voice for truth. Her first step toward her role as full-time antilynching activist came in May 1892 with the publication of another editorial on the subject. It certainly was not her first antilynching statement, but it was the first time she openly addressed the issue of rape. In the 21 May edition of the *Free Speech* she proclaimed the following:

> Eight Negroes lynched since last issue of the Free Speech—one at Little Rock, Ark., last Saturday morning where the citizens broke (?) into the penitentiary and got their man; three near Anniston, Ala., one near New Orleans—on the same old racket, the new alarm about raping white women.; and three at Clarksville, Ga., for killing a white man. The same programme of hanging, then shooting bullets into the lifeless bodies was carried out to the letter.
>
> Nobody in this section of the country believes the old threadbare lie that Negro men rape white women. If Southern white men are not careful, they will over-reach themselves and public sentiment

will have a reaction; a conclusion will then be reached which will be very damaging to the moral reputation of their women.[38]

The editorial became a ticking bomb, but Wells was out of town when it exploded.

Even before the March lynchings Wells had planned a three-week trip to Philadelphia and New York City. She had rarely traveled to the East and was excited to go. Bishop Henry McNeal Turner of the A.M.E. Church had urged Wells to attend the general conference of that denomination in Philadelphia. She stayed with Frances Ellen Watkins Harper, a well-known black poet, abolitionist, orator, and temperance advocate, who undoubtedly served as another female role model for Wells. Wells had also been invited by T. Thomas Fortune of the *New York Age* to visit his city. Although she was not "favorably impressed" by the A.M.E. conference, she "met all the big guns of the . . . church, who made a big fuss over our only female editor." Wells enjoyed visiting once again with Bishop Turner and was especially impressed by Bishop Daniel A. Payne. It was their first and last meeting, and Wells noted later that he "fulfilled my every ideal of what I thought a Negro bishop ought to be." She also relished her visit with Fannie Jackson Coppin, a leading black educator, and her husband L. J. Coppin, who edited the *A.M.E. Review*. On the Tuesday after the conference, she had breakfast with the couple, visited Fannie Coppin's famous school, and boarded the train for New York.[39]

While Wells relaxed on the train, Memphis was in turmoil. The local white papers expressed rage at her editorial, which they attributed to J. L. Fleming, the co-owner of the *Free Speech*. The *Memphis Commercial* printed part of Wells's editorial and declared:

> The fact that a black scoundrel is allowed to live and utter such loathsome and repulsive calumnies is a volume of evidence as to the wonderful patience of Southern whites. But we have had enough of it. There are some things the Southern white man will not tolerate and the obscene intimations of the foregoing have brought the writer to the outermost limit of public patience. We hope we have said enough.[40]

The editorial implied a threat of violence, but the *Evening Scimitar* was not so subtle. It published the *Commercial's* editorial and issued a graphic threat to Fleming as the presumed author of the *Free Speech* editorial.

Patience under such circumstances is not a virtue. If the negroes
themselves do not apply the remedy without delay it will be the duty
of those he has attacked to tie the wretch who utters these calumnies
to a stake at the intersection of Main and Madison Sts., brand him on
the forehead with a hot iron and perform upon him a surgical operation with a pair of tailor's shears.[41]

After the publication of these editorials, whites held an angry meeting
at the Merchants Exchange on 27 May 1892. Fearing a lynching, Fleming
left town—driven out once again as he had been from Marion, Arkansas.
Meanwhile, in New York City, Fortune greeted Wells at the train with an
account of the incident from the *New York Sun*. According to that account,
a mob had descended on the offices of the *Free Speech*, destroyed its fur-
nishings, and posted a death threat to anyone attempting to publish the paper again. Other accounts were not so dramatic, claiming the paper's
equipment had been sold to pay creditors. Either way white Memphians
made clear their determination to shut down the *Free Speech*.[42]

At first Wells thought of going back to Memphis, feeling she would be
safer than Fleming because she was a woman and a longtime resident of
the city. She wired her lawyer, B. F. Booth, for an assessment of the situation. Telegrams and letters from him and others urged her not to return and
described strange white men "abruptly inquiring" whether Wells was in
town. She noted that friends told her that "whites had declared they would
bleed my face and hang me in front of the Court House." Fearing a "conflict which would entail great slaughter," Wells decided to seek her fate
elsewhere.[43]

Even before the events of 27 May, Wells had been thinking of relocat-
ing. Soon afterward she proclaimed, "I had hoped to continue South or
West the work only a fearlessly edited Negro journal can do for the race."
According to that early account, the office had not been destroyed but instead "placed in the hands of the Sheriff and . . . sold to satisfy creditors."
Because Wells and Fleming were unable to collect debts owed to them, she
lamented that "in a few days, was destroyed what has taken years to build."
She was particularly perturbed because the *Free Speech* "was just getting . . . in shape to be profitable to all parties concerned." Without funds
to start a new paper, Wells accepted Fortune's offer to join the *Age* and let
that paper fill unexpired *Free Speech* subscriptions, which Wells numbered
at two thousand. She announced her connection with the *Age*, informed
the public that she would report on the "Southern field," and asked for her
readers' continued support.[44]

From the retrospect of her later years, Wells noted she had first thought that the destruction of her paper had been the result of "the white southerner's chivalrous defense of his womanhood." Decades later, however, she decided that whites had been plotting against the *Free Speech* before the offending editorial. Wells described the real source of their anger by saying, "For the first time in their lives the white people of Memphis had seen earnest united action by Negroes which upset economic and business conditions." She concluded, "In casting about for the cause of all this restlessness and dissatisfaction the leaders concluded that the *Free Speech* was the disturbing factor. They were right."[45]

As most autobiographers do, Wells likely exaggerated her influence by claiming her paper was *the* "disturbing factor." Other leaders and organizations protested the events. In fact another of the city's black newspapers was also threatened. In April it had seemed that the *Living Way* might well be the target of mob action. Threats were made to lynch its editor, who replied, "But one consoling thing to me which may be discouraging to the would-be lynchers, is that when I am lynched my soul will not go down to hell, where the souls of the lynchers will soon be."[46]

The triple lynching had raised the specter of mob law for all outspoken leaders of the African American community in Memphis. The impossible now seemed possible — even probable. Wells later wrote:

> I had bought a pistol the first thing after Tom Moss was lynched, because I expected some cowardly retaliation from the lynchers. I felt that one had better die fighting against injustice than to die like a dog or a rat in a trap. I had already determined to sell my life as dearly as possible if attacked. I felt if I could take one lyncher with me, this would even up the score a little bit.[47]

In the end, however, Wells would "even the score a little bit" with her pen, not her pistol. Instead of quieting her, the mob gave the fiery editor a larger audience for her attacks on lynching and more subtle forms of Jim Crow.

8

Indictment of Lynching

"The cold-blooded savagery of white devils"

"We cannot see what the 'good' citizens of Memphis gained by suppressing the *Free Speech*," the *St. Paul Appeal* declared in August 1892. "They stopped the papers of a few hundreds subscribers and drove Miss Ida B. Wells to New York, and now she is telling the story to hundreds of thousands of readers." Another black newspaper noted, "If those sneaking cowardly Negro hating Memphis copper-heads think they have gained anything by this arrangement they are welcome to it."[1] Memphis whites probably had no idea that driving the *Free Speech* from their city would be so harmful to them. They did not quiet Wells or J. L. Fleming but instead gave them the moral authority of martyrdom. Wells was even honored by the school she had left in disgrace: Rust College awarded her an honorary Master of Arts degree soon after her exile.[2]

African American editors across the nation expressed outrage at the ousting of the *Free Speech*. The sentiments were well expressed by the Coffeyville, Kansas, *Afro-American Advocate*.

> The fearless spirit of Ida Wells editor of the Memphis Free Speech [has been] spoken of in these columns and her bravery commended. Among all civilized people, courage commends itself to brave people but among the barbarians, of the Memphis stripe, her courage was a menace, so these brave, chivalrous southern people, made up their minds to drive this plucky little woman out of town.[3]

The editorial further noted the willingness of Memphis whites to assassinate both Fleming and Wells for "no other reason than the exercise of their rights of free speech." It sarcastically concluded, "This is a very striking example of the superiority of the white race."[4]

African Americans' anger was also fueled by the trials of the so-called Curve rioters soon after Wells and Fleming left Memphis. Editorials frequently linked the exile and the trials in their condemnations of the city. The *Plaindealer* proclaimed that "one outrage upon another has followed the Memphis massacre." The Indianapolis *Freeman* listed five of the black defendants and reported their sentences, which ranged from fifteen years in the penitentiary to eleven months in the county workhouse. It then noted that none of the white lynchers had yet been found. Another column in the 17 June *Plaindealer* angrily related, "Judge DuBose thought the punishment too light and, after lecturing the jury, ordered them out of the courtroom."[5]

Most black newspapers noted Wells's and Fleming's exiles and offered words of encouragement for their new endeavors. Although Wells received the most attention, Fleming was also praised for reestablishing the *Free Speech* in Chicago. The reborn paper was lauded by the *Topeka Weekly Call*, which declared, "The editorials, and general tone shows that the editor is equal to the task." Nevertheless, Fleming was not able to sustain his Chicago paper. Wells later recalled that with "little money and no help he soon gave up and went West, connecting himself with a journal in Kansas." After having been driven out of both Marion, Arkansas, and Memphis, Tennessee, Fleming was embittered. Wells regretfully noted, "To lose everything the second time when prospects were so bright was almost more than Mr. Fleming could bear. He blamed me very bitterly for that editorial, and perhaps he was justified in doing so."[6]

Fleming's fate evoked brotherly concern from his fellow journalists; Wells's predicament moved her male cohorts to chivalric defense. Several offered her jobs—at least in the columns of their papers. In Kansas City the *American Citizen* declared, "If Miss Wells will accept our editorial chair it is at her disposal." The *Langston City Herald* urged, "Come west, Miss Wells, come west."[7] The chorus of praise for her courage seemed overly effusive to some editors—especially those who had been at odds with Wells earlier. In July 1892 the Indianapolis *Freeman* noted her affiliation with Fortune at the *New York Age* and launched into a diatribe against all the attention given Wells. It followed the quote "Crown her with flowers/And sprinkle her with perfume" with "Until you carry it ad nauseum." The edi-

Picture of Wells made soon after she left Memphis, c. 1893–94 (courtesy of the University of Chicago Library).

torial also implored, "we must ask, gentlemen of the press, with no desire to repress your fraternal gallantry, that you do not take the bit into your eloquent mouths and ride this free horse of manly privilege to death."[8]

Although the *Freeman* acknowledged that "Miss Wells is a good writer, an earnest, industrious lady, who has been inconvenienced, made to suffer, and is an exile from home because of devotion to her wronged and persecuted people," the tone of the editorial infuriated other male journalists. Responding to attacks in August for not sufficiently praising her, the *Freeman* remarked on the "implication that Miss Wells is a fisher of compliments and praise from any source" and expressed hope it was mistaken. "We can conceive of women," the editorial continued, "yes, and of men too by the score, bewiskered, stentorian voiced barnacles of the press, who might cry their eyes out for compliments that never came, . . . but, of this somewhat unfortunate young woman, we had no thought of such a thing."

The *Freeman* urged Wells not to "allow the impression to obtain that she is a poser for attention."[9]

A few other papers echoed the *Freeman*'s charges. The *American Citizen* noted the same month that the *Boston Courant* "has at last found out Ida Wells [is a] fake" and commented, "Brother you are right. She seeks fame and gets notoriety."[10] Such criticisms led to further chivalric defenses by male editors. The *Langston City Herald* warned:

> The *Freeman of Indianapolis* and the Boston *Courant* will "get it in the neck" if they don't let up on Miss Ida B. Wells, of the *New York Age*. It is true that she is small in stature, but she is diamond pointed and a fighter "from the ground up," and the *Herald* stands ready to hold her bonnet whenever she sails into you cultured gentlemen.[11]

Even her critics realized her strength. One reason the *Freeman* admonished her defenders was because she did not need such help. It noted that "we have no thought, but that any half dozen of you, with all your mental brilliancy would fall an easy 'take' to her trenchant 'gray goose quill.'"[12]

Seldom was Wells not embroiled in some controversy. Even after leaving Memphis, she continued to upset the city. Her exile and the conviction of the "Curve rioters" rekindled the anger of the black community. Fearing further violence, a few black Memphians sought to douse the flames of passion with calm words. One was the Reverend B. A. Imes of the Second Congregational Church, who as an activist preacher and leader had won Wells's respect. In 1887 he had told Memphis whites, "A church which makes caste distinctions in ecclesiastical relations, or in the worship of God, thereby forfeits its right to be called a church of Jesus in Christ." After the lynchings, Imes had flirted with emigration and visited Oklahoma. He decided instead to stay in Memphis and play the role of peacemaker. In the week after the demise of the *Free Speech*, Imes wrote a letter to the editor of the *Langston City Herald* deploring "rash mutterings of violence" on the part of "certain ones who speak for the negro."[13]

Imes proposed a meeting between the white and black leaders of Memphis in June to discuss ways to restore harmony to the city's race relations. On 7 June a biracial group of more than sixty met at the Cotton Exchange. Imes addressed the group and criticized whites for blaming all Negroes for the actions of a few. He also declared that most black Memphians deplored the *Free Speech* editorial. While implying that black rapists were rare, Imes said African Americans denounced rape and called on white leaders to take a similar stand against lynching. "We cannot believe," he stated, "that any intelligent businessman, merchant, lawyer— any good citizen can honestly advocate lynching as a substitute for the legal process of dealing with crime."[14]

Imes won white support, and a few days later a biracial committee drew up a set of resolutions. As a member of the committee, Imes conceded much to win white condemnation of lynching. The statement recognized whites as the "dominant and ruling element" with the responsibility "to give adequate protection from outrage and wrong to the weaker and more helpless element, composed of colored people, whose former services and devotion to them through a trying ordeal, appeal so strongly for sympathy and kindness."[15] Peace was bought with the coin of paternalism.

Peacemaking became more difficult when Wells refused to be silenced. Using the front pages of the *New York Age* in late June, she described events in Memphis and discussed lynching in general. Previous subscribers to the *Free Speech* in Memphis all received copies. Thus the city's whites learned of Wells's role as author of the infamous editorial in the last edition of the *Free Speech*. Their rage escalated as she repeated her attack on the reputations of white women for a national audience. The *Memphis Appeal-Avalanche* explained that whites had mistakenly believed Fleming to be the author of the "scurrilous reflection upon the white ladies of the South." It then noted Wells's connection with the *Age* and charged "she has continued to publish matter not a whit less scandalous than that which aroused the ire of the whites just prior to her departure."[16]

Imes once again sought to calm the waters. He met with about a dozen black leaders in a private home to organize an "indignation meeting of all the colored people in the city." Even before the public meeting, Imes and two others drafted a response to Wells's articles for publication in the *Appeal-Avalanche*. While granting "the right of personal views as to the matter and manner of public discussion," the statement called for appeals to "reason and intelligence rather than to passion and prejudice." Claiming to be speaking for the "large portion of our people who are capable of exercising a sober judgment and foresight," the document proclaimed

we desire to put on record a most positive disapproval of the course pursued by Miss Ida Wells, through the medium of the *New York Age*, in stirring up from week to week, in this community and wherever that paper goes, the spirit of strife over the unhappy question at issue. We see no good to come from this method of journalism on either side. . . . Virtue cannot be encouraged by sowing scandal broadcast, polluting the minds of the innocent and pure.[17]

The charge of "polluting the minds of the innocent and pure" would be leveled in various ways at Wells and her discussions of sexual relationships and rape. Such topics did not seem appropriate for womanly discussion.

Publication of the resolutions brought criticism from Wells and other black journalists. In response, Imes and B. K. Sampson wrote letters to black newspapers to explain their actions. The Detroit *Plaindealer* acknowledged Imes's and Sampson's actions were taken in good faith and that their past record entitled the men to a fair-minded hearing. At the same time the *Plaindealer* asked "why should representative Afro-Americans cringe and coddle" and declared, "It is time the Afro-American ceased to stand before the world as a coward. It is more honorable, and it would be better for the race for a few to die honorably than to cringe before the unholy promises that are not intended to be kept."[18]

Even those words were mild, however, compared to the lambaste leveled by Wells. Her attacks were so brutal that they provoked a backlash of sympathy for Imes and Sampson from other black journalists, including the editor of the *Plaindealer*. After granting "due deference" to Wells, he noted that "it hardly seems fair, that standing as a refugee" Wells should criticize those who dared to stay "in a bloody city while looking along the barrel of a ready Winchester."[19]

The question of whether it is better to flee and denounce injustice or to stay and fight it was raised by others. One of the more ironic exchanges on the issue occurred when J. C. Duke of the *Pine Bluff Weekly Echo* criticized Fleming's editorial in the *Chicago Free Speech*. Fleming had noted that lynching in the South "will not be stopped with outside violent influence" but by people living in the region. Duke retorted that lynching would end only after all potential victims had been run out or "those less fleet of foot than Editor Fleming have been caught and killed." Duke's assertion that Fleming "should have staid [sic] in Memphis and assisted in settling that problem," was met with derision by W. Calvin Chase of the *Washington Bee*. Chase recalled that Duke had been driven from Montgomery for writing an editorial very similar to that of Wells and ridiculed him for demanding of Fleming what he was unwilling to do himself.[20]

Black journalists were often hard on one another and seemed to consider the exchange of barbs a natural part of their profession. Wells was very good at hurling insults, but not as good at accepting criticism. She reacted angrily to the *Plaindealer's* mild rebuke and charged the paper with being an apologist for Sampson and Imes. In response the *Plaindealer* accused Wells of misrepresenting what had been written and denied the paper had ever "sanctioned the current idea of temporizing with wrong." It also questioned the heroism of flight.

> The *Plaindealer* declared it was unfair for [Wells] to pose as a hero, while running as against others who for the sake of their families have pursued another course and staid. Neither party has accomplished anything so far and there has been no act that would stamp one as a hero and the other a coward.[21]

Although her words were forceful, some black journalists criticized Wells's use of caustic comments to make her points. The *American Citizen* claimed it could be published in Memphis with "no fear of being killed." The paper charged that Wells was at least partly responsible for her fate of exile and claimed the following:

> The method is the trouble. Some medicine will not stay in the stomach when taken. Small doses, sugar-coated, would do better. God could have made the world and all in it in one minute. He chose to take six days, in order, if for nothing else, to teach the Negro patience, moderation and conservatism.[22]

It was not the first, nor the last, time Wells would be rebuked for her militancy. Nevertheless, she felt she could do no less.

Her forced exile did not cow Ida Wells but instead added more fuel to her rage and strength to her determination. "Having lost my paper, had a price put on my life and been made an exile," she wrote, "I felt that I owed it to myself and to my race to tell the whole truth now that I was where I could do so freely."[23] She was grateful to T. Thomas Fortune and his co-owner of the *New York Age*, Jerome B. Peterson, for giving her a base of operations in her war against lynching. In return for the subscription list of the *Free Speech*, the two men gave Wells a one-fourth interest in their paper and paid her a salary for writing weekly articles on the "southern field."[24]

While she had peppered the *Free Speech* with antilynching articles and editorials, Wells focused and refined her arguments on lynching in the *Age*. She began with a description of the events of 24 May that had caused the demise of her newspaper. Wells not only reprinted her editorial but also those of the Memphis *Daily Commercial* and *Evening Scimitar* that led to the meeting at the Cotton Exchange at which "threats of lynching were freely indulged." The *Scimitar's* threats to "brand [the editor] in the fore-head with a hot iron and perform upon him a surgical operation with a pair of tailor's shears" were thus given a national audience.[25] Allowing the words of whites to damn themselves was an effective method of exposing racism and became a frequent tool of Wells.

In her attempt to reeducate America about lynching, Wells attacked the idea that lynching was the work of poor, ignorant whites whose actions were deplored by their "betters." Writing of the lynching threats at the Cotton Exchange on 24 May, Wells noted the actions were "not by the lawless element upon which the deviltry of the South is usually saddled—but by the leading business men, in the leading business center."[26] As long as those who actually had the power to stop lynching were exonerated from the responsibility for it, very little improvement would result. Wells would not allow elite whites to reap the benefits of black subordination while washing their hands of the unseemly methods by which it was enforced.

Next, Wells directly confronted the issue of rape and its relation to lynching. Using the arguments of lynching apologists that black rape of white women was not a problem before emancipation, she reinterpreted the meaning of that claim. One reason for the persistence of that myth was its usefulness to both sides of the lynching debate. Whites used it to explain why lynching had only just begun for a crime that they claimed was inherent in bestiality of Negroes. To them the recent emergence of rape as an issue reflected the rise of a generation of African Americans who had never known the restraining hand of slavery. Wells attacked their logic, exclaiming:

> The thinking public will not easily believe freedom and education more brutalizing than slavery, and the world knows that the crime of rape was unknown during four years of civil war, when the white women of the South were at the mercy of the race which is all at once charged with being a bestial one.[27]

Wells asserted, "I feel that the race and the public generally should have a statement of the facts as they exist." She often proclaimed her allegiance to the "facts" and argued a factual accounting would "serve at the same time as a defense for the Afro-American Sampsons who suffer themselves to be betrayed by white Delilahs."[28]

Whereas the *Free Speech* editorial had been subtle by hinting obliquely at the theme of voluntary sexual liaisons between white women and black men, Wells now became explicit. She told how J. C. Duke had voiced his suspicions of "the growing appreciation of white Juliets for colored Romeos" and was forced to leave Montgomery for "reflecting on the 'honah' of white women." Before leaving town, Duke had disclaimed any intention of "slandering Southern white women." Wells, on the other hand, boldly announced she would make no such disclaimer and instead asserted that "there are many white women in the South who would marry colored men if such an act would not place them at once beyond the pale of society and within the clutches of the law."[29]

Wells also attacked the irrationality of southern miscegenation laws that supposedly outlawed interracial sex. Such laws, she noted, were enforced only against "the legitimate union of the races." The laws did not prevent a white man from seducing "all the colored girls he can, but it is death to the colored man who yields to the force and advances of a similar attraction in white women." The black man, Wells claimed, was lynched "not because he is a despoiler of virtue, but because he succumbs to the smiles of white women." Her point was obvious. Protection of female purity might be honorable, but jealousy was not.[30]

To explain how consent was transformed into rape by white women, Wells related the story of the white Ohio woman who told her minister husband that while he was out of town working for the Prohibitionist party, she had been brutally attacked by a black man. She claimed the man had forced himself into the kitchen, chloroformed her, and raped her. The accused man was sent to prison, even though he vehemently denied raping the woman. Four years later the wife, overcome with remorse, admitted she had lied. Acknowledging that the accused rapist "had a strange fascination for me" and that he had visited several times "and each time I was indiscreet," the wife explained her lies to her husband: "I had several reasons for telling you. One was the neighbors saw the fellow here, another was, I was afraid I had contracted a loathsome disease, and still another was that I feared I might give birth to a Negro baby. I hoped to save my reputation by telling you a deliberate lie."[31] In recounting the story, Wells related names, dates, and places to give the account a quality of legitimacy—another tactic she frequently employed.

Wells also realized that a single story would not make her contentions credible. "A few instances to substantiate the assertion that some white women love the company of the Afro-American," she wrote, "will not be out of place." To convince the doubters, Wells assured her readers that most of the cases, she would give "were reported by the daily papers of the South." She realized that gleaning her examples from white sources would make them hard for white southerners to deny. Drawing from Memphis papers, Wells recounted six cases in that city where white women had voluntarily taken black lovers or black men had been proven to be innocent of rapes charged to them.[32]

To prove Memphis was not an aberration, Wells then recounted similar incidents from all around the South. In a rapid, staccato style she listed case after case, pausing occasionally to give the details of specific cases. The women involved represented a broad stratum of society—from prostitute to physician's wife. In a number of cases, women gave birth to dark babies but refused to name the father. Wells asserted that hundreds of other examples could be given and that there "is hardly a town in the South which has not had an instance of the kind which is well-known." Thus, she contended, her assertion that "nobody in the South believes the old thread bare lie that negro men rape white women" was not slander but reality.[33]

Very aware of most people's aversion to the crime of rape, Wells sought to divorce the actions of lynch mobs from the punishment of rape. One way she did this was by showing that white men "are not so desirous of punishing rapists as they pretend." To expose their hypocrisy, Wells noted how "the pulpits, officials and newspapers of the South" had become apologists for the lynchings of black rapists of white women, but "when the victim is a colored woman it is different." Following her previous method, Wells reported case after case where white rapists had attacked black women and girls without paying any serious consequences for their action. Some were acquitted despite evidence of their guilt. Others received short sentences— one served six months and was made a police detective for the city of Nashville after his release. In one case rumors of a black mob preparing to lynch a white rapist led to the posting of 250 white guards armed with Winchester rifles.[34]

Wells could be very graphic in her descriptions of lynchings. One case that especially enraged her was the lynching of Eph. Grizzard. He was accused of rape and brutally lynched in Nashville, Tennessee. Wells captured the horror of the event with forceful imagery of the events following his removal from jail by a white mob:

> . . . with Governor Buchanan and the police and militia standing by, [Grizzard was] dragged through the streets in broad daylight, knives plunged into him at every step, and with every fiendish cruelty a frenzied mob could devise, he was at last swung out on the bridge with hands cut to pieces as he tried to climb up the stanchions.

The barbarity of the lynching itself was horrifying, but Wells was further disturbed by another circumstance of the event. When taking Grizzard from the jail, the mob had left in his cell, unmolested, a white man who had raped an eight-year-old girl. "The outrage upon helpless childhood needed no avenging in this case; she was black," Wells wrote.[35]

After eliminating rape as the real reason for lynching, Wells then explained the roots of the practice. To her the evil resulted from "the well-known opposition growing out of slavery to the progress of the race." Whites had opposed blacks' voting and holding office, and the Ku Klux Klan and others had used violence to prevent or limit both. Wells noted that these "massacres were excused as the natural resentment of intelligence against government by ignorance." Some African Americans had believed political rights should be sacrificed for peace. They felt their race "should fit itself for government, and when that should be done, the objection to race participation in politics would be removed." Wells sadly reported, "But the sacrifice did not remove the trouble, nor move the South to justice." She then directly attacked the notion that white discrimination was the result of black backwardness by discussing the segregation of trains. "The race regardless of advancement," she wrote, "is penned into filthy, stifling partitions cut off from smoking cars."[36]

Disfranchisement negated a political justification for lynching. At that point, Wells asserted, the South needed a "new cry" and adroitly began "shielding itself behind the plausible screen of defending the honor of its women." The effect of the new cry was described by Wells: "It has closed the heart, stifled the conscience, warped the judgment and hushed the voice of press and pulpit on the subject of lynch law throughout this 'land of liberty.'" She denounced the silence of leaders as much as the violence of mobs. "They do not see that by their tacit encouragement, their silent acquiescence, the black shadow of lawlessness in the form of lynch law is spreading its wings over the whole country."[37]

Wells frequently noted that both the press and the pulpit not merely acquiesced but also sometimes abetted mob action by spreading the foul lies used to justify it. Again she used whites' own words to prove her point. Wells reproduced long quotes from two Memphis newspapers that appeared following the triple lynchings in that city. Both reiterated the rape myth. The *Commercial* regretted that even lynching did not adequately deter black rapists: "The facts of the crime appear to appeal more to the Negro's lustful imagination than the facts of the punishment do to his fears. He sets aside all fear of death in any form when opportunity is found for the gratification of his bestial desires." The *Evening Scimitar* came closer to the truth, but still found it necessary to include some allusion to rape. "Aside from the violation of white women by Negroes, which is the outcropping of a bestial perversion of instinct," it declared, "the chief cause of trouble between the races in the South is the Negro's lack of manners." Acts of independence on the part of African Americans were labeled "boorish insolence." Blaming the Memphis riot of 1866 on "the outrageous conduct of blacks towards whites on the streets," the *Scimitar* then revealed the true nature of its complaints.

> It is also a remarkable and discouraging fact that the majority of such scoundrels are Negroes who have received educational advantages at the hands of the white taxpayers. They have got just enough learning to make them realize how hopelessly their race is behind the other in everything that makes a great people, and they attempt to "get even" by insolence, which is ever the resentment of inferiors.[38]

To Wells the paper inadvertently revealed the true cause of lynching— white fear and resentment of black advancement.

At this point Wells introduced the story of the lynchings of Moss, McDowell, and Stewart to illustrate white reaction to black advancement and to dispel the notion that lynching victims were poor, ignorant criminals or political radicals. She called the Memphis victims "three of the best specimens of young since-the-war Afro-American manhood" and described them as "peaceful, law-abiding citizens and energetic businessmen." Painting them as conservatives, Wells noted, "They believed the [race] problem was to be solved by eschewing politics and putting money in the purse." In retrospect, their murder undoubtedly played a major role in Wells's later rejection of the accommodationist approach of Booker T. Washington, who counseled African Americans to put their energy toward economic and educational advancement rather than political agitation.[39]

After a brief account of the events in Memphis, Wells asked the rhetorical question: What lesson did whites seek to give by the lynchings? Her answer was "the lesson of subordination." She believed the whites were saying to themselves, "Kill the leaders and it will cow the Negro who dares to shoot a white man, even in self-defense." Wells also pointed out that the white papers misrepresented facts to make lynchings seem more justifiable. She told of an incident in which the lynching victim was reported to have raped the eight-year-old daughter of the sheriff. In fact the woman was eighteen and had been discovered by her father in the black man's room.

Wells repeatedly attacked the credibility of the news sources from which most Americans learned of lynchings—an important step in the reeducation of the nation.[40]

In her lynching articles, Wells next debunked the notion of a "New South." Henry Grady of the *Atlanta Constitution* and others had been touting the remaking of the region from the "Cotton Kingdom" into a land of opportunity for business investors. Seeking an infusion of northern capital, New South advocates sang the praises of the region's plentiful resources, cheap labor, and industrial potential. Out of the ashes of defeat, the South was said to be rising with a new vigor and outlook. In what Wells called "well-mannered speeches in New England and New York," Grady asserted the South's ability to solve its racial problems if freed from the meddling of northerners who did not understand the situation. Distracted by other issues and priorities, northerners increasingly accepted the idea of a "redeemed" South, which no longer required federal intervention. Wells sought to destroy that fabrication. "There is little difference," she proclaimed, "between the Ante-bellum South and the New South." She explained:

> Her white citizens are wedded to any method however revolting, any measure however extreme, for the subjugation of the young manhood of the race. They have cheated him out of his ballot, deprived him of his civil rights or redress therefor in the civil courts, robbed him of the fruits of his labor, and are still murdering, burning and lynching him.

The result, Wells claimed, was that the "South is brutalized to a degree not realized by its own inhabitants, and the very foundation of government, law and order, are imperilled [sic]."[41]

If whites wondered what they could do about the scourge of lynching, Wells provided some examples. She named groups and people who had taken forceful stands against "the frequent and revolting crimes against a weak people." Recipients of her praise included "the spirit of Christianity of the great M. E. Church," which led to the adoption of "strong condemnatory resolutions at its General Conference in Omaha last May." The Republican party received fainter praise for its "feeble declaration of the belief in human rights in the Republican platform at Minneapolis, June 7th." Wells also lauded President Benjamin Harrison, the governor and the chief justice of Georgia, and the citizens of Chattanooga for opposing or preventing lynching.

In her discussion of white opposition to lynching, Wells printed a long quote from Col. A. S. Colyar of Nashville, Tennessee. As a well-known "New South" advocate, Colyar's condemnation and descriptions of lynchings increased the credibility of her own accounts. His words were no less forceful: "Nothing since I have been a reading man has so impressed me with the decay of manhood among the people of Tennessee as the dastardly submission to mob rule." The actions of mobs, he believed, reflected "a degeneracy rapidly approaching savage life." Wells asserted the need for such strong, public stands against lynching. "The strong arm of the law must be brought to bear upon the lynchers in severe punishment," she argued, "but this cannot and will not be done unless a healthy public sentiment demands and sustains such action."[42]

Wells concluded her treatise on lynching with a message to African Americans regarding the weapons available to them in the battle against lynching. She stressed their strengths rather than their weaknesses. Trying to get them to realize their power, she explained:

> To Northern capital and Afro-American labor the South owes its rehabilitation. If labor is withdrawn capital will not remain. The Afro-American is thus the backbone of the South. A thorough knowledge and judicious exercise of this power in lynching localities could many times effect a bloodless revolution. The white man's dollar is his god, and to stop this will be to stop outrages in many localities.[43]

To prove the existence of that power and to demonstrate its effectiveness, Wells recounted events in Memphis and in Kentucky.

Following the triple lynching in Memphis, Wells noted, African Americans had remained peaceful and "waited for the authorities to act in the matter and bring the lynchers to justice." When this did not happen, they "left the city by thousands, bringing about great stagnation in every branch of business." Those who remained boycotted the streetcars in protest. As a result of the economic impact of these actions, whites held a meeting and passed resolutions condemning lynching. Persistence was required, however, because whites still refused to punish the lynchers. That failure caused Memphis to continue "losing her black population."[44]

In Kentucky, Wells claimed, a boycott of newly segregated railroad cars would cost the various railroads a million dollars in that one year. She encouraged such activities, claiming "the appeal to the white man's pocket has ever been more effectual than all the appeals ever made to his conscience." Rejecting an accommodationist approach, she proclaimed,

"Nothing, absolutely nothing, is to be gained by further sacrifice of manhood and self-respect." Indeed, lynchings had been prevented by armed self-defense in Jacksonville, Florida, and Paducah, Kentucky. "The lesson this teaches and which every Afro-American should ponder well, is that a Winchester rifle should have a place of honor in every black home," Wells declared. "The more the Afro-American yields and cringes and begs, the more he is insulted, outraged and lynched."[45] These were powerful words, but they demanded unrealistic resistance from a race in a region where all the powers of the state were arrayed against it.

Wells also issued a challenge to her fellow journalists to become investigative reporters and expose the falsified accounts of particular lynchings. Asserting that "there is no educator to compare with the press," Wells cited examples of how white coverage of lynchings from New York to Alabama had been proved biased and inaccurate by thorough investigation. "The race thus outraged," she exhorted, "must find out the facts of this awful hurling of men into eternity on supposition, and give them to the indifferent and apathetic country." Wells then concluded her treatise on lynching with the following challenge:

> Nothing is more definitely settled than [the Afro-American] must act for himself. I have shown how he may employ the boycott, emigration and the press, and I feel that by a combination of all these agencies can be effectually stamped out lynch law, that last relic of barbarism and slavery. "The gods help those who help themselves."[46]

The reference to barbarism is indicative of a recurring theme in the writing of Wells—and indeed of most apostles of antilynching in the late nineteenth century. A resurgence of colonialism by Europe and the United States was accompanied by increasing attention on the concepts of "civilization" and "barbarism." This interest was also compounded by the popularization of the Darwinian concepts of natural selection, survival of the fittest, and evolution. By applying those principles to humankind, peoples of European descent justified their positions of power. Human society was said to have evolved from a primitive, savage state of barbarism to a refined, cultured state of civilization. Some people believed that the advanced evolution of Europeans was rooted in genetics, and, therefore relatively permanent. To others the non-European peoples of the world merely lagged behind and would eventually follow the stages of development on the road to civilization that Europeans had already passed. Either way, for the present, most Europeans and European Americans agreed that "backward peoples" required the guiding hand of their "superiors." By emphasizing a sharp dichotomy between their own "civilized" natures and the "barbarity" of the rest of humankind, they justified imposing their government and economic control on others, calling it the "White Man's Burden."

At the same time, late-nineteenth-century industrialization and urbanization required a new degree of self-restraint and discipline. Businessmen became more dependent on access to capital for investment, so that strict control of one's expenditures was often a necessary first step up the ladder of success. As businesses grew larger so did responsibilities. Personal restraint, organization, and discipline were necessary in order to coordinate the activities of numerous employees. For the workers, factories brought new demands that curtailed spontaneity and required more self-discipline, bodily urges had to be sublimated to the time clock. Instead of personal whim or instinctual responses, the clock now told one when to rise, when to work, when to eat, and even when to go to the bathroom at work. These demands caused a reinterpretation of manhood. Physical strength, courage, aggressiveness, and strong will had defined masculine ideals in earlier frontier conditions, but now success depended on restraint and discipline. True manhood was redefined as responsibility, refinement, and restraint.

Concepts of manhood and civilization became closely linked. Manliness was also considered the result of the evolution from the primitive savagery of barbarism to the cultured refinement of civilization. Because civilization brought with it the right to rule others, political power was an element of true manhood. Lynching apologists argued that Negroes were a less evolved people still mired in animal-like savagery. Controlled by their lust rather than their intellect, bestial black men naturally lacked the self-restraint to wait for consent before sexual conquests. Such men surely could not be given the responsibility of voting. How could they govern others, when they could not even govern their own instincts? Was not any measure, no matter how extreme, justified in restraining assaults on white civilization by black barbarism? Because white women were the pure embodiment of that civilization, could there ever be greater barbarism that the defilement of that purity by the bestial act of rape? Such questions quieted protests to mob law.

In the battle for white support against lynching, Wells and others recognized that attacks on civilization and manhood would not win converts. They were too essential to whites' self-definition. Instead the principles of both manhood and civilization would have to be reaffirmed and redefined by antilynching advocates. Mob law had to be shown as the result of barbarism rather than the remedy for it.[47]

Although Wells was not the only one to use the issues of civilization and manhood to denounce lynching, she was perhaps the most effective. She accomplished this in number of ways. First, she exposed the mythical nature of the cry of rape, stripping away the most compelling "honorable" justification of lynching. Second, she questioned the manliness of those who would basely exploit true manhood's desire to protect womanhood to justify a barbaric practice. Third, she described lynching as a savage act of uncontrolled fury or as a throwback to outdated notions of manliness. Fourth, she contrasted the restraint shown by African Americans with the excesses of lynch mobs. Fifth, she warned of the destructive force of mob law on civilization and democracy. In short, Wells was able to cast lynchers as crude barbarians rather than as manly defenders of womanhood. As she later wrote, "No torture of helpless victims by heathen savages or cruel red

"OH! JUSTICE THOU HAS FLED TO BRUTISH BEASTS"

Cartoon illustrating the use of the concept of civilization against lynchers, from the Indianapolis *Freeman, 5 November 1898.*

Indians ever exceeded the cold-blooded savagery of white devils under lynch law."[48]

Wells later recalled that Fortune and Peterson had printed ten thousand of the first edition of the *New York Age* that contained her words on lynching. She indicated that a "thousand copies were sold in the streets of Memphis alone."[49] Clearly, the city's citizens had not quieted Wells. Numerous people remarked on how her audience had expanded.

In a book on African American women published the next year, Monroe Majors declared:

> Her readers remain the same, only the magnetic force of her pen enjoys a broader scope. Before her audience was a multitude. Now it is the nation. Ten thousand minds fly out to her in adoration and praise. Ten thousand hearts throb with exaltation in witnessing her triumphs.

The prophecy of the Detroit *Plaindealer* was realized when Wells was given a safer place than Memphis from which to speak. "The bourbons of Memphis, smarting under the . . . strictures of the *Free Speech* regarding lawlessness," the paper noted, "drove its editors from their homes by cowardly threats, but the *New York Age* which is yet more caustic will take its place."[50]

Ironically, if Wells had not been run out of Memphis, she would never have become the recognized leader of the antilynching movement—and thus Memphis and its lynchings would have likely been soon forgotten as new, bloodier massacres occurred across the South. Three months before Moss, McDowell, and Stewart were lynched, Edward Coy had been lynched in Texarkana. In its immediate aftermath that lynching received as much, or possibly more, attention as the one in Memphis. Coy was burned alive after being falsely accused of rape by a white woman who had willingly been intimate with him for months. It was an ideal case with which to prove the falsity of many rape charges.

Indeed, in an antilynching meeting held at New York City in April 1892, speakers gave more attention to the Texarkana lynching than to those in Memphis—or Ida B. Wells. Still a resident of Memphis, Wells was only one of many to occupy the platform while T. Thomas Fortune and others spoke. The Coy lynching also provoked a series of articles under the heading "Is God Dead?" in the Kansas City *American Citizen* written by its editor, C. H. J. Taylor. He appears to have believed he should have become the foremost antilynching advocate, which helps explain his comment about Wells, "She seeks fame and gets notoriety." Taylor was jealous not only of the attention Wells received after her exile but also of Frederick Douglass, who almost eclipsed both Taylor and Wells in the fight against lynching.[51]

Douglass had given militant speeches against lynching even prior to Wells's exile from Memphis. Immediately after her first antilynching article in the *New York Age*, he published "Lynch Law in the South" in the July issue of the *North American Review*. His article made many of the same points as Wells and Taylor had, but it received more attention because of both his international renown and the wider circulation of the *North American Review*. His own white wife provided tangible proof that white women could desire black men. Even in Memphis, Douglass's article provoked more rage than Wells's articles. The *Evening Scimitar* called the famous black abolitionist a "senile negro scoundrel" and labeled his article "the vilest assault on millions of his country['s] women that a black heart could conceive or a lying pen frame in words."[52]

Within two years, however, Ida B. Wells would be the best-known figure in the antilynching movement. A meeting called on her behalf in October 1892 by black women in New York launched Wells's speaking career. Her elocution lessons and drama experiences in Memphis helped her to give speeches with unusual force and power. Perhaps the fact she was a women discussing sexual matters in public added to her mystique. At any rate, demands for her lectures mushroomed and eventually sprouted across the Atlantic as well.

9

⌘

Antilynching Lectures

"The disturbing element which kept the waters troubled"

⌘

S oon after moving to Memphis, Ida B. Wells had become active in the literary and dramatic circles of that city's vibrant black community. Almost immediately she had discovered her love of the platform and stage. Although she toyed with the idea of becoming an actress, like other young women of her era, Wells soon realized that the stage could not provide adequate respectability or remuneration. Very few women speakers could support themselves on the lecture circuits either; for a long time, women had rarely been allowed to speak out in public at all. Nevertheless, while earning her living teaching and writing, Wells utilized the available forums in Memphis and spent scarce dollars on elocution lessons.

Her journalistic ties eventually provided Wells with opportunities to exercise her oratorical skills beyond her home town, at regional and national meetings. Her first lectures outside of Memphis were at National Press Association conferences. Her speeches there and at the meeting of the Afro-American League at Knoxville in July 1891 gained favorable coverage in the press. After moving to New York, her first public speech appears to have been "The Afro-American in Literature," given before the Concord Literary Circle of Brooklyn, New York, on 15 September 1892. Wells was said to have "completely captivated the large and cultivated audience."[1]

At the end of that month, Wells attended the National Press Association convention in Philadelphia. Usually a center of attention whenever she attended these meetings, Wells was proclaimed the "star of the convention," elected treasurer of the group, and called on to speak. Described as "modest in appearance," she was said to have "shone with intellectual brilliancy" and to have been "moved to grief" in relating the story of her exile. Before adjourning, the seventy-five delegates adopted a resolution to establish a fund "to prevent outrages on the Negroes in the South."[2]

The National Press Association was notorious for failing to follow up resolutions with positive action. Prior to the meeting, the *Atchison Blade* predicted, "Now they will go to Philadelphia, read ably written papers on 'The Race Problem,' denounce southern lynchings, give a ball, drink wine, eat a delicious dinner, and then go to their various homes feeling good and as though they had actually accomplished something worth talking about." Although the prophecy of the delegates' actions apparently proved true, the convention actually did lead to concrete action by a visitor at the meeting—Catherine Impey. An English Quaker, Impey was the editor of *Anti-Caste*, which was "Devoted to the Interests of the Coloured Races." She not only attended the sessions at the convention but also was the guest of honor at a tea given by Fannie J. Coppin, at whose house Wells had previously stayed. Impey left the meeting with a pledge to help the antilynching cause and with the memory of meeting Wells. Several months later she would find a way to aid both the cause and Wells.[3]

Meeting Wells now was undeniably memorable. As capable as her earlier speeches may have been, the subject of lynching was decidedly more suited to the fire and drama of Wells's temperament. With the rape myth as the centerpiece of her antilynching arguments, however, she was in danger of being scandalized for speaking so openly about sexual matters. Although forces of urbanization and industrialism were lessening sexual taboos, the Comstock Law of 1873 still barred distribution of loosely defined "obscene literature and articles of immoral use," and Margaret Sanger was forced to flee the country for giving out contraceptive information as late as 1914. Wells faced the dual suspicions of women speaking in public and of anyone speaking openly of rape. Fortunately, her first widely publicized address on lynching was made under the auspices of some of the most respectable women of her race. According to Wells, soon after her article in the *New York Age*, "two women remarked on my revelations during a visit with each other and said that the women of New York and Brooklyn should do something to show appreciation of my work and to protest the treatment I had received."[4]

The two women were Victoria Earle Matthews, a fellow journalist, and Maritcha Lyons, a schoolteacher. They called a meeting, where the group decided to rally the women of New York and Brooklyn through a series of meetings held in churches. Out of those meetings emerged a plan to raise enough money to allow Wells to start a newspaper of her own. A group of these women, called the Ida B. Wells Testimonial Reception Committee, then organized a meeting in honor of Wells that was held at Lyric Hall on 5 October 1892.

The meeting was a huge success. Not only did most of the leading black women of New York and Brooklyn attend, but sizable delegations also came from Boston and Philadelphia—swelling the audience to over two hundred. Among the members of the black elite who attended were fellow journalist Gertrude Mossell, physician Susan McKinney, social activist Josephine St. Pierre Ruffin, and the widow of the famous Episcopal clergyman, Henry Highland Garnet. In her autobiography, Wells recalled that these women "were all there on the platform, a solid array behind a lonely, homesick girl who was in exile because she had tried to defend the manhood of her race." As Wells was thirty at the time and had traveled widely, her portrait of herself as a "lonely, homesick girl" reflects a desire to cast herself as a tragic heroine—perhaps like the heroic literary characters she had always read about.[5]

The event was well planned and executed. Advertising was provided free of charge by the black press; the *New York Age* and the *New York Review* gave extensive attention and support to the preparations. The committee spent over $150 to make the event successful and memorable. Gas jets spelled out "Iola" at the back of the stage, and programs were printed on miniature copies of the *Free Speech*. The ushers and committee members wore white silk badges lettered with "Iola." Floral arrangements included a horn of plenty donated by the ushers. Victoria Earle Matthews presided over what Wells called "a beautiful program of speeches, resolutions, and music."[6]

In her memoirs Wells recalled being terrified of giving her address to the assemblage. She admitted, "I had some little reputation as an essayist from schoolgirl days, and had recited many times in public recitations which I had committed to memory." She also confessed to having made talks asking for subscriptions to her paper, but she insisted that this was the first time she "had ever been called on to deliver an honest-to-goodness address." Wells avowed that although "every detail of that horrible lynching affair was imprinted on my memory," she had "to commit it all to paper" so she would only have to read the words. Again, Wells appears to have played down her maturity and experience for dramatic effect. Her account portrayed a poignant pathos:

> As I described the cause of the trouble at home and my mind went back to the scenes of the struggle, to the thought of the friends who were scattered throughout the country, a feeling of loneliness and homesickness for the days and the friends that were gone came over me and I felt the tears coming.
>
> A panic seized me. I was afraid that I was going to make a scene and spoil all those dear good women had done for me. I kept saying to myself that whatever happened I must not break down, and so I kept on reading. I had left my handkerchief on the seat behind me and therefore could not wipe away the tears which were coursing down my cheeks.

Wells continued to describe her attempts to signal behind her back to the women on the platform who could not see her face or tears, until finally Matthews brought her a handkerchief. "I kept on reading the story which they had come to hear," Wells proclaimed.[7]

Wells remembered being "mortified" to have "not been able to prevent such an exhibition of weakness." Her consternation appears genuine; over thirty years later she went to some length to explain why it happened. "It came on me unawares," she declared. "It was the only time in all those trying months that I had yielded to personal feelings." Wells noted that she had especially wanted to "be at my best in order to show my appreciation of the splendid things those women had done!" Their very kindness seems to have been the stimulus. Wells explained, "They were giving me tangible evidence that although my environment had changed I was still surrounded by kind hearts."[8]

It is likely that the expression of acceptance by these black elite women did have a profound impact on Wells. Since the death of her parents, Wells had been a frequent target of salacious rumors, expelled from Rust College, fired from teaching, and run out of town. Respectability was among the highest goals of middle-class black women after the degrading experiences of slavery, and for Wells it had been especially elusive. Despite her religious devotion and high moral standards, something always seemed to happen to tarnish the reputation she worked so hard to maintain. While in Memphis, she had also despaired of her seeming inability to sustain close relationships with women. Without the backing of wealth and family,

Wells had probably felt at times like an outsider in the elite social circles of Memphis. The endorsement of so many women — some of whom were undisputed members of the elite — was a precious gift at that point in her life.

One reason scandal haunted Wells was her frequent outbursts of anger, which led her to say things she soon regretted. Not surprisingly, emotional control came to be very important to Wells in her quest for respectability. "After all these years," she wrote late in life, "I still have a feeling of chagrin over that exhibition of weakness. Whatever my feelings, I am not given to public demonstrations." Interestingly, in the handwritten autobiography manuscript, she concluded the same paragraph, "And only once before in all my life have the tears forced their way uncontrollably to the surface when I was before the public." In her final version, however, Wells changed the second half of the sentence to "had I given way to woman's weakness in public."[9] Accounts of her later speeches bear out this assertion; her oratory was usually described as forceful, earnest, and effective but also as quiet, educated, and unimpassioned.

Her reasons for ascribing what she considered "weakness" to her gender were as complex and contradictory as her own self-image often was. Even after overcoming numerous obstacles for more than a half century, Wells still blamed her infrequent moments of "weakness" — but not her strength — on her womanhood. When a woman as independent, liberated, and strong-willed as Wells could still belittle her sex, the power of patriarchy in the socialization of nineteenth-century women is abundantly evident. However, in the particular setting of her Lyric Hall speech, a failure to display emotion may have led the audience to question Wells's credibility or her femininity. Among her "sisters" Wells may have seemed unnaturally cold if she had not wept. Wells noted, "But the women didn't feel that I had spoiled things by my breakdown. They seemed to think that it made an impression on the audience favorable to the cause and me."[10]

The reception was a financial success. The committee eventually tabulated the receipts as $613.90, out of which $150.75 was deducted to cover expenses. One of those expenditures was the purchase of a brooch in the shape of "a beautiful gold pen engraved with the legend 'Mizpah,'" which was presented to Wells at the reception. On the back of the pen, according to the *American Citizen*, were engraved the words "Afro-American women of New York and Brooklyn Oct. 5 1892." Wells prized this "emblem of my chosen profession" and claimed to have worn it "for the next twenty years on all occasions." She was probably even more grateful, however, for the $450 that the women deposited in an account for her.[11]

The meeting received favorable attention in the black press. The *Washington Bee* called it "one of the finest testimonials ever rendered an Afro-American." The *American Citizen* described it as "one of the most successful affairs ever managed by the 'fairer sex'" and proclaimed Wells worthy of the honor, declaring: "She is a heroine; would we had more with such zeal and nobility of womanhood."[12] The New York speech brought not only praise but also invitations to speak. Indeed, Wells soon embarked on a frantic tour of eastern cities, where she lectured and was toasted and entertained. Her schedule caused the *Atchison Blade* to remark, "It's a wonder the eastern women haven't become jealous of the banquetting Miss Ida B. Wells is receiving. . . . Miss Wells tells our people to go west and grow up with the country and at the same time she goes east and grows up with beneficial banquets and fulsome adulation."[13]

Somewhere along the way, in such cities as Boston; Wilmington, Delaware; Chester, Pennsylvania; New Bedford, Massachusetts; Providence, and Newport, Rhode Island; New York; and Washington, D.C., Wells encountered Frederick Douglass. He apparently praised her article on lynching because on 17 October, Wells wrote to ask him "to put in writing the encomiums you were pleased to lavish on my article on Lynch Law in June 25 issue of the Age." She explained that she was preparing that article for publication as a pamphlet and would "feel highly honored" if Douglass would write his opinion of it to serve as an introduction.[14]

Douglass promptly replied. His 25 October letter was included in Wells's pamphlet *Southern Horrors, Lynch Law in All Its Phases*, which was released soon afterward. Douglass strongly praised Wells's work:

> Let me give you thanks for your faithful paper on the lynch abomination now generally practiced against colored people in the South. There has been no word equal to it in convincing power. I have spoken, but my word is feeble in comparison. You give what you know and testify from actual knowledge. You have dealt with the facts with painstaking fidelity and left those naked and uncontradicted facts to speak for themselves.
>
> Brave woman! you have done your people and mine a service which can neither be weighed nor measured. If American conscience were only half alive, if the American clergy were only half christianized, if American sensibility were not hardened by persistent infliction of outrage and crime against colored people, a scream of horror, shame and indignation would rise to heaven wherever your pamphlet shall be read.[15]

Douglass clearly recognized the power of personal experience; his accounts of his life as a slave had been among the most potent antislavery tools. He also highlighted an effective component of Wells's talks and writings—her decision to use white sources for "naked and uncontradicted facts."

Southern Horrors was dedicated to the women who had given the New York testimonial. Their contributions paid for its printing, so she did not have to engage in extensive fund-raising activities for printing costs, as she often did for later pamphlets. Wells was also grateful to be able to borrow some of their respectability. In her preface the assertion, "It is with no pleasure I have dipped my hands in the corruption here exposed," acknowledged that the subject was not totally proper for a woman. "Somebody must show that the Afro-American race is more sinned against than sinning," Wells explained, "and it seems to have fallen upon me to do so." The black press praised the pamphlet. The *Chicago Conservator* wrote, "We commend it to all who desire to give this phase of the Southern question serious thought."[16] Wells must have been exhilarated by the show of support by Douglass, the New York women, and the press; nevertheless, her next speech was a disappointment.

On 31 October Wells spoke at the Metropolitan A.M.E. Church in Washington, D.C. Although the meeting was given extensive advertising and support by the *Washington Bee* as well as by Frederick Douglass and T. Thomas Fortune, the turnout was quite small. An advertisement noted that Mary Church Terrell would preside and Fortune would introduce Wells. The lecture was scheduled for 8:00 P.M., and the cost of admission was set at twenty-five cents. Though the *Bee* called for a turnout of "three to four thousand" and proclaimed it "the duty of every citizen to go and hear her," the *Cleveland Gazette* reported that the meeting "was not a financial success" and noted that "fashionable colored society did not turn out *en masse*." Some blamed the failure on Fortune's connection with the event, because of his unpopular political support of the Democrats. J. E. Bruce, however, declared that "the Washington Negro is no good." Douglass was embarrassed by the reception Wells had received and promised to reschedule and deliver a larger crowd.[17]

Before Washington hosted Wells again, however, she returned to Philadelphia for the November convention of the A.M.E. Church. After a number of bishops had spoken, including Henry McNeal Turner, Wells went to the podium. Her efforts won effusive praise. In his account of the convention, *A.M.E. Church Review* editor Dr. H. T. Johnson noted,

"RIGHTEOUSNESS EXALTETH A NATION; BUT SIN IS A REPROACH TO ANY PEOPLE."

ALL EYES WERE TURNED ON IDA B. WELLS, FOR IT WAS SHE, HERSELF A VICTIM OF THE PORTRAYED OUTRAGES AND SHE WAS MOVED TO GRIEF. MISS WELLS WAS THE STAR OF THE CONVENTION; THOUGH MODEST IN APPEARANCE SHE SHONE WITH INTELLECTUAL BRILLIANCE.—PROVIDENCE (R.I) TORCHLIGHT, OCT. 1, 1892.

The way to Right Wrongs is to turn the Light of Truth upon Them.

Yours for Justice,
IDA B. WELLS.

"SOUTHERN MOB RULE;" The Simple Story of an Eloquent Woman.

Miss Ida B. Wells

(of the Editorial Staff of THE NEW YORK AGE)

WILL DELIVER

A LECTURE

AT

Metropolitan A. M. E. Church

M Street, between 15th and 16th Streets,

MONDAY EVENING OCT. 31st, 1892.

Mrs. Robert H. Terrell will preside.

Admission   25 cents

DOORS open at 7 o'clock   Exercises will begin at 8 o'clock.

Subject:—"SOUTHERN MOB RULE."

T. THOMAS FORTUNE

Will introduce the Lecturer.

Miss Wells made a National Reputation as Editor of the Memphis Free Speech, the publication of which she was compelled to suspend because of her Bold, Fearless and Intelligent Denunciation of Mob Violence and the enactment and enforcement of malicious and degrading class laws.

As a platform orator, Miss Wells takes high and commanding rank as an earnest and eloquent speaker. No woman of the race has greater power than she exercises to hold the attention of an audience. In a public address before the Afro-American League at Knoxville, in July, 1891, she astonished her hearers by her impassioned denunciation of the Separate Car Law and Mob Rule. In her lecture on "The Afro-American in Literature," delivered before the Concord Literary Circle of Brooklyn, New York, September 15, 1892, she completely captivated the large and cultivated audience; and at the Testimonial tendered her by the women of New York City and Brooklyn, at Lyric Hall, New York, October 5, 1892 she moved the vast assemblage to tears by the pathetic recital of the terrible lynching of three of her friends at Memphis, in March, 1892, and the forced suspension of her newspaper.

(Fortune and Peterson, Managers.)

Col. Geo. M. Arnold, Manager of the Washington Engagement.

Announcement appearing in the *Washington Bee*, fall of 1892.

the climax of which was capped by the dauntless but exiled "Iola," whose unique and inimitable speech won the conference, and so excited sympathy in her behalf that it were [sic] well for her Memphian adversaries that they were in their distant safety in the lower regions of the Mississippi Valley.[18]

In a later account of this Philadelphia visit, Wells recalled that she had stayed at the home of William Still, the great operator and chronicler of the "Underground Railroad," which had aided slaves escaping to freedom. While Wells was at the Still house, Catherine Impey came to call, and they discussed the lynching plague. Impey expressed shock over Wells's lynching stories and white indifference to such occurrences. Wells noted, "She was especially hurt that this should be the fact among those of her own sect and kin. We deplored the situation and agreed that there seemed nothing to do but keep plugging away at the evils both of us were fighting."[19] Thus another link was forged in the chain that would tie their efforts together and move their labors across the sea.

News of the testimonials for Wells and her lectures on the Memphis lynching trickled back to the white community of Memphis. Retaliation was vicious. In December the *Memphis Commercial* launched an attack on her credibility and morality. The paper claimed "this Wells wench" had not even written the infamous editorial bringing her such attention. Instead it depicted her as "the mistress of the scoundrel" who authored it and implied she was raising money for personal gain under false premises. The lowest blow was the charge that she was a "black harlot" seeking a white husband.[20]

The *Commercial* described her audience as members of Boston's "effete civilization" made up of "thin-legged scholars" and "glass-eyed females." The reference to Boston was natural. Of all the towns Wells visited, none welcomed her more warmly. She made at least three visits to Boston from November 1892 to March 1893. On Thanksgiving morning, Wells spoke at the Women's Department of the Mechanics' Fair, and she returned in January to address the Moral Educational Association at the Ladies' Physiological Institute. That month she also lectured a large crowd at Wesleyan Hall on "Sufferings of the Colored People of the South." The next month, in response to the *Commercial*'s attack on Wells, the black women of the city organized to show their support for her. They formed a local branch of the National Colored Women's League, chose Josephine St. Pierre Ruffin as president, and unanimously adopted resolutions condemning "the foulest aspersion of one of the daily papers of Memphis."

They recorded "our indignation at the slander" and asserted "our confidence in Miss Wells' purity of purpose and character."[21]

Her visit to Boston in mid-February 1893, however, was her greatest triumph. "It was during this visit to Boston," Wells recalled, "that I had my first opportunity to address a white audience." A famous preacher of that day, Joseph Cook, sponsored a lecture series titled the "Boston Monday Lectures" at Tremont Temple and invited Wells to speak on 13 February. Her speech was covered in the white newspapers of the city and later printed in the May 1893 edition of *Our Day*. As the only known talk preserved in full text, it illumines Wells's oratorical approach for speeches on lynching for white audiences. Regarding her lecture tour, Wells later claimed, "In these meetings I read my paper, the same one that I had read at the first meeting in New York."[22] While this is *substantially* true, the Tremont Temple speech shows that the talk was updated as new lynchings occurred and was modified to suit the various audiences.

Wells began with her standard disclaimer that she approached the subject "through no inclination of my own, but because of a deep-seated conviction that the country at large does not know the extent to which lynch law prevails." She proclaimed faith in the decency of white Americans by asserting that "the apathy and indifference" over mob rule had to be the result of "ignorance of the true situation." As Martin Luther King, Jr., would later do, Wells appealed to both whites' consciences and self-interests—by holding up American ideals.

> Repeated attacks on the life, liberty and happiness of any citizen or class of citizens are attacks on distinctive American institutions; such attacks imperiling as they do the foundation of government, law and order, merit the thoughtful consideration of far-sighted Americans; not from a standpoint of sentiment, not even so much from the standpoint of justice to a weak race, as from a desire to preserve our institutions.[23]

Wells then described the "omnipresent and all-pervading" impact of the "race problem or negro question," calling it "Banquo's ghost of politics, religion, and sociology."[24]

With the sentence, "Born and raised in the South, I had never expected to live elsewhere," Wells moved into the body of her speech—an account of her life, the triple lynchings, and her exile. She recognized the emotional impact of a well-told story and infused it with details that gave the narrative richness and texture. She told of how she had worked as a teacher and journalist in the faith that the "doctrine of self-help, thrift and economy" provided the key to acceptance and justice for her people. In the beginning, Wells asserted, "This sentiment bore good fruit in Memphis. We had nice homes, representatives in almost every branch of business and profession, and refined society." Although proscribed by segregation, black Memphians believed the city would remain free of lynchings. "But there was a rude awakening," Wells continued, launching into her account of the lynchings. One of her longest descriptions of those events, it was filled with heartrending details. "The baby daughter of Tom Moss," Wells declared, "too young to express how she misses her father, toddles to the wardrobe, seizes the legs of the trousers of his letter-carrier uniform, hugs and kisses them with evident delight and stretches up her little hands to be taken up into the arms which will nevermore clasp his daughter's form."[25]

Wells further described the responses of the black community to the lynchings. She admitted that they considered vengeance but realized it would mean "certain death for the men, and horrible slaughter for the women and children." She reminded her audience, "The power of the State, county and city, the civil authorities and the strong arm of the military power were all on the side of the mob and lawlessness." Instead they decided to leave, and white Memphians felt the impact of their departure. "There were a number of business failures and blocks of houses were for rent," Wells explained. "To restore the equilibrium and put a stop to the great financial loss," she continued, "the next move was to get rid of the *Free Speech,* — the disturbing element which kept the waters troubled."[26]

After detailing the events that led to her exile, Wells assured her audience, "The lawlessness here described is not confined to one locality. In the past over a thousand colored men, women and children have been butchered, murdered and burnt in all parts of the South." She then described a number of grisly lynchings and listed the statistics from 1882 to 1892. Her account made clear that "neither age, sex nor decency are spared" and that in only one-third of lynchings were charges of rape even made. Lynchers had come to believe nothing would be done to punish them. Wells cried that:

> So bold have the lynchers become, masks are laid aside, the temples of justice and strongholds of law are invaded in broad daylight and prisoners taken out and lynched, while governors of states and officers of law stand by and see the work well done.
>
> And yet this Christian nation, the flower of the nineteenth century civilization, says it can do nothing to stop this inhuman slaugh-

ter. The general government is willingly powerless to send troops to
protect the lives of its black citizens, but the state governments are
free to use state troops to shoot them down like cattle, when in des-
peration the black men attempt to defend themselves, and then tell
all the world that it was necessary to put down a "race war."[27]

Wells then compared slavery with lynching and the nation's reaction
to it. She noted that few had been willing to confront the evil of human
bondage for many years. Only the martyrdom of white abolitionists and
threats to freedom of speech convinced the nation "that slavery was not
only a monster [but also] a tyrant." Wells proclaimed, *"The very same forces
are at work now as then."* After appealing to the abolitionist sentiment of
white Bostonians, Wells blamed the North's current moral blindness on a
desire to prevent another Civil War. However, the efforts to win back the
allegiance of the South had failed, she explained:

> With all the country's disposition to condone and temporize with the
> South and its methods; with its many instances of sacrificing princi-
> ple to prejudice for the sake of making friends and healing the
> breach made by the late war; of going into the lawless country with
> capital to build up its waste places and remaining silent in the pres-
> ence of outrage and wrong—the South is as vindictive and bitter
> as ever.[28]

Wells not only defined the problem for her audience but also provided
a solution. "Do you ask a remedy?", she asked, then answered, "A public
sentiment strong against lawlessness must be aroused. Every individual can
contribute to this awakening. When a sentiment against lynch law as
strong, deep and mighty as that aroused against slavery prevails, I have no
fear of the result." Wells then appealed to Republican party strength in
Boston by blaming the party's defeat in the 1892 presidential election on its
failure to meet "the issues squarely for human rights." She closed with a
ringing appeal and reference to white abolitionists.

> The voice of the people is the voice of God, and I long with all the
> intensity of my soul for the Garrison, Douglas [sic], Sumner, Wit-
> tier, and Phillips who shall rouse this nation to a demand that from
> Greenland's icy mountains to the coral reefs of the Southern seas,
> mob rule shall be put down and equal and exact justice be accorded
> to every citizen, who finds a home within the borders of the land of
> the free and the home of the brave.
> Then no longer will our national hymn be sounding brass and

tinkling cymbal, but every member of this great composite nation will be a living, harmonious illustration of the words, and all can honestly and gladly join in singing:

> My country! 'tis of thee,
> Sweet land of liberty
>   Of thee I sing.
> Land where our fathers died,
> Land of the Pilgrim's pride,
> From every mountain side
>   Freedom does ring.[29]

Her words are eerily prophetic of King's "I Have a Dream" speech during the "March on Washington" in 1963. Both orators, like Thomas Jefferson, realized that effective propaganda appeals to deeply felt values and "self-evident truths." Both drew from the Bible and hymns as well as patriotic songs and literature. Wells's description of "this great composite nation" celebrates the cultural diversity with which the United States continues to struggle.

Following her speech, the audience at Tremont Temple passed resolutions of support and pledged to work "to arouse public sentiment in indignant condemnation of the increasing prevalence of lynch law in our land." The resolutions referred to Wells's "pathetic and unimpassioned recital of the horrible atrocities perpetuated in various parts of the South" and expressed "thanks to this cultivated Christian lady for the important information she has imparted." The audience further declared "our admiration for her intelligent, reasonable and heroic advocacy of the rights of American Citizens and our sympathy with her and her people in the injustice they are suffering." Such a public display of support helped rehabilitate Wells's reputation of respectability after the attack by the Memphis *Commercial*. During the next three days, Joseph Cook continued to demonstrate his approval by accompanying Wells at her lectures at Charles Street A.M.E. Church and at Malden.[30]

The black press also came to the defense of Wells. The *Topeka Weekly Call* criticized the *Commercial* for "wantonly and ruthlessly slandering the good name of Miss Ida B. Wells." It labeled the attack on her as "evidence that boasted southern chivalry is a thing of the past." The *Weekly Call* proclaimed, "Miss Wells is a lady, the peer of any in the land and the *superior of many whose only stock in trade is a white skin.*" Whites, not Wells, were guilty of "inhuman brutality and insensate laciviouness [sic] and lecherousness."[31]

Wells was not only personally outraged by the *Commercial* article but also recognized that besmirching the morality of black women was an important component of the racist ideology used to justify white Southerner's actions. She decided to confront the *Commercial*'s aspersions with legal action. As she began her search for an attorney to file libel charges, Wells remembered her disappointment with the representation of black lawyer T. F. Cassells during her suit against the railroad in 1884. She also felt that the leading attorneys of Memphis—both black and white—were hostile to her. Cassells had not forgiven her for replacing him with a white lawyer, and J. T. Settle continued to resent her criticisms of him in the *Free Speech*.

When Wells realized the need to go outside of Memphis for representation, she thought of Albion Tourgee. In her twenties she had read his book, *Bricks Without Straw*, about Reconstruction and race relations. A white Chicago lawyer, Tourgee was well-known among African Americans for founding a civil rights organization and for confronting racial issues in his "Bystander" column in the Chicago *Inter-Ocean*. Wells had been pleased to receive a congratulatory letter from him about her lynching article in the *New York Age*. She had also distributed information about Tourgee's National Citizens' Rights Association among the black women of New York.[32]

When Wells wrote Tourgee in February, she referred to her dilemma in obtaining representation by Memphis attorneys. He evidently questioned her about it, for she later explained the situation more fully and noted of Settle and Cassells, "Both are sycophants and do not half defend their clients." Wells asked whether Tourgee believed she could succeed in getting "vindication" of her character. Although Tourgee declined to represent Wells because of financial constraints, he did give her advice. He thought that filing her complaint in Chicago would give her a better chance of a fair trial and a *"very large verdict."* To win, however, he noted her need to prove she had not engaged in an affair with Taylor Nightingale, and also to "deny and sustain a denial of impropriety *with any man*."[33]

Most important to Wells, Tourgee recommended another Chicago attorney to handle the case—Ferdinand L. Barnett. A native of Nashville, Barnett was a graduate of Union College of Law in Chicago. He owned the *Chicago Conservator*, practiced law with S. Laing Williams, was active in Republican party affairs, and held a number of government appointments.[34] Although he had been a supporter of the antilynching movement and Wells, he apparently knew little of her personally when he took the case. After Tourgee cautioned him to be sure of the facts before he proceeded, Barnett expressed faith that "the libelous article was entirely without foundation" but assured Tourgee he would "find out before we take any steps in the matter." His conversations with her friends from Memphis and Wells's willingness for him to consult such "enemies" as Cassells, convinced Barnett of her integrity; however, he and Wells eventually decided not to pursue the case because they feared the damage that a loss would cause.[35] Nevertheless, working on the case together proved to be the start of a relationship that would flower into romance.

Perhaps because of the attack on Wells, the black community of Washington, D.C., rallied to support her return engagement at the Metropolitan A.M.E. Church on 3 February. Douglass's promise to Wells that if she came back, he would guarantee a large crowd came true; the church filled with what Wells called "one of the biggest audiences I had ever seen." Douglass's success was partially due to his recruitment of the city's prominent black women to take a role in the event. Douglass presided, aided by Anna J. Cooper, the principal of Washington's black high school, and Lucy Moten, the head of Miner Normal School. Mary Church Terrell, perhaps the city's most prominent black woman, introduced each speaker.[36]

The daughter of Robert Church of Memphis, Terrell had first met Wells while they were both in their twenties. Wells had thought them kindred spirits before Mollie had left to tour Europe and then married Robert Terrell, who became a judge in Washington. Although the two women did share many interests and goals, the friendship never blossomed—but rivalry grew abundantly. Many years later Terrell considered Wells an ingrate and claimed to a friend, "I did everything I could for that lady years ago when she had very few friends." Terrell's words that night in Washington were certainly supportive: "We admire Miss Wells for her undaunted courage, and laud her zeal in so worthy a cause, we encourage her ambition to enlighten the mind and touch the heart by a thrilling . . . recital of the wrongs heaped upon her oppressed people in the South." Terrell continued to extend Wells "a cordial welcome" and to "offer her our hearty support." Nevertheless, the bulk of her introduction was comprised of her own indictment of lynching as well as more fulsome and extensive praise for the other speaker, T. Thomas Fortune.[37]

In her autobiography, Wells did not allude to their rivalry and noted that Terrell "was president of the Bethel Literary and was just beginning her public career" at the time of the introduction. She also noted that Terrell was the daughter of Robert Church, "who had shown himself a friend while I was a teacher in Memphis," which was probably an allusion to his loan to her when she was in California. All in all, Wells was thrilled by the event, writing that it "ended in a blaze of glory and a donation of nearly two hundred dollars to aid the cause."[38]

Wells soon found a use for the purse. While she was in Washington, she learned of a particularly gruesome lynching in Paris, Texas. The *New York Times* provided the grisly details of the death of Henry Smith, who was accused of assaulting a four-year-old girl. After his capture, the train carrying the prisoner was met by a "mass of humanity 10,000 strong." Smith was placed on a scaffold "within view of all beholders" and "tortured for fifty minutes by red-hot irons being thrust against his quivering body." Thinking him dead, the crowd doused him with kerosene and set him on fire. When Smith "wriggled and tossed out" of the fire, he was shoved back in, twice. The *Times* further noted "the vast crowd still looked calmly on" and reported the presence of participants from eight other cities, including Dallas, Fort Worth, and Texarkana.[39]

In her autobiography, Wells elaborated on the lynching. She told of how "the mob fought over the hot ashes for bones, buttons, and teeth for souvenirs" and recounted a mother's calm response to her eight-year-old daughter's words, "I saw them burn the nigger, didn't I Mamma?" (Wells also described the lynching during her Boston speech in mid-February as evidence of the corrupting influence of mob law.) Suspicious of the charges against Smith, she decided to use the money raised at the Washington meeting to investigate the lynching. "I had said in newspaper articles and public speeches," Wells declared, "that we should be in a position to investigate every lynching and get the facts for ourselves." She used the money "to have Pinkerton's [detective agency] send an honest, unprejudiced man from the Chicago office to bring unbiased facts." Although Wells was disappointed with the quality of the report, the Paris lynching launched another phase of her antilynching crusade, and she continued to investigate lynchings for many years.[40]

The visit to the nation's capital also raised Wells's hopes that she might get the attention of the men who governed the nation. In May 1892, President Benjamin Harrison had penned a timid reply to a memorial against lynching from the black Virginia Baptist Convention. Some began to look to Congress. Before Wells's lecture, the *Washington Bee* predicted, "Several members of Congress will be present." Immediately afterwards, the *Christian Banner* noted that Wells "is stiring [sic] up the country" about lynching and reported, "it is possible she will get a hearing before a Congress committee appointed for that purpose." The report probably referred to an unsuccessful attempt by Frederick Douglass and some Washington women to get Wells a hearing before the Senate Judiciary Committee.[41] The inability to get the federal government to move against lynching continued to frustrate the antilynching movement until its death.

By this time Frederick Douglass had become an important ally to Wells. She visited his home on several occasions and won his gratitude by treating his second wife with respect. Following the death of his first wife in 1882, Douglass married a white coworker, Helen Pitts, in 1884. Many African Americans echoed the words of a writer in the *Pittsburgh Weekly News*: "We have no further use for him. His picture hangs in our parlor, we will hang it in the stables."[42] According to Wells, Douglass told her that except for Charlotte Forten Grimke, whose husband Francis had married the Douglasses, Wells was the only black woman to treat Helen "as a hostess has a right to be treated by her guest." "I, too," Wells wrote, "would have preferred that Mr. Douglass had chosen one of the beautiful, charming colored women of my race for his second wife. But he loved Helen Pitts . . . and it was outrageous that they should be crucified by both white and black people for doing so."[43]

Wells's support for the couple is easily understandable because she had also felt the sting of public disapproval by both whites and African Americans. Their union also upheld her contentions about interracial sex: She noted that they sought to "live together in the holy bonds of matrimony rather than in the illicit relationship that was the cause of so many of the lynchings I had noted and protested against."[44] Finally, like Douglass, Wells remained at heart an integrationist. Militancy was often coupled with support for integration in that era. Only in the next century would militancy become synonymous with separatism.

Perhaps the criticism he received made Douglass more sensitive to the plight of Wells. At any rate, their relationship seems to have flowered after the slanders in the *Commercial*. A year later, Wells reminded Douglass, "At that juncture you comforted me with your counsel and gave me your protection."[45] Although sometimes disappointed in the extent of protection and defense provided by Douglass, Wells appears to have reciprocated his support. In several instances, Wells sought to counter rumors critical of Douglass. In February 1893, she wrote Douglass that "many people in Boston asked me as to the truth of the published account that you had given a thousand dollars toward Will Cook's World's Fair Concert Co." After assuring Douglass that to have done so would be all right, Wells continued, "if not, the use of your name is misleading many." Eight months later, the Indianapolis *Freeman* noted, "Ida B. Wells denies that Frederick Douglass is an applicant for political office." Wells lamented, "I think this nagging of Mr. Douglass should cease."[46]

Wells's reference to Will Cook reflects a common interest that drew her closer to Douglass. To celebrate the voyage of Christopher Columbus, a world's fair, the World's Columbian Exposition, opened in Chicago on 12 October 1892. From its beginning, the fair provoked anger and controversy among African Americans. Issues included the fair's omission of black contributions to the United States, its failure to note racist activities, and the holding of a segregated "Negro Day"—at which the celebrated black violinist Will Cook was to perform. According to the *Cleveland Gazette*, it was at Wells's October lecture in Washington that Douglass conceived the idea of "an exposition, by paintings, drawing and written accounts of lynchings, hangings, burnings at the stake, whippings and all southern atrocities" to be held concurrently with the Chicago fair.[47] Wells wholeheartedly agreed, and the result would be a joint pamphlet, but first Wells was sidetracked by an offer too appealing to refuse.

The gruesome nature of the lynching in Paris, Texas, had drawn attention abroad. Among those who reacted was Isabelle Fyvie Mayo, a Scottish author who provided shelter to students from Ceylon and India. She and *Anti-Caste* editor Catherine Impey had been corresponding for some time about racial issues. In March 1893, Mayo invited Impey to Scotland to get to know a fellow opponent of the caste system in India. Having just received news of the Paris lynching, Mayo asked Impey, as Wells told it, if she had learned during her American travels "why the United States of America was burning human beings alive in the nineteenth century as the red Indians were said to have done three hundred years before."[48]

Impey's reply caused Mayo to inform the British public of the outrages. Impey asserted, "The chief difficulty over here is that people *don't know* & therefore *don't care* about the matter." As a remedy, the two women decided to form an "Emancipation" organization to attack all the evils of caste. Although they intended to "declare war against it any & everywhere," they agreed to begin combat against lynching in America, because the "evil is so *glaring, so terrible*." Some asserted that lynching was "purely an American question," but Impey proclaimed, "where evils of such magnitude exist—& helpless people suffer wrongs unspeakable—we can't stand on ceremony." Based on Impey's contacts with Wells in Philadelphia, they decided to ask Wells to come and help them launch their movement.

Mayo agreed to pay Wells's expenses, and Impey drafted the invitation on 19 March 1893.[49]

In her letter Impey declared, "Our English press has been getting hold of some of those Texas lynchings, and our people are beginning to feel that there is something very wrong somewhere." She urged Wells to aid them "to set on foot a living effort to remedy the cruel wrongs now suffered." The letter reached Wells while she was visiting Frederick Douglass. According to Wells's autobiography, Impey noted that Douglass was too old to come and asked Wells to do so or to ask Douglass to suggest someone else. Douglass told Wells, "You go, my child; you are the one to go, for you have a story to tell."[50]

Wells already recognized the potential of drawing the English and Scots into the antilynching movement—as Douglass had once done for the abolitionist movement. Her pamphlet *Southern Horrors* had been republished in London in 1892 as *U.S. Atrocities*. The invitation was "like an open door in a stone wall" to Wells. She had despaired the failure of white northern newspapers to mention her movement; all had ignored her except those in Boston. She hated to interrupt her work on the world's fair pamphlet, and she also had to cancel plans to confront a meeting of southern governors in Richmond that month.[51] Nevertheless, she felt compelled to respond to the call. On 5 April 1893, Wells embarked on a journey across the sea that would catapult her and the antilynching movement to widespread prominence.

10

Taking the Message to the World

"An open door in a stone wall"

B y April 1893, Ida B. Wells had lived through numerous adventures and received widespread publicity in the black press as a martyr in the antilynching cause. In some ways, however, her life until then was but a dress rehearsal for a play performed on the stage of England. Until the voyage across the sea, Wells had been one of many outstanding African American women being celebrated in the black community. Proclaimed the "Year of the Black Woman," 1893 witnessed the publication of *Noted Negro Women* by Monroe Majors and *Women of Distinction* by L. A. Scruggs. The next year Gertrude Mossell published *The Work of the Afro-American Woman*. At the start of 1893, Wells was merely one of the brighter stars in a galaxy of black women activists and artists—all of whom were generally ignored by the white media and public.

Anyone who shone brightly enough to catch the attention of whites quickly ascended to a paramount position among African Americans. White praise brought the most prominence, but even criticism—when it came from contemptible sources—could enhance one's status. In a society permeated with white supremacy, white recognition was an important step in obtaining legitimacy both in and outside the black community. Until 1893 only white newspapers in Boston praised Wells; the slanderous insults from Memphis won Wells far more attention in the black press. In England, however, Wells got glowing reviews from English papers. Such attention made Wells possibly the most discussed individual in the black press—aside from Frederick Douglass. For decades thereafter, few important events happened in black America without Wells's participation.

Aware of the significance of the invitation from Catherine Impey and Isabelle Mayo, Wells saw herself as a modern-day Frederick Douglass sent to enlighten the world about the new evils confronting African Americans. Less than two weeks after receiving Impey's letter, Wells boarded the *Teutonic* for Liverpool, England.[1] On her arrival, Wells went to Impey's home, which Catherine shared with her mother and sister. At the time Impey was forty-seven—about fifteen years older than Wells. A Quaker and vegetarian, Impey was deeply committed to justice and reform, participating in the temperance movement and humanitarian efforts on behalf of the poor. At some point she became especially engrossed in the subject of race and caste. Beginning in 1878, Impey had made four trips to the United States during which she "learned enough to have our sympathies keenly alive & to really feel ourselves *more black than white*," as she wrote Frederick Douglass in 1883. For years she cultivated relationships with most African American leaders, including Frederick Douglass, Booker T. Washington, T. Thomas Fortune, Daniel Payne, Fannie J. Coppin, and William Still. Impey wished to share all she had discovered through her visits and contacts; she told Douglass, "if English people knew one-hundredth of what I have learned . . . America would be *stung* into activity by the indignation that England would give voice to." To spread her ideals, she established *Anti-Caste* in March 1888. Its masthead read "Devoted to the Interests of Coloured Races" until August 1889, when it changed to "Advocates the Brotherhood of Mankind Irrespective of Colour or Descent." Most likely its circulation was limited to those who already agreed with Impey's ideals.[2]

The national day of prayer organized in the wake of the Memphis lynchings piqued Impey's interest in mob justice. In the July 1892 issue of *Anti-Caste*, she noted the prayer meetings of 31 May as well as the appeal to "put an end to the cruel hangings, burnings and other tortures inflicted upon the coloured race in the South." The next issue announced Impey's fourth trip to America. Her arrival in the States coincided with Wells's ouster from Memphis, and their paths crossed in Philadelphia. The union of these two women in the antilynching cause was another unintended consequence of the actions by Memphis whites. The attempt to muzzle Wells continued to backfire on the city.[3]

After Wells recuperated from her voyage, she and Impey journeyed to Mayo's home in Aberdeen in northern Scotland. Almost fifty years old,

Mayo was a successful novelist. Beginning in the late 1870s, she wrote about a book a year—at first under the pen name Edward Garrett. Her writings often appeared as serials in the religious press and stressed morality and self-sacrifice. One reviewer described her characters as "good, kind, wise women, who seem to be sent into the world to put things straight and lift everybody to a higher plane of existence." Mayo devoted her energies to such causes as pacifism, antiracism, and vegetarianism.[4] Mayo, Impey, and Wells shared bonds of idealism that transcended race.

Living with Mayo were three young male boarders—a German music teacher, a student from Ceylon, and the student's relative, Dr. George Ferdinands, who had attended the University of Aberdeen and was then practicing dentistry. According to Wells, all three "threw themselves whole-heartedly into the work of helping to make preparations for our campaign: writing letters, arranging meetings, seeing the press, helping to mail out ten thousand copies of Anti-Caste." A special edition of Anti-Caste announced their plans, and Wells made her first presentation at 3:00 P.M. on 21 April in Mayo's drawing room. She later recalled, "When introduced to speak, I told the same heart-stirring episodes which first gained me the sympathy and good will of my New York friends. The facts I related were enough of themselves to arrest and to hold the attention. They needed no embellishment, no oratory from me."[5]

The Society for the Recognition of the Brotherhood of Man (SRBM) emerged from that meeting. It was formally established on 24 April at the Aberdeen Music Hall, after Wells's first public lecture. Mayo agreed to head the organization, which adopted a three-part declaration. The document denounced any "system of race separation" that cut "despised members of a community" off "from the social, civil, and religious life of their fellow-men"; censured "lynching and other forms of brutal injustice"; and required "its members to refrain from all complicity in the system of Race Separation, whether as individuals, or by co-membership in organizations which tolerate and provide the same."[6] These were bold, uncompromising words that, nevertheless, allowed room for black separatist movements.

Mayo also took Wells to a gathering of about fifteen hundred men in Aberdeen, known as the Pleasant Saturday Evening meeting. Although the women were seated on the platform, no one had asked Wells to speak. During the singing, however, the chairman approached Wells, explaining that their scheduled speaker had canceled and asking her to talk for about fifteen minutes. Wells gladly lectured on "conditions in the South since the Civil War, jim crow laws, ballot-box intimidation, and laws against intermarriage" before describing "the cruel physical atrocities vented upon [her] race." In her enthusiasm, she talked ten minutes longer than allotted, but no one seemed to mind. Afterward, Wells recalled, "Mrs. Mayo was elated, said that it was the best I had done, and urged me to continue along those lines."[7]

On 25 April, Mayo and Wells traveled to nearby Huntly while Impey went to arrange meetings in England. In Huntly they established a branch of the SRBM and left for Edinburgh. Arriving there on Thursday, 27 April, they were the guests of Eliza Wigham, who had aided Frederick Douglass in his antislavery campaign. The next day Wells addressed the Edinburgh Ladies' Emancipation Society in the Bible Society Rooms at St. Andrew Square. Her lecture was reported by the Edinburgh *Scotsman*, which black newspapers reprinted in America. Summarizing her talk, the article recounted that Wells "described how the troubles of the colored people in the south did not end . . . at the close of the Civil War." After quoting a claim that more African Americans were killed during Reconstruction that during the war, Wells declared, "Nor . . . had matters improved in recent years, but on the contrary, the Negroes had been terrorized into abstaining from voting, and the legislation had all tended towards the social degradation and exclusion of the colored people." A discussion of lynch law followed with an account of the Memphis lynchings and her exile from the city. At the close of the meeting, Impey and Mayo asked for and received support for the SRBM.[8]

On Saturday Wells gave two talks—at a "drawing-room meeting" at the Free Church Manse and at the "crowded assembly hall" of the Carubbers' Close Mission. The *Edinburgh Evening Gazette* observed that Wells "has everywhere been heard with deep attention and interest, and has evoked unanimous expressions of sympathy." Apparently resting on Sunday, Wells spoke at the YMCA on Monday.[9] Her hectic schedule became even more exhausting after she spent a sleepless night—seeking answers to a dilemma regarding her hosts.

While in Edinburgh, Mayo received correspondence that profoundly influenced the remainder of Wells's overseas tour. Mayo's male boarder and fellow worker, Dr. Ferdinands, forwarded her a letter he had received from Impey. The son of a British father and Ceylonese mother, Ferdinands had been shocked by Impey's letter. According to Wells, Impey had

> . . . declared that she returned the affection she felt sure he had for her; that she was taking this advance step because she knew he hesi-

tated to do so because he was of a darker race; that she had written to her family acquainting them with the state of affairs, and telling them to prepare to receive him as her husband and that she rejoiced to give this proof to the world of the theories she had approved—the equality of the brotherhood of man.[10]

Mayo's reaction was to demand that Impey withdraw from SRBM and destroy all copies of *Anti-Caste* in which both their names appeared. Wells questioned how a letter known only to the four of them hurt the cause, but Mayo insisted Impey was a "nymphomaniac" and the "type of maiden lady who used such work as an opportunity to meet and make advances to men" and was likely to do so again. Wells was distressed by Mayo's "scorn and withering sarcasm" and called the encounter "the most painful scene in which I ever took part." Wells admired both women and wrote: "To see my two ideals of noble womanhood divided in this way was heartrending. When it was demanded that I choose between them it was indeed a staggering blow."[11]

Wells "spent a sleepless night praying for guidance." Although she could be prudish and judgmental of others, Wells simply could not reject a friend and advocate of justice for African Americans. Wells had the good sense and compassion to see that Impey's actions had been indiscreet but not immoral. She tried to make Mayo understand and reminded her of Impey's "many years of faithful, honorable service." All was to no avail. Wells regretfully remembered, "Mrs. Mayo, stern upright Calvinistic Scotchwoman that she was, could not see anything but that I was hurting the cause, and parted from me in what to her was righteous anger. She cast me into outer darkness with Miss Impey and I never saw her again."[12] Wells later wrote Mayo and "begged her to have a kinder feeling." Instead, Mayo publicly attacked Impey in *Fraternity*, a journal of the SRBM that she and Mr. S. J. Celestine Edwards founded as a replacement for *Anti-Caste*.[13]

With Mayo's defection, Impey first relied on her Quaker ties to make arrangements. On Tuesday, 2 May, Wells addressed an audience in the Society of Friends' Meeting House of Glasgow. The *Scottish Pulpit* described how a large audience listened "with rapt attention" and declared, "Nothing more harrowing has been for years related from a Glasgow platform than the narrative she gave of the cruelties and outrages perpetrated upon her people." A week later she and Impey were in Newcastle, where Wells once again spoke at a Friends' meetinghouse in the afternoon and evening of 9 May. The *Newcastle Leader* noted that the crowd was so large in the evening that two sessions had to be held. It described Wells as "a young lady with a strong American accent, and who speaks with an educated and forceful style." The paper observed that Wells "gave some harrowing instances of the injustice to the members of her race, of their being socially ostracized and frequently lynched in the most barbarous fashion by mobs on mere suspicion." The article closed by quoting Wells as saying that "England has often shown America her duty in the past, and [I have] no doubts that England will do so again."[14]

In preparation for a trip to Birmingham, Impey and Wells mailed announcements and literature about the movement to influential citizens of that city. One recipient, a city councilor, questioned the appropriateness of the proposed meeting in a letter to the *Birmingham Daily Post*. "My time is valuable," he wrote, "my powers are limited and I feel justified in asking what possible practical object can be attained by such meetings?" Not questioning Wells's motives, he noted that she "has come four thousand miles to raise a question which could be dealt with effectually only on the spot." He ended his letter, "I protest against being expected to give my attention to matters of municipal detail in a civilised country at a great distance, any interference with which by English people would be an impertinence."[15]

Wells penned a reply, which appeared on 16 May—the day before her scheduled talk. After reviewing the injustices faced by African Americans, Wells explained why she raised these issues in England.

> The pulpit and press of our own country remains silent on these continued outrages and the voice of my race thus tortured and outraged is stifled or ignored whenever it is lifted in America in demand for justice. It is to the religious and moral sentiment of Great Britain we now turn. These can arouse the public sentiment of Americans so necessary for the enforcement of law. The moral agencies at work in Great Britain did much for the final overthrow of chattel slavery. They can in like manner pray, write, preach, talk and act against civil and industrial slavery; against the hanging, shooting and burning alive of a powerless race.
>
> America cannot and will not ignore the voice of a nation that is her superior in civilization, which makes this demand in the name of justice and humanity. . . . I am in Great Britain today because I believe that the silent indifference with which she has received the charge that human beings are burned alive in Christian (?) Anglo-Saxon communities is born of ignorance of the true situation, and that if she really knew she would make the protest loud and long.[16]

As Martin Luther King, Jr., did so eloquently in his "Letter from the Birmingham Jail" in 1963, Wells appealed to the values and pride of her audience in the English city from which the Alabama city drew its name.

Even before her response, the councilor's letter had an impact. On Sunday the members of the Coventry Road Congregational Church reacted to the letter with a resolution that the growing prevalence of lynch law in America "is in danger of lowering the high and deserved esteem in which the powerful Government of that country is held by the most advanced nations and tends to dim the glory of some of the splendid traditions of the Republic." The congregation then mailed a copy of the resolution to Wells.[17]

Wells believed the controversy brought "a splendid audience" to her talk at the YMCA assembly room in Birmingham on 17 May. Another city councilor presided—and read an alderman's letter of support. The *Daily Post* reported the presence of "several ministers, members of the Society of Friends and ladies and gentlemen interested in local philanthropic work." In "a quiet but effective address," Wells used the disgruntled councilor's letter as a rhetorical foil to penetrate English indifference or reticence. As always, she opened with graphic depiction of the civic and political degradation of African Americans. She demonstrated the irrationality of segregation through such observations as, "A colored man might be employed as a janitor or to ring the bells, but would not dare walk into the same church simply to hear the preacher." Wells highlighted obstacles to a fair hearing in African American's own homeland. Congress and a meeting of southern governors both spurned delegations seeking a hearing on lynching. Wells concluded that "Southerners appeared totally unable to realize the common humanity of the Negroes with themselves, and that is why it was desirable that they should learn the views of Englishmen whom they regarded as their equals and whose good opinion they valued."[18]

A two-page editorial in another paper ruefully predicted Wells might not convince everyone that African Americans "are being inhumanly treated, because there is, unfortunately, a class of people which imagine that no treatment can be too vile for anyone whose lot it is to be born black." The lynching of over a thousand black "men, women, and children" in America exposed the hypocrisy of "citizens of the country which claims to be the most advanced, most elevated, and the most progressive and enlightened in the world." The editorial appealed to a British sense of moral superiority and concluded, "Open slavery was sternly denounced in this country years ago; ought not the covert tyranny now prevailing equally to be censured?"[19]

At a second meeting held in Central Hall, Reverend J. C. Street presided and also referred to the councilor's letter. Admitting too many organizations already existed, Street questioned when had the city ever been "irresponsive to a cry for mercy and an appeal to justice." Even if English people could not change the laws of America, "they would find in the future, as in the past, that moral force was more powerful than swords and cannons." After Wells spoke, the audience passed a resolution of support and established a branch of the SRBM.[20]

Impey and Wells then proceeded to Manchester where they were the guests of the editor of the *Manchester Guardian*. Here again Wells worked her oratorical magic. The *Guardian* proclaimed, "Her quiet, refined manner, her intelligence and earnestness, her avoidance of all oratorical tricks and her dependence upon the simple eloquence of facts make her a powerful and convincing advocate in her plea for equal justice and fair opportunity." The audience was especially shocked to hear the details of the torture of Henry Smith in Paris, Texas. The account of the meeting concluded with another slap at the hypocrisy of the United States:

> Americans have never hesitated to criticise freely the conduct and institutions of other nations, and we do not doubt their criticisms have been useful. They, in turn, may very well profit by international criticism and make an effort to change a condition of affairs that brings upon their country the condemnation of the civilized world.[21]

Word of Wells's tour trickled home to Memphis. The *Appeal-Avalanche* reprinted the *Manchester Guardian* editorial to show that "Ida Wells is continuing her career of triumphant mendacity." The Memphis writer complained that only one side of the question was being heard—that of "the negro adventuress who has so deftly gulled a number of credulous persons in England." He lamented that "Ida Wells does not go into the cause of this horrible chapter of death." Denying that it had ever defended lynch law, the *Appeal-Avalanche* proceeded to blame the victims. Mistakes had been made, it claimed, "only when the negroes have, by their crimes, stirred up the people beyond all restraint." Negroes had the remedy for lynch law: "Let them stop committing rape and midnight murder." The editorial sarcastically concluded:

We have no objection to the organization of a society of credulous Englishmen under the ministrations of a negro adventuress of decidedly shady character, and we suggest that they erect a monument to the negro who was burned at Paris, Texas. We would further suggest that the monument contain the following inscription: "Erected to the memory of the colored martyr, _____ , who ravished a baby and then cut her to pieces with an ax."[22]

Later that month the *Washington Post* published a more temperate critique of Wells's tour in a lengthy account of her Birmingham talks. The *Post* did not attack Wells's personal morality—just the truth of her assertions. Noting her claim that "the American people virtually indorse [sic] mob law by the indifferent manner in which those who participate in it are prosecuted," the *Post* replied, "In this Miss Wells, whose heart is evidently all right, is mistaken in judgment." Instead opposition to lynch law was strong, and Wells was "specific in her misrepresentations" when she declared that only the Chicago *Inter-Ocean* "had the courage to denounce such crimes." The column also implicitly labeled Wells a racist because she "studiously ignores the lynching of white men, and devotes all of her time to denunciation of the lynching of blacks." Without agreeing to lead any movement, the *Post* proclaimed, "let all semblance of race prejudice be thrust to one side, and let there be a united effort against the evil." Sometimes African Americans were expected to display a degree of color blindness not required of whites.[23]

As much as Wells hated criticism—especially attacks on her character—she recognized that such verbal assaults were victories to celebrate. Upon her return to the states in June, Wells proclaimed, "I know that the work has done great good, if by no other sign than the abuse it has brought me from the Memphis Appeal Avalanche, Atlanta (Ga.) Constitution and Macon Telegraph and Washington City Post."[24] She correctly diagnosed that English criticism had made southerners—and indeed many northerners—more defensive. Attacks on Wells indicated how important the South and the nation considered British opinion.

The year 1893 was an especially effective time to bring attention to racism in the United States and the barbarity of lynching. The nation was in a celebratory mood. In the observance of the country's centennial in 1876, North and South had worshiped at the shrine of nationalism, while black rights appeared to be the sacrificial offering in the cause of unity. In 1893 Americans celebrated the "discovery" of America by Christopher Columbus with the world's fair in Chicago, where exhibits trumpeted the great advances in "civilization" and heralded American leadership in the progress of the world. Such claims did not seem extravagant in light of the nation's emergence as the world's foremost economic power.

The sanctification of "civilization" by the Western powers justified the subjugation of so-called backward nations to their rule. Defining civilization as being like them, Europeans and Americans labeled as "primitive" or "barbaric" all countries that did not share their political, technological, and military power. Nevertheless, cherished democratic principles were ignored in the rush to colonize. In such an atmosphere, Wells exploited both British and American sensitivities. The English alleviated lingering guilt over their mistreatment of colonials by focusing on American atrocities. On the other hand, the barbarity of mob rule exposed the hypocrisy of American celebrations of superiority. White Americans hated for anything to blemish the image so carefully polished for display to the world. Although the United States was indeed on the road to world dominance, its people still felt that their nation had not won proper respect from the European powers. America was falling behind in the acquisition of colonies, which seemed to be the yardstick to measure national greatness. Therefore Americans especially desired affirmation by the English, who had established a great colonial empire and with whom Americans claimed racial kinship.

To succeed in England, Wells needed meetings with prominent groups and publicity in the British press. London was the ideal place to get both, as many organizations held annual meetings there in May. Wells described the setting, "Parliament is in session, the society season is at its best, and everyone is in town." Several London journals announced her impending arrival. Unfortunately, as Wells and Impey headed toward London, a change occurred that dramatically diminished the momentum of the tour. At every stop, Mayo had protested Impey's organizing activities for the SRBM. Because Mayo was the major financial backer of both the organization and tour, Wells finally acquiesced to demands to go to London without Impey.[25]

Mayo sent a "German maiden lady," described by Wells as "a fine companion and chaperon but . . . not well enough known to secure entrance for me at [the] important meetings." Without contacts, they scanned the papers for news of influential group gatherings. Only the Women's Christian Temperance Union (WCTU) granted Wells an audience. The group's British president, Lady Henry Somerset, placed Wells on her left on the platform and invited Wells to speak on temperance.

Wells replied that "she had only one excuse for being before the British public, and that was to protest against 'lynch law.'" Although Wells was allotted only a few minutes to speak, after her speech Somerset's group adopted an antilynching resolution.[26]

Mayo fulfilled her promise to pay tour expenses, but her withdrawal and insistence on the German chaperone created some doubts about Wells. Without a prominent advocate by her side, Wells could not solicit invitations like those she had received in other towns. She ruefully noted, "My duty was to tell the story wherever an opening had been made, so when the time came for no more meetings it was the appropriate time for me to return." Deciding to sail home from Southampton, Wells rejoined Impey and headed for the coast. While waiting for the ship, the two friends undoubtedly discussed the successes and failures of the tour. According to Wells, Impey "blamed herself bitterly for the sudden ending of what had promised so well."[27]

Impey was able, however, to arrange one last audience in Southampton. She took Wells to the local cathedral to meet Canon Wilberforce, and Wells was "especially glad to meet" the grandson of a "great antislavery agitator." During their half-hour visit, Wilberforce expressed regret that there was no time to organize a meeting in his city. When Wells left, he gave her an autographed photograph of himself, wished her a "safe journey across the water," and restored some of her faith in the clergy.[28]

Wells's spirit was also refreshed by her voyage, on which there "were few if any white Americans on board." Instead of confronting hostility, Wells met a party of fifteen young Englishmen on their way to the world's fair. Two of them were Quakers and had heard of Wells's activities. She later remembered, "They were as courteous and attentive to me as if my skin had been of the fairest." The "delightful experience" continued as they accompanied her "practically all the way to Chicago" and "seemed to take great pleasure in shocking the onlookers by their courteous and respectful attention." Wells declared, "I enjoyed it hugely, because it was the first time I had met any of the members of the white race who saw no reason why they should not extend to me the courtesy they would have offered to any lady of their own race."[29] Being treated like a "lady" was reassuring after the assaults on her respectability and character.

White acceptance—except by bigots—provided a powerful boost to status among the black elite; therefore, the British tour enhanced Wells's image in the black press for most of 1893. As soon as Wells announced Impey's invitation, praise by editors began. The Detroit *Plaindealer* called her "the most aggressive worker in that direction" and expressed confidence that "her peculiar mission there ought to raise up many friends for the oppressed."[30] As news of the Scottish and English response reached the states, the chorus of commendation increased. The *Cleveland Gazette* proclaimed that Wells "is making the welkin ring with an eloquence which carries conviction."[31] After southern white newspapers began to criticize Wells, the black press leapt to her defense. The St. Paul *Appeal* described the motivation for the attacks on Wells:

> They seem to think that by doing so they disprove or destroy the effect of the statements she makes. But, in fact, Miss Wells does not give those statements on her own authority, but proves them by the Southern newspapers themselves. She is a respectable and talented lady, but that has little to do with the truth of her statements, as she proves her statements by Southern newspapers. Her witnesses are Governor Hogg, Fishback and Tillman and the official publications of the Southern states.[32]

After reprinting the *Appeal* editorial, the *Parsons Weekly Blade* gave its own assessment of the impact of the efforts by the southern press. "The Southern journals who have such little regard for one of the most noble ladies that ever lived," the paper predicted, "may kick and sweat until they have killed their fool selves and her truthful statements concerning race prejudice in the South will ever live to make known to the world the cussedness of Southern prejudice and mob law." Most black editors seemed to think that the attacks on Wells would backfire on the white press. Many agreed with the Huntsville, Alabama *Gazette* when it proclaimed that Wells "has returned home and not empty handed either."[33]

Because the overseas tour had convinced Wells that world opinion could be a potent force in the fight against lynching, she returned with a renewed commitment to use the world's fair as a platform for her message. Twenty-seven million people from all over the world attended the five-month celebration, which in many ways was a paean to white males. Struggling to redefine masculinity when economic and cultural changes threatened previous sources of male power, middle-class white men in the late nineteenth century began to link racial domination with manhood. The Columbian Exposition provided physical representations of the boasted cultural, political, and economic superiority of white men. The Court of Honor housed six large buildings with white Italian classical facades. Their architectural styles and contents gave the label the "White City" a dual meaning. All six venerated the technological and economic dominance of the Western world. Located on the fringes of the fair, the midway exhibits seemed designed to highlight the "backwardness" of the rest of the world with exotic depictions of the peasant peoples of Africa, Asia, the Middle East, and the Pacific. Visiting journalist Marian Shaw noted, "These people are they who, in the mad race of nations for power and pelf, seem to have been left far behind, and, compared with the nations of today, are like untutored children."[34]

Given the era's fascination with the concepts of civilization and barbarism, Wells shrewdly made the dichotomy an integral part of her attack on lynching. There could hardly be a better site to challenge white Americans' boasted superiority than the Columbian Exposition. Wells saw ironic possibilities in forcing visitors, who came to celebrate the progress of white men, to confront the blood-lust of white lynch mobs. At the same time she and other black leaders realized that the near exclusion of African American cultural and economic contributions from exhibits was not merely an oversight. White Americans wanted nothing to detract from their shrine to Anglo-Saxon superiority. Both black achievement and white denial of opportunity to African Americans contradicted the themes of the gleaming "White City."

From the fair's inception, black leaders had fought unsuccessfully to be included—symbolically and physically. They were excluded from both the World's Columbian Exposition Commission and the Board of Lady Managers.[35] In reply to an attempt by the black women of Chicago for representation, the secretary of the Board of Lady Managers, Susan G. Cooke, blamed the failure to appoint a black woman on "dissensions among the colored people." Actually, a division of thought did exist in the black community. The disagreement was related to another contention by Cooke: "No color line is drawn, consequently there is no suggestion of superiority; [black women] are placed upon a basis of equality."[36]

Then, as later, whites invoked the ideal of "color blindness" to justify the exclusion of African Americans. In regard to the fair, Frederick Douglass noted, "We are as usual overlooked in quarters where we should have expected consideration and when we ask for what in all fairness is our due we are taunted with drawing the color line." Black leaders struggled with whether to ask for separate exhibits or not. Some believed that without such exhibits African Americans' contributions would be excluded or, if merged into general exhibits without ascription, overlooked. On the other hand, many felt separate exhibits would be demeaning and to ask for them would be "abandoning the very principle for which we have been contending in the newspapers and in the Courts."[37] Nevertheless, all agreed that with or without separation, African Americans deserved representation.

In June 1892, an Ohio representative in Congress decried the lack of black representation and unsuccessfully proposed an $100,000 appropriation for an exhibit to show what African Americans are "accomplishing under freedom." A southern congressman retorted that any such exhibit should show "what progress the colored race has made from the period since they come [sic] in contact with the white race. They made none before." African Americans feared the southern view would prevail. Their alarm escalated as the shape of the fair became clearer between its dedication in October 1892 and its official opening the following April. Some exhibits, such as the reproduction of antebellum plantation scenes, were "intended to be a standing insult to the present condition of the race."[38] The fair contained no hint of the violence and repression African Americans confronted.

After Wells's February 1893 speech in the Metropolitan Church of Washington, D.C., ideas for a response coalesced into a call for a pamphlet to make the truth known. Frederick Douglass quickly gave his support to a proposal by Frederick J. Loudin to bring "the whole panorama of the lawless, cruel and barbarous persecution to which our people are subjected to the attention of the civilized world at Chicago."[39] Loudin and Douglass joined with Wells to issue a circular letter soliciting donations for the production of "a carefully prepared pamphlet, setting forth the past and present condition of our people and their relation to American civilization, [to] be printed in English, French, German and Spanish." The three calculated the costs would be about five thousand dollars and subscribed a hundred, fifty, and twenty-five dollars respectively. The black press widely published the letter and debated the merits of the idea. In mid-April the *Cleveland Gazette* noted that Wells's departure for England "leaves the bulk of the work to be done by Messrs. Douglass and Loudin" and urged its completion. The *Washington Bee*, however, sarcastically noted Wells's work on the pamphlet and claimed she had "demonstrated her great love and interest in the negro race, by throwing up the great (?) and important (?) work in which she was engaged to accept a position that will be of greater personal benefit to her."[40]

During Wells's absence, the pamphlet elicited more debate than donations. One journalist criticized the donation campaign as bringing "a matter of high race importance down to the level of a washer-woman's church collection." The *Washington Bee* proclaimed, "The race have [sic] too much in pamphlets and too little in their pockets" and agreed with the *Savannah Tribune* that a boycott of the fair made more sense than attending and giving out pamphlets. Wells's return, however, reinvigorated the pamphlet movement. Its production became her highest priority.[41] The Indianapolis *Freeman* noted,

> Her labors ended, Miss Wells turned her face homeward, and like a comet, if not of 'tremendous size' of great velocity, she sped through New York, turned her back upon the Age office and its poetic and captivating monarch, and hastened to Chicago, loudly proclaiming her intention to get out that 'pamphlet.'[42]

Douglass reported a lack of success in fund-raising and suggested abandoning the project. Fresh from her English success, Wells refused to surrender. She insisted money could be raised both at the fair and in black churches. Leaving New York and T. Thomas Fortune behind, Wells made Chicago her home base to launch her campaign, while remaining a correspondent for the *Age*.[43]

Wells used her column in the *Age* to solicit donations but was disappointed with the results. "Yet of all our wealthy educated men and women . . . who should be interested in the vindication of the race, the only response to that appeal [in the *Age*] I yet received," she wrote, "has come from a poor uneducated hard working farmer." A circular letter to black newspapers yielded little more, and Wells turned to church meetings without much more success.[44] Wells reported $275.13 in hand as of 22 July. Far short of the estimated five thousand, she and Douglass decided to do only one pamphlet in English, but with prefaces in French and German. In late August at a meeting at St. Stevens Church, Mary Church Terrell presided as the two once again made their pitch and raised another $34.59. About a week later, the pamphlet went to the printers.[45]

The pamphlet campaign thrust Wells back into the maelstrom of controversy that swirled around her during her entire adult life. The *American Citizen* called Wells anxious "to exhibit the sores and wounds of the Negro race" and predicted that her efforts would arouse whites "to attack upon a helpless and defenseless people in many ways." Many papers forecast that the pamphlet would never be issued or not before the fair's end. When it went to the printers, the *Freeman* chastised Wells for using a white printer, and the *American Citizen* grumbled, "It remains to be seen what good it will do." Both critics and supporters agreed the pamphlet was primarily the product of Wells's endeavors.[46]

Although Wells was chief architect, she had several collaborators in the writing of the eighty-one-page *The Reason Why the Colored American Is Not in the World's Columbian Exposition*. Frederick Douglass wrote the introductory chapter and two chapters on "Class Legislation" and "The Convict Lease System." Wells wrote chapter four, "Lynch Law"; Garland Penn contributed chapter five, "The Progress of the Afro-American Since Emancipation"; and Ferdinand L. Barnett penned the final chapter, which outlined the efforts of African Americans to get representation at the Exposition. Wells's chapter reiterated her antilynching arguments and highlighted two lynchings that had occurred during the summer of 1893. She also reprinted a postcard that a proud lynching committee had sent to Albion Tourgee with a picture of their victim, C. J. Miller. Tourgee had supplied encouragement as well as the postcard, and Wells sent him an inscribed copy of the pamphlet in appreciation.[47]

To dispense the pamphlets, Wells daily manned a desk at the Haitian Building, which that nation's government had asked Douglass to supervise. Fund-raising difficulties, however, had an impact on the effectiveness of the pamphlet. Its late printing meant that less than two months remained to distribute it. Although twenty thousand copies were printed, Wells apparently could hand out only about half before the fair's closing. At the back of the pamphlet she gave her address in Chicago with a promise to send a copy to all who enclosed three cents postage.[48]

A controversial issue strained the collaboration of Wells and Douglass; they disagreed on the desirability of a "Colored Jubilee Day" set aside for African Americans at the Exposition. The movement for the day began at about the same time as the pamphlet campaign. Although many papers linked the two—Douglass supported both—Wells was vehemently opposed from the beginning. The *Freeman* congratulated Wells for her stand and used her opposition to undermine Douglass's support. Unlike some editorialists, Wells never named Douglass in her attacks on "Jubilee Day," which she described as "lacking in dignity, self-respect and judgment, to say nothing of good taste."[49] Her words, however, offended Willetta Johnson, a Boston resident and secretary of the "Colored Jubilee Day" committee, who was angry that Wells "should attack this committee," comprised of "the people of Massachusetts who have rallied round and supported her in her hour of sorrow and need."[50]

Wells was not ungrateful but was offended by the image of the day and the people who would attend. In a widely published editorial in July, she decried the promise of free watermelons and called the day a scheme to enrich the railroads and the world's fair people. Her words reflect the class bias of the black elite.

> The self-respect of the race is sold for a mess of pottage and the spectacle of the class of our people which will come on that excursion roaming around the grounds munching watermelons, will do more to lower the race in the estimation of the world than anything else. The sight of the horde that would be attracted there by the dazzling prospect of plenty of free watermelons to eat, will give our enemies all the illustration they wish as excuse for not treating the Afro-American with the equality of other citizens.[51]

Although Wells often called for race unity, she joined many of the elite in distinguishing herself from poor, unsophisticated blacks and resented behavior that reinforced stereotypes. More affluent, refined African Americans were acutely aware that the white public usually judged the whole race by the actions of the black poor or criminal classes. The simultaneous pulls of race unity and class identity often created ambivalence in Wells and others.

Despite the criticism, "Colored American Day" took place on 25 August and featured black musicians and entertainers as well as a speech by Frederick Douglass. Glowing press reports of the event caused Wells to rethink her position. Wells later noted that Douglass had "persevered with his plans without any aid whatever from us hotheads and produced a program that was reported from one end of the county to the other." After reading of Douglass's speech, Wells claimed, "I was so swelled with pride over his masterly presentation of our case that I went straight out to the fair and begged his pardon for presuming in my youth and inexperience to criticize him." Very rarely did Wells admit error and apologize. Her willingness to do so indicates her high regard for the "grand old man," as she called Douglass.[52]

A number of conventions, congresses, and conferences took place during the fair, and Wells participated in several. In July she and Douglass spoke before a Congress of Colored People, at which Wells was elected vice president of the sponsoring National Colored People's Protective Association. In early September, she joined Booker T. Washington, American Federation of Labor officials, and white reformers Henry Demerest Lloyd and Henry George as speakers at the Labor Congress. In her address

Wells explained southern opposition to black migration by noting that "the black man is the wealth-producing factor of the South."[53]

The Columbian Exposition provided Wells with another platform for her protest and antilynching campaign—another "open door in a stone wall." Her involvement also caused her to relocate her home base to Chicago and furthered her relationship with Ferdinand Barnett, who would become her husband in June 1895. For the next eighteen months, however, Wells stayed on the road and in the middle of controversy.

11

∞∞∞

The Continued Crusade

"Not myself nor my reputation,
but the life of my people"

∞∞∞

The World's Columbian Exposition drew Ida B. Wells to Chicago in 1893, and the lure of the Windy City convinced her to relocate. Chicago was becoming a northern mecca for black southerners, who were rapidly losing basic rights in the South. After the Civil War, each decade brought increasing numbers of African Americans, and between 1880 and 1900 the city's black population soared from 6,480 to 30,150. The largest segment of that population (41.2 percent) came from the upper southern states—mainly Tennessee and Kentucky. Those who migrated tended to be more literate, urban, and militant than those who remained in the South. For such migrants a major attraction was an Illinois civil rights law that guaranteed equal access to all public accommodations.[1] By 1893 a flourishing black middle class enjoyed a rich social and cultural life. To enter that group, Wells eagerly accepted an offer to join the *Chicago Conservator*, which was edited by R. P. Bird and owned by Ferdinand Barnett.

Wherever Wells moved, controversy was her companion. Her affiliation with the *Conservator* provoked the most vicious attack ever launched against her by a black editor. C. H. J. Taylor of the Kansas City *American Citizen*, who resented Wells's getting credit for the antilynching crusade, which he felt he deserved, wrote an 1893 editorial that reached a new level of nastiness.

We are sorry for the *Conservator*. It was once a clean paper, worthy of entering any home. Surely it can not be that the 'crazy addition' from Memphis has ruined it. We never fight women and children, but, really, Brother Bird, you had better put a muzzle on that animal from Memphis. We are onto her dirty, sneaking tricks. If we get after her we will make her wish her mother had changed her mind ten months before she was born.[2]

Such an attack naturally elicited support for Wells from other editors, and some wanted Taylor punished. The *Washington Bee* reprinted an editorial that labeled the attack as "too vile to be reproduced in a decent newspaper." In self-defense Taylor blamed the words on a subordinate. By mid-January, Wells thanked "her newspaper brothers, generally, for the chivalric defense made against the 'office boy' of the *American Citizen*."[3]

Wells wanted more than rebukes for Taylor; she wanted revenge. She wrote to the one man with the power to exact it: Frederick Douglass. After quoting the entire editorial, Wells cried, "In my distress, wounded to the quick and utterly unable to help myself, I turn to you." She asked Douglass to use his influence to quash Taylor's political aspirations and "teach him a lesson he will not forget." Douglass had played a key role in establishing Wells's legitimacy after her expulsion from Memphis. By 1894, however, he was becoming a little less enthusiastic in his support and failed to take action against Taylor.[4] Constant controversy continued to erode Wells's credibility.

Once again an English invitation rescued her reputation, but not without another dose of controversy. In September 1893, Isabelle Mayo forwarded to Wells a request for American newspapers from Celestine S. J. Edwards, who edited *Fraternity*, the organ of the Society for the Recognition of the Brotherhood of Man (SRBM). Mayo also informed Wells that Edwards had suggested a second tour by her, beginning in February. After assuring Wells that all expenses would be paid and that she would "not be asked to work for absolutely nothing," Mayo asserted that "Mr. Edwards' arrangements would do you justice,—and you would work *unblighted*!!"[5]

Wells requested two pounds per week in addition to her expenses, and the executive council of the SRBM accepted her terms. When a glitch delayed the appropriation of money for her passage, Wells borrowed twenty-five dollars from Frederick Douglass toward her passage. Then, however, the split between Mayo and Catherine Impey once again complicated matters. Wells was called on to decide between her duty to a friend and to the cause. To ensure that the tour was "unblighted," Mayo wanted Wells to repudiate Impey publicly. Refusing to do so, Wells almost did not go to England, until Edwards assured her that the council desired only her silence on the dispute. However, once Wells arrived in Liverpool on Friday, 9 March, Mayo learned of the council's decision and withdrew her financial support. Meanwhile, Edwards had become very sick and could not take care of arrangements. Thus Wells found herself in England without adequate funds or support.[6]

Nevertheless, she gave her first address two days after her arrival — to an audience of thirteen hundred at Pembroke Chapel (Baptist) in Liverpool. In his introduction, the Reverend Charles F. Aked told of her ouster from Memphis, and she was greeted by what a reporter called "most un-Sabbatarian applause." The journalist noted, "She is slight of build, distinctly good-looking, speaks fluently and with grace, and tells her story with a simple directness which is most affective." The report also declared, "She is accredited to the friends of progress by the Hon. Frederick Douglas [sic]."[7]

Reverend Aked and his wife befriended Wells when she told them of her difficulties. She became their house guest and, at Aked's suggestion, wrote Douglass for a letter of recommendation. Enclosing a clipping of the article about her talk, she told Douglass of the circumstances and noted, "I am compelled to depend upon myself somewhat." Apparently the cumulative effects of the attacks on Wells had eroded the black leader's confidence. He wrote a very guarded letter to Aked and a brief, suspicious one to Wells. He resented the use of his name by the *Liverpool Daily Post* and doubted Wells's version of events. Asking her for more details about who had invited her to England, he closed by saying, "I am ready to hold up your hands, and want to do so, but I wish to do so intelligently and truthfully."[8]

Wells was devastated. "With all the discouragements I have received and the time and money I have sacrificed to the work," she wrote, "I have never felt so like giving up as since I received your very cool and cautious letter this morning, with its tone of distrust and its inference that I have not dealt truthfully with you." She filled eight pages with a detailed explanation of events and a promise to pay back the twenty-five dollars she borrowed.[9] Wells was painfully aware that a defection by Douglass would irreparably cripple her tenuous claims to legitimacy and respectability. As an unmarried woman, she was vulnerable to slander because of her frank and shocking discussions of female sexuality.

Wells was relieved to receive a reassuring letter from Douglass, who apparently chided her for the tone of her letter and the mention of his loan. She was encouraged enough on 6 May to ask for stronger letters of support and to inform him that she needed an extension on the loan. Once again multiple duties plagued her. Her sisters in California needed money for school, and Wells sent the funds she had earmarked for Douglass. In a second letter on 10 May, Wells added urgency to her pleas. She informed Douglass of a proposed meeting at the Lord Mayor of London's house "to which members of Parliament and other influential persons would be invited," for which she needed letters of recommendation from "persons of influence in America." That same day she wrote to Senator William B. Chandler, who had spoken against lynching during a congressional session in February. Reflecting her new confidence in Douglass's support, Wells referred Chandler to him as a reference in her request for a letter of support from the senator.[10]

Douglass was reassured not only by Wells's letters of explanation but also by letters from others. Aked wrote him that Wells was "a charming woman" and that "to have her in the house and talk with her has been an education." Even more important was a letter from a dear English friend, Ellen Richardson, who had arranged the purchase of Douglass's freedom in 1846. After Wells had called on her, Richardson wrote "you have done well to send her here" and described Wells as "agreeable in her manner— earnest in her speech." On 22 May Douglass wrote Aked; John Clifford, a Baptist minister; and Richard A. Armstrong, a Unitarian clergyman who had proposed an antilynching resolution at the denomination's conference. In all three letters Douglass strongly endorsed Wells, telling Armstrong, "I regard Miss Wells as a brave and truthful woman, devoted to the cause of her outrageed [sic] and persecuted people."[11]

At first English doubts about Wells arose from the fact she was largely unknown and apparently without sponsorship. Later, however, her fame rather than her obscurity caused controversy. In some ways the partial defection of the SRBM freed Wells to make other contacts and solicit other sponsors.[12] In less than five months she delivered more than a hundred lectures and was the subject of numerous interviews. Over fifty accounts of her talks and activities filled British newspapers, most of which praised Wells profusely and offered support. Her voice also reverberated across the sea. In the United States, both the *Conservator* and the *New York Age* frequently published long letters from Wells. Her longest accounts went to the white-owned Chicago *Inter-Ocean*, which was paying Wells to write of her experiences. The London correspondent to the *New York Times* frequently mentioned her activities. Such attention made Wells a formidable foe. Her perceived power led the objects of her scorn to seek to limit her effectiveness. Her major opponents included defenders of the South and defenders of Frances Willard, the American president of the Women's Christian Temperance Union (WCTU), who was widely admired in both America and the British Isles.

On her first English tour, Wells had met Willard, who was the guest of Lady Henry (Isabel) Somerset for a two-year tour to rally British support for the temperance movement. Years earlier Willard had toured the southern United States and given an interview published in October 1890 by the *New York Voice*. In it Willard expressed pity for southerners and noted, "The colored race multiplies like the locusts of Egypt. The grog-shop is its center of power." She also declared, "'Better whiskey and more of it' has been the rallying cry of great dark-faced mobs in the Southern localities where local option was snowed under by the colored vote." The temperance leader seemed to condone lynching and to accept the usual charge of black bestiality, when she declared, "The safety of women, of children, of the home is menaced in a thousand localities at this moment, so men dare not go beyond the sight of their own roof-tree."[13]

Willard's words were widely quoted among African Americans. About six months after the interview, Wells remarked, "Miss Willard's statements possess the small pro rata of truth of all such sweeping statements." Writing for a temperance symposium in the *A.M.E. Church Review*, Wells rejected Willard's claim of the black man's menace to white society. "In his wildest moments he seldom molests others than his own," she wrote, "and this article is a protest against such wholesale self-injury." To Wells the dangers of black intemperance were not to whites but to the black community, which needed all available intellectual and financial resources for advancement. She asserted, "It is like playing with fire to take that in the mouth which steals away the brains." Buying whiskey wasted precious resources and gave "judges and juries the excuse for filling the convict camps of Georgia alone with fifteen hundred Negroes." Money spent on alcohol produced "enormous profits flowing into Anglo-Saxon coffers," and African Americans who entered "the nefarious traffic" in whiskey were "sacrificing to the Moloch of intemperance hundreds of our men."[14]

Although many black leaders recognized the negative influence of alcohol on African American advancement, some also realized that a thread of racism ran through organized temperance and prohibition movements. Prohibitionist scare tactics included horrifying accounts of the effect of "demon rum" on the "Negro brute." Often WCTU leaders followed the pattern of many white-dominated reform movements of subordinating issues of racial justice to win southern support for their causes. Prior to Wells's English trip, black newspapers criticized the WCTU for drawing the color line in meetings. The *Parsons Weekly Blade* pronounced, "Shame on a religious union that would prove itself a mockery to Christianity."[15]

Because of the deep importance of religion in her own life, Wells found racism in religion especially abhorrent. According to the Church of Christ, all divisions among Christians were mistakes. Belonging to a church that embraced all denominations reinforced her beliefs in the unity of believers regardless of race. She often expressed her profound disappointment in white churches' failures to attack the evils of prejudice and discrimination and was especially appalled when religious leaders or church bodies actually embraced segregation or defended racism. Just before leaving for England in 1893, Wells wrote, "These Christian bodies have always cringed, with few exceptions, to this spirit [of segregation or exclusion], and nourished in the church, the viper which secular organizations like the G. A. R., repudiate and cast out."[16] In her British speeches, Wells continued her condemnation of white Christian leaders, often accusing them of condoning lynching.

Because both Wells and Willard were American women reformers touring Great Britain, audience members in 1893 had asked Wells about the temperance leader's position on lynching. Remembering the *Voice* interview, Wells answered that Willard excused lynching as a response to black rapists. Asked similar questions about the famous American evangelist Dwight L. Moody, Wells related his acquiescence to segregation at religious services in the South. She claimed to have named neither person in her general condemnations of white American Christians' failure to support black rights. "But," she explained, "when someone in the audience would ask the pointed question naming these two persons, there seemed nothing else for me to do but to tell the truth as I knew it."[17]

As Wells prepared to return to England in 1894, she recalled encountering skepticism regarding her comments on Willard, who was greatly revered by the British public. With Willard still touring England, Wells knew more questions were likely and, therefore, brought a copy of Willard's interview in the *Voice* on her return trip. Not only did Wells quote from the interview but she also gave it to the SRBM's *Fraternity* for publication with the comment, "here we have Miss Willard's words in full, condoning fraud, violence, murder, at the ballot box; raping, shooting, hanging and burning." The article also noted that Frederick Douglass had denounced Willard's comments as false. Although warned that Lady Somerset "would instantly resent what might seem to be an attack on her," Wells refused to back down.[18]

Somerset was furious. In a letter to Frederick Douglass, she lambasted Wells for "vituperation, bitterness, and unfairness" and claimed "already there is a growing feeling of distrust in the judgment and methods of her presentations." Somerset also published an interview with Willard in the 20 May edition of the *Westminister Gazette*. In the introduction Somerset called Wells's charges against Willard the result of an "exaggeration of mind" and "race hatred," which Somerset claimed was reflected in Wells's earlier comment: "I tell you if I have any taint to be ashamed of at all it is the taint of white blood." In response to questions by Somerset, Willard insisted that her words in the *Voice* article related to the "colored vote," not "what our paper at home calls southern outrages." She described her previous support of Wells and countered claims of white Christian indifference by citing one antilynching resolution and proclaiming, "I know that the concurrent opinion of all good people North and South, white and black, is practically united against the taking of any human life without due process of law." Nevertheless, Willard admitted and reiterated her claims of the black menace to women and children before asserting that "no crime however heinous can by any possibility excuse the commission of any act of cruelty or the taking of any human life without due course of law." The interview closed with Willard's assertion, "I think that British justice may be trusted to guard my reputation."[19]

Wells was exceptionally adroit in using attacks against her character or credibility to further her cause. In a reply in the next day's paper, Wells impugned the women's motives as "not to determine how best they may help the Negro who is being hanged, shot and buried, but 'to guard Miss Willard's reputation.'" In contrast Wells noted, "With me it is not myself nor my reputation, but the life of my people which is at stake." She once again borrowed credibility from Douglass by referring to his words on Willard's 1890 interview. Most significantly, Wells utilized Willard to prove her original point, noting that Willard "is no better or worse than the great bulk of white Americans on the Negro question," all of whom were afraid to speak out. "It is only British public opinion which will move them," she declared.[20]

Wells recognized white reformers' willingness to subordinate black rights for southern support. Only direct confrontation and public exposure could prevent many from evading questions of racial justice. The power of Wells's words caused some to criticize Willard as "a temporizer when it comes to questions relating to Afro-Americans." The temperance leader felt Wells was being unfair because following Wells's criticisms during her first British tour, Willard had denounced lynching for the first time at the 1893 national WCTU convention. In her presidential address, she spoke of "our duty to the colored people" at a time when "the antagonism between them and the white race have [sic] seemed more vivid than at any previous time, and lurid vengeance has devoured the devourers of women and children." Wells, however, realized that support for the rape myth by those who opposed lynching legitimized the justifications of lynchers.[21]

An ideological chasm that could not be bridged separated the two women, and they continued to snipe at each other for years. Willard undermined the fundamental issue in Wells's campaign to prove that lynching sought to maintain white supremacy rather than to deter rape. On the other hand, Wells jeopardized Willard's use of female purity as a basis for public action. In an era that considered women's proper sphere to be the home, early women reformers stressed women's "special talents" as guardians of morality to justify their entrance into political debates. Wells undermined white women's claims to moral superiority by insisting some willingly engaged in illicit activities with black men. The amazing effectiveness of Wells is evident in her ability to threaten Willard's reputation. After all, the black antilynching campaigner flouted convention by publicly discussing sex, while the white temperance leader's issue was eminently respectable.[22]

Of course, Wells did not remain unscathed by her criticisms of American religious leaders. The *Christian Commonwealth* called it "simply absurd to suppose the Christians of America are indifferent to the reign of lynch law" and warned that Wells would "kill her cause by imprudent speeches." Even a strong Wells supporter wrote Douglass, "We think she has done very well—but we feel that she will suffer from her courage in showing how white religious people who go South are deceived & led to betray the cause of justice." Wells's criticisms of Willard in her letters to the Chicago *Inter-Ocean* led that paper to declare, "Miss Wells has the weakness of most agitators who lose sight of everything else but the cause they advocate, and misunderstand those not willing to blindly follow them." On the other hand, the paper pointed out that the same was true of Willard.[23] Undoubtedly, Wells did subordinate other issues of class, gender, and poli-

tics to those of race, but most white reformers subordinated race to everything else.

The debate with Willard allowed Wells to illustrate the damage done
to the antilynching cause by religious and reform leaders. Even more dramatically, Wells utilized criticism by defenders of the South to damn them
by their own words. The flurry of attention given by the white American
press to her first overseas crusade became a blizzard when Wells returned
to England. The earliest American accounts occurred in articles by the
London correspondent to the *New York Times*, who tended to discredit
Wells by distorting her words into an exaggerated parody of her message. In
April he charged Wells with making "sensational charges" in a "lurid two-
column interview" and claimed that Wells asserted that "in all these cases
where negroes are summarily punished for outrages on white women, it is
the women themselves who have tempted the blacks." Noting the "inherent meddlesomeness" of the English, he opined that the "more salacious
she can make her revelations," the more effective she would be. Coverage
in the *New York Times* continued in this vein, and the paper summarized
her motives in August "to have been an income rather than an outcome."[24]

Such tactics were hard to refute, but the southern press offered a more
inviting target for Wells. Once again Memphis papers sought to discredit
the message by slandering the messenger. In two heavy-handed articles on
26 May, the Memphis *Daily Commercial* strung together an amazing number of unflattering epithets for Wells: notorious negro courtesan, disreputable colored woman, half-cultured hater of all things Southern, saddle-
colored Sapphira, intriguing adventuress, strumpet, malicious wanton,
paramour to both J. L. Fleming and Taylor Nightingale, unimportant adventuress, and infamous slanderer and traducer. The paper also charged
that "rumors had been rife of her unchastity" in Holly Springs. The next
month the *Appeal-Avalanche* claimed: "She has no social standing here
among respectable colored people." It characterized her as a con artist out
to make a fortune, after which "perhaps she will buy some broken down
English roué for husband."[25]

Ironically, by trying to cast Wells as without social standing in the black
community, the Memphis papers undermined southern white assertions of
black degradation. Wells was a living contradiction to their lies; the English
were astonished by the cultured demeanor of this daughter of former
slaves. The *Liverpool Daily Post* called her "a distinguished lady" who was
"adorned by every grace of womanhood." Richard Armstrong noted that
Wells spoke "with singular refinement, dignity, and self-restraint." The

*Drawing of Wells, c. 1893–94
(courtesy of the University of
Chicago Library).*

London Daily Chronicle labeled her "a woman of culture." Charles Aked
referred to her as "a lady of great personal charm." The *Inter-Ocean* quoted
another press account that called Wells "a good-looking mulatto, dressed
with uncommonly good taste." In addition she possessed the social graces
to move with ease among the British elite. If white southerners called such
a woman a contemptible representative of her race, all their charges
against African Americans were suspect.[26]

The Memphis *Daily Commercial* also quoted the *Free Speech* editorial
that had led to Wells's exile and proclaimed the "vileness of this utterance."
To the English, her words seemed very discreet compared to those of the
two *Commercial* articles. The *Liverpool Daily Post* declared, "Both articles
are very coarse in tone, and some of the language is such as could not possibly be reproduced in an English journal." In her letter to the Chicago
Inter-Ocean, Wells noted her label of "adventuress" for merely telling the
truth. "However revolting these lynchings, I did not commit a single one of
them, nor could the wildest effort of my imagination manufacture one to
equal their reality." Wells recognized her vulnerability as a woman who
spoke so openly of sexual matters and deliberately tried to separate herself

from her message. One device she used to distance herself was to quote the words of southern newspapers. She also realized the tactic added credibility to her message. "Out of their own mouths shall the murderers be condemned," Wells exclaimed.[27]

The details of many lynchings titillated the Victorian public for whom frank discussions of violence and sex bordered on pornography. Such details played an important role in arousing a passion for justice but were also capable of alienating Wells's audiences. She sought to counteract the sensational nature of her material by adopting a dispassionate mode of speaking. The oratorical impact was powerful. Accounts by her listeners contain remarkably similar descriptions of both her style and effectiveness. The *Liverpool Daily Post* described her delivery as "quiet and unimpassioned but earnest and forcible." One reporter noted that Wells "spoke in the quiet undemonstrative style which is more eloquent than any of the tricks of oratory." Another wrote, "Her indictment is all the more telling from the absence of rhetoric." Richard Armstrong's letter in the *Christian Register* not only described her "singular refinement, dignity and self-restraint" but also continued to observe, "nor have I ever met any 'agitator' so cautious and unimpassioned in speech. But by this marvelous self-restraint itself, she moves us all the more profoundly."[28]

The shock of hearing such grotesque tales from the lips of an unmarried young woman probably increased the impact of her words. Indeed, British press accounts often stressed and exaggerated her youth and "girlishness." One British reporter described her as "a young lady of little more than 20 years of age, a graceful, sweet-faced, intelligent, courageous girl." He also remarked on her "slim, youthful figure" and declared "if her pleasant face is not a guarantee of absolute truthfulness, there is no truth in existence." The *London Chronicle* declared, "She is under thirty years of age, very vivacious in manner, and decidedly good looking." Wells seems to have realized the impact of her apparent youthfulness; in one letter to an editor, she referred to "my 28 years" in the South, which can be interpreted in a number of ways, but appears to shave two to four years from her actual age of thirty-two. Ellen Richardson described the situation to Frederick Douglass: "It astonishes me," she wrote, "how she has made her way into the hearts of our Editors—especially the 'Chronicle'—had it been a Gentleman I doubt if equal success would have been achieved."[29]

To counter Wells's effectiveness, defenders of the South utilized the testimony of both British travelers to the region and other African Americans. On 12 May a long letter signed "An Englishman" appeared in the

Westminister Gazette. The writer, who claimed to have lived in the South for four years, disputed many of Wells's statements with descriptions of both black degradation and white kindness. In response to Wells's criticisms of segregation, he noted, "Let anyone take a long journey in America with negroes—especially if the weather is hot—and then judge the Southern people for making this restriction." Wells again adroitly used words of a critic to further her cause. Her response, published three days later, demonstrated point by point the absurdities of his arguments. Using his statement on segregation, she argued that the practice reflected whites' desire to subordinate African Americans rather than to separate from them. Wells explained that colored people "cook and serve the food of the white Southerner, nurse his children, launder his clothes, tidy his house, and drive his carriage, and never once does he object to the negro—no matter how hot the day—till he doffs the servant [role] and assumes the role of the man."[30]

The use of black critics had far more potential to discredit Wells than most other tactics. Realizing this, the editor of the Memphis *Daily Commercial* quoted Thomas Turner of the *Memphis Watchman* as saying that Memphis blacks "repudiate [Wells] and her statements utterly." Wells also believed that someone was paying a black man, J. W. A. Shaw, to give speeches and interviews in London to contradict her. When asked in a meeting about him, Wells retorted, "as our Savior had his Judas, Caesar his Brutus, and America her Benedict Arnold, it should not surprise us that the Negro race [is] no exception to the rule in producing its cowards and traitors and leeches." Wells ignored Turner's quote in her published reply to the article sent to the English press. Perhaps she did not want to give it more publicity; she also did not discuss the claim she had been the "paramour" to two men.[31]

Nevertheless, criticism by African Americans deeply wounded her. Writing to the *New York Age*, Wells rebuked Fleming and Nightingale for not repudiating the charges. "It would seem," she declared, "that if they cared nothing for my painful position and feelings, truth, honor and a true regard for race welfare would cause [them] to make a public statement." Apparently, she was as concerned for "race welfare" as her own honor. When Shaw tried to contradict an antilynching speech by Aked at the National Baptist Union, Wells was "speechless with rage." She was prepared to be attacked by white people but found opposition from a black man "monstrous." To the black press, Wells lashed out at African Americans "wishing to gain favor in the eyes of Mr. White Man" and proclaimed:

These Negroes who run when white men tell them to do so, and stand up and let the white man knock them down or kill them if it suits his pleasure, are the ones who see no good in "fire-eating speeches." Such Negroes do nothing to stop lynching, are too cowardly to do so, and too anxious to preserve a whole skin if they could, but never fail to raise their voices in deprecation of others who are trying to do whatever can be done to stop the infamy of killing Negroes at the rate of one a day. [Nevertheless, she proclaimed] the barking of a few curs cannot make me lose heart or hope.[32]

The "barking of a few curs," however, created quite a debate in African American newspapers. Wells's tirade no doubt referred in part to J. L. Fleming's editorial comment, "Fire eating speeches no where on the globe will help the situation." A number of other black editors also doubted the wisdom of Wells's campaign. One argument was that she should campaign in America, not Britain. The Leavenworth (Kansas) *Herald* contended, "British gold and British interference are obnoxious to the independent and liberty loving spirit of American citizens." Noting segregation and the "cramped condition of the colored people of New York City," the *Herald* suggested, "Come home, Ida, and help Fortune to redeem New York." Some editors also questioned the motives of Wells. The Wichita *People's Friend* asserted, "No one will be benefited by it but Miss Wells, who no doubt will return to her native land with a well filled pocket." The *Kansas State Ledger* answered queries regarding her motivation: "a conundrum; we give it up."[33]

The overwhelming majority of black editors, however, supported and defended Wells. A letter to the Indianapolis *Freeman* chastised Fleming for seeking "to impede the progress of the greatest woman the race has produced." The *Parsons Weekly Blade* responded to the charge that Wells could be more effective at home by suggesting, "It would be another case of casting pearls before the swine." The paper also disparaged "the midget attempts of inferior aspirants who seek to ruin her reputation." Even her old nemesis, the *Washington Bee*, declared Wells "should be defended by the negro press" and exclaimed, "No matter what her faults may be she is honest." The *Cleveland Gazette* was especially upset by Turner's comments in the Memphis *Commercial* and suggested he "ought to be given a suit of tar and feathers." For other "traitorous Afro-Americans" the *Gazette* suggested ostracism. Most seemed to agree with J. G. Robinson that "the Negro who can stand amid the shot and shell of the wrongs perpetrated upon the Negro in this country, and say a word against her, is not worthy of the name Negro, and should be condemned by every lover of the race."[34]

One reason even former enemies in the black community began to defend Wells was her success in bringing lynch law to the forefront of the nation's attention. The English press was filled with accounts of prominent individuals and groups endorsing the antilynching campaign, and Wells and her hosts made sure America knew it by sending copies to "the president of the United States, the governors of most of the states in the Union, the leading ministers in the large cities, and the leading newspapers of the country." Americans could no longer ignore the evil. They were embarrassed by British attacks on the savagery and backwardness of a nation that condoned lynching. For example, an article in the *Spectator* proclaimed, "If they [Americans] were so many savage tribes to whom civilisation and the restraints of civilization were only known by report, this [lynching] would be no cause for wonder." Such words cut deeply and caused Americans to lash out against the British, whose "hands are yet dripping with the blood of massacred Africans." Noting the "'British characteristic' to assert absolute mastery and dominion over every inferior race," the Memphis *Daily Commercial* asserted Americans had "no particular complaint to make of this," because they "have never been affected by . . . maudlin sympathy for barbarians." Nevertheless, it seemed hypocritical for the English to get "wrought up to such a pitch of frenzy by the blood-curdling tales of a nigger wench."[35]

Assailing the credibility, character, and motivation of critics was the major tactic employed by the defenders of the South, but occasionally they attacked Wells's ideas and arguments as well. Her assertion that white women sometimes were willing sexual partners to black men was especially contested. To cast doubts on her arguments, Americans exaggerated Wells's statements, accusing her of claiming that black men never raped white women and that all victims of lynchings were innocent. White newspapers protested "the vile insinuations against the white women of the South" and sought to exploit sexual fears of the British. "If Englishmen can imagine," the *Commercial* wrote, "their own daughters or sisters violently deflowered by ignorant, unclean men, lower in the scale of morality and intelligence than the basest peasantry of the world, . . . they can form some slight conception of the vileness of this utterance."[36]

Wells insisted that southerners sought "to save not so much the white woman's reputation, as the white man's ferocious pride of race." She depicted the women as victims, explaining that

the white man has never allowed his women to hold the sentiment "black but comely," on which he has so freely acted himself. . . .

white men constantly express an open preference for the society of black women. But it is a sacred convention that white women can never feel passion of any sort, high or low, for a black man. Unfortunately facts don't always square with the convention; and then if the guilty pair are found out, the whole thing is christened an outrage at once and the woman is practically forced to join in hounding down the partner of her shame. Sometimes she rebels, but oftener the overwhelming force of white prejudice is too much for her, and she must go through with the ghastly mockery.[37]

In attacking this sexual double standard, Wells had to be careful not to appear to condone interracial sex. Both she and white southerners were very aware that most Britons were repulsed by miscegenation. When an English reporter admitted as much, her "retort came like lightning":

Which race has sought it? Not ours. It is yours who forced it upon our women when they were your slaves; and now having created a mulatto population, you turn and curse it. Even today, whatever may be the truth about the white women, you can not deny that the white man is continually mixing his blood with black; it is only when he seeks to do it honorably [by marriage] that it becomes a crime.[38]

Such words further increased the controversy, which increased publicity — the aim of her mission to England.

The more attention Wells received the more the South fought back. Soon even southern governors joined the fray. "She has succeeded in stirring up a 'hornet's nest,'" one of Wells's supporters wrote, "and one of them has stung Missouri's Governor." Governor W. J. Stone charged that Wells was part of a plot "to keep capital and emigration [sic] from this section of our Republic." He also asserted, "Memphis is too high in the scale of civilization to be guilty of the crimes alleged by Miss Wells."[39] Governor W. J. Northen of Georgia echoed Stone's words, calling Wells an agent for a group of investors who sought to lure immigrants away from the South to the West, for personal gain. South Carolina Governor Benjamin Tillman also took note of Wells's London activities and wrote that he "would lead a mob to lynch any man, white or black, who had ravished any woman, white or black."[40]

The more white southerners protested, the more publicity Wells received. Black newspapers reported the campaign against her, which included "a raft of letters" to the London Daily Chronicle. One paper noted that Americans had paid more attention to questions of black rights "during the past ninety days than they have given the matter since 1876." The Indianapolis *Freeman* argued that Wells's standing should rise in proportion to southern indignation and charged, "What she needs most, if anything, other than her dauntless heart, and the inspiration of her self-selected mission, is to be made to feel by every means within our power that we are with her." Many rushed to defend and support Wells as well as to chastise those who did not. A.M.E. Bishop Henry McNeal Turner proclaimed, "Her detractors will be lost in oblivion, when her name shall blaze upon the pages of the future."[41]

Many African Americans vicariously enjoyed Wells's triumphs as they followed her widely reprinted accounts of the journey. They celebrated the many antilynching resolutions passed by church and civic groups and sent to American Ambassador Thomas F. Bayard and other prominent Americans. They relished the growing list of prestigious supporters, including newspaper editors, members of Parliament, wealthy socialites, novelists, famous clergymen, an African prince, reform leaders, and members of the nobility. Especially marvelous was the social acceptance Wells received. Not only was she the houseguest of celebrated editors and authors but also Wells was widely entertained by the British elite. Her accounts took her readers into drawing rooms filled with "the wealthiest and most cultured classes of society." She described the "gorgeous costumes, blazing diamonds, general small talk, social prestige and gracious high-bred bearing" of the women she met at a reception. Living in a society that sought hundreds of ways to remind them of their supposed inferiority, African Americans filled with pride as they read:

> When my hansom reached the big iron gates surrounding the Houses of Parliament, the policeman at the gate was on the lookout and cleared the way almost as if I had been a member of royalty. I was met at the entrance by those who were watching for me and hurried to Mr. Woodall's private dining room. When I entered the room, the guests were all seated and rose at my entrance.

The *American Citizen* exulted, "Miss Wells has been escorted to Parliament by white friends, has dined and sat in the drawing rooms with members of the nobility and gentry, including men and women prominent in public and literary life."[42]

The crown jewel of the tour was the formation of the Anti-Lynching Committee in the home of Wells's London host, P. W. Clayden, editor of the *London Daily News*. Committee president was Sir John Gorst, Duke of

Argyle and member of Parliament from Cambridge University. Members included many prominent Britons and membership was extended to such Americans as Frances Willard; Samuel Gompers, president of the American Federation of Labor; Carl Schurz; and numerous bishops and archbishops. The group was organized to raise money for the investigation and exposure of lynching. Sir Gorst noted that its goals were not merely "consideration for the Negro" but also "regard for the law" and "the moral effect of such a spectacle as a lynching."[43]

Soon after the committee's formation, Wells returned to America. Exhausted from her hectic tour, Wells sailed with British friends on a more leisurely cruise home to the Gulf of Saint Lawrence and then took the train to New York. Her arrival on 24 July in New York was triumphal; she was greeted with attention from the white press as well as black. The *New York Sun* published a long interview accompanied by flattering comments from the white interviewer. Wells utilized her new access to the white press of America to further her cause by stressing British scorn for mob violence done "not by savages, not by cannibals, . . . but by people calling themselves Christian, civilized American citizens." She also emphasized English social acceptance of African Americans, noting that her trip "was like being born again in a new condition." Her words spoke of genuine amazement at her treatment in England. Wells later recalled that her London hostess had remarked that her effectiveness would have been even greater had Wells "been a few shades blacker." However, the *New York Times* reminded Wells things were different at home by noting that the *Sun* interview appeared on the same day as the report of an assault by a black man on a white woman in the city. "The circumstances of his fiendish crime," the *Times* exclaimed, "may serve to convince the mulatress missionary that the promulgation in New York just now of her theory of negro outrages is, to say the least of it, inopportune."[44]

Several days after her return, the black community of Brooklyn officially welcomed Wells. Hosted by T. Thomas Fortune, the gathering at Bethel A.M.E. Church on 29 July filled the sanctuary and contained numerous whites and several reporters. The *New York Times* wrote a surprisingly flattering account of the meeting, and an Associated Press release was widely published—including by the Memphis *Commercial Appeal*, without comment. In her speech Wells recounted her travels, restated her case, and appealed for help. "The press is in the control of the whites," she declared, "and the attacks upon us are colored to suit themselves." To counter this, Wells suggested, "It is our duty to see that every story published from the South in which a Negro is accused of some fiendish act and lynched for it, is run down by our own detectives, if necessary, and the other side published." She also pledged a year of her life to the movement if supporters provided adequate funding.[45]

Black leaders discussed how to finance a continued crusade. The *Cleveland Gazette* suggested, "When Miss Ida B. Wells arrives in this country a monster ovation and a fat purse ought to be given her." The paper listed people who had "secured fortunes" with "large salaried positions" from the Republican party and asserted that they owed contributions "because they were supposed to be representative Afro-Americans." Opining that "this little woman has done more within the last four months . . . than had resulted prior to her tour from the combined efforts of all the 'big men' of the race," the Indianapolis *Freeman* launched a drive to establish the "Ida B. Wells Expense Fund." A letter to that paper proposed 30 September be set aside for all churches, social clubs, and civic organizations to donate to the fund. Wells wrote to express her gratitude but declared, "I enter a veto to it." She suggested instead that local antilynching leagues be established for the "three fold purpose of carrying on the agitation against lynching, publishing literature and investigating lynchings as they occur." The contributions received on 30 September should then be channeled to the central executive committee. "If this is done," Wells concluded, "the anti-lynching Committee will have the funds with which to pay me a salary for work yet to be done."[46]

The fund failed to grow significantly. Almost a year later, Wells was still plugging the idea and noted sarcastically that people "seemed to suppose strong resolutions of indorsement [sic] would pay her expenses in the work." Nevertheless, Wells was able launch a yearlong lecture tour that spanned the continent. While waiting without success for an antilynching network to materialize, she received numerous invitations from all over the nation. "These invitations I accepted," Wells later remembered, "and I charged a fee for doing so at each place I visited." In addition, in every town she appealed to white editors and clergymen for she believed "it was the white people of the country who had to mold the public sentiment necessary to put a stop to lynching." Thus she was able to make her promised tour.[47]

Her activities kept lynch law in the public eye and provoked a barrage of both praise and criticism. The "lynch law queen," as one of her detractors called her, spoke from coast to coast, while publishing articles and a new pamphlet.[48] Although she enjoyed her many adventures, Wells was becoming weary of being constantly on the road without any real home. She was tired of having her sexuality and chastity constantly questioned. Finally finding a compatible man who lived up to her exalted standards, Wells overcame her reluctance to marry. For her, however, forsaking all others did not include giving up her crusade. She was to learn more of the dilemmas of divided duty.

12

Balancing Womanhood and Activism

"I was not to be emancipated from my duties"

B efore embarking on her journeys, Wells returned to her new home of Chicago, in which she had scarcely resided. Soon after her arrival, the leading churches and civic groups sponsored a grand reception for her on 7 August. Quinn Chapel could not hold all who wished to attend, and Wells received ovation after ovation from an audience that good-naturedly hurried the opening speakers to bring on the guest of honor. She then had to wait several minutes for the applause to end before she began her speech. After finishing her talk, she received flowers from the church stewardesses and resolutions of support drafted by Ferdinand Barnett.[1]

From then until late June 1895, Wells stayed busy—mostly on lecture tours. Her itinerary took her practically everywhere but the South. On the East Coast she visited such cities as Providence, Philadelphia, Washington, Pittsburgh, New York, and Rochester. During a two-month tour in the West, Wells sojourned in Denver, Los Angeles, San Francisco, Santa Cruz, and elsewhere. She spent even more of her time in the Midwest. She returned again and again, speaking in such places as St. Louis, Indianapolis, Des Moines, Kansas City, and Omaha. During several lengthy tours in Kansas, Wells stopped at Topeka, Wichita, Lawrence, Emporia, Parsons, Atchison, Leavenworth, and other small towns. Although most of her audiences were black, she also spoke before white churches and groups. Helping to open the doors of white churches was an appeal signed by "the leading ministers of all denominations in Great Britain" asking American clergymen to extend Wells a welcome. She later recalled, "Rarely was it unsuccessful, because our American ministers knew that this powerful committee in London would receive reports as to their attitude on this burning question."[2]

Wells shared platforms with other celebrities, such as Frederick Douglass and suffrage leader Susan B. Anthony. Her reviews were usually fulsome. One noted that she spoke "for two hours, without manuscript, holding the undivided attention of her hearers." Another described how Wells held her audience spellbound: "All were eager to catch every word, even the little infants on their mother's laps seemed to realize what she said, her voice resembled the low strains of pathetic music which steals in upon the soul and touches the very heart."[3] Wells's success was chronicled in black and white papers around the nation and even some from abroad. Admirers wrote poems about her, named clubs after her, and even founded a town called Wellsford in Florida.[4] Group after group at home and overseas passed resolutions supporting Wells or condemning lynching. Local anti-lynching leagues sprouted in the wake of her lectures. Newspaper coverage of lynchings increased in such northern white papers as the *New York Times*.

White southerners sought comfort by highlighting the rare black criticism of Wells. They freely quoted the words of such people as H. C. C. Astwood, who was a former consul to Santo Domingo and secretary of the National Negro Democratic League. Asked about Wells, he charged, "I speak for the honest and intelligent masses of my race when I call her a fraud. She has been going about the country gathering notoriety." Astwood further proclaimed that African Americans who knew the facts about lynching "approve of them to the extent that the white people of the South do." He and other black Democrats were widely accused of downplaying southern racial violence to further their political careers. Such words simply stimulated more resolutions of support for Wells and her cause.[5]

Some of those resolutions drew angry criticism from whites. For example, in September the National Press Association met in Richmond, Virginia. The group asked Wells to speak on lynch law and passed a resolution against lynching, crediting her with "the arousing of the civilized world."[6] Afterward, a delegation invited Virginia Governor Charles T. O'Ferrall to speak to the group. Replying by letter, O'Ferrall declared, "I would not think of accepting an invitation to address any convention or assembly that endorses . . . the course of Ida Wells in her slanders of the people and civil authorities of the South." The long letter detailed many of the allegations against Wells by white southerners. O'Ferrall charged that she "stirred up a feeling against her own race which did not exist prior to her crusade" and accused her of sympathizing with the "brutes who commit [the] crime, too horrible to mention" rather than "their victims who have suffered more than death."[7]

Black newspapers widely reprinted the governor's letter as well as the Press Association's response, which insisted the Association had merely done its duty to "a brave little woman who has dared champion our cause." Most agreed with the *National Baptist World*'s assertion: "If there was not so much truth to Miss Wells' statements, O'Farrell [*sic*] would not squirm as he does." The *Huntsville Gazette* gloated that his refusal would attract "more widespread attention than his acceptance would have done."[8] Many white southerners inadvertently aided the cause of African Americans with publicity-causing hostility.

The South made another tactical mistake. In attacks on Wells's credibility, several southern papers urged Britons to come see for themselves the falsity of her words. The first major campaign of the Anti-Lynching Committee did just that. A committee, headed by the Duke of Argyle, Sir John Gorst, arrived in late August to investigate mob action in America. The committee made quite an impression on white America — mostly negative. The *New York World* polled state governors for their reaction to the group's investigation. In republishing the results, *Literary Digest* noted that only three welcomed the men — including two southerners who felt their states would be vindicated and Illinois Governor John Altgeld, who also suggested that southerners return the favor by going to Ireland "to stop the outrages there." Most of the governors, from all regions, labeled the British efforts as "presumptuous effrontery," urged the English to "purify their own morals," and reminded readers of Jack the Ripper and other evils that better deserved Britons' attention.[9]

Major white newspapers covered the investigation and the South's response to it. The governors of Georgia and Arkansas made lengthy comments about the English committee, which the *New York Times* published. Georgia Governor W. J. Northen charged that the Britons had "received their information from irresponsible sources" and noted that "the people of this state are quite able to administer their own affairs." Continuing to stress the irrepressible southern cry of states' rights, he lamented, "We have already endured more outside interference in our local matters than we will submissively tolerate in the future." Arkansas governor W. M. Fishback claimed to support the committee's objectives but questioned its methods and inquired, "What civilized country on the globe has shown less regard for human rights . . . than England?" The *London Times* noted both the committee's work and an apologia of the governor of Alabama.[10]

Declaring its desire to get the truth about lynching in America, the committee queried governors about lynchings in their states. The committee also sought to get statements of opposition to mob violence from political leaders in the United States. The investigation raised much interest in the black press, which discussed its progress and celebrated its victories. The *Parsons Weekly Blade* expressed the sentiments of most African Americans regarding outrage expressed by southern governors: "The whole uproar simply shows that something is radically wrong in the South and it is feared that an investigation will bring a dead dog out of the bushes that will cast a decidedly offensive odor over the garments of such great men as Gov. Northen."[11] Most black journalists credited Wells for the Britons' action and the white South's discomfort.

The discomfort increased after a sextuple lynching near Millington, Tennessee—fifteen miles from Memphis—on 31 August. Accused, but not convicted, of burning down some barns, six manacled black men were riding in a wagon on the way to jail when a mob shot and killed them. A white Ohio newspaper proclaimed, "If Ida B. Wells had desired anything to substantiate the charges against the south that she has been rehearsing before English and American audiences, nothing more serviceable could have come to hand." Interviewed the day after the lynching, Wells observed that even had the men been guilty, "there is no other place in the world where a capital offense is made of burning barns." She pointed out that the murders illustrated the falsity of the usual excuse of rape. The white men in the South, she charged, "do not think any more of killing a Negro than they do of slaying a mad dog." In conclusion, Wells declared:

> The South has more than once insisted upon being left alone with the Negro problem. The nation has obligingly accommodated her, and to-day the spectacle is presented of a so-called civilized country standing idly by and seeing one section disgrace the entire country. I think it is high time the justice-loving and law-abiding people should take some steps to make such acts impossible.[12]

The impact of Wells's crusade on the attitude of white southerners was displayed by their reactions to the Millington murders. The Memphis *Evening Scimitar* exclaimed, "Every one of us is touched with blood guilti-

Picture of Wells from her pamphlet, A Red Record.

ness in this matter unless we prove ourselves ready to do our duty as civilized men and citizens who love their country and are jealous of its good name." After earlier having slandered Wells, the Memphis *Commercial-Appeal* cried out:

> Men of Memphis, men of Shelby county, brave, chivalrous men of the South, shall this bloody record stand against us? Can we look civilization in the face while we stand thus accused? Can we be silent and inactive and remain guiltless of the bloodshed of these poor wretches and guiltless of the crimes that are to follow?[13]

The apparent determination to rectify the wrong led to the arrest of the two deputies who were in charge of the murdered men. African Americans rejoiced over such responses, but disillusionment soon followed. As early as 2 November Wells's new employer, the *Chicago Conservator*, announced, "Already it is confidentially declared that every murderer will soon be free." The words proved true, and in January the British Anti-Lynching Committee issued a denunciation of the refusal of an all-white jury to convict any of the men even though, as the Memphis *Commercial* declared, "there was no moral doubt whatever in the ghastly, cowardly and brutal massacre." White concern for the opinion of the "civilized world" did not immediately translate into justice for African Americans.[14]

Wells, nevertheless, asserted the impact of public opinion on Memphis in *A Red Record*, issued early in 1895. The desire "to escape the brand of barbarism," she explained, prevented the city from being "just as calm and complacent and self-satisfied over the murder of the six" as it had been during the 1892 lynchings there. A *Red Record* was her longest antilynching work. Its hundred pages contained a listing of all known lynchings of African Americans in 1893 and 1894, organized by the accusations made against the victims. Wells also gave detailed accounts of specific lynchings in which rape was charged, showing the flimsiness of those claims. One of her major points was the hypocrisy of southern white claims to chivalric protection of women, which "confines itself entirely to women who happen to be white." She proclaimed, "Virtue knows no color line, and the chivalry which depends upon complexion of skin and texture of hair can command no honest respect."[15]

Perhaps responding to criticisms that she only recited atrocities without providing a cure, Wells closed the book with "The Remedy." She recommended five specific actions: (1) bring the facts in the book to the attention of all acquaintances; (2) get churches and civic groups to pass antilynching resolutions and send copies wherever outrages occur; (3) call the South's attention to "the refusal of capital to invest where lawlessness and mob violence hold sway"; (4) "think and act on independent lines in this behalf"; and (5) send resolutions to Congress supporting the Blair bill to create an investigatory commission.[16]

The reference to the Blair bill illustrates that Wells's crusade was winning some powerful allies. In August 1894, Congressman Henry W. Blair of New Hampshire offered a resolution to the House of Representatives calling for an investigation of all the rapes and lynchings of the previous ten years. Fearing the influence of southern Democrats would prevent acceptance of the resolution, African Americans mobilized to rally support. In mid-December they presented Blair with a batch of petitions "containing 10,000 names of citizens from all parts of the country." Wells also testified before the House committee to which the resolution had been referred, but all efforts failed to launch a congressional investigation.[17]

Another recruit to the cause by Wells was the influential clergyman and editor Lyman Abbott. An editorial in the February 1895 *Woman's Era* noted that his congregation had been added to the "audience after audience [that] have found her simple, forceful presentation of facts convincing and her eloquence irresistible." After Wells's speech at his church, Abbott began giving "authentic reports of lynching with trenchant comment" in his paper, *The Outlook*.[18] Few people could listen to Wells and remain unconvinced of the evil of lynching. For example, in the aftermath of her address at the Boston Monday Lectures, lynching remained the topic of the forum for the next two years. Coverage of lynching in white periodicals and newspapers, including the *New York Times*, became more extensive and condemnatory.[19]

These were heady days for Wells as more and more famous people joined the chorus of praise for her efforts. On a trip to Rochester in April 1895, she was the houseguest of Susan B. Anthony, who fired her stenographer for refusing to take dictation from Wells. At a public meeting in the First Baptist Church of Rochester, a listener from Texas sarcastically asked Wells if all lynched Negroes were innocent. Wells replied, "I never said that. I simply claim that they were innocent in the eye of the law; no man is guilty until found so by trial." He then asked why black southerners did not come North if conditions were so bad. She explained, "They are not able to emigrate, because they are always in debt to their landlords, being paid in checks for provisions only good at plantation stores." At this point, Wells later recalled, Anthony sprang to her feet and declared it was "because we, here in the North, do not treat Negroes any better than they do in the South, comparatively speaking." The suffragist then proceeded to tell a moving story of a little black girl in Rochester who had been told by her teacher she could not attend the school dance because of her color.[20]

Wells was impressed by Anthony's refusal to accept segregation in the North but could not understand why the suffragist accepted it in the South. In discussing the conflict with Frances Willard, Anthony had tried to get Wells to "see that for the sake of expediency one often had to stoop to conquer on this question of color." To illustrate her point, Anthony described how although Frederick Douglass had been the earliest and most consistent male supporter of women's rights, she had asked him not to attend a National Women's Suffrage Association meeting in Atlanta because she did not "want anything to get in the way of bringing the southern white women into our suffrage association." When Anthony asked Wells if she thought the action had been wrong, Wells recalled, "I answered uncompromisingly yes, for I felt that although she may have made some gains for suffrage, she had also confirmed white women in their attitude of segregation. I suppose Miss Anthony had pity on my youth and inexperience, for she never in any way showed resentment of my attitude."[21] Even with age and experience, however, Wells continued her refusal to compromise on issues of black rights.

In the end her uncompromising attitude won Wells far more enemies than friends. Among them was former U.S. Senator Blanche K. Bruce, whom she had singled out for scorn in 1891 by claiming he had forsaken black interests for personal ambition. As editor of the Leavenworth *Herald*, Bruce returned the favor constantly in the mid-1890s. He was one of the few to question her motives during the English tour and continued his assault after her return. His account of her lecture in Leavenworth ridiculed the effort and emphasized her desire for money. It must have especially galled Bruce to have his nemesis called a leader. "Ida B. Wells," he wrote, "has become so spoiled by the Afro-American press that she has delegated to herself the care and keeping of the entire colored population of the United States." Bruce charged she tried to tell black editors what to do and asserted, "We should think that the autocrats of the press would resent this egotistic, self-appointed, bossing principle which seems to underlie Ida B.'s makeup."[22]

Male editors throughout these attacks defended Wells—in ways that belittled her more subtly than Bruce. An editorial in the *Kansas State Ledger* responded to Bruce's attacks: "Well, you know that some men who fear their equals in every particular, always satisfy their lust and low ambition by striking a defenseless woman." Other editorials were full of such phrases as "noble little heroine," "solitary little woman," "brave little woman," "brilliant little being," and "her slandered womanhood." Stressing her diminutiveness and womanliness seemed to lessen the threat Wells posed to their manhood. George Knox of the Indianapolis *Freeman* exclaimed that "one of the chief charms of Miss Wells' crusade [is] that she has not permitted the cares and labors of the same to unsex her. The full blown rose of a blameless womanhood abideth with her."[23] Both Wells and her male observers struggled to reconcile the competing claims of womanhood and activism on her. The "little woman" occasionally claimed for herself heroic qualities usually reserved for men. When asked by a reporter if she would lecture in the South, Wells reportedly answered, "They [southerners] would probably try to run me away and I would not run if I once went there and of course you know what would happen."[24]

Black male leaders feared Wells in part because of a pending leadership vacuum as Douglass drew closer to death. When Douglass entered his seventies in the late 1880s, no black figure came close to commanding the attention and respect he received from both blacks and whites at home and abroad. As long as he was alive and competent, all others would remain in his shadow, but in the 1880s various men sought to position themselves to be his successor. They often savaged one another while jockeying for power. In the last years of his life, Douglass sometimes appeared to be handing his mantle to Wells. No other African American came nearly as close to assuming the role of Douglass in the white mind—and white recognition played a key role in race leadership. The *Nashville Citizen* even endorsed her as "the proper person to succeed Frederick Douglass as leader of the Afro-American race."[25]

Many African American women gloried in Wells's heroic status. A poem by Katherine Davis Tillman compared Wells to "Charlotte Corday for the English" and "Joan of Arc for the French." Black males, however, were torn between their appreciation of Wells's efforts to defend their honor and their embarrassment over this reversal of roles. Several deplored the fact that "none of our representative and most prominent men would take up the lead." One lamented "The hour had come, where was the man? Unfortunately, the man was not forthcoming—but Miss Wells was!" When Douglass died in February 1895, Wells wrote a tribute to him that she closed with the words: "For the first time since the burden of race defense was laid upon me, I cannot have the help and support of Frederick Douglass." Bruce immediately parodied her words. Later that year, after Booker T. Washington's speech in Atlanta catapulted him to fame, Bruce exulted that Wells was not "the star attraction in Atlanta" and asked, "Can it be that this new Mrs. Moses has been shelved so quickly?" As late as 1902, E. E. Cooper of the Indianapolis *Freeman* expressed continued resentment at her assumption of the role of "uncrowned queen of the Negroes of America" and her "boldly insisting the Negro men had not sufficient intellectual fibre or courage to shape thought or mould opinions for the race."[26] Other men were likely just as uncomfortable with Wells as their defender, but rather than attack her, they rhetorically stripped away her power to defend herself, much less the race. Just as white males often did, they employed chivalry to deny a woman the power of self-defense and thus independence.

Although Wells apparently appreciated being defended by men, she did not surrender her right to defend herself. An April 1895 *Freeman* article, titled "In Her Own Defense," reprinted Wells's letter to a California paper. In it she discussed a debate among Methodist ministers in San Francisco on her request for an antilynching resolution. Among other things, she disputed a bishop's attempt to exclude her and other women from the meeting to protect them from "horrible stories." Wells asserted her right to be there and proclaimed, "Whatever the Bishop's disability in that respect is I flatter myself that I have sufficient command of the English language to tell my stories, horrible as they are, without shocking 'ears polite.'"[27]

Just how "defenseless" Ida B. Wells was can also be seen in two inci-

1. T. Thomas Fortune, Journalist. 2. Booker T. Washington, Educator.
3. Hon. Frederick Douglass, Statesman.
4. I. Garland Penn, Author, Orator; 5. Miss Ida B. Wells,
Chief Commissioner, Atlanta Exposition. Lecturer, Defender of the Race.

Illustration in Henry Davenport Northrop, The College of Life *(1895), reflecting Wells's ranking among the top leadership group.*

dents at conventions of clergymen that she related in her autobiography. Wells appeared before many ministerial associations, most of which adopted resolutions of support with little discussion. However, after she spoke at a meeting of A.M.E. pastors in Philadelphia, one member argued that "they ought to be careful about endorsing young women of whom they knew nothing." Wells rose in protest, told of the white support she had received, and questioned the need for their endorsement as she had God's. She recalled telling them, "I feel very deeply the insult which you have offered and I have the honor to wish you a very good morning," before she "walked out of the meeting and left them sitting with their mouths open."[28]

The second incident occurred at a biracial meeting of evangelical ministers in Kansas City. This time it was a former white resident of Memphis who objected to the resolution of support for Wells and a heated debate followed. A newspaper account of the event noted,

> All this time Ida Wells had been listening to the discussion with manifest excitement. She now rose and in spite of objections, insisted upon being heard. She said all she wanted was the endorsement of her work. If any of those present objected to her they could leave her name off; it was the condemnation of lynching that she asked for.

The resolution was tabled until the regular meeting was over. A rump group of ministers "who wanted to consider the resolution" then met separately. At that time Wells insisted that her name be placed back on the document, as its removal was no longer necessary to thwart the actions of "southern sympathizers." Although the "meeting was inclined to be surprised," it granted her request.[29]

Such assertiveness undoubtedly "surprised" many men. One man, however, never seemed to be surprised or threatened by Wells's strength or independence. Ferdinand Lee Barnett was the man who finally convinced the independent Miss Wells to enter the bonds of matrimony. Ideologically indistinguishable and temperamentally compatible, they appear to have been drawn to each other from the beginning of their collaboration on the World's Fair pamphlet in 1893. The demands on Wells the activist, however, prevented a conventional courtship for Wells the woman. Her return to England and her American lecture tour led to what their daughter later referred to as "a long distance correspondence courtship." Barnett knew even before Wells left for England that he wanted to marry her, and fortunately for him, he could write "a beautiful love letter," one of which awaited Wells at every stop along her itinerary in America. At the end of her promised year of antilynching activism, she accepted Barnett's proposal. Unlike earlier suitors, Barnett was strong enough to win her respect without threatening her independence.[30]

Although not as well known nationally as Wells, Barnett was a prominent and successful attorney in Chicago. Born about 1856 in Nashville, Tennessee, he was the son of a slave who had bought his freedom and moved his family to Canada. The elder Barnett brought his family to Chicago in 1869, where he worked as a blacksmith and a cook on steamboats. Ferdinand was very bright and after graduating from high school taught school in Missouri for two years. He then returned to Chicago and read law with Attorney Morton Culver while enrolled in the law department of Northwestern University. In 1878 he graduated from law school and established the *Chicago Conservator*. Four years later he began the active practice of law in partnership with S. Laing Williams. In 1882 Barnett married Mary Graham of Ontario, Canada, who was the first black woman to graduate from the University of Michigan. She died in 1888, leaving Barnett with a three-year-old son and a five-year-old son to raise. His mother then moved in with him and helped to raise his sons.[31]

Barnett became an activist as soon as he became an adult. He served as recording secretary of the National Conference of Colored Men of the United States held at Nashville in May 1879. There he voiced two themes that were central to both Wells's and his brand of militancy. "Race elevation can be attained only through race unity," he exclaimed. "White people grant us few privileges voluntarily. We must wage continued warfare for our rights, or they will be disregarded and abridged."[32] Barnett continued his activism by participating in both black groups and local politics. In 1881 he served as the second president of the National Colored Press Association and the following year became its treasurer. That year the circulation for his paper was reported at 3,200, and he also ran for South Town clerk in Chicago. In 1884 Barnett chaired a "large public mass meeting" regarding the treatment of Senator Blanche K. Bruce's wife by Washington society. By then his growing legal practice had curtailed his active involvement in the *Conservator*. Those legal activities and victories were noted by the black press, as was his clerkship in the registry department of the Chicago post office and his presidency of the Colored Men's Library Association in 1887.[33]

The ideology and rhetoric of Barnett during his editorship of the *Conservator* paralleled that of Wells to a remarkable degree. Like Wells, he criticized the monopoly of black government appointments by a handful of

*Ferdinand Barnett, c. 1906
(courtesy of the University of
Chicago Library).*

African Americans. "Senator Bruce and Fred. Douglass," Barnett wrote in
1881, "will receive the loaves, John M. Langston, Smythe and Elliot will
gobble up the fishes, and the rest of us will get the 'taffy.'"[34] With Wells, he
attacked the loose morals and extravagant living styles of the black masses
as well as the failures of black churches. Much like her, Barnett deplored
the casual mixing of the refined and coarser classes "all in one motley mass
for the sake of money." They also shared a prudish Puritanism, reflected in
his words, "We will endeavor to tear the gilded sophism from vice and
show its gilded mien and to establish a social line — on one side of which is
purity, virtue, and happiness; and on the other side social death." Although
generally Republican in politics, he advocated the same "race first" loyalty
and political independence as Wells. They both attacked secret societies
and fraternal orders as a waste of precious resources. Most remarkable was
the convergence of the two journalists on the issue of white violence
against African Americans. In the early 1880s, Barnett wrote:

> Not long ago, a colored man was lynched upon the charge of an
> attempt at outrage. An attempt, mind you. This is a comprehensive
> term in the South. It embraces a wink by a colored man at a white
> girl a half mile off. Such a crime is worthy of lynching, but a beastly

attack upon a colored girl by a white man is only a wayward indis-
cretion. The colored people have stood such discriminations long
enough.[35]

If one shuffled unmarked clippings written by the pair, it would be difficult
to determine who was the author of each. Both espoused a brand of protest
growing from the antebellum black convention movement that led to Barnett's being called "Resoluting Ferd."[36]

Unsurprisingly, their union began in protest rather than marriage.
From the beginning of the planning for the Chicago fair, Barnett played
the leading role in that city's movement to ensure black representation. He
drafted resolutions opposing a separate black exhibit in 1890 and lobbied
the president of the Board of Lady Managers to appoint a black representative to her group. Barnett had corresponded with Frederick Douglass,
who apparently brought Barnett and Wells together to produce *The Reason
Why*. On all the issues of the Columbian Exposition, as on other ones, the
two agreed completely, and Barnett soon became a partner in Wells's antilynching campaign. He was founder and president of the Illinois Anti-
Lynching League and wrote Senator William Chandler on her behalf
while Wells was in London.[37]

In temperament, Barnett and Wells complemented rather than duplicated each other. A family friend later told their daughter, Alfreda Duster,
"Your father was full of wit and dry humor that always endeared him to his
audience and your mother was full of fire and uncompromising." Duster
remembered "my father was a very mild-mannered man, he was not aggressive . . . or outspoken like my mother." Barnett and Wells shared many
characteristics, however, including their moral standards. Barnett would
not allow liquor or wine to be served in the house because he did not want
anyone to "say that they took their first drink at our house." Both felt great
compassion for the underdog. Barnett not only represented people who
could not pay for his legal services but also "paid the carfare of the charity
client to and from court."[38]

Whereas Wells's strong personality intimidated some men, it was precisely what Barnett was looking for in a wife. Several years earlier, when he
had erroneously been romantically linked with a young employee, Barnett
was reported to have said, "Bell is a dear sweet child but I am not thinking
of marriage as I have not forgotten my first wife enough, yet, and when I do
think of marriage it will be to a *woman*—one who can help me in my career." In the end, however, he probably did more for Wells's career than she

did for his. He made her editor of the *Conservator* soon after their wedding and relieved her of her financial worries. Barnett never expected Wells to stay at home and play housewife for him. He employed housekeepers and did most of the cooking himself, having learned how from traveling with his father as a cook on steamboats. Not only was he better in the kitchen than his wife, he apparently enjoyed cooking as much as she hated it.[39]

Theirs was a marriage grounded in protest. News of it spread like wildfire through the black press, and even such white journals as the *New York Times* and *Chicago Tribune* commented on the wedding. Some black editors asked how Wells would balance her roles as activist and wife. In the *Woman's Era*, Fannie Barrier Williams declared that Wells's "determination to marry a man while still married to a cause will be a topic of national interest and comment." John Mitchell of the *Richmond Planet* noted the name Wells had made for herself as "a single lady" and opined that "her opportunities for good so far as the race is concerned are by no means lessened by this union of heart and hand." At the same time, some editors focused on the fact that Wells finally had a full-time male protector. The *American Citizen* dared evangelist Sam Jones to go to Chicago now and repeat the attacks on Wells he had reportedly made elsewhere. Her nemesis Blanche K. Bruce suggested that Wells had married the "sly old 'duck'" Barnett because of his attacks on her attackers.[40]

Fortunately, Barnett seemed perfectly willing to be overshadowed by Wells. Even before their marriage, after she affiliated with the *Conservator*, black editors began to attribute articles written by others to her. Afterward, Barnett was often referred to by designations, such as the "husband of the brilliant Ida B. Wells Barnett," even though he was influential in his own right—holding down the position of assistant state's attorney from 1896 to 1911 and advising Republican presidents on black appointments. He also became the butt of editor Bruce's jokes that claimed Wells "gives Ferd her skirts and dons his trousers." Calling him Ferdinand Barnett-Wells in response to her adoption of Wells-Barnett, Bruce claimed Barnett was to go on a lecture tour and sell excess silver spoons received as wedding presents in an "endeavor to raise money enough to get a bedstead."[41]

The wedding itself was a major social event. Five hundred invitations were mailed, and guests came from all over the nation to the ceremony, which was held at eight o'clock on Thursday evening, 27 June, in Chicago's Bethel A.M.E. Church. Wells's two sisters, attired in "lemon colored crepe" with white ribbons, slippers, and gloves, were the bridesmaids. They and a flower girl preceded Wells, who was dressed "with white satin entrain trimmed in chiffon and orange blossoms and the regulation veil." She carried "a bouquet of bride roses." Barnett's two groomsmen included R. P. Bird, the current editor of the *Conservator* and S. J. Evans. The bride and groom made a striking couple; both have been described by contemporaries as "regal" in appearance. Since Wells had no parents to host the reception, the chore was fulfilled by members of the Ida B. Wells Club, which Wells had founded before her second English tour. They transformed the double parlors of the home where Wells boarded into "a bower of beauty with ferns and palms and roses."[42]

Wells-Barnett later recalled, "The interest of the public in the affair seemed so great that not only the church filled to overflowing, but the streets surrounding the church were so packed with humanity that it was almost impossible for the carriage bearing the bridal party to reach the church door." Included in the guests were white women members of the Women's Republican State Central Committee and their husbands. Wells made talks at their request for the 1894 elections and considered it "a very great honor" that the women had asked to attend and "were dressed in honor of the occasion in evening attire, just the same as if they had attended a wedding among themselves."[43]

Wells's hectic schedule for 1894–95 not only caused numerous reschedulings of the nuptials but also exhaustion. She was on the road when the announcement was made and continued speaking until within a week of the wedding. Wells-Barnett later recalled, "I did not know how utterly worn out I was physically until I reached the point when I could rest quietly without the feeling that I must be either on the train or traveling through the country to some place of meeting where I was scheduled to speak." At first, setting up house occupied her time—and reflected Barnett's willingness to accommodate her needs. When it became apparent that his mother and wife could not comfortably share the house, Barnett moved his mother and two sons Ferdinand, Jr., and Albert (then aged twelve and ten, respectively) into a nearby house. At the same time he allowed his wife to move in her two sisters, from whom she had been separated during her travels. Perhaps Wells-Barnett felt guilty for shirking her duty to raise her sisters and now had a chance to rectify her perceived neglect of them. Already young women by then, Lily and Annie could hardly help being drawn into the excitement of the city. Eventually, Annie met and married a Chicago man, Bernard W. Fitts, and the two couples remained close. Lily, however, married a man from California and could only return occasionally to visit Chicago.[44]

Less than a week after her marriage, Wells-Barnett assumed the editorship of the *Conservator*, whose offices were across the hall from Barnett's law offices. The paper was the first black one in the city and had boasted several editors, including Barnett's first wife. The extent of Barnett's involvement had risen and fallen over the years, but the paper had remained closely tied to him in the public's mind. By the early 1890s, the *Conservator* employed about ten people, and its offices were described as a "magnet which drew most all of the well known and important leaders of not only the city but of the nation." Black editors all around the country predicted the paper would "flourish as never before" under Wells-Barnett's editorship. Evidently unwilling to give up independence and control entirely, she bought the paper from her husband and remained its editor for several years.[45]

Wells-Barnett was back on the lecture circuit less than two months after the wedding, speaking in Buffalo, New York. In December the *National Reflector* announced, "Mrs. Ida B. Wells-Barnett is again speaking in the interest of law and order." In addition to speaking and her editorial job, she also wrote articles for white Chicago papers and spoke at white women's clubs in and around the city and served as president of the Ida B. Wells Club. The Indianapolis *Freeman* exulted that Wells-Barnett "is still giving sledge-hammer blows to the lynching industry." As busy as she was, Wells-Barnett later recalled, "I was not too busy to find time to give birth to a male child the following 25 March 1896." Predictably, the "advent of the baby King" was widely reported in the press and provoked such comments as, "Too bad, it isn't a second Ida B."[46]

Wells-Barnett had been offered birth control advice but refused to take it, even though, as she later admitted, "I had not entered into the bonds of matrimony with the same longing for children that so many other women have." She further explained:

> It may be that my early entrance into public life and the turning of my efforts, physical and mental, in that direction had something to do with smothering the mother instinct. It may be that having had the care of small children from the time I was big enough to hold a baby also had its effect.

Eventually, Wells-Barnett rejoiced that she had "realized what a wonderful place in the scheme of things the Creator has given women." Nevertheless, she was reluctant to allow motherhood to interfere with activism and soon began to feel the pressures confronted by most working mothers.[47]

Wells-Barnett with her first-born son, Charles Aked Barnett, 1896 (courtesy of the University of Chicago Library).

Naming her son Charles Aked Barnett in honor of the British clergy-man, Wells-Barnett began to carry him with her on her travels. Her husband paid for a nurse to accompany them to some meetings, but the new mother soon began to ask those who invited her to bear that expense. One group to do so was the Illinois Republican Women's State Central Committee, who had a nurse available at all the stops Wells-Barnett made throughout the state on behalf of the party in the 1896 elections. At one stop, however, a black nurse wanted to hear the talk herself and asked if she could bring the baby to the meeting. Wells-Barnett recalled, "The baby, who was wide awake, and failing to see me but hearing my voice, raised his voice in angry protest." The chairwoman immediately carried Charles Aked out in the hall beyond his mother's voice.[48]

Wells-Barnett carried her son with her because she had refused the suggestion not to nurse him. Although glad to have fulfilled her "duty as mother to my first-born," she admitted she "looked forward to the time when I should have completely discharged my duty in that respect." Relief was short-lived, because eight months after weaning Charles, Wells-Barnett gave birth to her second son, Herman, in November 1897. "I was not to be emancipated from my duties in that respect," she later recalled.[49]

With the birth of a second child, Wells-Barnett claimed that "all this public work was given up and I retired to the privacy of my home to give my attention to the training of my children." Nevertheless, she was unable to remain in seclusion for very long because she felt the call of duty to her race. Susan B. Anthony diagnosed the dilemma. While Wells-Barnett was staying with her to attend a meeting to reactivate the Afro-American League in 1898, she noticed that Anthony "would bite out my married name in addressing me." Wells-Barnett later reminisced:

> Finally I said to her, "Miss Anthony, don't you believe in women get-ting married?" She said, "Oh, yes, but not women like you who had a special call for special work. I too might have married but it would have meant dropping the work to which I had set my hand." She said, "I know of no one in this country better fitted to do the work you had in hand than yourself. Since you have gotten married, agitation seems practically to have ceased. Besides, you have a divided duty. You are here trying to help in the formation of this league and your eleven-month-old baby needs your attention at home. You are dis-tracted over the thought that maybe he is not being looked after as he would if you were there, and that makes for divided duty."

Wells-Barnett reflected that Anthony had not realized "it was because I had been unable . . . to get the support which was necessary to carry on my work that I had become discouraged in the effort to carry on alone."[50]

Undoubtedly, the double duties of activism and motherhood slowed the pace of Wells-Barnett's activities. However, her prickly personality and her need to be the leader of movements in which she participated played just as large a role in her failure to become a significant factor in the new organizations that emerged to deal with the racial crises of the 1890s.

13

Organizational Efforts and Problems

"Lest I might become a contender for the position"

The 1890s were bloody, discouraging years for African Americans. Since the last shot fired in the Civil War, white southerners had tried to construct upon the ruins of slavery a new institution with its benefits and privileges. Reconstruction slowed their success by providing political power to the former slaves. That power was not great enough, however, to protect black southerners from sporadic economic and physical intimidation or intermittent exclusion and segregation. By the 1890s, the North was withdrawing its efforts to remake the South. Each retreat by the North was met with new white determination to transform chaotic discrimination based on custom into a legalized system of repression. *Plessy v. Ferguson* merely put a constitutional seal of approval on those efforts in 1896. Determined to stem the rising tide of racism, African Americans battled each new step toward systematic disfranchisement and segregation. Their fight produced the most violent decade in the history of southern race relations. Black northerners began the decade protesting the outrages of the South and ended it defending their own rights in the North.

The era was also marked by massive growth in national organizations to accomplish goals that seemed elusive to individuals or local organizations. Revolutions in transportation, communication, and economics created both opportunities and problems beyond the scope of one's self or community. The convergence of black problems and the spirit of organization led to increased efforts to harness scattered cries of protest into a unified plea for justice. Of course, African Americans had long realized that their individual rights were virtually inseparable. Slavery circumscribed the status of free blacks as it controlled the bodies of the enslaved. This realization led to the emergence of the black convention movement in the 1830s and to a flurry of organizational efforts at the turn of the century. Ida B. Wells-Barnett participated in many of these efforts, yet she seemed unable to exert her leadership or sustain her involvement in many national movements for a variety of reasons—both ideological and personal.

Before her marriage, Wells-Barnett had sought unsuccessfully to rally African Americans into a centralized movement against lynching. Soon after her wedding, she received an invitation to a national conference of black women at Boston in August 1895. Although Wells-Barnett was too busy and exhausted to attend, the meeting was rooted in her antilynching campaign. The secretary of the British Anti-Lynching Committee, which she had helped found, sent a letter to American journalists recruiting their efforts in the battle against lynching. John W. Jacks, president of the Missouri Press Association, replied with a scathing attack on the morals of African Americans in general and black women in particular:

> The Negroes in this country are wholly devoid of morality. They know nothing of it except as they learn by being caught for flagrant violations of law and punished therefor. They consider it no disgrace but rather an honor to be sent to prison and to wear striped clothes. The women are prostitutes and all are natural liars and thieves. . . . Out of 200 in this vicinity it is doubtful if there are a dozen virtuous women of that number who are not daily thieving from the white people.

He also quoted one black woman as saying of another, "She won't let any man, except her husband, sleep with her, and we don't 'sociate with her."[1]

Such words echoed countless attacks against black women, who were called barriers to race advancement and corrupters of white youth.[2] Those accusations ignored African American women's efforts to better themselves and their world. They had organized groups as early as 1793, when some established the Female Benevolent Society of St. Thomas in Philadelphia. They founded antislavery groups, literary groups, sewing groups, and a plethora of others. Most of their efforts just before and after the Civil War were centered in the church and sought to provide the basic necessities of life to poor people. Rooted in the cooperative efforts of slaves, these mutual benefit societies collected dues and helped members in times of crisis with medical bills, funeral expenses, and temporary shelter. Although considered corrupt by white society, black women were expected by their own people to be the saviors of African American souls and healers of dark bodies. When public agencies and northern philanthropists began to ignore the cries of their needy, they sought to fill the void with private kindergartens, health clinics, old folks' homes, and orphanages. They entered into movements of reform—from abolition, to temperance, to suffrage, to education, and to many more. Black women built most of the infrastructures that supplied the needs of black communities. Such nurturing roles seemed appropriate to the "proper sphere" for women. Men, on the other hand, were expected to lead protest movements. As late as 1893, leader Fannie J. Coppin described the men's "part to perform" as the protection of the Fifteenth Amendment. "The right to petition is a powerful weapon of defense," she continued, "Lawlessness, insubordination and hatred are the bloody angle of our race battle."[3]

The first generation of freedom found men in all significantly visible leadership roles. The two dominant sources of authority in the black community were the Republican party and the black church—each controlled by men. Women did much of the day-to-day work to make both successful but received little recognition or power. In the 1890s a new generation, reaching adulthood after the Civil War, emerged from the shadows of the abolitionist generation. Declining support for black rights by the Republican party and the diminishing importance of the church in urban settings set the stage for the rise of more secular women's groups that were less likely to shy away from political issues. Most importantly, women began to want forums to discuss *their* needs as black *women*. From 1892 to 1895, such women's groups sprouted everywhere. Although some took the name of Ida B. Wells and others openly spoke of her inspirational influence, these groups were the logical next step in a movement with long roots. Excluded from leadership or even participation in most male-dominated groups and white women's organizations, black women did not so much imitate those groups as to build upon their own traditions to confront problems.

John Jacks's letter crystallized the determination of black women to speak for themselves against the "base aspersions to blight and dwarf the spirit of the Negro woman."[4] The idea was not new; in 1892, Anna J. Cooper deplored the tendency of others to speak for black women, when "not many can more sensibly realize and more accurately tell the weight and the fret of the 'long dull pain' than the open-eyed but hitherto voice-less Black Woman of America." The call for the 1895 convention in Boston included a copy of Jacks's letter and cited the need to educate "the public to a just appreciation of us."[5] Most agreed with a delegate from the Omaha Women's Club: "There was a time when our mothers and sisters could not protect themselves from such beasts as this man Jacks and it is to him, and his kind, that the morality of colored women has been questioned. But a new era is here and we propose to protect and defend ourselves."[6]

Although Wells-Barnett did not attend the Boston meeting, her spirit lingered over it. Her success inspired women and, according to Fannie Barrier Williams, "strongly suggests the importance of a greater sense of conscious dignity and self-respect among colored women." For several years, Wells-Barnett had served as a lightning rod for white males' contempt toward black women. A number of local clubs sprouted from the 1892 meetings organized by black women on behalf of the exiled journalist. Among these was the Boston Woman's Club, which called the 1895 conference under the leadership of Josephine St. Pierre Ruffin. Its *Woman's Era* announced in July the group's invitation to Wells-Barnett and noted, "Being with them at their formation, and also being in every sense of the word a club woman, the congratulations waiting to be showered upon Mrs. Barnett will be heartfelt indeed."[7] Responses to the call also indicate the importance of the new bride in the minds of its recipients. One saw the conference as an attempt to "second the efforts of our leading women such as Ida B. Wells-Barnett." A group of women from Bethel Church in New York, however, feared the meeting would become "the sounding board of mere 'agitators.'" Making clear which agitator they had in mind, they labeled the Jacks letter as "the natural result of the resentment provoked by the fierce denunciations of 'southern white women' that have been injudiciously indulged in by some of the 'mercurial persons' of our race."[8]

At the convention, the women passed a resolution that expressed their admiration for "the noble and truthful advocacy" of Wells-Barnett "against the lying charge of rape," congratulated her on her marriage, and hailed her "in the face of all her assailants, as our noble 'Joanna of Arc.'" Congratulations, however, were mingled with controversy. Aware of her dispute with Frances Willard, a Missouri delegate sought to discredit Wells-Barnett indirectly with a resolution supporting "the work and methods of the W.C.T.U." Ruffin ruled her out of order but was overridden by "the Washington delegation." Although the resolution passed with protest, it was never published. The next month the Boston Woman's Club publicly deplored the WCTU's lynching position, and the *Woman's Era* proclaimed, "let it be understood that the editors of this paper stand by Mrs. Wells-Barnett squarely in her position on this matter and fully endorse it."[9]

The conflict between the Washington and Boston women grew from more than their positions on the WCTU. Before departing, the conference delegates voted to form the National Federation of Afro-American Women with Margaret Murray (Mrs. Booker T.) Washington as president. Washington, D.C., women had already sought to establish a national organization. By 1896, over one hundred women's groups had joined the National League of Colored Women; however, eighty-five were located in the District. The rivalry manifested itself when both groups scheduled meetings for July 1896 in Washington. As a result of those meetings, however, the groups united to form the National Association of Colored Women (NACW), with Mary Church Terrell as president.[10] This time Wells-Barnett was present in flesh as well as spirit, playing an important role in its deliberations.

Ferdinand Barnett hired a nurse to accompany his wife and four-month-old son to the Washington meeting. The famous abolitionist Harriet Tubman, as the oldest attendee, introduced the youngest, Charles Aked Barnett, to the audience, which elected him "Baby of the Federation." His mother was busy. Representing both the Ida B. Wells Club as its president and the Anti-Lynching Society of London as a fraternal delegate, she gave a speech on "Reform"; read the report of the committee on resolutions, which she chaired; and offered numerous resolutions regarding the formation of the permanent organization. Wells-Barnett received new tasks at the convention—appointment to the editorial staff of the *Woman's Era*, selection as secretary of a committee to publish the minutes of the 1895 and 1896 conferences in pamphlet form, and designation as representative to the next Prison Congress of the United States. She even helped take up the collection at meeting's end.[11]

The merging of any two groups creates problems and rivalries, but the proceedings seem to have gone remarkably well. The *Cleveland Gazette* expressed doubt "if there ever assembled a more thoughtful, earnest body of persons." The *Woman's Era* exulted over the "utter absence of frivolous personalties" and observed, "The all important question, 'Is my bonnet straight?' was never even dreamed of." That paper gave credit to Wells-Barnett for helping maintain unity:

> History is made of little things, after all. It was a pretty little scene in
> one of the committee rooms, that ought to go down in the history of

the Afro-American woman—if one should be written. Mrs. Ida Wells-Barnett, whom every one knows, is positive and determined in her opinions, and her expression of them, gracefully and gently, yielded . . . when the question of endorsing in an unqualified manner the work of the W.C.T.U. was raised. Considering the differences of opinion between Miss Willard and Mrs. Barnett, and the utterances of the former in regard to the work of the latter, the introduction was somewhat after the fashion a slap in Mrs. Barnett's face. But she gracefully gave her approval, and thus added another heroic act to the list of self sacrificing acts done at Washington.

The *Washington Bee* declared, "Mrs. Barnett was the politician among the delegates."[12]

Wells-Barnett did not realize that the 1896 meeting was the last time she would play a significant role in the NACW. In 1897 NACW held its first biennial meeting in Nashville, Tennessee. Wells-Barnett was not one of the two delegates sent from Illinois, who invited the group to hold its second meeting at Chicago in 1899. To prepare for the event, Chicago clubwomen formed the "Woman's Conference." It became the nucleus of the Illinois Federation of Colored Women's Clubs with Fannie Barrier Williams as president. Wells-Barnett was not among them, and these women notified NACW president Mary Church Terrell that they would not cooperate in the 1899 meeting if she included Wells-Barnett. Terrell acquiesced, and when Wells-Barnett learned of the request, she called it "a staggering blow."[13]

Wells-Barnett was as disappointed with Terrell as with the Chicago women. In her autobiography she blamed the action on the president's ambition, claiming Terrell "used the narrow-minded attitude of my own home women to ignore me lest I might become a contender for the position she wanted again." Wells-Barnett must have felt great satisfaction when Terrell's reelection caused a brouhaha that was reported in the press. She claimed the effort "somehow seemed to kill her [Terrell's] influence." Terrell, on the other hand, insisted then and in her 1940 autobiography that she had not wanted the position and had to be talked into taking it.[14]

The two women's autobiographies also differ on another incident at the 1899 convention. According to Wells-Barnett, she promised Terrell "not to inflict my presence upon the organization." However, Jane Addams of Chicago's Hull House called Wells to invite the NACW officers to lunch. Wells-Barnett did not inform Addams that she "had no part or lot with the organization" and promised to extend the invitation. When she went to Quinn Chapel to do so, Wells-Barnett declined an invitation by

Terrell to come to the platform until the "Memphis delegation" insisted on it. Then she delivered the invitation and later escorted the group to the luncheon. Terrell's book does not mention any part played by Wells-Barnett. Indeed, her autobiography never mentions her fellow Memphian at all—but, then, it rarely mentions any black women.[15]

The incident reflects Wells-Barnett's continuing difficulties in making and maintaining friendships with women that she had noted during her twenties. After the 1899 convention, Terrell wrote a crony that "our 'Virtuous Friend' had done all in her evil power to prejudice the minds of Illinois delegates against me." Into the 1920s, Terrell and her friends wrote snide comments about Wells-Barnett in personal letters, which indicate the Chicagoan had been much more public in her criticisms of Terrell.[16]

Wells-Barnett's problems with women were both personal and ideological—as were troubles among other black women. The *Washington Bee* asserted in 1896, "Women like men, are ambitious for fame and notoriety." So soon after slavery, it is not surprising that the black elite remained small enough to form a national network. With such a small pond, many naturally wanted to be big fish. Both Fannie Barrier Williams and Terrell had been two of the biggest fish when Wells-Barnett's antilynching work catapulted her ahead of them in the public's minds. Both developed bitter relationships with her that worsened as they became affiliated with the accommodationism of Booker T. Washington and she sided with the anti-Bookerite militants. By 1902 the Chicago *Broad Ax* noted Wells-Barnett and Williams "hate each other like two she rattlesnakes."[17]

There were differences of style as well as substance between Wells-Barnett and most women of the black aristocracy. While Wells reworked dresses in the 1880s because she could not afford new ones, Mollie Church wrote of a European trip for which her "travelling dress was made at Lord and Taylors." Williams also came from a very privileged background. Even marriage to the successful Ferdinand Barnett did not close the "respectability gap" between Wells-Barnett and the others. All three were activists, but Wells-Barnett's manner was much more aggressive and confrontational. Both Terrell and Wells-Barnett had been close to Tom Moss and deeply affected by his lynching in 1892 spoke out against lynching. However, according to one rhetorical scholar, Terrell maintained a "feminine" oratorical style, while Wells-Barnett did not.[18]

One black woman who consistently supported Wells-Barnett was Josephine Ruffin. Twenty years older than Wells-Barnett, she may have considered her a protégée. An observer in February 1893 noted, "Miss Ida Wells has been pretty influenced by Mrs. Ruffin who will rule or ruin." At any rate, as editor of *Woman's Era*, Ruffin defended Wells-Barnett while other prominent black women, such as elocutionist Hallie Q. Brown and journalist Mary E. Britton, criticized her antilynching efforts. Most black women were likely ambivalent about Wells-Barnett—proud of her fame and distressed by the accompanying scandal. After all, to defend themselves against the defamation of their womanhood, they surrounded themselves with white middle- and upper-class trappings of respectability.[19]

The women of NACW clearly saw themselves as flesh-and-blood refutation of the charges of black inferiority. They knew they were atypical of black women but asserted that "the few show the possibilities of the many."[20] They thus rejoiced over favorable accounts by whites who visited their meetings. A *Chicago Times Herald* reporter declared of the 1899 meeting, "These women of color were a continual revelation, not only as to their appearance, but as to intelligence and culture." Another white observer of an 1901 meeting marveled that the black women "had the faces of ladies—strong, sweet, thoroughly refined faces" and also the "manners of ladies, sweet and dignified." A Buffalo paper described the impact of such revelations, noting that the "good breeding of these women . . . put at once on the defensive anyone who undertook to apply the term 'inferior' to them."[21] Wells-Barnett was unlikely to be called "sweet" by anyone, and the negative reactions to her by many whites jeopardized the respectability campaign of the NACW.

NACW and Wells-Barnett also began to diverge in interests and focus. In 1896, when she chaired the resolution committee, the organization protested numerous injustices. By the turn of the century, many black leaders were becoming disillusioned with the effectiveness of protest. As ideologies of self-help became ascendant, NACW women turned their attention to improving the home environment of African Americans. Elizabeth L. Davis, the Illinois state organizer for NACW, explained in 1900, "Home is an[d] ever will be the chosen kingdom of woman." In 1906 the *Colored American Magazine* rejoiced that, unlike among white women, club work "has been the means of drawing the women of the colored race into closer touch with the individual home life." Mary Church Terrell noted that "the real solution of the race problem, both so far as we, who are oppressed and those who oppress us are concerned, lies in the children." All the women contributing to "Woman's Part in the Uplift of the Negro Race" in that journal the next year stressed variations of the theme: "The greatest work, the hardest work and the most vigorous efforts of the Negro woman should be done at the home."[22]

Although important to Wells-Barnett, home was not her "chosen kingdom." Of course, many black women explored other "kingdoms," and she shared their community involvement in establishing kindergartens and settlement house work. Nevertheless, Wells-Barnett continued to feel more at home in male-dominated protest organizations. In fact, while NACW women deliberated at Quinn Chapel, she was busy preparing for a meeting of the National Afro-American Council, which opened the day that the NACW convention concluded. As a young journalist, Iola had supported T. Thomas Fortune's efforts in the late 1880s that led to the formation of the National Afro-American League in 1890. A year later she spoke at the group's convention in Knoxville. After that group petered out in 1893, various black men and white liberal Albion Tourgee attempted to form other national organizations to confront deteriorating race relations. During April 1898, A.M.E. Zion Bishop Alexander Walters called on Fortune to revive the League. The result was a September meeting at Rochester, New York, in conjunction with the unveiling of a monument to Frederick Douglass.[23]

Having just weaned her second son, Wells-Barnett felt she "could safely leave him with his grandmother" to attend the events in Rochester, where she stayed with Susan B. Anthony. Quite a number of women attended the organizational meeting of the Afro-American Council, as it was renamed. Wells-Barnett, however, was the only woman to be elected to office (secretary) or to serve on the executive committee. As usual, she made her presence known. She successfully challenged the election of Fortune to the presidency, following what one observer called an "onslaught" in which he "denounced the race in the bitterest language possible." Wells-Barnett later recalled that Fortune had "spent more time trying to point out the shortcomings of the race than in encouraging us to unite." Regarding her election as secretary, she lamented, "So despite my best intentions, when I got back home to my family I was again launched in public movements."[24]

After being elected president, Bishop Walters called a meeting for 29 December in Washington to solidify the organization. The turnout at Rochester had been disappointing, and he hoped that advance notice and a more convenient setting would enlist more support. Among those mentioned by the *Freeman* as potential recruits were a number of women as well as Booker T. Washington. A race riot in Wilmington, North Carolina, in November sparked interest in the Council, following the reports of white mobs killing eleven African Americans. Although the *Colored American* worried that the "Negro is in danger of overdoing the mass-meeting business," it added its support. Most African Americans believed, with the *Cleveland Gazette*, "If we remain silent and surrender all that has been given us as citizens, we shall prove ourselves unworthy of the name of freemen." Many more people attended, and a number who did not, including Booker T. Washington, wired their regrets and support.[25]

Among the frequently quoted speeches was Wells-Barnett's "Mob Violence and Anarchy." Referring to the Wilmington riots, she deplored "the indifference manifested by the people of the North to these wrongs." Booker T. Washington was mistaken to believe African Americans could win rights by becoming factors in economic growth, she asserted. Success sometimes made them targets of lynchings instead. "President McKinley," Wells-Barnett exclaimed, "was much too interested just now in the national decoration of Confederate graves to pay any attention to the Negroes' rights." Addressing the expansion debate following the recently ended Spanish-American War, she asserted, "We are eternally opposed to expansion until this nation can govern at home." On the meeting itself she proclaimed, "If this gathering means anything, it means that we have at last come to a point in our race history where we must do something for ourselves, and do it now. We must educate the white people out of their 250 years of slave history."[26]

Wells-Barnett's criticisms of McKinley's failure to respond to the Wilmington riots were part of a larger debate within the Council regarding its relationship to partisan politics. One faction wanted to denounce McKinley and the Republican party in the group's "Address to the Nation," while according to the St. Paul *Appeal*, "certain federal office holders, aided by sundry bishops and ministers [wanted] to have incorporated in the address an indorsement of the Republican party in general, and the McKinley administration in particular." The end result was a compromise that expressed "regret" for the president's silence and "indulge[d] the hope that the President will use his good office in adjusting the matter." Nevertheless, charges of partisanship continued to echo in the Council during its entire existence.[27]

The debate also brought out another issue that would deeply divide the organization. John P. Green charged that McKinley had failed to act because certain colored men had advised him not to speak out on the subject. His speech was met with "hisses, groans and hoots." Although Green did not reveal the names of those advisors, most people assumed that he meant Booker T. Washington.[28] By that time, Washington had stepped into the void created by Douglass's death. The success of his school, Tuskegee

Institute, and his ability to raise funds among white philanthropists caught the attention of the black community, but he did not emerge as chief spokesperson until after a speech at the Atlanta Cotton States Exposition in 1895. Referred to as the "Atlanta Compromise," Washington's talk spelled out a basis for interracial cooperation in the South. He advised black southerners to concentrate on acquiring wealth and education rather than on agitating for rights. In return for aiding black educational and economic efforts, whites' reward would be a richer and more peaceful South. In time African Americans' success and contributions to the economy would win white support for black rights.

At first both the white and black communities praised the Atlanta speech. However, it soon became clear that they did not interpret Washington's words in the same way. To African Americans the emphasis on self-help echoed a growing chorus. Because of the fickleness of white allies and failure of protest to penetrate public indifference, many called for self-sufficiency. Whites focused on one unfortunate phrase: "In all things that are purely social we can be as separate as the fingers, yet one as the hand in all things essential to mutual progress." They misinterpreted the sentence as an endorsement of segregation in public accommodations. From the beginning, some black militants had viewed Washington as too conciliatory to white southerners. Others came to agree that he conceded too much; some became alienated by his emphasis on industrial education at the expense of higher education. However, in 1899 distinct camps of supporters and critics had not yet emerged.[29] Like many others, Wells-Barnett was ambivalent toward the "Wizard of Tuskegee."

Even though their positions on Washington were not clearly defined, black leaders began to diverge into what the *Freeman* called "radicals and conservatives" as early as the 1899 meeting of the Afro-American Council. The *Freeman* clearly put Wells-Barnett into the radical category, noting that the Council "had as its presiding officer a bishop and as its secretary an agitator." It further asserted the conservatives had dominated and the "chronic agitators and sensationalists received the reward of passing applause and a corresponding lessening of influence."[30] The debate over Washington would soon escalate, however, dividing the Council and decreasing Wells-Barnett's role.

In 1899, E. E. Cooper of the Washington *Colored American* already believed that Wells-Barnett had too large a role. He claimed that she "seemed to possess an ardent desire to be 'the whole thing.'" Her gender rather than her ideology bothered Cooper. Calling her election as secretary, the "Council's One Mistake," he asserted it was a man's job and said Wells-Barnett's "splendid abilities" could best serve the Council by organizing a women's auxiliary. "The proprieties would have best been observed," he declared, "by giving her an assignment more in keeping with the popular idea of woman's work, and which would not interfere so disastrously with her domestic duties."[31] Some men and women did not approve of the way she handled her "divided duties."

Even though obviously an agitator, Wells-Barnett was not yet an opponent of Washington. She had written a letter of support to him in 1890, and she declared in 1894 that his "quiet, earnest work is a shining light in the Black Belt of Alabama, where it is so needed." In January 1899, Wells-Barnett spoke at a pro-Washington rally in Boston, and in that same month Washington praised Wells in a speech at the Unitarian Club of New York.[32] The lynching of Sam Hose near Newnan, Georgia, in April began their estrangement. Hose was burned alive after he killed a white man, apparently in self-defense, and erroneous rumors circulated that Hose had raped the man's wife. It was a particularly grisly lynching because of its premeditation, the long torture of the victim, the picniclike atmosphere, the involvement of prominent whites, and the sale of charred body parts as souvenirs. Numerous papers, including the *New York Times*, graphically described the gruesome event.[33]

Wells-Barnett immediately organized a committee in Chicago to raise money for a detective to investigate. His report to a mass meeting in Chicago clearly showed that whites had lied in their accounts of the lynching. Many black newspapers and some white ones noted his report and the speech by Wells-Barnett that followed it. She also published the pamphlet *Lynch Law in Georgia* to publicize the findings as well as reproduce newspaper accounts of the event. "Samuel Hose was burned," she asserted, "to teach the Negroes that no matter what a white man does to them, they must not resist."[34]

Booker T. Washington failed to comment on the Hose lynching until after the Afro-American Council appealed to southern politicians and judges to protect black citizens. Fearful that Washington's silence would be criticized, T. Thomas Fortune, who had become one of the principal's ardent supporters, urged Washington to respond. The resulting letter to southern newspapers probably did more harm than good. Washington asserted that lynching injured the "moral and material growth" of the region and that most lynchings were not the result of rape. However, he closed with an acknowledgment of widespread black crime and urged African

Americans to repudiate "the beast in human form guilty of assaulting a woman."[35]

Soon afterward Wells-Barnett began to criticize Washington. In September Fortune informed Washington of a "sassy letter" from her complaining about the removal of a "disparaging reference" to the Tuskegean from her article in the *New York Age*. Fortune's relations with Wells-Barnett had been strained since she had criticized him for a speech he made in Texas the winter of 1895. He warned Washington that she was "a sort of bull in a China Shop."[36] Perhaps the clash of Wells-Barnett and Washington was inevitable given their ideologies and temperaments. Although they agreed on much, her long-held idea of lynching as a white tool to prevent black advancement could not coexist comfortably with his idea that black success brought white acceptance. His career was marked by a willingness to compromise; hers by an unwillingness to concede. She criticized almost everyone; he resented criticism from anyone. He tried to calm troubled waters; she sought to disturb still waters. Nevertheless, they sought—increasingly without success—to work together for several years.

The division within the Council over Washington's accommodationism became more apparent in the August 1899 meeting at Chicago. For that gathering the Barnetts were central actors in its preparation. The planning committee met at the *Conservator* offices and Ferdinand Barnett presided. Wells-Barnett chaired the local publicity and promotion committee and was a member of the national program committee. Both spoke at the meeting—he on disfranchisement and she on lynching. To expand the participation of women, Wells-Barnett asked several to be on the program and invited both Mary Church Terrell and Margaret Washington to a banquet in the Sherman Hotel at which she presided. When she called on Mrs. Washington to speak, however, the principal's wife declined, citing criticism of her husband in the meeting the previous day.[37]

Although Wells-Barnett later expressed surprise at that action, the issue of the Tuskegean's leadership had haunted the meeting even before it began. Fortune had advised him not to attend any sessions of the Council because he could not control the resolutions and speeches—some of which might embarrass him. Instead, Washington met privately with President Walters in his hotel room during the convention. When that action was questioned by Reverdy C. Ransom at the next meeting, press accounts claimed that "the famous Negro educator, was roundly criticised." Ransom, pastor of Chicago's Bethel A.M.E. Church, immediately repudiated the accounts. Among others who came to Washington's defense was Harvard Ph.D. recipient W. E. B. Du Bois. The denials, however, did not reassure the Tuskegean's supporters and angered others, who accused the Council of being "as bad as Mr. Booker T. Washington . . . a southern apologist and trimmer." The Barnetts seem to have remained uncharacteristically quiet about the issue, but Wells-Barnett saw her influence in the group decline as she moved from the secretary's position to head of the new antilynching bureau.[38]

Hoping to use the new bureau to expand her antilynching work, Wells-Barnett set up office on Princeton Avenue and mailed out circular letters "asking for 10,000 persons to enlist themselves in the work of disseminating correct reports throughout the community of the lynchings that happen." In the letter she asked for contributions of twenty-five cents from everyone in order to fund lynching investigations. She noted that the two hundred dollars spent by black Chicagoans to hire a detective in the Sam Hose case and to publish *Lynch Law in Georgia* had "done much to revolutionize public sentiment on that case." Her letter also pointed out, "The work of that bureau is to be the same as that which I have individually conducted for the past seven years: agitating, investigating and publishing facts and figures in the lynching evil."[39]

Several lynchings in the previous few years had especially engaged Wells-Barnett. One occurred in the neighboring state of Ohio. On 4 June 1897, an Urbana mob of five thousand attacked the jail in which Charles "Click" Mitchell was being held for allegedly assaulting a white woman. Guards fired into the crowd, killing three. This further enraged the crowd, which finally succeeded in capturing and hanging Mitchell. The initial reports described Mitchell's crime as a horrible attack in which the victim's nipple was bitten off and included an assertion that Mitchell had confessed after being identified by the victim. Wells-Barnett was suspicious. She went to Urbana to investigate and issued a report debunking the nature of the attack and the confession. Mitchell's family filed suit under a state antilynching law that state legislator and *Cleveland Gazette* editor H. C. Smith had marshaled through the legislature the previous year. The law, which held a county liable for five thousand dollars for any lynching occurring within its borders, was at first declared unconstitutional. Smith enlisted Wells-Barnett's aid in raising money for legal appeals, which ultimately proved successful in defending the law's constitutionality.[40]

Another lynching to enrage Wells-Barnett was the February 1898 murder of Frazier B. Baker and his infant child in Lake City, South Carolina. A mob of several hundred burned down his house and shot at his family because they were angered at his appointment as local postmaster. Wells-Barnett spoke at a mass protest meeting in Chicago, which raised money to send her to Washington where she sought federal action against the murder of this government official. She also solicited compensation for Baker's widow. Carrying along her five-month-old son Herman, she spent five weeks lobbying in the nation's capitol—exhausting the money raised and spending Barnett family funds in the cause. Typically, her critics used her womanhood to denounce her activism. One charged, "Mrs. Ida Wells Barnett has given the babies the bottle to nipple at, and is making frequent trips to Washington, to bother the president in behalf of a lot of men who are dead and in their graves."[41]

Seven Illinois congressmen and one senator accompanied Wells-Barnett to see President McKinley. Among other things, she told him:

> To our appeals for justice the stereotyped reply has been that the government could not interfere in a state matter. Postmaster Baker's case was a federal matter, pure and simple. He died at his post of duty in defense of his country's honor, as truly as did ever a soldier on the field of battle. We refuse to believe this country, so powerful to defend its citizens abroad, is unable to protect its citizens at home.

The president assured the group that he had launched a federal investigation.[42]

In seeking compensation, Wells-Barnett encountered some difficulties with North Carolina Congressman George White, the last black legislator elected from the South until after the Voting Rights Act of 1965. He had introduced a bill asking for one thousand dollars compensation, believing that the small amount would be less likely to meet southern opposition. Wells-Barnett believed any amount would be opposed. She wanted him to withdraw his bill so that Illinois Senator William E. Lorimer could submit one for a larger amount. The outbreak of the Spanish-American War, however, diverted attention and waylaid her efforts.[43]

Later that year violence struck closer to home. It came as the result of the widespread practice of using African Americans to break labor strikes. After coal miners struck in the Illinois cities of Virden and Pana, company owners brought in black Alabamians to take their places. Fearing violence, mine owners appealed to Governor John R. Tanner for protection, but he replied that he "did not propose to render military assistance in protecting the colored ex-convicts and scalawags of Alabama." On 12 October 1898, an angry crowd of miners fired into a train bearing two hundred strikebreakers. Wells-Barnett immediately went to Virden to investigate and made arrangements to bring several black miners to the state capitol to tell their side of the story. She called on the governor and then brought five miners back to Chicago to participate in an "indignation meeting" at Quinn Chapel. One black state appointee tried to block resolutions condemning Governor Tanner, but Wells-Barnett freely attacked the governor despite her own husband's lucrative position as assistant state's attorney. The *Illinois Record* reported that during her speech, "Barnett, her husband, was twitching and pulling his whiskers and the people said, 'Oh! his job . . . is gone,' but she kept on and the people were with her." Her speech did anger Tanner but did not cost Barnett his job.[44]

Wells-Barnett had promised to agitate as well as investigate, and one way she did so was by writing antilynching pamphlets and articles for white periodicals. Following her *Lynch Law in Georgia* in 1899, she published *Mob Rule in New Orleans* in 1900. It detailed the death of Robert Charles, who had violently resisted what he considered to be an unlawful arrest. For her information she relied on two white newspapers and correspondence. Again, she positioned herself as an objective reporter, writing that she "does not attempt to moralize over the deplorable condition of affairs shown in this publication, but simply presents the facts in a plain, unvarnished, connected way." Her words often belied that claim, however. The conclusion declared, "The white people of this country may charge that he was a desperado, but to the people of his own race Robert Charles will always be regarded as the hero of New Orleans."[45]

"Lynch Law in America," published in the January 1900 *Arena*, blatantly appealed to the pride and honor of white males. Wells-Barnett asserted that lynching may sometimes be justified by the absence of courts but not where "centuries of Anglo-Saxon civilization had made effective all the safeguards of court procedure." Now "butchery is made a pastime and national savagery condoned." Wells-Barnett did not deny that black men sometimes did rape: "The negro has been too long associated with the white man not to have copied his vices as well as his virtues." Referring to the "home of the brave," she noted, "Brave men do not gather by thousands to torture and murder a single individual, so gagged and bound he cannot make even feeble resistance or defense." Irony is obvious in her reference to the cost of lynching to the federal government, which had paid "nearly a half million dollars" of indemnities to China, Italy, and Great Britain for its inability to protect their citizens from mob violence on American soil.[46]

Two of Wells-Barnett's other articles were responses to white liberals' writings on lynching. "The Negro's Case in Equity," published in the April 1900 *Independent*, was a rejoinder to a previous article in that journal. After a few African Americans had participated in a lynching, the *Independent* published a plea to African American teachers, preachers, and editors "to tell their people to defend the laws." Wells-Barnett reminded readers of all that black Americans had done to end lynch law and of the horrors they had witnessed against their own before declaring, "Theoretically the advice is all right, but viewed in the light of circumstances and conditions it seems like giving a stone when we ask for bread." A year later she again responded to an *Independent* article—this one by Jane Addams on lynching. The two women were colleagues and worked together a number of times. Addams was one of the best-known white racial liberals and her article attacked lynching. Nevertheless, Wells-Barnett felt compelled to challenge "an unfortunate presumption used as the basis of her argument [that] works so serious, tho doubtless unintentional, an injury to the memory of thousands of victims of mob law." Addams had rhetorically accepted some southern assertions about rape to show that even if they were true, lynching still could not be justified. Wells-Barnett, however, asserted that any kind of acceptance of southern myths was unacceptable.[47] In her mind the more fame and power one had, the more care should be given in choosing words regarding African Americans.

Wells-Barnett's willingness to take on the powerful brought her into conflict with Booker T. Washington before the 1900 meeting of the Afro-American Council in Indianapolis. In 1899 Du Bois had become the director of the group's Negro business bureau, largely because of a conference he had called at Atlanta University that year on "The Negro in Business." At that meeting he had suggested forming local black business leagues to be united into a national federation. However, in 1900 Washington preempted his idea by establishing the National Negro Business League. In the *Chicago Conservator*, Wells-Barnett asserted that Washington had stolen the idea to establish an "organization of which he will be president, moderator and dictator," declaring he "is determined to help no movement he does not inaugurate." She later recalled that at the Council meeting "we made the best of the matter, since Mr. Washington himself had hitherto given us the impression that he could not ally himself with us because we were too radical."[48]

At the end of the 1900 Indianapolis meeting, Wells-Barnett remained an important force in the Afro-American Council, adding the title of national organizer to that of director of the Anti-Lynching Bureau. Early the next year she was the only woman on a Council committee "appointed to visit the President in the interest of the race." However, at the time of the 1901 convention Wells-Barnett was busy at her role as woman—very pregnant with her daughter Ida, who was born right after the convention. Washington's secretary, Emmett J. Scott, declared he was "glad Mrs. Barnett was not there to complicate the situation." Ferdinand Barnett attended and praised the Tuskegean. In her absence Wells-Barnett retained her anti-lynching bureau position but was replaced as national organizer. In 1902 the Chicago *Broad Ax* called her a "lonely leader treading a lonely path." At the Council meeting in St. Paul that year, her influence further declined as that of Booker T. Washington climbed. Sure of being able to control the group, he actually attended in 1902. A group portrait in the *Appeal* showed him at President Waters's right and Wells-Barnett on the president's left.[49]

The 1902 meeting marked a turning point for the Council. Fortune replaced Waters as president, causing William Monroe Trotter of the *Boston Guardian* to assert that the presidency "will now be Mr. Booker T. Washington's in everything except name." Although Wells-Barnett remained chair of the Anti-Lynching Bureau, most of the new officers were Bookerites. By that time her antilynching post was mainly honorific. In a January appeal for support to members of the bureau, Wells-Barnett admitted, "there are absolutely no funds in the treasury to pay postage much less the printer." In 1903 Wells-Barnett appears to have withdrawn completely, for the Indianapolis *Freeman* asked, "Won't Mrs. Ida B. Wells-Barnett relent and undertake her old trust of running the Afro-American Council?"[50]

After the St. Paul meeting, W. Calvin Chase of the *Washington Bee* noted with disgust that Washington's "satallites [sic] were in the saddle" and that they "trotted and pranced just as he pulled the reins." Emmett J. Scott exulted to his boss that "we control the Council *now*" and that it "was wonderful to see how completely your personality dominated everything at St. Paul." "From the moment you reached there," he exclaimed, "you were the center of attention, much to the chagrin and regret of our friends, the Barnetts—especially." The next year in Louisville, Washington's supporters shouted down Trotter's attempt to introduce anti-Washington resolutions, and Scott, whom the *Broad Ax* called "Washington's head chambermaid," joined the executive committee.[51]

In 1902 Trotter had noted that Fortune would furnish "whatever brain the combination needs, and Washington the boodle."[52] The comment reflected Washington's increasing power. His standing among white Americans burgeoned after McKinley's assassination passed the presidency to Theodore Roosevelt, who made Washington his political advisor on issues affecting African Americans. Wells-Barnett noted the irony of a political advisor coming from a state in which African Americans had no political power. The Tuskegean's impact also grew because of his ties with northern philanthropists. For a period of time, he had extraordinary influence over the dispensation of political offices and the granting of charitable contributions to the black community. Many northern blacks felt that this accommodating, white-selected spokesperson should not speak for them, and opposition grew after the 1902 Council meeting.

W. E. B. Du Bois and the Barnetts soon joined Trotter and Chase in the anti-Washington camp as the battle lines between the "radicals" and "conservatives" formed. The first widely published critique of Washington's leadership was an essay in Du Bois's 1903 book, *The Souls of Black Folk*. In it Du Bois questioned the principal's disparagement of protest and the vote as vehicles of black advancement. He also believed Washington overemphasized industrial education at the expense of higher education. The book created quite a sensation among white as well as black Chicagoans. White Unitarian minister Mrs. Celia Parker Wooley "had a gathering of the [white] literati at her home near the university to discuss it." She invited the Barnetts and six other black Chicagoans to lead the discussion, which focused on the criticisms of Washington. According to Wells-Barnett, when the discussion began, most of both the black and white guests "thought the book was weak because of [the criticism]." In a letter to Du Bois and in her autobiography, she claimed that she, her husband, and Mrs. C. E. Bentley spoke in Du Bois's defense and "came away feeling that we had given them an entirely new view of the situation."[53]

The Barnetts hosted another discussion of the book in their home in June 1903, and joined in a local Equal Opportunity League to sponsor a lecture by the Atlanta University professor the following December. During that fall E. E. Cooper, editor of the Washington *Colored American* and an ardent Bookerite, referred to a critic of Washington as "a fourth edition of Ida. B. Wells." The next April she launched a public attack on Washington's leadership, which was published in *World Today* as "Booker T. Washington and His Critics." First, she decried his willingness to demean the race. "The Negro is the butt of ridicule with the average white American," Wells-Barnett wrote. Knowing nothing but of the black lower classes, white humorists could be somewhat excused for their jokes, but what they "did unintentionally Booker T. Washington has done deliberately." Knowing "intimately the ablest members of the race," Washington could not be excused for jokes like one he told "a cultured body of women" at the Chicago Woman's Club. In that joke, Washington compliments a black farmer for growing his own hogs, and the farmer replies, "Yes, Mr. Washington, ebber sence you done tole us bout raising our own hogs, we niggers round her hab resolved to quit stealing hogs and gwinter raise our own." Wells-Barnett considered it an insult to "the hundreds of Negroes who bought land, [and] raised hogs . . . long before Booker Washington was out of school."[54]

Washington's emphasis on industrial education to prepare African Americans for work also appalled Wells-Barnett.

> This gospel of work is no new one for the Negro. It is the South's old slavery practice in a new dress. It was the only education the South gave the Negro for [the] two and a half centuries she had absolute control of his body and soul. The Negro knows that now, as then, the South is strongly opposed to his learning anything else but how to work.

She did not deny that industrial education was appropriate for many but believed Washington's emphasis had disastrous effects—decreasing the availability of higher education without a corresponding increase in industrial education programs.[55]

Wells-Barnett characterized the Tuskegean's answer to lynching as: "Give me some money to educate the Negro, and when he is taught how to work, he will not commit the crime for which lynching is done." To her, Washington ignored the fact that "lynching is not evoked to punish crime but color, and not even industrial education will change that." She recognized that the principal avoided "radicals" to protect his school, but insisted that if he refused to defend the rights his race "for fear of injury to his school by those who are intolerant of Negro manhood, then he should be just as unwilling to injure his race for the benefit of his school."[56]

As criticism of Washington escalated, so did his efforts to silence it. He ruthlessly sought to use his influence over political appointments and charitable contributions to win converts and crush opponents. In addition, he endeavored to control as many black newspapers as possible through investment, subsidy, and advertising money. Behind the scenes, Washington joined with militants to oppose disfranchisement and segregation as a secret partner in court challenges and legislative lobbying. Publicly, he continued to counsel attention to work and education rather than protest and politics. As his fame grew and the world's attention focused on Tuskegee

Institute, Washington increasingly felt that any criticism of himself or his school hurt the image of all African Americans. To his critics, however, the Tuskegean seemed to value his personal power and prestige above his duty to race. His takeover of the Afro-American Council left militants without an effective voice.

In 1905 Du Bois and Trotter joined together to form a new protest organization, which came to be called the Niagara Movement. Both Barnetts were supporters, but the group floundered in the face of Washington's efforts to destroy it. For Wells-Barnett, national platforms for her protest dwindled as she lost influence in the major organizations through personal and ideological conflicts. As a result, she turned her attention increasingly to her local community and to her family to meet her duties as an activist and woman. Believing that black women were "unwilling that one of their own race should occupy a position of influence," Wells-Barnett also turned to the group that had given her so much support in England—white women.[57]

14

⊸∞⊸

Community and Interracial Activities

"To break down the barrier of race prejudice"

⊸∞⊸

B lack novelist Richard Wright wrote of Chicago, "there is an open and raw beauty about that city that seems either to kill or endow one with the spirit of life." In the 1890s, Chicago had the virility and untamed rambunctiousness of an adolescent experiencing rapid growth spurts. When Ida B. Wells moved there in 1893, the city was only twenty-five years older than she but had already become home to more than a million people. The peculiar American habit of dividing people into two catagories— black and white—lost some of its hold where foreign-born immigrants and their children comprised nearly 80 percent of the population. Although it had rarely lived up to its antebellum label as a "sinkhole of abolition," Chicago expanded black rights after the war, eliminating segregated schools and granting the vote to African American males. During the 1890s, black newspapers across the nation extolled its racial openness and enumerated its many black officeholders, city employees, and professionals. It was the home of both a vibrant black aristocracy and famous white liberals, such as Jane Addams and Albion Tourgee, who sought to bridge the chasm of race. At the same time Chicago did much to earn its label as "a modern Sodom and Gomorrah." Vice was rampant and politicians could be bought. Rarely has there been a more arresting mixture of crime, corruption, and crusades.[1]

For Wells-Barnett, Chicago's social problems and its possibilities were inspirations for activism. The city was experiencing growing pains that challenged city services and threatened racial tolerance. Housing and job competition created hostility that was beginning to erode black rights. Nevertheless, white reformers offered Wells-Barnett new experiences of integration, and black protest frequently brought tangible results. It was a fertile field for her militancy. At the same time marriage brought new responsibilities as well as new respectability. By the young city's standards, her husband was an "old settler" whose prominence and prosperity gave the couple stature within the socially active black elite. Relieved of her gnawing financial worries, Wells-Barnett had to apportion another scarce commodity—her time.

Although she did not stop traveling after the birth of Charles Aked in 1896, Wells-Barnett began to spend more time in Chicago. At that time she had two major outlets for her activism: the *Conservator* and the Ida B. Wells Club. The editorship of the *Conservator* provided both a local and national platform, as black editors continued to quote her pithy comments. Marriage did nothing to soften her stridency. Defending a fellow journalist charged with disrespecting the flag, Wells-Barnett exclaimed, "Bah! With the smell of the burning flesh of his race in his nostrils, how can any man with an ounce of blood in his veins defend the flag under whose folds such things regularly occur." When a row was raised over the burial of a black woman in a white Richmond cemetery, she wryly noted, "At the Judgment Day there will be many American white christians [sic] who will refuse to go to heaven it is feared, because there will be Negroes admitted." She regularly criticized a racial double standard in the administration of justice, once proclaiming, "If justice is blind in America it is blind in only one eye." To make that point, Wells-Barnett brought to her readers' attention the prosecution of a black man and the freeing of his white wife for violating an Indiana law prohibiting interracial marriage. She continued to be critical of black leaders for timidity and lack of unity, labeling one gathering as "a small body of men who are anxious to pose as 'white men's niggers'" and deploring the failure of many African Americans to remember that "no man builds well whose foundation is laid upon another's ruin."[2]

Just before the birth of Herman in November 1897, Wells-Barnett decided that she could no longer be a full-time editor and mother and stepped down from her position at the *Conservator*. Black newspapers noted her retirement with "surprise" and " heart-felt regret." The *Charleston Enquirer* expressed the "lasting gratitude of her people" for the "plucky agitator." The *Cleveland Gazette* noted that the *Conservator*, "under her management, maintained a dignified and forceful position." Most referred to her work in the past tense. The *Freeman* declared that she "wielded a fearless pen in the interest of her race," and the *Michigan Representative* proclaimed, "She was an able, fearless and staunch supporter of her race."[3] Anyone who expected motherhood to silence Wells-Barnett was misguided. She continued to write letters to both white and black newspapers as well as articles for the *Conservator*. Although that paper changed editors and owners many times, some competitors rightly noted that the Barnetts continued to have indirect control of the journal most of the time. In 1903 the Indianapolis *Freeman* asked the Barnetts to "end confusion by hoisting their names fairly and squarely at the editorial mast-head."[4]

The Ida B. Wells Club had grown out of the Columbian Exposition in 1893. During the fair, a group of prominent black men organized the Tourgee Club and established a clubhouse on Dearborn Street primarily to entertain fair visitors. The club invited Wells that September to speak and host a "ladies day," which led to continued women's meetings in the Tourgee Club's parlors every Thursday. Soon the women formed their own organization, naming it for the antilynching agitator and electing her president. The Ida B. Wells Club undertook such projects as raising money to ensure prosecution of a police officer who had killed an African American.[5]

As president of the Ida B. Wells Club and a new mother, in 1896 Wells-Barnett launched a project that seemed innocuous and in keeping with her motherly role—establishing a kindergarten. Even when not protesting, however, she remained controversial. Kindergartens were new and rare at the time. Only a few private ones existed, and only one was available to the black residents of South Side. The Armour Institute accepted black children but had few openings. Although not legalized, housing segregation confined most African Americans to one of four neighborhoods (out of which whites began moving when black neighbors began arriving). South Side was the largest of these and to place a private kindergarten there meant all its pupils would be black. Wells-Barnett only saw a need and an opportunity to meet it when a black female graduate of the Chicago Kindergarten College approached the club for help in establishing one. Another member also had kindergarten training but had been unable to find a job. Armed with a staff, the group set out to raise funds.

Calling a mass meeting at her church, Bethel A.M.E., Wells-Barnett met unexpected opposition. One witness recounted that "she was made to understand we do not want nor need any separate organizations or institutions for the colored people." Wells-Barnett recalled, "To say I was surprised does not begin to express my feeling." She noted that people were "so afraid of the color line" that they preferred "to let our children be neglected and do without kindergarten service than to supply the needs of their own." Wells-Barnett saw duty to the children as more important than any duty to the abstract ideal of integration. Opponents, however, charged that "it was just such methods on the part of a few narrow-minded men that brought about [a] separate school system in this city many years ago which took the ability and time and large sums of money of some of our best men and women to break up." Never one to be easily deterred, Wells-Barnett succeeded in raising funds and persuading the church to let them use its lecture room. The resultant kindergarten was open to all but was patronized only by African Americans.[6]

The incident illustrates the ambivalence of many African Americans regarding separatism and integration. Most black leaders at the close of the century remained philosophically committed to integration but repeatedly encountered the barrier of white exclusion. The agonizing dilemma was how to meet black needs without implicitly endorsing segregation. For Wells-Barnett and others, the answer was an uneasy coexistence of both doctrines in their minds and hearts. Some fought the implied degradation of segregation but had little desire to mingle with whites as long as they were not barred from doing so. Many of the black elite, including Wells-Barnett, eagerly cultivated relationships with whites, while simultaneously fostering race unity and self-help. With color determining their status in most white minds, they could not afford the luxury of color blindness.

Despite the charges of her opponents on the kindergarten issue, Wells-Barnett usually refused to acquiesce to segregation and clearly cherished her triumphs over the color line. At the close of the World's Fair in 1893, Frederick Douglass had come to the *Conservator* offices to invite Wells to lunch. The closest restaurant was the Boston Oyster House, which she had heard did not serve black customers. The pair decided to seek admittance anyway, and Wells-Barnett later recalled, "The waiters seemed paralyzed over our advent, and not one of them came forward to offer us a table. Mr. Douglass walked up to the nearest table, pulled out a chair, seated me, then took a seat himself." The owner recognized the old abolitionist and fawned over him — much to her delight. A year later, however, soon after her return from London, she and another woman on the *Conservator* staff sought service there and would have been denied access, except for the intervention of the white editor of the *Inter-Ocean*.[7]

The importance of such incidents to Wells-Barnett is seen in the attention she gave them in her autobiography. She spent a page and a half describing how her English friend, Charles Aked, who was a guest minister at the University of Chicago on Thanksgiving 1895, had invited her to attend a school football game with him and the university's president after the services. "Although I did not understand football," she wrote, "and did not especially fancy sitting out in the cold November wind, I could not resist the opportunity to aid in giving a lesson in real democracy to our American friends." She agreed with Aked that the white elite had contact only with "the menial class" and needed to be exposed to members of the black elite to dispel their false impressions. "When we could do so without sacrificing self-respect," she wrote, "we should make it a point to be seen at lectures, concerts, and other gatherings of public nature and thus accustom white people to seeing another type of the race as well as their waiters and cooks, seamstresses and bootblacks."[8]

Like the black aristocracy elsewhere, the Chicago elite sought to distinguish itself from not only black criminals and "menials" but also from the lower middle class. In the nineteenth century, the northern black elite emphasized family roots and called themselves "old settlers" in contrast with the new migrants from the South. A white observer in 1908 noted, "Even in Chicago where there is nothing old, I found the same spirit." Ferdinand Barnett was an "old settler" by virtue of his family's residency there since 1869, and his wife became an honorary member. An 1898 article listed him among the pioneer "colored aristocracy" and referred to "his able and fearless wife." Wells-Barnett recognized very early the importance of class in Chicago. When forming the Ida B. Wells Club, she recruited Mrs. John Jones to be the honorary head of the movement because "as an old citizen, her husband being the wealthiest colored man in Chicago at that time, it would lend prestige to have such a genteel, high-bred old lady of the race to lead them."[9]

The black elite of the older cities in the East questioned whether Chicago had a "true aristocracy" because of its youth and the fact that "money talked" there more. Fannie Barrier Williams, however, asserted in 1905 that the city's aristocracy was "better dressed, better housed, and better mannered than almost anywhere else in the world." Its wealth was apparent in a 1902 article describing one woman's dress as costing $275 and in an 1899 description of a charity ball:

Down the great hall they came in stately measured tread, brave men
by the side of beautiful women, as lovely as the daughters of the gods,
and each as fit to be a queen. To the right and left swept the brilliant
calvacade, the air scintillating with the gleam of diamonds and precious jewels, not brighter than starry eyes that flashed gloriously.
There was a sweep of silk and satin, the perfume of a thousand
flowers.

The article noted, however, "Never before had the great people, blessed
with an abundance of goods, been willing to indulge in the frivolity of the
dance for the sake of sweet charity." One of the "great people" explained in
1907 that "society proper" included less than a score of Chicagoans, who
eschewed ostentation and preferred "discussing music, drama or literature
or whiling away an hour or so at cards" among "small circles of friends."
The Barnetts were frequently mentioned in press accounts of both types of
gatherings.[10]

Their popularity was undoubtedly enhanced by Ferdinand Barnett's
political clout. In 1896 the Republican party established separate black an-
nexes in New York and Chicago to direct the election campaign among
African Americans. Barnett headed the western office. Among black editors the idea of separate offices was controversial, and Barnett drew fire
from some for asking them to run campaign literature free of charge. The
party's success, however, cemented Barnett's influence. Soon afterward,
black Cook County Commissioner Edward H. Wright used his clout to
force the state's attorney, Charles S. Deneen, to deliver on a political bar-
gain and appoint Barnett as the first black assistant state's attorney at the
generous salary of $150 a month. The new appointee quickly demon-
strated his competence: first, by running the newly established juvenile
court, and then by taking sole charge of cases involving antitrust violations
and of extradition and habeas corpus proceedings. Becoming a recognized
expert in these fields, Barnett continued to be reappointed by every state's
attorney until 1911.[11]

In 1900 Barnett again headed the Republican Negro Bureau and received a request from a white party leader in Missouri for assistance by
Wells-Barnett in the state campaign among African Americans. When she
arrived, plans had become muddled and some black party leaders objected
to the party's paying for help that was not needed. Nevertheless, a county
chairman decided to go ahead with a meeting since the antilynching agitator was already there. It was so successful that he paid her expenses to the
next county. "So in this way," Wells-Barnett later wrote, "I was handed from

one town to another, each county chairman paying the expenses of the trip." Women did not have the vote yet, but she attempted to stimulate black women to "use their moral influence to see that their men voted and voted right."[12]

In the late 1890s, Ferdinand Barnett's influence was reflected in his being named as a possible candidate for a cabinet position in the federal government and in his consultation with President William McKinley on black patronage. However, as Booker T. Washington's star ascended, it began to eclipse Barnett's. Theodore Roosevelt's succession to the presidency in 1901 increased the Tuskegean's political strength, and in 1904 Washington challenged the reappointment of Barnett by the national Republican committee. The members of the so-called Tuskegee Machine clearly saw Wells-Barnett as a partner in her husband's party role. In letters Emmett J. Scott discussed "the effort to block Barnett and his wife," and Washington referred to replacing "Barnett and his wife" with the Chicagoan's former law partner and now a Bookerite, S. Laing Williams. The Tuskegean also considered T. Thomas Fortune for the position, to which the New York editor replied, "I want it, and it will make the Chicago hyenas wild."[13]

Washington believed he could persuade Republican party leaders to dump Barnett because of the Chicago couple's criticisms of both McKinley and Roosevelt's early administrations. He noted with disgust that "in both cases at the proper time they laid low and proclaimed themselves loyal supporters of the administration." Washington failed, however, because Chicago was a center of anti-Washington sentiment and Williams did not have the political clout to overcome the Barnetts' popularity or the influence of Barnett's boss, Charles Deneen. Nevertheless, the Bookerites succeeded in getting their man in New York and diminishing Barnett's position into what one Chicago paper referred to as a "janitor's job." In 1908 the Barnetts' open opposition to William Howard Taft completed the destruction of their influence in the national Republican party.[14]

Their work in the Republican party was not the only interracial effort of the couple. In 1902 Wells-Barnett had much hope in the activities of white women "who were trying to break down the barrier of race prejudice." When NACW President Josephine S. Yates came through Chicago, Wells-Barnett entertained her with "a small luncheon at which were present an equal number of white and colored club women." One of the white guests, Mrs. George W. (Mary R.) Plummer, issued an invitation for a similar luncheon at her house when Yates came back to Chicago. Before

Yates's return, however, some Chicago black women informed the NACW president about rumors of white opposition to such a gathering. Plummer assured Wells-Barnett that only the smallness of her house had limited the guest list, but Yates at first refused to attend. Wells-Barnett reminded Yates to "not forget that white women who try to be our friends risked friendships and social prestige by doing so and that we ought not add to their burdens by taking a narrow viewpoint ourselves." Yates relented and the luncheon with six white club presidents was "a great success socially." Nevertheless, Wells-Barnett refused to reveal the participants' names to "reporters of the daily press, looking for sensation."[15]

The friendship of Plummer and Wells-Barnett also led to the inclusion of black women in the founding of the League of Cook County Clubs by Chicago women. Before the organizational meeting Plummer extended an invitation to Wells-Barnett, thinking she was still the president of the Ida B. Wells Club. Later claiming that circumstances prevented notification of Agnes Moody, the club's actual president, Wells-Barnett attended and became a member of the nine-person board of directors, after receiving the most votes of all the candidates. She and a friend were the only African Americans in attendance and paid the dues for their club. When Moody learned of those actions, she was furious. Wells-Barnett claimed, "My only thought at the time had been that we must not fail to respond to the invitation extended by our white sisters." More likely, she could not resist the opportunity to represent black women after she had failed to win influence in the NACW. After spending four days "visiting and explaining to the members of the club," Wells-Barnett won ratification of her actions over the protest of Moody. Nevertheless, she withdrew from her namesake club and became estranged from another of the city's leading black clubwomen.[16]

Wells-Barnett turned increasingly to the white community for allies against the growing hostility of prejudiced white citizens. The city's public schools had been legally integrated since 1874, but beginning about 1900 segregation proposals began occurring in newspapers and school board meetings. According to Wells-Barnett, after her husband complained about segregationist statements in the *Chicago Tribune*, she wrote a letter noting that "everybody had been quoted on the subject of separate schools except those most vitally concerned—the Negroes." She asked if the editor would receive a delegation from the black community. Getting no response, she personally called on Editor Robert W. Patterson, who mistook her for "one of the women from one of the colored churches coming to solicit a contribution." Their conversation convinced her that he was "southern" on the "subject of racial equality."[17]

Thinking over her options, Wells-Barnett realized black Chicagoans did not have the numerical or financial strength to force a modification in Patterson's position. "I knew," she later wrote, "that if every Negro in Chicago taking or advertising in the *Tribune* should fail to take it, the result would be so small it would not even be known." Therefore, she asked Jane Addams, "Will you undertake to reach those of influence who would be willing to do for us what we cannot do for ourselves?" Addams called together white liberals to hear Wells-Barnett's story, and they formed a committee of seven to call on Patterson. Writing in the late 1920s, Wells-Barnett declared, "I do not know what they did or what argument was brought to bear, but I do know that the series of articles ceased and from that day until this there has been no further effort made by the *Chicago Tribune* to separate the schoolchildren on the basis of race."[18]

Asked to speak on "The Afro-American Woman: Her Past, Present and Future" at the Chicago Political Equality League in early 1903, Wells-Barnett expressed a faith in biracial contacts to diminish prejudice. She told her predominantly white audience that the greatest work for African American women was "to emancipate the white women of the country from the prejudice which fetters their noblest endeavors and renders inconsistent their most sacred professions." Black women would accomplish this, Wells-Barnett predicted, "by a bearing so dignified and courteous, and withal so tempered by a nature absolutely incapable of race hatred; by a genius which shall delight the world; by a love which beareth all things, believeth all things, hopeth all things, endureth all things."[19]

One white woman who agreed was Celia Parker Wooley, the Unitarian minister who hosted the biracial discussion of *The Souls of Black Folk* in 1903. Around that time she came to Wells-Barnett with the idea of establishing "a center in which white and colored persons could meet and get to know each other better." According to Wells-Barnett, the city's black leaders opposed the idea and "Mr. Barnett and I had to become militant champions in the effort to put the movement over." Unable to find a landlord willing to rent to such an interracial group, Wooley got white friends to donate a down payment to buy a house on Wabash Avenue. Wells-Barnett organized the black community to help make the payments. In late 1904 the Frederick Douglass Center began under controversy. Some whites considered it an "astonishing attempt to force social equality," because light refreshments were served at the biracial business meetings.[20]

In 1905 Wooley called on Wells-Barnett for advice on forming a Frederick Douglass Center Women's Club. Wells-Barnett gave her wholehearted support but was surprised when Wooley suggested making Mary

Plummer the group's president. "I saw very clearly," she later wrote, "that she had determined not only that I should not be president but that she wanted a white woman." Citing the demands of her family to which a fourth child, Alfreda, had been added in September 1904, Wells-Barnett declined to take any office but agreed to preside over the organizational meeting, which elected Plummer president in absentia and convinced Wells-Barnett to accept the vice presidency. The group formally organized in mid-September, when Plummer returned from summer vacation.

The club joined a growing list of center activities that included a kindergarten, sewing classes, a Young People's Lyceum, a Men's Forum, sociology and English classes, an exhibit of "African curios," a vacation school for black children during the summer, and Athletic Clubs for boys and girls, organized by Ferdinand Barnett. Both Barnetts were heavily involved in the center, often speaking or teaching classes. The Phyllis Wheatley and Ida B. Wells Clubs as well as others began to meet at the center. Some saw it as part of the settlement house movement, and membership included such prominent white settlement house workers as Jane Addams, Graham Taylor, and Mary McDowell.[21]

One of Wells-Barnett's attempts to raise money for the Frederick Douglass Center created quite a furor because of the venue. Her longtime love for the theater and race pride led her to seek to bring black artists, writers, and entertainers to the Chicago public and also to encourage cultural activities. She invited such authors Charles W. Chestnut and Samuel Coleridge-Taylor to speak in Chicago, raised money for musical prizes and scholarships, and established an Afro-American Historical Society.[22] Thus Wells-Barnett was delighted when Robert T. Motts decided to turn his saloon and amusement hall into the Pekin Theater, and she and her husband attended the opening night. Pleased with the quality of the production and disappointed in the small turnout, Wells-Barnett had the inspiration to stage a benefit for the Frederick Douglass Center at the Pekin in May 1906. It was a huge success. Attended by the "cream of the four hundred," it raised over five hundred dollars. Because of the Pekin's shady background and Motts's continuing ties to gambling, however, many ministers opposed the theater and chastised the Barnetts for their support. A number of black leaders were concerned with the influence of gambling interests in city politics, which was considerable at the time. Nevertheless, from 1906 to Motts's death in 1911, the Pekin Theater thrived and launched the careers of numerous famous black entertainers.[23]

Prominent whites attended the Pekin benefit, but Wells-Barnett's faith in interracial cooperation received numerous blows during 1906. The first came in January. Asked at the last moment to arrange a replacement to a canceled program for the Frederick Douglass Center Women's Club, Wells-Barnett chose the topic "Motherhood." After she, an artist, a doctor, a minister, and an attorney spoke, Wooley requested an opportunity to address the group. According to Wells-Barnett, Wooley downplayed motherhood by pointing out that many influential women were not mothers. Her words "seemed like a dash of cold water" to Wells-Barnett, who complained:

> From that time on Mrs. Wooley never failed to give me the impression that she did not propose to give me much leeway in the affairs of the center. I felt at first that she had been influenced by other colored women who, strange to say, seemed so unwilling that one of their own race should occupy a position of influence, and although I was loath to accept it, I came to the conclusion before our relations ended that our white women friends were not willing to treat us on a plane of equality with themselves.[24]

The experience was very similar to that which Frederick Douglass had with white abolitionists who sought to keep him in a protégé role.

Other African Americans, most notably editor Julius Taylor, were also suspicious of Wooley's attitude toward them. Taylor was outraged by an article in the *Boston Transcript*, which he quoted as saying that Wooley had left her comfortable home to move into the center, "where she is content to reside with her commanding presence, simply to benefit the poor, uncouth, ill-bred, and repulsive-appearing Colored people, who are so much in need of her love and unbounded sympathy." That was hardly an accurate rendition of the center's clientele, but Wooley had the article reprinted to use in fund-raising. Taylor also noted that when Wooley "lectures to her overgrown Colored boys and girls, who pose as the great leaders of their race," she invariably referred to them as "you people or your people," which demonstrated she did not "regard them as part and parcel of herself." He agreed with Wells-Barnett that Wooley was "not willing to treat us on a plane of equality" and singled out the treatment of Well-Barnett herself as proof that Wooley believed all black women "lack executive ability." The editor noted Wells-Barnett's status as vice president and declared, "in all honesty and sincerity, we believe she is a lady of too much prominence to accept such a minor or unimportant position in any woman's club."[25]

After her disappointment with Wooley, Wells-Barnett continued to have a good relationship with club president Plummer, but by the end of 1906 racial tensions drove a wedge between them also. It was a year of profound disillusionment for African Americans. Several events shook their faith in white allies' commitment to ending racial violence. In August longstanding hostility toward black troops stationed at Brownsville, Texas, led to a shoot-out resulting in white casualties. President Roosevelt, who had been seen as friendly to African Americans because he made some key black appointments and invited Booker T. Washington to dine in the White House, dismissed an entire battalion. Without any kind of trial, the black soldiers were dishonorably discharged and barred from any further military or civilian jobs in the federal government. That outrage was followed the next month by a race riot in Atlanta, during which white mobs attacked any African American they encountered and destroyed black property in their wake.

One of the many black Atlantans to leave in the riot's aftermath was J. Max Barber, who moved his magazine *Voice of the Negro* to Chicago. According to Wells-Barnett, after he told the story of violence in Atlanta to the Frederick Douglass Center Women's Club, Plummer responded, "I do not know what we can do or say about this terrible affair, but there is one thing I can say and that is to urge all of you to drive the criminals out from among you." Wells-Barnett immediately protested her comments and asked for a strong resolution condemning the riot. Several black women came to Plummer's defense, and the meeting adjourned without passing the resolution. Stunned, Wells-Barnett approached Plummer, who pointed to the large number of black criminals in the city and noted that every white woman she knew in the South feared going out at night. When Wells-Barnett denied the southern charges, Plummer retorted, "My dear, your mouth is no more a prayer book than that of any other of my friends who have talked with me about this subject." Soon afterward, Wells-Barnett tried to mend fences but recalled that "her reply showed me very clearly that I had sinned beyond redemption with her when I had dared to challenge a statement of hers in public."[26]

Wells-Barnett's connection with the center further diminished after a number of white members, including Wooley, appeared to condone an invitation issued by a local hospital board to the bigoted, prolynching U.S. Senator Benjamin Tillman of South Carolina. The rupture was completed by Wooley's manipulations to ensure Wells-Barnett would not be elected president when Plummer resigned. "It seemed to me," Wells-Barnett later wrote, "such a case of double-dealing that my temper, which has always been my besetting sin, got the better of me." After presiding over the election, she "closed the meeting, officiated in the tea room as was my duty as presiding officer, then put on my things and left the Douglass Center never to return."[27]

The year 1906 delivered another blow to the Barnetts' faith in interracial cooperation, after Barnett won the Republican nomination for municipal judge. He was the only African American candidate for the citywide election and was apparently selected because of merit rather than color. Comprising less than 2 percent of the city's population, black Chicagoans had little political clout and had only succeeded in electing representatives for the wards into which housing discrimination corralled them. Barnett's credentials won him the support of the white attorneys of the Chicago Bar Association, which voted one hundred to forty-four to endorse him. However, most white newspapers—both Republican and Democrat—protested the nomination. The *Chicago Chronicle* declared, "The bench is a position of absolute authority and white people will never willingly submit to receiving the law from a negro." According to the Portland *New Age*, opponents issued postcards "picturing a trembling white woman being tried in a court in which brutish, black, anthropoid apes, supposed to be Afro-Americans, were judge, counsel, jury and bailiff." The black press, on the other hand, rallied around Barnett. Earlier, Democrat Julius Taylor had often lambasted Republican Barnett in the Chicago *Broad Ax*, writing in August 1903 that "if Barnett's record will permit him to go into court with clean hands, then the devil has the right to wash his face in holy water." In November 1906, however, Taylor urged all black voters to rally around Barnett "to secure this big honor to our race" and commended the candidate "as a worthy man by experience, education, temperament, integrity and fitness to fill the place."[28]

When the election returns came in, it appeared that the entire Republican judicial slate had won. Although Barnett received twenty thousand less votes than the other candidates, he had five hundred more votes than the Democratic challenger. Whites were astounded and angry. The *Evening Post* agreed with a letter writer who protested: "His nomination was a blunder; his election is an accident." It suggested that Barnett follow the example of Booker T. Washington and "refuse to seek or to accept public office." The Democrats demanded a recount, after which Barnett was declared the loser by 304 votes. African Americans believed he had been robbed of his victory by fraud and were bitterly disappointed in Chicago whites. They agreed with S. Laing Williams that "No colored candidate could have been treated much worse in the South." Wells-Barnett, however, blamed her husband's defeat on the lukewarm support he had received from black A.M.E. pastors as the result of her support of the Pekin Theater.[29] No matter how disillusioned she became with white allies, she was more bitterly disappointed by the abandonment of black leaders, from whom she expected more.

African Americans rarely felt more deserted by Republicans than in 1906. Roosevelt's treatment of the black troops at Brownsville was especially galling and led to massive defections. Bookerite S. Laing Williams wrote, "Things in Chicago are at fever heat in the race matter. You cannot find a Negro who is not denouncing the President in frightful terms of abuse. I never saw anything like it. Mass meetings are held in which the President's acts and motives are held up to scorn." For years the president's close ties with Booker T. Washington had been noted in the black press, often with admiration, but also with scorn. Although generally supporting Roosevelt in 1903, William Monroe Trotter declared he "has injured the race by making Booker Washington the race's dictator." Declining support for Roosevelt naturally diminished approval of Washington's leadership.[30]

Although the Tuskegean had critics long before Brownsville, they had been unable to rally any effective counter-movements. Most African Americans had remained ambivalent about Washington and his critics. For example, in December 1903, Ferdinand Barnett participated in a dinner for Du Bois hosted by the Equal Opportunity League and five months later attended a banquet honoring Washington.[31] By 1904 Trotter, Du Bois, and Wells-Barnett had publicly rebuked Washington, but neither the Equal Opportunity League nor Trotter's National Negro Suffrage League had flourished. In that year white liberal John Milholland formed the Constitution League to protest black disfranchisement. In 1905 Milholland's group joined the newly formed Niagara movement to push for legislation to reduce congressional representation in states that disfranchised African Americans. Washington's refusal to endorse the Platt bill angered Wells-Barnett and other supporters of the legislation.[32]

During the disappointments of 1906, the Niagara Movement furnished an outlet for what Du Bois labeled "plain, blunt complaint, unfailing exposure of dishonesty and wrong [which] is the ancient, unerring way to liberty." Both Barnetts supported the activism of the Illinois branch, headed by political ally Dr. C. E. Bentley. Its greatest achievement was getting an African American appointed to the new charter committee of Chicago, which helped thwart a move to segregate the city's schools. It also recruited the help of Jane Addams to see that the racist play, "The Clansman," was ignored by the drama critics of the local press. The next year, when the Illinois branch sponsored a talk by Reverdy C. Ransom, the list of "honorary vice-presidents" read like a "Who's Who" of Chicago's black elite and included Wells-Barnett. Nevertheless, Du Bois's "Talented Tenth" had little success rallying the masses or overcoming Washington's efforts to sabotage the movement. The Tuskegean's ability to hush his critics began to slip, however, as race relations deteriorated.[33]

Washington's influence suffered further decline in 1907, when the so-called radicals wrested control of the Afro-American Council from the Tuskegee machine. The greatest blow, however, came in 1908 when "outrages were perpetrated under the very shadow of Lincoln's tomb." The Springfield, Illinois, race riot in August proved that white mob violence had not been quarantined to the South. The *Broad Ax* lamented, "The hydra-headed monster, the murderous and destructive mob spirit, nurtured and bred in the haunts of vice, has broken out in the home and resting place of the Great Emancipator." Coming only two years after the Atlanta riots, the Springfield riot indicated to many that accommodationism was not working.[34]

The *Broad Ax* asked, "Where are our leaders?", and then listed five wrongs that demanded attention: "The Clansman," the defeat of Barnett, the address of Ben Tillman, the Brownsville incident, and the Springfield riot. White liberals joined the soul-searching. In the *Independent*, William English Walling asked, "Yet who realizes the seriousness of the situation and what large and powerful body of citizens is ready to come to [the Negroes'] aid?" He called for a revival of "the spirit of the abolitionists." One descendant of white abolitionists, Mary White Ovington, decided those questions needed answers. She prodded Walling and several other prominent white progressives to "call upon all the believers in democracy to join in a national conference for the discussion of present evils, the voicing of protests, and the renewal of the struggle for civil and political liberty." Written by another abolitionist's descendant, Oswald Garrison Villard, "The Call" was issued on the hundredth anniversary of Abraham Lincoln's birth in February 1909. Among its signers were Du Bois and Wells-Barnett.[35]

Although the white organizers allied with members of the Niagara Movement and the Constitution League, they sought to avert active opposition by Booker T. Washington. "If you wanted to raise money in New York for anything relating to the Negro," Ovington wrote, "You must have Washington's endorsement." Thus they issued an invitation to the

Tuskegean, but were relieved when he declined. Still not wanting to alienate him, they sought to prevent the gathering from appearing anti-Washington. Du Bois and Wells-Barnett, however, met just before the conference opened on 31 May with other "radicals," perhaps to ensure that Bookerites would not control the conference or the resultant organization. At the same time, Washington had informants watching the developments closely.[36]

About three hundred people attended the opening meeting of the National Negro Conference in the Charity Organization Hall at New York. Speakers included eminent scientists and scholars who sought to refute charges of black inferiority; white liberals, such as Villard and Milholland; and three black speakers—Wells-Barnett, Du Bois, and Zion Bishop Alexander Walters. In her speech, "Lynching: Our National Crime," Wells-Barnett opened with "three salient facts":

> First: Lynching is color line murder.
> Second: Crime against women is the excuse, not the cause.
> Third: It is a national crime and requires a national remedy.

She then gave proof of those statements and talked of the remedy. "Agitation, though helpful, will not alone stop the crime," she explained, "Year after year statistics are published, meetings are held, resolutions are adopted and yet lynchings go on." Wells-Barnett asserted, "The only certain remedy is an appeal to law. Lawbreakers must be made to know that human life is sacred and that every citizen of this country is first a citizen of the United States and secondly a citizen of the state in which he belongs." Her proposals included federal antilynching legislation and "a bureau for the investigation and publication of the details of every lynching."[37]

Wells-Barnett envisioned such a bureau as providing her an organizational base for continuing her crusade, but she was to be bitterly disappointed during the deliberations of the second day. One account notes, "On the second day . . . interracial good will evaporated." Another called the final session "a stormy meeting which lasted until midnight."[38] Two issues caused dissension: the adoption of resolutions and the nomination of a "Committee of Forty" to affect a permanent organization. Black and white perspectives on the resolutions debate indicate a wide gap in perception. Writing to Francis J. Garrison, Villard accused Trotter and the Reverend J. M. Waldron of "behaving very badly, speaking incessantly, and making the most trivial changes in the language, always with a nasty spirit." Du Bois, on the other hand, reported, "The black mass moved forward and stretched out their own hands to take charge. It was their problem. They must name the condition." He also recalled the response of an unnamed woman (most likely Wells-Barnett) to a proposal to put Booker T. Washington on a committee as crying "in passionate, almost tearful earnestness—an earnestness born of bitter experience—'They are betraying us again—these white friends of ours.'"[39]

Certainly these whites, who represented the most advanced thinkers on race relations, displayed an annoying paternalism. In his letter Villard lamented, "I suppose we ought really not to blame these poor people who have been tricked so often by white men, for being suspicious, but the exhibition was none the less trying." He also admitted their suspicions were correct that "the whole proceeding was rigged up in advance—which naturally it had to be." Ovington admitted to Villard, "I find myself still occasionally forgetting that the Negroes aren't poor people for whom I must kindly do something, and then comes a gathering such as last evening and I learn they are men with most forceful opinions of their own." She later explained, "Every white person who came to the first conference . . . was sympathetic but the most of them expected to meet belated people who would primarily arouse their pity."[40]

The naming of the Committee of Forty was even more controversial than the resolutions. The only black member of the nominating committee was Du Bois, who read the committee's report about midnight at the stormy last session. Session chair Charles Edward Russell rushed through the report's adoption but could not prevent a bedlam of backlash. Wells-Barnett was stunned when her name was not among those read. According to her autobiography, Milholland told her that Du Bois must have deleted her name from the original list. She blamed both Du Bois and Ovington, who she claimed "swept by me with an air of triumph and a very pleased look on her face." Wells-Barnett recalled being pursued by various allies after she left the meeting, finally returning, and being told by Du Bois that she had been omitted because her associate at the Frederick Douglass Center, Celia Parker Wooley, could represent her interests. Thus C. E. Bentley, as president of the Illinois chapter of the Niagara movement, had replaced her. Refusing to have her name added, Wells-Barnett admitted, "I did a foolish thing. My anger at having been treated in such a fashion outweighed my judgment and I again left the building." She insisted, however, that Ovington's influence in the founding of the National Association for the Advancement of Colored People (NAACP) limited the group's effectiveness. While granting that her intentions were good, Wells-Barnett asserted that Ovington "made little effort to know the soul of the black woman; and to that extent she has fallen short of helping a race which has suffered as no white woman has ever been called upon to suffer or understand."[41]

Wells-Barnett's two antagonists had their own explanation of the events. Discussing the omission of Wells-Barnett as well as Trotter, Ovington declared the nominating committee "took a middle course and suited nobody" by also omitting Booker T. Washington. Of the radical agitators, she wrote, "They were powerful personalities who had gone their own ways, fitted for courageous work, but perhaps not fitted to accept the restraint of organization." On another occasion Ovington explained, "She [Wells-Barnett] was a great fighter, but we knew she had to play a lone hand. And if you have too many players of lone hands in your organization, you soon have no game." In *Dusk of Dawn*, Du Bois noted that all the Niagara leaders "save Trotter and Ida Wells Barnett came to form the backbone of the new organization." Much later he explained that the two "refused to join the new organization, being distrustful of white leadership."[42]

Although Du Bois may have been reluctant to share power, he did not have the clout to impose his will on the committee. Villard was most likely responsible for the small number of African Americans on the Committee of Forty, which Milholland called a "stupendous error." Walling and Milholland lobbied for more black members. Even before their request, however, Russell responded to Wells-Barnett's complaints, and in the words of Ovington, "quite illegally, but wisely, put her on the Committee." The leaders continued to court the Chicago agitator, paying her way to the next year's meeting, where the NAACP was formally organized. She had a prominent role in the program, "was shown every courtesy and attention possible," and became a member of the executive committee. Du Bois, however, was the only black officer—serving as director of publicity and research and as editor of the organization's journal, *Crisis*.[43]

As the first decade of the twentieth century came to a close, Wells-Barnett had plenty of reasons to be "distrustful of white leadership" but remained active in the NAACP, which was then controlled by whites. Within a few years she totally withdrew from participation. Involvement in other biracial movements heightened her disillusionment and led her toward self-help as a solution to African American problems. Increasingly, she would form local organizations that she could control and would undertake personal crusades—often for unpopular causes.

15

⌒⚬⚬⌒

New Crusades for Justice

"Do the work that the others refuse"

⌒⚬⚬⌒

D uring the emergence of the NAACP, Ida B. Wells-Barnett embarked
on a more solitary crusade for justice. In 1909 the specter of mob violence again haunted Illinois. After a young white woman was found stran-
gled in a Cairo alley, the city's sheriff arrested William "Frog" James on cir-
cumstantial evidence. Fearing a lynching, Sheriff Frank Davis and a single
deputy took James out of town and hid in the woods where a mob found
them and returned James to Cairo. After the mob placed a rope around
James's neck and forced a confession, the victim's sister rushed forward to
take the rope. The men in the ten-thousand-person mob stepped back, let-
ting her and about five hundred women pull the rope to hang James.
Members of the crowd then riddled the body with hundreds of bullets,
drug the mutilated corpse to the scene of the crime, burned the body, and
placed James's head on a fence post. Still in a frenzy and unable to locate
a second black suspect, the mob broke into the jail and hanged a white
man accused of killing his wife.[1]

As Wells-Barnett pointed out in an *Original Rights Magazine* article,
"How Enfranchisement Stops Lynching," black political power in Illinois
offered some remedy. In 1905 African American state legislator Edward D.
Green pushed through antilynching legislation. One provision stated that
the lynching of any person in custody was "conclusive evidence of the failure on the part of such sheriff to do his duty." It required the governor to re-

move the sheriff from office until a subsequent hearing to determine whether the official had taken all possible measures to protect the prisoner. Cairo offered a test of that legislation. Because Sheriff Davis was friendlier to the county's black population than his successor, a number of prominent African Americans wrote Governor Charles S. Deneen to express support for Davis's reinstatement.[2]

According to Wells-Barnett, her husband reported the pending hearing at the family dinner table and declared to his wife, "And so it would seem that you will have to go to Cairo and get the facts with which to confront the sheriff next Wednesday morning [at the hearing]. And your train leaves at eight o'clock." She recalled objecting "very strongly because I had already been accused by some of our men of jumping in ahead of them and doing work without giving them a chance." Her perceived duty as a mother increased her reluctance to take on more "men's work," and Wells-Barnett protested, "I don't see why I should have to go and do the work that the others refuse." However, her son came to where she had fallen asleep while singing to her youngest daughter, Alfreda, and reminded her of another duty. "He stood by the bedside a little while," she wrote, "and then said, 'Mother if you don't go nobody else will.'"[3]

The next day Wells-Barnett left for Cairo, where she encountered resistance in the black community because of Sheriff Davis's popularity and James's reputation as "a worthless sort of fellow." She rallied support by stressing how failure to enforce the antilynching law for guilty victims jeopardized the protection of innocent ones. Armed with signed petitions and a letter from a prominent black citizen retracting his previous support for Davis, she went straight to Springfield. There Wells-Barnett used both the results of her investigation and a legal brief written by her husband to argue persuasively against the reinstatement of Davis. In the end her lone voice prevailed over those of prominent whites testifying for Davis—including a state senator and a United States land commissioner. Deneen refused Davis's petition, causing the *Chicago Defender* to proclaim, "If we only had a few men with the backbone of Mrs. Barnett lynching would soon come to a halt in America." Apparently her effort did halt the lynching of prisoners in Illinois. The next year an attempted lynching in Cairo was thwarted by the sheriff's firing at the mob and killing a prominent white citizen. Twenty years later, Wells-Barnett claimed that all threatened lynchings since Cairo had been averted by prompt requests for state troops.[4]

Failing to find an adequate institutional base for her crusades, Ida B. Wells-Barnett began creating her own vehicles for activism in 1910. She

Wells-Barnett with her children Charles, Herman, Ida, and Alfreda in 1909 (courtesy of the University of Chicago Library).

continued to fight injustice through protest, but became increasingly involved in self-help programs and legal action for racial advancement. Because she still believed in racial unity, Wells-Barnett persisted in her efforts
to affiliate with such national organizations as the NAACP and NACW
and joined new protest movements. Personality conflicts continued to
plague her, and she increasingly felt forced to "trod the wine-press alone"
in order to "do the work that the others refuse."[5]

In 1910, however, Wells-Barnett had hopes of playing major roles in
both the NAACP and NACW. After the 1899 NACW meeting at Chicago,
in which Wells-Barnett had not been included, she had attended no further meetings. In 1910 NACW president, Elizabeth Carter, sought recon-
ciliation with the Chicago agitator by inviting her to speak about the
NAACP at the biennial NACW meeting in Louisville and by placing her
at the head of the committee on resolutions. Wells-Barnett came and
brought controversy as her companion. By that time she was a leader in the
opposition to Booker T. Washington and was encouraged by the formation
of the Niagara Movement and NAACP. Anti-Bookerites had also wrested
control of the Afro-American Council from the Washington faction in
1907; Wells-Barnett apparently attempted to wean NACW from the Tuskegean's influence.

Debate arose over NACW's *National Notes*, which for more than a
decade had been edited by Margaret Murray Washington and printed by
Tuskegee Institute students at no cost to the NACW. Wells-Barnett believed it had become another of many organs controlled and subsidized by
Booker T. Washington to tout his doctrine and silence his critics. Some
women complained that articles and editorials critical of Washington
failed to appear; others grumbled about missing issues and lax delivery of
paid subscriptions. Wells-Barnett capitalized on that discontent to support
a move to place the *National Notes* directly under the organization's control and to elect an editor. She claimed the motion was carried by rising
vote but was overruled by the chair and tabled. The parliamentary wran-
gling led some of the delegates to hiss at her. Afterward, Wells-Barnett
recalled, "I went home and went to bed instead of appearing at the big banquet which was given to the delegates that night."[6]

Despite that setback, Wells-Barnett seemed destined to play a major
role in the NAACP in 1910. After her initial exclusion from the Committee of Forty, she became a member of the executive committee and on 25
May was one of nine members who met and perfected the plan of organization.[7] That meeting, however, marked the apogee of her involvement, al-

though she continued to participate for a number of years. The first step in her disillusionment with the organization was the Steve Green extradition case—in which the NAACP duplicated her efforts and failed to acknowledge her role.

Green was a black Arkansas tenant farmer who moved when his landlord, Will Seidle, practically doubled his rent. After Seidle found Green working for a neighbor, he came to Green's cabin, began shooting, and inflicted several wounds before his victim returned fire, killing his attacker. Knowing African Americans were not supposed to slay white men even in self-defense, Green immediately went into hiding on an island in the Mississippi River. For three weeks his friends brought supplies and raised money to finance his escape. Like a fugitive slave, he eluded bloodhounds by rolling in a hog pen and made his way to Chicago in August 1910, only to be betrayed, arrested, and extradited. Like the abolitionists of old, Wells-Barnett mobilized a rescue, securing a writ of habeas corpus and wiring sheriffs along the route back to Arkansas with offers of a one hundred dollar reward for Green's return to Chicago. A sheriff in Cairo reclaimed Green and returned him for judicial action in Chicago. Still fearing extradition for Green, Wells-Barnett led a group that arranged for his escape to Canada.[8]

The Steve Green case caught the attention of white liberal Joel E. Spingarn, who sent the NAACP a check for one hundred dollars and wired Green's black attorney, Edward H. Wright, to notify him of his contribution to the Arkansas farmer's defense. NAACP treasurer, Oswald Garrison Villard, telegraphed Wells-Barnett to ascertain the status of the case and inquire whether money was needed. She informed Villard of Green's escape and scathingly noted, "It will be necessary for him [Spingarn] to state whether he wishes the money to be used for Steve Green's personal expenses, or whether it is to be used as a contingent fund for the lawyers and others who are seeking to make notoriety as well as money out of the case." Villard informed Spingarn of her response and lamented that black lawyers "usually take advantage of philanthropic interest of this kind to make money for themselves." Despite her prominent efforts, for which the *Chicago Defender* called her "that watchdog of human life and liberty," the NAACP's *Crisis*, under W. E. B. Du Bois's editorship, failed to mention Wells-Barnett in its account of the case.[9]

The Steve Green case brought Spingarn into the NAACP, where he became one of Wells-Barnett's closest allies and confidants as her relations with other members eroded. In April 1911, she wrote him of her frustrations with the organization. After telling of a Chicago branch meeting called by Villard, who did not inform her, Wells-Barnett continued:

> Both Mr. Villard and Prof. DuBois gave me the impression that they rather feared some interference from me in the Chicago arrangements. They also gave me very clearly to understand at the executive meeting there in New York that I was not expected to do anything save to be a member. Candidly, I don't expect a great deal to result from their activity, for the very good reason that Miss [Jane] Addams whom they desire to mother the movement [in Chicago] simply has not the time nor strength even if she had the inclination to lead this new crusade.

Wells-Barnett also asserted that black participation in the Chicago NAACP had become limited to the "exclusive academic few" who sought to "bask in [Addams'] reflected glory and at the same time get credit for representing the race that they ignore and withdraw themselves from on every occasion of real need." She conceded, "I am not very popular with the exclusive few, and I can not say that I look with equanimity upon their patronizing assumptions."[10]

Wells-Barnett's harsh critique of the "exclusive few" reflected both her keen intellectual insight and her continuing sense of alienation from the black elite. Scholars have echoed her assertions. The old black elite in Chicago and elsewhere had close ties to the white community either by kinship or through service professions. Its members generally prided themselves in their adoption of the gentility displayed by the white upper class. By 1910 their social prominence was threatened by southern black migration to northern cities and the rise of a black *nouveau riche* society. Many adopted a defensive posture and drew distinctions between themselves and "the rabble, the ignorant and the uncouth," as Fannie Barrier Williams labeled the black nonelite. Black aristocrats often withdrew from clubs that opened their membership to the newcomers and sought social prestige from membership in white-dominated biracial organizations—such as the Chicago NAACP branch.[11]

Several factors alienated Wells-Barnett from the Chicago elite even though she and her husband were active participants in the "colored society" of Chicago. Foremost were her flouting of gender conventions, her assumption of "male" leadership roles, her identification with unpopular causes, her lack of a college education, and her ideological ambivalence to class issues. Although Wells-Barnett shared the elites' desire for respectability and white approval to counter white racist assumptions, she had little faith that respectability was the path to rights—the lynching of Tom Moss dispelled that notion. She advocated forcing, rather than imploring, whites to grant justice.

Ironically, white recognition of Wells-Barnett was a major reason African Americans were compelled to include her in biracial movements. Among white radicals and even some liberals her name lent credibility to a cause, just as Frederick Douglass's had. Wells-Barnett was not immune to the balm of white acceptance to soothe the sickness of the soul brought on by the virus of racial prejudice. However, she seemed to cultivate white allies more for their power than their approval, and she was unwilling to serve as a junior partner in biracial coalitions. Her refusal to curry white favor with deference is evident in relationships with reformers, such as Frances Willard, Jane Addams, and Susan B. Anthony.

In 1912 both Barnetts were members of the local arrangements committee for the national meeting of the NAACP to be held in their city in late April. Soon, however, their participation ceased as the local group became dominated by Washington supporters. By 1914 (a year before his death) Washington rejoiced that "all the old, strong forces have either been put out of Villard's organization, or have withdrawn" and listed Wells-Barnett as one of those forces. In addition to ideological incompatibility, Wells-Barnett was also not well suited to play the role most black women played in the NAACP—as grassroots organizers who left the formal leadership roles to whites and black men. The exclusion of black women from visible leadership roles helped to make them historically invisible for a long time—despite Mary White Ovington's assertion in 1947 that the NAACP would never have survived without their organizing efforts.[12]

Unwilling to play merely a supporting role, Wells-Barnett established her own outlet for activism in 1910—the Negro Fellowship League. Its origins and activities reflect the expansion of her role from integrationist agitator to include more race-based programs of self-help. The move was a natural progression, stemming from her changed status and environment. Becoming a wife and mother focused her concern more on the local community and its needs. Although she remained too unconventional to assimilate well, Wells-Barnett's activities as a "clubwoman" drew her attention to the traditional functions of African American women to nurture the black community and care for its weak and sick.[13] The needs of that community in Chicago were far different from those in Memphis and other parts of the South. Soon after moving to the Windy City, the Memphian recognized that racial barriers in the North were far more subtle than the blatant, state-sanctioned segregation and disfranchisement of the South. Replying to a white woman's criticism of black orators' failure to distinguish the backwardness of the South from the more democratic North on racial issues, Wells-Barnett wrote:

> It is true that the schools and colleges are open to [the Northern Negro], but it is not true that "every opportunity is given to him to engage in any business or profession he may select." These schools graduate him and the economic conditions force him to become a railway porter, a hotel waiter or bootblack. The trades unions, by law, have shut him out from the trades and factories and stores of the North. If he takes a profession there are not enough of his own race in most Northern cities to insure him a living by patronage, and the accursed caste system prevents white custom.[14]

She quickly learned that legal rights could not feed families. For many southern migrants, Chicago was proving less than the promised land.

Chicago's phenomenal growth at the turn of the century—like that of other northern cities—was fueled by the arrival of rural folk ill-equipped for urban life. Immigrants with their foreign tongues and dress had the most visible adjustments to make in cities growing too fast to meet the needs of citizens. Settlement houses, such as Jane Addams's Chicago Hull House, arose to solve their problems. Living in immigrant neighborhoods, white middle-class workers provided social services, educational opportunities, and recreational facilities to the newcomers. As foreigners crossed over settlement house bridges to citizenship, jobs, and better housing, African Americans frequently moved into the poorer neighborhoods they left behind. For a variety of reasons, most settlement houses excluded the black newcomers and eventually either moved with the immigrants or shut their doors. Many argued that poor whites would not use facilities open to African Americans.[15]

Even though settlement house workers were frequently more tolerant than most whites, they also were infected with the era's insidious racism, which permeated all the nation's institutions. White liberals and bigots rarely argued *whether* African Americans were inferior; they only debated *why*. The latter blamed heredity; the former named slavery. To some liberals, slavery had caused a moral degeneracy and a breakdown of families. Others claimed Africa's climate had failed to produce any "civilization" to be destroyed by slavery. Most agreed Negroes were the most "backward" of the newcomers to the northern cities. Unlike many charitable organizations that asserted poverty's solution lay in individual effort and hard work, settlement house workers tended to blame the environment and call for social change; however, these beliefs were often tainted with racism. Whereas they considered immigrants' poverty the result of current environmental factors modifiable by reforms, they believed that African Americans had first to overcome a pathological culture rooted in the past and amenable only to self-help.

Those settlement house workers for whom the answer to immigrant problems was "Americanization" did not see their efforts as pertinent to black newcomers. Most of the cultural pluralists, for whom ethnic diversity was a strength rather than a problem, saw little to be admired or incorporated from black culture. Perhaps because of her working relationships with Wells-Barnett and others of the black elite, Jane Addams was an exception and wrote:

> What has been and is being lost by the denial of opportunity and free expression on the part of the Negro, it is now very difficult to estimate; only faint suggestions of that waste can be perceived. There is, without doubt, the sense of humor, unique and spontaneous, so different from the wit of the Yankee, or the inimitable story telling prized in the South; the Negro melodies which are the only American folk-songs; the persistent love of color expressing itself in the bright curtains and window boxes in the dullest and grayest parts of our cities; the executive and organizing capacity so often exhibited by the head waiter in a huge hotel or by the colored woman who administers a complicated household; the gift of eloquence, the mellowed voice, the use of rhythm and onomatopoeia which is now so often travestied in a grotesque use of long words.[16]

In another article, however, Addams lamented that segregation prevented the spread of European "inherited resources" of "custom and kindly intercourse" that produced "social restraint" to the "newer group [African Americans] which needs them most." The result was that "in every large city we have a colony of colored people who have not been brought under social control."[17]

Chicago was home to some of the most racially aware settlement workers, who seemed to understand more than most whites that African Americans suffered not only from the shocks of urban living but also from forms of discrimination not faced by immigrants. Sophonisba Breckinridge, a professor of Social Economics at the University of Chicago, noted, "The Negro is not only compelled to live in a segregated black district, but this region of Negro homes is almost invariably the one in which vice is tolerated by the police." Black tenants paid twelve dollars or more a month in rent, which was two to four dollars more than immigrants paid. At the same time, she declared, "No other group suffered so from decaying buildings, leaking roofs, doors without hinges, broken windows, insanitary plumbing, rotting floors, and general lack of repairs."[18]

Breckinridge's words were echoed by Louise deKoven Bowen, who was affiliated with Hull House and the Juvenile Protective Association. Bowen also noted that because it was "so very difficult for a skilled colored man to secure employment," industrial education provided little opportunity. In addition, the limited fields open to black men created greater competition, which depressed wages. At the same time, young black women with high school educations and "refined appearance" were sent by employment agencies to "serve as domestics in low class hotels and disreputable houses." Some were even sent to houses of prostitution. Bowen was surprised that the percentage of black criminals was so low given the barriers they faced: lack of opportunity, limited recreational facilities, working mothers, scarce social services, and law enforcement officials with "apparently no scruples in sending a 'nigger up the road' on mere suspicion."[19]

Chicago's white women activists were better at diagnosing the problems than addressing them. Only Celia Parker Wooley opened anything resembling a settlement house for African Americans. Her Frederick Douglass Center, however, was located in a racially mixed area and sought primarily to bring together the "better classes" of white and black Chicagoans in order to promote understanding. Attacking the problems of poor African Americans was not a priority. Since city government also failed to provide many basic services, black Chicagoans founded such institutions as orphanages and homes for the aged. Although not as predominantly as in the South, black churches continued to function as social agencies as well. Among the most activist clergy was Reverdy C. Ransom, minister of Bethel A.M.E. Church, to which the Barnetts belonged in 1900. In that year Ransom left Bethel to establish Institutional Church, which functioned very much like a settlement house with a day nursery and industrial classes. The Chicago *Inter-Ocean* called it a "Hull House or Chicago Commons founded by Negroes for the help of people of that race."[20]

Although Ferdinand Barnett was on Institutional's board of managers and his wife participated in activities there, they kept their membership at

Bethel until disagreements with the new pastor led Wells-Barnett to go church shopping. Charging the Bethel pastor with immorality, she refused to expose her children to him and moved to Grace Presbyterian Church. Still espousing the unity of all Christians, Wells-Barnett admitted, "I was not Presbyterian by doctrine, but since all Christian denominations agreed on a standard of conduct and right living it seemed to me to matter very little what name we bore." Joining Grace with her daughters, she soon accepted a request to teach a Sunday school class—from which the Negro Fellowship League emerged.[21]

Wells-Barnett continued to prefer the company of men—as she had in her twenties when she taught a boys' Sunday school class. The Grace class, which she taught for ten years, had about thirty young men from the ages of eighteen to thirty. According to her autobiography, Wells-Barnett was upset about the lack of concern in the black community regarding the Springfield riot of 1908. "As I wended my way to Sunday school that bright Sabbath day, brooding over what was still going on in our state capital," she wrote, "I passed numbers of people out parading in their Sunday finery. None of them seemed to be worried by the fact of this three days' riot going on less than two hundred miles away." During her lesson she gave "vent to a passionate denunciation of the apathy of our people," and one young man asked, "What can we do about it?" That afternoon three of the members met at the Barnett home and formed what became the Negro Fellowship League (NFL).

In the beginning the NFL continued to meet at the Barnett house. The young men brought their girlfriends, and the group discussed current issues and heard addresses by prominent people. Then, the 1909 Cairo lynching and the 1910 Steve Green extradition case transformed the group from a debating society into an activist organization. Wells-Barnett mobilized its members and acted, through the group, in Green's behalf. Inmates at Joliet Penitentiary were soon asking her to come hear their stories, and she became a prisoners' advocate with the NFL as her arm of action. Her contacts with prisoners also led Wells-Barnett to perceive the destructive power of the city on young male migrants from the rural South. Local police had allowed State Street to become the vice district of the city. She explained what happened when young men arrived.

> They knew no one in Chicago, but made for State Street, the Great White Way of our people. Here they found only saloons, buffet flats, poolrooms, and gambling houses, and many of them had gotten in

trouble in these places. With no friends, they were railroaded into the penitentiary.

As president of the Negro Fellowship League, Wells-Barnett declared, "I thought it was our duty to try to see that some sort of lighthouse was established on State Street where we could be on the lookout for these young people and from which we could extend to them a helping hand."[22]

Although conceived as a self-help organization, the NFL Reading Room and Social Center on State Street received its start-up funds from sympathetic whites. Wells-Barnett attended a Congregational Union dinner where Dr. J. G. K. McClure, the head of the Chicago Theological Seminary, spoke on "The White Man's Burden" and cited the disproportionate numbers of black criminals in Chicago. Already scheduled to give a talk on lynching at the dinner, Wells-Barnett responded to queries about McClure's statistics. Asked to refute the charges, she replied, "I am sorry I cannot do so . . . for that is what the figures seem to indicate." She continued:

> The statistics which we have heard here tonight do not mean, as it appears to mean, that the Negro race is the most criminal of the various race groups in Chicago. It does mean that ours is the most neglected group. All the other races in the city are welcomed into the settlements, YMCA's, YWCA's, gymnasiums and every other movement for uplift if only their skins are white. The occasional black man who wanders uninvited into these places is very quickly given to understand that his room is better than his company. Only one social center welcomes the Negro, and that is the saloon. Ought we to wonder at the harvest which we have heard enumerated tonight?[23]

Among her listeners was the wife of Victor F. Lawson, owner of the *Chicago Daily News* and a large donor to the YMCA. Appalled by what she had heard, Mrs. Lawson notified her husband of Wells-Barnett's charges of discrimination by the YMCA. He checked into the charges, found them true, discontinued his donations, and agreed to give Wells-Barnett the money needed to rent a place on State Street. On 1 May 1910, the Negro Fellowship League Reading Room and Social Center opened its doors at 2830 State Street with an open house at which lemonade was served by members of the Ideal Woman's Club.[24]

Wells-Barnett remembered opening day as being too hot to close the doors. The din of boisterous State Street began to interrupt the program and the janitor suggested calling the police. She quickly replied, "Oh, no, we have come over here to be friends to these people and it would never do for us to start in by sending for the police." Instead she went to where several men were shooting craps and drinking a bucket of beer, introduced herself, and invited the men to join in the activities. Claiming to be too dirty to shake her hand or enter the building, the men nevertheless agreed to leave and several promised to clean up and come to the Sunday afternoon programs in the future. Wells-Barnett claimed, "I was never again disturbed or molested" at that location.[25]

The NFL place on State Street began modestly as a reading room with tables, chairs, books, and magazines—especially featuring "race literature." Manned by one paid professional and young male volunteers, the room stayed open daily from 9:00 A.M. to 10:00 P.M., and its functions gradually increased. Sunday programs remained a key feature with a diversity of topics and speakers, including such prominent whites as Jane Addams, Mary White Ovington, William English Walling, and prominent Chicago politicians. Black speakers included elected officials; activists, such as William Monroe Trotter; editors I. Garland Penn and Robert S. Abbott; outstanding scientist Ernest Just; and educators, such as Benjamin Brawley and Carter G. Woodson. Despite their support for the Reading Room, Wells-Barnett later insisted that few of the elite would have anything to do with State Street's problems.[26]

Soon after opening the reading room, the NFL turned the upstairs into a men's lodging place with beds at a cost of fifteen to twenty-five cents. Because forty to fifty young men utilized the reading rooms daily to read, write letters, play checkers, etc., employers began dropping by to find workers, and the NFL evolved into an employment bureau as well. Eventually, the League was placing so many people that private employment offices insisted that Wells-Barnett pay fifty dollars for a business license. The NFL also sponsored cultural activities, including a League orchestra and chorus as well as literary contests. The group hosted Christmas services, Emancipation Day exercises, and July Fourth celebrations.[27]

In 1911 Wells-Barnett was criticized, in terms that were now familiar, for taking an inappropriate leadership position within the League. In June the president noted that some of "our manhood object to the leadership of a woman." She replied that as no one else had stepped forward, she "could no longer sit quietly by and see the interest of the race sacrificed because of the indifference of our manly men." Although Wells-Barnett pledged to step down if an appropriate man emerged, she remained president during the NFL's ten-year existence and made it a major vehicle for

Wells-Barnett with Ida and Alfreda, September 1914 (courtesy of the University of Chicago Library).

her activism. Through it she even returned to journalism, founding the *Fellowship Herald* in May 1911 and serving as editor the several years it was published.[28]

Julius Taylor of the *Broad Ax* welcomed the new paper and proclaimed, "It is ably and brilliantly edited by Mrs. Ida B. Wells-Barnett, who has no superior as a keen, logical and forcible writer." Four years later the *Chicago Defender* quoted a Danish visitor who called Wells-Barnett "the Jane Addams among the Negroes," and noted of her paper, "This weekly publication, although somewhat handicapped, is, no doubt, the best paper the Negro has here in Chicago. It has 500 subscribers and is not filled with the silly nonsense so generally met with in the public press." Such praise and a personal invitation in 1912 to join the Colored Press Association of Chicago, however, seemed to do little to lessen the stings of her critics and her growing sense of alienation.[29]

The publication of a weekly paper marked Wells-Barnett's transition from a busy but flexible schedule of activism to full-time work outside the house as her children grew up. From the start neither parent had separated their work from their home. In 1978 their youngest daughter, Alfreda Barnett Duster, recalled a hectic household. She noted that her father made the house "his extended office" and "always had a succession of people coming to the house." On holidays he brought home clients to share in family celebrations. Her mother, Duster remembered, "always kept some-thing going for the young people" and the presence of so many teenagers thrilled the young girl. Their home also welcomed visiting dignitaries— William Monroe Trotter was the most frequent. The disadvantage, Duster admitted, was "there wasn't too much time for intimate family life in the home, since it was almost a business."[30]

Wells-Barnett took her role as mother very seriously. She recognized the importance of the home to black advancement as well as the assaults made on it by white attitudes and actions. In a 1910 article, Wells-Barnett celebrated black motherhood and noted, "If slavery could not crush the mother-love out of the hearts of Negro women, the race prejudice of the present cannot do it."[31] As her own mother had done, she often went to her children's schools to check on their progress. Concern for her children even outweighed Wells-Barnett's usual bluntness. According to Duster, "whenever rough spots appeared upon the surface of school waters, she was the interested and devoted parent who always smoothed the troubled waters." For her daughters she was both protective and ambitious. Duster recalled that her mother did not want her to go to a coed school and had urged her to go to law school. Her mother had always wished to become a lawyer so, Duster explained, "vicariously she wanted me to be a lawyer." Ferdinand Barnett never punished the children. "That was my mother's job," Duster noted.[32] She described her mother's disciplinary tactics as follows:

> During our growing up years, I remember mother as a kind and lov-ing, though stern and exacting parent. She did not use force to obtain obedience. She did not need to. Her "look" was enough to straighten any misdoer into the correct behavior, and she stressed the importance of behaving in her absence better than in her presence.[33]

Beginning on 28 May 1913, Wells-Barnett was absent from the home more as she took a full-time job as Chicago's first black adult probation of-ficer. Later that summer she described her duties to Joel Spingarn, "This work requires that I shall be on duty at the Harrison St. Municipal Court room from 9 to 12 every day and out in the field looking after my 85 pro-bationers for the balance of the day and far into the night." The job inter-fered with her practice of taking the children further north during the sum-mer, and she described herself as "one who is condemned to be burned alive in this great city for the entire Summer season."[34]

By this time, Charles was seventeen, Herman not yet sixteen, Ida almost thirteen, and Alfreda nine. According to Duster, all four were quite different. She described Charles as mild, quiet, and kind; Ida as "a very studious young lady" who read all the time; and Herman as a manipulator who "pulled the wool over Mother's eyes." Alfreda depicted herself as a tomboy who, away from her mother's eyes, both skated and had water balloon fights with Herman inside the house. Although rambunctious, Alfreda was also responsible for starting dinner, which she and her father finished after he got home. Cooking gave them time together; her minutes with her working mother were more limited. Duster remembered that her mother would come home and read the paper to catch up on what was happening. After fetching her glasses and slippers, Duster reminisced, "I would climb up on the chair in back of her and take her hair down and comb it, you know, and braid it up."[35]

Wells-Barnett needed those quiet moments as her workload increased. She continued to edit the *Fellowship Herald* and stayed busy in club work while working full-time. Indeed, she never separated her paid and volunteer work. Her job as a probation officer was closely intertwined with her efforts at the Negro Fellowship League and actually grew out of that work. Victor Lawson maintained his support of the NFL until 1913, giving a total of nine thousand dollars. Then a YMCA branch opened in the black community, and he shifted his funding to it. Although supportive of it, Wells-Barnett did not see the YMCA as an adequate alternative to the NFL. Its twelve dollar membership fee could not be paid by most of the men using the League. Without Lawson's support, however, the League could no longer afford the $175 monthly rent and moved into cramped quarters at 3005 State Street that cost thirty-five dollars. Chief justice Harry Olson of the municipal court was aware of the NFL's work with potential criminals and wanted it to continue. Therefore, he appointed Wells-Barnett as a probation officer so that her $150 monthly salary could be used to meet expenses. The NFL became her office to which her probationers reported.[36]

Her job grew increasingly demanding. In 1914 she reported having two hundred probationers under her charge. As that number remained consistently over 150, Wells-Barnett began lobbying for additional black probation officers. The request seemed reasonable; the juvenile court had four African Americans as case workers. In December 1915, her request was denied and her contract not renewed, probably because of her support of Judge Olson's losing bid for the mayor's office. Although leaving the ranks of paid employees, Wells-Barnett remained busy in volunteer work and somehow kept the NFL functioning for five more years without Lawson's support or her salary to meet expenses.[37] She later wrote of that work: "All I can say of that ten years I spent on State Street is that no human being ever came inside the doors asking for food who was not given a card to a restaurant across the way. No one sought a night's lodging in vain, for after his case was investigated, a card to the Douglass Hotel was given him." The NFL derived its income from the placement bureau, but "nobody who applied for a job was ever turned away." Although many left with a promise to pay and failed to return, Wells-Barnett explained, "we took what satisfaction we could out of the fact that we had helped a human being at the hour of his greatest need."[38]

The NFL served as a vehicle for Wells-Barnett's activism as well as providing self-help. Through its offices, she continued to take on cases in defense of accused criminals' rights. The longest-running case that Wells-Barnett brought to the League and her husband for action was that of Joseph "Chicken Joe" Campbell. An inmate accused of setting a fire in Joliet Penitentiary that killed the warden's wife in 1915, Campbell was charged mainly because he had access to the warden's quarters as a trusty. Without any physical proof of rape, the authorities asserted that Campbell tried to obliterate the evidence of rape by arson. The charge was all too familiar, and Wells-Barnett worried that Campbell was being railroaded because he was black. She approached James Keeley, the new editor of the *Record Herald*, and told him that the other white papers "have stopped printing what I have to say on the subject of mobs and I wouldn't be guilty of uttering the namby-pamby stuff they try to put in my mouth." He agreed to print her letter, in which she described Campbell's treatment in solitary confinement and asked, "Is this justice? Is it humanity? Would we stand to see a dog treated in such fashion without a protest?"[39]

After visiting Campbell, Wells-Barnett became convinced of his innocence. Six months later the NFL announced it had raised over five hundred dollars for the case, which hardly compensated Ferdinand Barnett for the six-week trial that resulted in a guilty verdict and death sentence. Barnett's efforts continued through almost three years of appeals, until Governor Frank Lowden granted clemency. Although unable to get his release, the Barnetts and the NFL saved Campbell's life.[40]

The League and the Barnetts became involved in numerous legal cases. Their daughter noted that her father "spent much, too much of his time and legal ability . . . defending those who not only had no one to defend them, but who had no money to pay for such services." Although not a lawyer, Wells-Barnett also invested much time and energy to providing le-

gal assistance. For example, she appeared before the Pardon Board on behalf of William Smith and secured his release from prison on charges of
kidnapping. At the NFL meeting in which Smith expressed his gratitude,
the group also considered "the cases of George Thomas who has been arrested three times in the month he has been here from Georgia for walking
on the street, and also that of Alfred Bradford." In 1912 the NFL took up
the case of famous prizefighter Jack Johnson, who was accused of abduct-
ing a white woman who later became his wife. League efforts were not confined to cases involving black males. In 1915 it aided a "young colored
woman" who served a white family "for fourteen years at a dollar a week
and was never allowed to associate with other Colored people," and in
1917 it raised money to pay the fine of Bertha Thomas, a "white woman
who was horse whipped in the road because she stood up for Negro children's right to attend school at Palos Park."[41]

The assistance the Barnetts rendered to those caught up in the criminal justice system extended far beyond that of a lawyer or a probation officer. Their daughter noted that both brought home young men who were in
trouble or needed a place to stay after being paroled. "All through my
childhood," Alfreda Duster wrote, "I can remember this stream of under-
privileged boys and young men who formed a part of our home life." Although friends and neighbors warned of the "ill things which would result
from this good-heartedness," Duster claimed that with all her parents'
"dealing with this element, there was not one who betrayed the trust placed
in him by molesting anything in our home, or anyone who lived there."
She compared her mother's work to that of the later Big Sister and Big
Brother movements. When legal remedies failed and a young man went to
prison, Wells-Barnett continued to "keep the inmate encouraged by writing letters, or by appearing before the Board of Pardons at the earliest possible time to plead for a chance."[42]

The League provided Wells-Barnett with a vehicle to utilize two methods of racial advancement: self-help and legal recourse. Previously, she
concentrated her efforts in protesting injustice; her temperament led her
naturally to militant activism. The qualities that made her an effective agitator ensured she would never abandon that role—no matter how many
others she might play. Through the NFL and other organs, Wells-Barnett
continued to combat prejudice through protest. At the same time she
sought to use another weapon: political power.

16

Prejudice, Protest, and Politics

"When principle and prejudice come into collision"

Although the Negro Fellowship League usually used the tools of self-help and legal redress for black advancement, Wells-Barnett's leadership ensured that protest and politics would not be ignored. The League agitated against prejudice and injustice—especially in Chicago and Illinois. To fight for rights on the national level, its president affiliated the organization with William Monroe Trotter's Equal Rights League in 1913. To promote political activity, the NFL hosted candidates' forums and urged voter participation. By 1913 Wells-Barnett increased her efforts to get franchisement for women as well as African Americans, founding the state's first black women's suffrage organization. Late in the decade, her activism began to focus on issues growing out of World War I, including a rash of race riots. Many of her experiences confirmed her 1913 assertion that "when principle and prejudice come into collision, principle retires and leaves prejudice the victor."[1]

In 1911 Wells-Barnett sought to stem the rising tide of racism in American popular culture. White supremacy infected all of American life. Although the South lost the Civil War, the region succeeded in selling the stereotypes of slavery to the victors. African Americans became objects of both fear and ridicule. The burly black beast coexisted in the public's mind with grinning, watermelon-eating Sambos and Aunt Jemimas. At the same time, the slaveowner's image began to change from cruel torturer to patient father. Reconstruction became seen as a tragic mistake. An effective purveyor of these myths was writer Thomas Dixon, Jr., whom the *Broad Ax* labeled "the most bitter and the greatest arch enemy of the Negro race." When his play "The Sins of the Father" was set to open in Chicago in March 1911, Wells-Barnett led a delegation to city hall to block its showing, but Dixon argued his case effectively and prevailed over her pleas.[2]

The play caused barely a ripple compared to a movie based on Dixon's books, *The Clansman* and *The Leopard's Spots*. Produced in 1915 by D. W. Griffith, *Birth of a Nation* was a cinematic masterpiece, but its glorification of the Ku Klux Klan led to a reincarnation of that terrorist organization, which was more powerful than the original. African Americans nationwide were outraged by its depiction of a black rapist and his lynching. In some northern cities, they succeeded in blocking the picture's showing, even though President Woodrow Wilson had screened it in the White House and praised it as "writing history with lightning."[3]

In Chicago the controversy became another factor in the schism between Wells-Barnett and the NAACP (which claimed the lead in the movement against the movie). She believed the organization had not prepared adequately for the unsuccessful court hearing. "It was a veritable farce of a trial," she wrote, "with a number of persons attempting to do something about which they knew nothing and refusing to call into conference those who had made a business of such things." Wells-Barnett was especially disgusted when black attorney S. A. T. Watkins questioned her right to be at the hearing, asking if the city was paying the probation officer to sit in court all day. Inexplicably, she insisted that the fight against the film was "something in which a woman cannot function" and unsuccessfully sought to enlist Edward H. Wright to lobby city hall. After the film opened, the NFL lobbied without success for the passage of a state law "to prohibit Acts tending to incite ill-feeling or prejudice or to ridicule or disparage others on account of race."[4]

By 1915 the Barnetts had withdrawn from participation in the NAACP after joining Trotter's National Equal Rights League (NERL) in 1913. The NERL grew out of a conference in 1908 and went through various reincarnations as well as names, but remained, in Trotter's words, "an organization of the colored people and for the colored people and led by the colored people." Like Wells-Barnett, Trotter refused to accept a subordinate position within the NAACP and remained a fiery militant throughout his life. In November 1913 the two agitators led a delegation that visited

President Woodrow Wilson to protest the segregation of federal offices taking place in his administration. The president received them politely, accepted a petition with about twenty thousand signatures, assured them that "it will be worked out," but took no action. A year later Trotter returned without Wells-Barnett. That meeting was more heated, Wilson became furious, and the white press labeled Trotter insolent and disrespectful. Identifying with his crucifixion by the media, Wells-Barnett invited the Boston radical to speak to the Negro Fellowship League a little over a month later. Following that address, the audience established a Chicago branch of the NERL with George Ellis as president and Wells-Barnett as vice president.[5] From that point forward, the NFL and the NERL in Chicago became closely intertwined and served as platforms for Wells-Barnett's protest.

Both Barnetts remained active in the NERL for many years, and Wells-Barnett and Trotter became allies against compromise and accommodation. Although most of her efforts for the remainder of the decade were made in organizations she headed and were centered on local problems, Wells-Barnett and Trotter's long period of collaboration on the national level indicates she was willing and able to participate in organizations she did not control—under the right circumstances. She did not mind playing a supportive role to strong black men who treated her as their intellectual equal and were comfortable with her assertiveness. She remained active in the Afro-American League/Council as long as men as militant as she was remained in control. Such men seemingly were not threatened by her activism; their own radicalism kept them from appearing timid or "unmanly" by contrast. On the other hand, her style threatened the respectability of black women, and her uncompromising ideology conflicted with the moderation and expediency of most white liberals and black male leaders.

The NFL and NERL became so linked in Wells-Barnett's mind that she included NERL activities in her NFL press releases and used NFL stationery to conduct business for both.[6] Under their auspices, she fought creeping segregation on the local, state, and national levels. In 1913 she led a successful campaign to prevent the passage of a law segregating public transportation in Illinois. In its account of the victory, the *Defender* capitalized her name in the list of those responsible and declared:

> The name of Mrs. Barnett stands out alone because that constant and fearless champion of equal rights was on the firing line all the time. Her eloquent pleas in private conferences with the legislators and in open session were eloquent and forcible. Ida B. Wells-Barnett has again endeared herself to the world.[7]

That same year, and in 1915, she and the NFL/NERL fought bills in Congress that would have prohibited interracial marriage in the District of Columbia. In 1915 they also led the battle against segregation of social activities at Chicago's integrated Wendell Phillips High School and instigated a letter-writing campaign against a proposed national immigration law that would have excluded Africans. The union of these forces is also seen in the NFL's electing Wells-Barnett as its delegate to the national NERL meetings in 1916 and 1917, as well as its hosting the 1918 meeting at Chicago.[8]

Protest had long been a potent weapon for Wells-Barnett; politics evolved as a second important tool for her. Beginning with her move to Chicago, Wells-Barnett became increasingly interested in politics for several reasons. In a period of darkening hopes for African Americans, who seemed to be losing rights daily, growing black political power in Chicago and Illinois was one bright light in the night of despair. As southern legislatures were turning lily-white, African Americans began moving into northern cities where they became part of political machines, which were organized to meet the needs and take advantage of ethnic neighborhoods peopled with immigrants. In that context even numerical minorities could have a political voice, and the 1909 Cairo lynching taught Wells-Barnett the power of political clout in combating racial violence. Until 1913, her role in politics had been limited to urging men to vote, protesting southern black disfranchisement, stumping for the Republicans in Illinois, and endorsing the efforts of such women suffragists as Susan B. Anthony.

For example, in 1910 Wells-Barnett published "How Enfranchisement Stops Lynching" and organized the Women's Second Ward Republican Club "to assist the men in getting better laws and having representation in everything which tends to the uplift of the city and its government." By 1910 the population of the Second Ward had become 25 percent black and five years later black voters would be the majority. Although two white politicians still dominated the ward in 1910, both had to woo black voters to retain power. One of them, U.S. Representative Martin Madden, became a leading advocate for African Americans in Congress and obtained over five hundred jobs for them in the Chicago post office. Black political power was evident in Illinois. After 1882 the state legislature always had black members and attempts to pass discriminatory legislation all failed. African American political leaders still faced prejudice, as Ferdinand Barnett's defeat for a judgeship in 1906 had proven, but the vote was seen as a potent weapon for advancement.[9]

Also, in 1910 a change occurred that would alter Wells-Barnett's political focus. Grace Wilbur Trout became president of the women's suffrage organization, Chicago Political Equality League, and began a dramatic expansion of the membership and activities in Illinois. Two years later, Trout became president of the Illinois Equal Suffrage Association (ISEA). Her vigorous leadership brought increased press attention as women urged the state legislature to enact women's suffrage. Although Wells-Barnett had long been a member of both groups, the suffrage movement in Illinois before 1913 was overwhelmingly white and upper class in its leadership and orientation. That year the campaign's growing strength caught Wells-Barnett's attention, and she shifted some of her efforts from trying to influence the political process to seeking to participate. In January 1913 she formed the Alpha Suffrage Club (ASC), the state's first suffrage organization among black women.[10]

The group's initial action was sending Wells-Barnett, as its delegate, to a national suffrage parade held on 3 March 1913 at Washington, D.C., in conjunction with the inauguration of Woodrow Wilson. There she encountered the problem facing black women suffragists: White leaders often insisted that they place gender interests above those of race. As the Illinois delegation organized to begin the march, Trout announced that southerners had protested the inclusion of black women in state delegations and insisted all colored suffragists march together. Facing the threat of a southern white boycott, Trout suggested acquiescence to the request to exclude Wells-Barnett, even though she was personally opposed to exclusion. The *Chicago Daily Tribune* dramatically described Wells-Barnett's reaction:

> Mrs. Barnett's voice trembled with emotion and two large tears coursed their way part way down her cheeks before she could raise her veil and wipe them away. "The southern women have tried to evade the question time and again by giving some excuse or other every time it has been brought up," she said. "If the Illinois women do not take a stand now in this great democratic parade then the colored women are lost."

She issued the ultimatum, "I shall not march at all unless I can march under the Illinois banner," but an apparent compromise was reached when white delegates Virginia Brooks and Belle Squire announced they would join her in the colored delegation. Relief turned to alarm when Squire and Brooks appeared—without Wells-Barnett—to take their places within the Illinois delegation. However, instead of boycotting the parade, as many feared, the lone black delegate slipped out of the crowd along the parade route and joined the two women, successfully integrating the march without the consent of its leaders. As usual Wells-Barnett placed her duty to her race above her duty to her gender.[11]

Following the parade, Squire and Brooks continued their support by speaking at an ASC fund-raiser. The black community celebrated the two "noble young women who stood for the right" and praised Wells-Barnett as "always to be found along the firing line in any battle where the rights of the race are at stake." The *Chicago Defender* also noted that she "enjoyed a period of publicity not to her liking."[12] Apparently this assessment was true because, inexplicably, the parade was the only major expression of her militancy that Wells-Barnett did not mention in her autobiography. Perhaps the exclusion reflects her ambivalence regarding race and gender issues.

The fights for black and women's rights have always been inextricably linked in complex and often contradictory ways—complicated further by class issues. In the United States, the women's movement originated from the raised consciousness of white women abolitionists. In the fight against slavery, they became increasingly aware of their own status as the property of fathers and husbands. Overwhelmingly from the middle class, these women (and the white suffragists who followed them) experienced discrimination exclusively because of their gender. Privileged by class and race, they naturally viewed sexism as the most significant form of oppression. Although they recognized economic and racial injustice, they subordinated both to the fight for women's rights. Depending on expediency, white suffragists either courted, ignored, or rejected black allies.[13]

During the antebellum and Reconstruction eras, white males supported the expansion of black rights more than women's. Thus white suffragists compared their status to that of African Americans and linked the battles against racism and sexism. In doing so, they ignored their close ties to white men based on economic and racial privilege as well as the unique position of black women. While white women sought to escape dependency *upon* white male protection, black women sought to win protection *from* white men. The key ingredient in the sexual exploitation of black women was their race, not their gender. White men raped them to demonstrate power over not only them but also their fathers, brothers, and husbands. Only after black men had the power to protect them could black women protect themselves. Wells-Barnett's lynching investigations convinced her that the experiences of black and white women—though intertwined—were fundamentally different. White women's sexual natures were denied and black women's exaggerated.

The strategy of linking the fight for black and women's rights failed when the Fifteenth Amendment extended suffrage to black men but not to women. Many white suffragists resented being told it was the "Negro's hour" and determined to subordinate race to gender—just as African Americans had subordinated gender to race. The issue helped to divide the suffrage movement until 1890 when the National American Woman Suffrage Association (NAWSA) reunited the movement and adopted an official policy of neutrality on racial issues. NAWSA leaders recognized that ratification of a constitutional amendment on woman suffrage required winning the South. The price of southern support was segregation, and white suffragists were willing to pay it. When Susan B. Anthony had tried to explain in 1895 the expediency of asking Frederick Douglass not to attend the NAWSA convention in Atlanta, Ida B. Wells had chastised her. In 1913 Wells-Barnett again refused to temporize on segregation for the good of the larger cause. She recognized that suffrage purchased with segregation would not guarantee the vote for black women in the South any more than the Fifteenth Amendment had for black men. To her the larger issue was not woman suffrage but democracy. Principles that supported women's right to vote were inseparable from those promoting black suffrage.

To Anthony and other white suffragists, votes for women would not only expand democracy but also bring a "womanly" influence to government, making it less corrupt and more compassionate. Viewed this way, woman suffrage became a transcendent issue—the cause that would make all other causes possible. Wells-Barnett, however, did not accept that premise. She knew that southern white women could be expected to support their husbands' cries of white supremacy. Thus suffrage extended only to white women would make racial reform less, not more, likely to succeed. In her autobiography Wells-Barnett explained her differences with Anthony:

> Whatever the question up for discussion as to wrongs, injustice, inequality, maladministration of the law, Miss Anthony would always say, "Well, now when women get the ballot all that will be changed." So I asked her one day, "Miss Anthony, do you believe the millennium is going to come when women get the ballot? Knowing women as I do, and their petty outlook on life, although I believe it is right that they should have the vote, I do not believe that the exercise of the vote is going to change women's nature nor the political situation."[14]

More than most women—white or black—Wells-Barnett was ambivalent about her gender identification. She viewed it as "women's nature" to
have a "petty outlook on life." Her actions challenged gender roles largely
because she identified with men rather than women. Predominantly male
national organizations elected her to offices; women's groups did not. In
some ways Wells-Barnett viewed women's actions as an outsider—writing
of "knowing women as I do" rather than of "being a woman." The power of
the "cult of true womanhood" in the socialization of nineteenth-century
women is evident in her acceptance of women as essentially weak and
passive creatures of limited horizons. The conflict between that image
and her own assertiveness and activism likely caused Wells-Barnett to continue to see herself as she had in her twenties: "an anomaly to myself and
others."

With her refusal to compromise principles to prejudice, Wells-Barnett
would never become a key player in the NAWSA. In the 1910s the organization moved from ignoring race to exploiting it. In the battle for the ratification of the Nineteenth Amendment, white suffragists increasingly portrayed woman suffrage as an antidote to the political power of immigrants
and African Americans. At the same time they courted northern black
women's support, seeking to explain their stances on race privately to black
suffragists. When the Northeastern Federation of Women's Clubs, an affiliation of about six thousand black women, applied for NAWSA membership in 1919, white suffragist Ida Husted Harper confidentially sought
Mary Church Terrell's support in getting the black women to withdraw
their application.[15] Although Terrell and Wells-Barnett shared similar ideologies regarding black and women's rights, Terrell's voice of supplication
was more palatable to whites than her fellow Memphian's cry of condemnation.

An uncompromising militancy and "race first" attitude doomed Wells-
Barnett's influence in the national suffrage movement but did not prevent
her from playing significant political roles in her home city and state. Unlike NAWSA, the Illinois Equal Suffrage Association (IESA) openly included her in their receptions and parades.[16] Self-interest rather than justice probably motivated IESA. In 1912 an advisory vote on woman suffrage
was conducted in Cook County and lost primarily because Democrats
voted against it in large numbers.[17] As president of the Women's Second
Ward Republican Club, Wells-Barnett could be a force in getting out the
Republican vote.

On 26 June 1913 the Illinois legislature enacted a limited suffrage law;
among the voters in favor was black Republican Senator Robert R. "Major"

Jackson and the Alpha Suffrage Club hosted a reception for him as a gesture of their appreciation.[18] The 1913 law extended suffrage to women for all offices not mentioned in the state constitution, which could be accomplished without an amendment. Included were all local offices and presidential electors. Amid celebration of the passage, a white Chicago settlement house worker announced, "We have already started the process of educating the women in foreign wards." Soon afterward, the ASC announced its intention to provide instruction to black women. It noted the movement among immigrants and warned, "If the colored women do not take advantage of the franchise they may only blame themselves when they are left out of everything." Noting that meetings would be held every Wednesday night, the announcement reflected Wells-Barnett's "race first" policy by declaring that "the women on the whole are nonpartisan. What they do hope to do is to become strong enough to help elect some conscientious race man as alderman. We are not looking for his politics, but we hope to elect a good man."[19]

Weekly meetings in the NFL Reading Room could not ensure that black women would register in large numbers. Wells-Barnett therefore organized women for a door-to-door campaign. "The women at first were very much discouraged," she later recalled. "They said the men jeered at them and told them they ought to be at home taking care of babies. Others insisted that the women were trying to take the place of men and wear the trousers." Neither black nor white men were united on the issue of women's participation in politics. Most black male leaders, such as Douglass and Du Bois, were ardent supporters of woman suffrage. Some, however, agreed with Howard professor Kelly Miller who wrote on "The Risk of Woman Suffrage." Many were ambivalent. Robert S. Abbott of the *Chicago Defender* did not find woman suffrage objectionable but insisted, "The woman does not need to leave her home to rule the nation." He later declared, "Men are not losing their prestige, they are not being run over, but simply aided and strengthened by the advent of the gentle sex into their realms."[20]

Black and white women of Chicago responded to the efforts of their leaders. On the first day they were eligible to register to vote, more than 153,000 did so. The *Defender's* account belittled their efforts by focusing on their reluctance to give their ages and included a list of women with their "right age" and their "registration age." (Forty-one and thirty-two were the respective ages given for the fifty-two-year-old Wells-Barnett.) The *Broad Ax*, on the other hand, marveled at the women's success and exulted that as a result the "wisest and the smoothest old line machine politicians in Chicago are at sea." Editor Julius Taylor especially praised the "Colored ladies" for winning about a dozen positions as election officials.[21]

Success soon brought the ASC respect. Wells-Barnett recalled, "Our men politicians were surprised because not one of them, not even our ministers, had said one word to influence women to take advantage of the suffrage opportunity Illinois had given to her daughters." She remained true to the nonpartisan pledge to work for any good black man running for alderman from the second ward. In spite of her friendship with Martin Madden, the white Republican political boss of the ward, the ASC backed the independent black candidate, William R. Cowan, in the primary. Wells-Barnett later asserted that because of the women's vote Cowan came within 167 votes of victory. The next day two representatives of the regular Republican organization came to the ASC meeting to plead with the women not to support an independent candidate in the election but instead to back the white Republican nominee to prevent a Democratic victory. Black politician Oscar DePriest assured the women that Madden and his organization would support a black candidate for the next opening for alderman, which would occur the next year when one of the ward's two white aldermen planned to resign.[22]

During 1914 Wells-Barnett worked hard to expand ASC's political clout. By then the group's membership numbered more than one hundred. The organization brought a voting machine to its meeting and had the election commissioner give lessons in electoral procedures, held a mass rally to encourage women to register and vote, hosted candidates' nights for potential municipal judges and county commissioners, and arranged a reception for candidates for state, district, and county offices. The extent of ASC's influence was seen when mayoral hopeful William Hale Thompson accepted its invitation and "told of his plan to get work for Colored people."[23]

In 1915, as promised, the white alderman resigned, launching a scramble among three African Americans to be the city's first black alderman. The number of candidates worried some, who feared division would doom victory for any. Ferdinand Barnett chaired a committee formed to deal with the problem, while his wife utilized the ASC to unify the women behind one candidate. Before picking a candidate, the women agreed that "any member of the club known to be working for the white alderman candidates should be expelled." After all three black candidates stated their cases before the ASC, the women held a "pre-primary" primary and voted to support Oscar DePriest, who also had the backing of the Madden organization. ASC's organ, *Alpha Suffrage Record*, announced on 18 March that "we endorse our young giant Oscar DePriest." After DePriest's primary victory, Wells-Barnett helped quash an independent candidacy to ensure his victory in the general election. He duly credited his win to the women's votes.[24]

Chicago was also choosing a new mayor in 1915. William Hale "Big Bill" Thompson began early to court the black vote, as evidenced in his appearance before the ASC in November 1914. According to Wells-Barnett, Thompson sent someone to find out "who the masses of colored people accepted as leader" and found out "it was not a man but a woman, and that I was the woman." He invited her to speak at a political meeting in the Sherman Hotel. She warned him that she could not endorse his candidacy until she learned more and, when called upon at the meeting, declared she "was tired of having white politicians come out in the Second Ward just before or on election day and buy up the votes of Negroes who had no higher conception of the ballot than to make it a question of barter and sale." Thompson strongly endorsed her words and won her support. The ASC became the first organization to endorse him. Wells-Barnett dedicated considerable energy, using personal contacts to secure pledges to vote for Thompson. After six months of work, however, she learned that Judge Harry Olson, who had appointed her as an adult probation officer, was going to challenge Thompson for the job.[25]

Thompson's staff tried to keep her onboard with allusions to the influence she would have in the mayor's office if she stuck with him to the end. Wells-Barnett later recalled that she could not work against her benefactor, Olson. "All my life I have been the victim of ingrates," she wrote. "I have constantly affirmed that I agree with the old time Spartans in spirit, anyhow, when they put ingrates to death." She withdrew from the campaign, but her prior efforts continued to benefit Thompson, who won almost seven thousand votes in the Second Ward to defeat Olson by less than three thousand votes citywide.[26]

In her early forays as a political power broker, Wells-Barnett soon learned that principles and politics do not always mix. She tried to parlay her work for DePriest into support for a judgeship for her husband but noted that "he never made the slightest effort to keep his promise." Thompson had promised to make the NFL Reading Room and Social Center "an auxiliary of the city" and to use the employment bureau to give African Americans "street-cleaning jobs and work in other departments of the city." Her principled defection cost her not only political clout in the new administration but also, she believed, her job with the city. Nevertheless, she retained her faith in black political power as a powerful weapon for justice.[27]

In 1916 she cast her first vote in a presidential race and convinced the NERL, which was meeting in Washington, D.C., to endorse Republican Charles Evans Hughes in his race against Woodrow Wilson. Some delegates regretted having endorsed Wilson four years earlier and argued that the group should remain nonpartisan. Wells-Barnett carried the day with arguments foreshadowing those of Black Power advocates in the 1960s. Upon her return she wrote:

> I tried to show them that we must so mass our political strength and so wield it in our own defense at all times and in all places, that no President again would ever dare to offer us such insults as we had suffered the past four years, and thus teach them to fear our vote as they now do the labor vote.[28]

Never one to advocate a single approach to race advancement, Wells-Barnett made the ASC an organ of protest and self-help as well as political power. The ASC often joined the NFL in causes, such as the fight against segregation at Wendell Phillips High School. It also sponsored educational and cultural programs for self-improvement. Program topics ranged from "The History of Woman Suffrage" to "The Menace of the House Fly." Speakers included prominent women suffragists; Lucy Laney, founder of Haines Institute in Augusta, Georgia; Lucy Parsons, the wife of a man killed as the result of an anarchist rally at Haymarket Square in 1886; and Marcus Garvey, who solicited money for an industrial school in Jamaica at a 1916 ASC meeting. Early in 1917, however, Wells-Barnett announced "it an impossibility for her accept the presidency" for another term. Close friend and ally Dr. Fannie Emanuel took over the helm, and was followed by Laura Covington, but Wells-Barnett remained active in the club's work.[29]

For much of the decade, Wells-Barnett remained extremely busy in her multiple roles as mother, probation officer, president of two major local organizations, editor of the *Fellowship Herald*, and general agitator. Her varied activities included organizing with her husband an exhibit of paintings by black artist William A. Harper at Chicago's Art Institute. She joined with the city's black and white elite on numerous other projects. During the second week in February 1913, she joined Jane Addams, Illinois Governor Edward Dunne, and others to celebrate the fiftieth anniversary of Abraham Lincoln's Emancipation Proclamation by organizing about one hundred singers in an "Emancipation Chorus," which performed unthe direction of J. A. Mundy. It was a great success; one member of the audience reported that "many were turned away in great disappointment." Later that year Wells-Barnett joined in a movement to host a national emancipation celebration in Chicago. She also remained in demand as a speaker, appearing before numerous church and civic groups both in Chicago and elsewhere.[30]

Throughout her life, Wells-Barnett remained a journalist at heart. Before the creation of the *Fellowship Herald* in 1911 and following its demise about 1914, she wrote letters to the editors for both white and black papers to make her voice heard. In them she protested incidents of segregation and discrimination in Chicago, sometimes suggesting boycotts as remedies. Regarding Provident Hospital, which served black clientele but had only recently hired a black superintendent of nursing, she asserted, "After fifty years of freedom, the Negro certainly should have developed sufficient race pride to insist on putting members of his own race at the head of institutions established for race benefit." She also wrote the *Chicago Tribune* in May 1914 to protest its use of the phrases "old Negro newsboy" and "aged darkey" to describe a seventy-year-old veteran of the Civil War. Wells-Barnett recognized the power of words and the linkage between

The Barnett Family in 1917 (courtesy of the University of Chicago Library).

racist language and racist violence. The letter closed, "This may seem a small matter to a large number of readers, but it is a part of the great whole, and, after all there is only a difference in degree between taking a man's self-respect and taking his life."[31]

By the end of the decade that difference, however, was made painfully obvious in Illinois and elsewhere by an outbreak of race riots. After World War I broke out in Europe during 1914, the flood of European immigration quickly dried up. By 1916 European demand for goods and the beginnings of the preparedness program at home created an economic boom, especially in the industrial centers of the North. The shrinking labor pool caused northern industrialists to begin recruiting black southerners. Black migration to states such as Illinois rapidly increased, causing concern in the white-dominated labor movement. A month after the United States entered the war in April 1917, racial tensions erupted in East Saint Louis, Illinois, as a result of economic competition between black and white workers. Although that incident was quickly squelched, in early July a bloody race riot practically leveled the city's black community and caused the deaths of at least thirty-nine African Americans. Wells-Barnett quickly mobilized a fight for justice that would span several years.[32]

Enraged by early reports on the morning of 3 July that about one hundred African Americans had been slaughtered in East Saint Louis, Wells-Barnett immediately rallied the NFL to circulate handbills announcing a meeting that very evening. Two hours after the distribution, the NFL Reading Room was packed for the 8:30 gathering. After adopting resolutions to be carried to Governor Frank Lowden by the group's president, the attendees donated $8.65 to defray Wells-Barnett's expenses for an investigatory trip before her visit to the governor. She left late the next day and arrived in East Saint Louis early on the morning of 5 July in time to accompany a group of black women under military escort as they returned to their homes to get some of the belongings left behind in their flight from the white mobs. Their stories as well as the vandalism, looting, and destruction of their homes convinced Wells-Barnett not only of the brutality of the mobs but also of the criminal negligence and complicity of the local police and state militia.

Upon her return on Sunday, 8 July, two meetings—at the NFL and at Bethel A.M.E. Church—raised fifty-eight dollars to send Wells-Barnett and four others to Springfield with a list of demands for the governor. These included an investigation of the failure of the militia to protect African Americans and soldiers' participation in the riot; court martial of those implicated; state funds for the relief of the refugees camping across the river in Missouri; and action to restore order and safeguard those who wished to return. Lowden promised action in all particulars except relief funds, which he stated were not available. However, he also urged the delegation to refrain from "incendiary talk" and asked for names of potential witnesses for legal actions. Thus Wells-Barnett returned to East Saint Louis, taking with her Delores Johnson Farrow, a black nurse, to check on the efforts of the all-white nursing contingent of the Red Cross. They gathered more horrifying stories from victims.[33]

National outrage grew as news of the riot circulated. The horror of the event was evidenced by eyewitness accounts, such as that of a white reporter in St. Louis, who wrote:

> "Get a nigger," was the slogan, and it varied by the recurrent cry, "Get another!" It was like nothing so much as the holiday crowd, with thumbs turned down, in the Roman Coliseum, except that here the shouters were their own gladiators, and their own wild beasts.[34]

Wells-Barnett sought to stoke the fires of protest by publishing the pamphlet *The East St. Louis Massacre, The Greatest Outrage of the Century.* As in previous pamphlets, she sought to maintain the role of reporter by providing victims' stories and white accounts of the riot.

Expressions of outrage induced Congress to launch an investigation, but Wells-Barnett believed more remained to be done. In a letter to the *Broad Ax* she commented on a silent protest parade in Providence, Rhode Island, and credited such actions with forcing Congress to act. However, to her "the first step of our effort, prayers, protests and passing resolutions has passed." To illustrate the need for further action, she made an analogy to the current war:

> It is almost the same as if our soldier boys had contented themselves with enlisting to fight for this country and feeling that they had done their duty in defending their country when they had taken part in a great parade, with flags flying and bands playing. But we all know that unless these parades are followed up by hard work in the trenches, all the firing of guns by every conceivable active physical movement possible, the war will not be won.

Wells-Barnett urged African Americans to raise money to have people observe the congressional hearings and the trials of riot participants to see that the truth was told and justice done.[35]

The need for follow-up became quickly apparent. When the congressional hearings ended, the chairman of the investigating committee decided not to go to the expense of publishing the evidence, which would be available in a file room. The NFL quickly began to lobby Illinois congressmen to overrule the chair.[36] Disgust also followed news that black participants in the riot seemed to get disproportionately longer sentences compared to those received by whites.[37] Both Barnetts were outraged when black dentist Leroy Bundy seemed to become a scapegoat in the riot. The spark that ignited the 2 July riot was an incident eerily reminiscent of the Memphis lynching of 1892. African Americans had fired at a car and killed two policemen, mistaking them for white rowdies who had earlier been shooting from a similar car. As the investigation unfolded, Bundy was tagged as the ringleader of a group that had urged black residents to arm themselves following the governor's failure to respond to the attacks of the previous May. Their efforts were labeled as a conspiracy to riot, and Bundy was charged with the murder of the police officers.

In early November, at the request of the NFL, the *Defender* sent Wells-Barnett to interview Bundy in his jail cell at Bellville. She returned convinced of his innocence and joined with the *Defender*, the NFL, and her husband in a fight to win Bundy's freedom. By this time the Barnetts had emerged as crusaders for the rights of the accused, and they doggedly stayed with the case for years through lost trials and appeals until Bundy's freedom was finally won. Wells-Barnett raised money for the cause and her husband provided legal counsel.[38]

Although ultimately victorious in the Bundy defense, the Barnetts' fight for justice in the East Saint Louis riots cost them dearly. In addition to the financial drain, their efforts undermined their relations with leading Chicago politicians and the NAACP. Wells-Barnett later charged that when her delegation went to see Governor Lowden, a group of influential black Chicago politicians had preceded them. Oscar DePriest, Edward H. Wright, Louis B. Anderson, and Major Jackson assured Lowden that "he need pay no attention to the resolutions which [the NFL] had published in the daily papers, that the Barnetts were radicals." The NAACP had originally agreed to represent the black defendants from the riot, but when Wells-Barnett interviewed Bundy, she discovered no preparations had been made for his trial. NAACP leaders seemed to resent the incursion; almost a year later Bundy publicly replied to their criticisms and declared that "after repeated [requests] to officials of your organization which brought no response, I deemed it absolutely necessary to seek aid elsewhere." Wells-Barnett charged that the NAACP had only gotten involved because her quick response to the crisis embarrassed the group.[39]

The Barnetts' actions also earned them the label of "subversive" by federal agencies, such as the Federal Bureau of Investigation (FBI) and the Military Intelligence Division (MID). Outraged by the riot, Ferdinand Barnett had urged his listeners at a mass meeting to "Get guns and put them in your homes. Protect yourselves. And let no black man permit a policeman to come in and get those guns." Sending a newspaper clipping about the speech, the division superintendent in Chicago informed the chief of the Bureau of Investigation that Barnett "is rabidly pro-German" and offered as proof that he "in fact speaks German." No legal action, however, could be taken because under Illinois law "a citizen may keep practically any amount of firearms and ammunition in his residence." In her pamphlet Wells-Barnett urged "Negroes everywhere to stand their ground and sell their lives as dearly as possible when attacked." A copy was forwarded to the inspector general of the War Department with the notation that "it is being used to stir up a great deal of inter-racial antagonism."[40]

War often endangers individual rights, and World War I went further than most. Congress passed the Espionage Act in 1917 and the Sedition Act in 1918, which made it illegal to use "disloyal, profane, scurrilous, or abusive language" about the nation's form of government, the Constitution, the flag, or the military uniform. Practically any criticism of the nation or war effort was considered disloyal and the result of pro-German propaganda. Legitimate grievances became subversion. With increasing racial violence against African Americans and blatant discrimination against black troops, few groups had more legitimate grievances. The MID collected files labeled "Negro Subversion" and employed agents to investigate every allegation of black "disloyalty" against such publications as the *Chicago Defender* and such organizations as the NAACP. At times the MID and FBI seemed to consider complaints about lynching as more un-American than the actual act of lynching. Some operatives suggested remedying legitimate grievances in order to diminish the Germans' power to exploit them, but the MID's most pro-black agent, NAACP leader Joel E. Spingarn, found his influence limited and short-lived.[41]

The MID and the FBI frequently sent agents to interview African Americans charged with being pro-German or disloyal. Confronting a federal agent usually caused most—including W. E. B. Du Bois, Robert S. Abbott, and Kelly Miller—to temper their criticisms of lynching, segregation, and discrimination. Such tactics had no chance of success, however, with the uncompromising Wells-Barnett, who was approached regarding her support of black soldiers charged with mutiny and murder in Houston,

Texas, in the fall of 1917. Her unwillingness to be cowed caused one agent to label her "a far more dangerous agitator than Marcus Garvey," who was considered dangerous enough to be deported in 1927.[42]

The Houston affair began when the Third Battalion of the Twenty-fourth Infantry arrived in Houston on 28 July 1917. The black-manned Twenty-fourth Regiment originated during the Civil War and had remained active in war and peace ever since. The men of the Third Battalion were not green recruits but experienced soldiers with a proud tradition. Nevertheless, like black troops elsewhere in the South, they became the targets of abuse by the city's white residents and police when they refused to abide by racial etiquette that required segregation and subservience. Indicative of the army's response was a bulletin posted by an officer at Camp Funston, Kansas, in which he recognized the legal right of a soldier attempting to enter a segregated theater but declared that "the sergeant is guilty of the greater wrong in doing *anything*, no matter how legally correct, that will provoke race animosity." The army's acquiescence to segregation hurt the morale of all black troops; in Houston some soldiers reacted with violence.[43]

On the night of 23 August 1917, about one hundred soldiers engaged in a three-hour riot in which twenty people died. Court martials soon followed. With bitter memories of the 1906 Brownsville affair and scanty convictions of whites who killed blacks, many African Americans were outraged when thirteen soldiers were hanged on 11 December 1917—before they had a chance to appeal their death sentences. Their executions were shrouded in secrecy and seemed especially odious coming so soon after the failure to hold any white soldiers responsible for the part they played in the East Saint Louis riots. Widespread protest alarmed the MID, which sought to diminish its impact. For example, agents called on the mother of one executed soldier to have a "quiet funeral."[44] Naturally, Wells-Barnett launched a protest that caught the attention of federal agents.

Like many African Americans, Wells-Barnett saw the thirteen soldiers as martyrs. She attempted to organize a memorial service, but she could not find a preacher willing to let her use his church. Instead, she began to distribute buttons with the words, "In Memorial MARTYRED NEGRO SOLDIERS." Soon after she gave one to a white reporter from the *Herald Examiner*, two men came to her office, identified themselves as Secret Service men, and threatened her with arrest if she continued to distribute the buttons. After Wells-Barnett refused to back down, they tried instead to

Wells-Barnett with the "Martyred Negro Soldiers" button during World War I (courtesy of the University of Chicago Library).

confiscate the remaining buttons and informed her that other African Americans did not agree with her. Later she recalled telling them:

> Maybe not. They don't know any better or they are afraid. . . . As for myself I don't care. I'd rather go down in history as one lone Negro who dared to tell the government that it had done a dastardly thing than to save my skin by taking back what I have said. I would consider it an honor to spend whatever years are necessary in prison as the one member of the race who protested.[45]

Her intransigence, however, went unpunished—probably out of the fear of creating yet another martyr. Threats had worked against other leaders, but Wells-Barnett proved those threats were mostly hollow. Nevertheless, a year later MID intelligence agent W. H. Loving mentioned the button incident in his suggestion to withhold a passport from this "known race agitator." Even British intelligence, a year after the war was over, called Wells-Barnett "a race agitator of some twenty years standing" and referred once again to the buttons.[46]

In the climate that spawned the Red Scare of 1919, being a "known race agitator" helped to diminish Wells-Barnett's influence on the national level. After the United States entered the war, President Wilson became aware that black disaffection could handicap efforts to mobilize African Americans in the war effort. Actually, as in every other war, most black citizens patriotically supported their nation. At the same time, many saw Wilson's proclaimed war goal, "to make the world safe for democracy," as an excellent opening to press for democracy at home. East Saint Louis and Houston, as well as discriminatory policies toward black troops, threatened black support. Strictly as a war measure, Wilson sought to allay African Americans' discontent in order to maximize their wartime efforts—without threatening the racial status quo. He chose as his allies Booker T. Washington's closest confederates: Emmett J. Scott, who had been the Tuskegean's private secretary, and Robert R. Moton, who became president of Tuskegee Institute when Washington died in 1915. Private organizations, such as the Women's Committee of the Council of National Defense, also sought black colleagues who would be acceptable to the South. Neither Barnett fit the mold of those recruited to aid mobilization efforts in the black community.[47] Actually, Wells-Barnett did feel a duty to support the war effort—just not at the expense of black rights. But her patriotic activities, such as selling Liberty Bonds and organizing a campaign to make up Christmas kits for soldiers, did not offset her agitation in the minds of intelligence agents.[48]

17

⚛⚛

Defending Freedom until Death

"Eternal vigilance is the price of liberty"

⚛⚛

I da B. Wells-Barnett began the last, unfinished chapter of her autobiography with the words, "Eternal vigilance is the price of liberty." From the close of World War I until her death in 1931, she remained the most persistent black voice for justice and power. By that time, however, the Chicago radical was alienated from most African American leaders and organizations and her style of agitation seemed dated. Although she had once rivaled Washington and Du Bois for the leadership role that Frederick Douglass had played, in the 1920s she found her contributions largely ignored. During her last years, she began an autobiography that reflected a disillusionment born from her sense of isolation.

As the war came to an end, Wells-Barnett joined other African Americans in a broadly based movement to have their voices heard in the peace process and aftermath of the war. Congresses and conventions sprang up all over, and many groups elected delegates to attend the peace conference at Versailles. Military Intelligence Division (MID) agent W. H. Loving reported that "more than one hundred delegates have been elected by the various societies" and that "people were filled with excitement over the fiery addresses of the radicals." Not surprisingly, two of the more radical organizations, both of which met in December 1918, elected Wells-Barnett as a delegate.[1]

The first to meet was the Universal Negro Improvement Association

(UNIA) in New York on 3 December. Its founder, Marcus Garvey, was a Jamaican who had traveled to the United States in 1916 to visit Tuskegee Institute and to raise money for an industrial school in his homeland. In November 1916 Garvey came to Chicago and met Ferdinand Barnett, who invited him home for dinner—as he so often did with black travelers of all classes. At the Barnett house the Jamaican guest described the domination of ninety thousand black Jamaicans by a mere 15,000 whites. His hostess was appalled and asked how they let that happen. When Garvey told of the lack of economic power, Wells-Barnett invited him to speak at the Negro Fellowship League to raise money for his proposed school. Both leaders seemed impressed with the dedication of the other; in *Champion Magazine* a couple of months later Garvey listed Wells-Barnett among the men and women in the United States "who are conscientious workers and not mere life service dignitaries."[2]

Soon after, Garvey postponed returning to his homeland and established in Harlem a chapter of his Jamaican group, the UNIA. His was an uncompromising voice that disturbed intelligence agents with talk of the next war—one that would be fought between the white and black peoples of the world. The UNIA became the first successful mass movement among African Americans, largely because of the appeal of Garvey's vision of a powerful, united Africa under black rule for the benefit of all the African diaspora. Africans in America had been taught to hate their origins and be shamed by their color. Such cultural brainwashing led to color prejudices among themselves in favor of those with more European ancestry and paler skin. Garvey turned that notion upside down and preached that white ancestry tainted rather than beautified. The UNIA instilled pride and self-respect through such symbolic trappings as uniforms and titles. Its popularity with the black masses threatened the credibility of many elite and middle-class claimants to leadership, and they increasingly became critical of its president. His separatist ideology appalled those fighting for integration.

Seeing herself also as a target of jealous criticism, Wells-Barnett was drawn to Garvey's fiery and uncompromising rhetoric. By 1918 she was disillusioned by white allies in both the NAACP and the woman suffrage movement. She shared Garvey's cries for self-help and economic independence even though she never embraced his separatist extremism, which later led him to endorse the Ku Klux Klan in its fight for racial purity. She gladly accepted an invitation to the December 1918 UNIA meeting and rejoiced in her election as one of its delegates to the Versailles conference. Chosen with her was another black leader outside the mainstream: A. Philip Randolph, a proclaimed socialist.[3]

Later Randolph would join the chorus of Garvey critics, who were particularly disgusted with the UNIA's grandiose scheme to establish the Black Star Line, a black-owned shipping company that failed, costing hundreds of African Americans their modest savings. Black criticism legitimized the federal government's pursuit of Garvey, which led to his being convicted of mail fraud in 1924 and deported in 1927. The Barnetts, on the other hand, remained supportive of Garvey. Ferdinand Barnett served as his legal counsel in an unsuccessful civil suit against the *Chicago Defender* for libel. Wells-Barnett continued to defend him after his exile. In her autobiography, she noted his ability "to solidify the masses of our people and endow them with racial consciousness and racial unity." She lamented his failure to take her advice against starting a shipping business and laid the blame for his downfall on the lack of "support which his wonderful movement deserved" and on his becoming "drunk with power too soon." Her evaluation concluded: "It may be that even though he has been banished to Jamaica the seed planted here will yet spring up and bring forth fruit which will mean the deliverance of the black race—the cause which was so dear to his heart."[4]

The other group to elect Wells-Barnett as a delegate to Versailles was the National Colored Congress for World Democracy, hosted by William Monroe Trotter's NERL. During its sessions in Washington between 16 and 19 December, Wells-Barnett gave an address, which an MID agent labeled as "intended to arouse the feeling of the persons present." Typically, she also imposed her will on the group's deliberations. When Trotter was not selected to go to France because his presence might offend President Wilson, Wells-Barnett lambasted the group and his name was included. Later she discovered that although elected as a delegate, she would be one of two whose expenses would not be provided. According to her recollection, Wells-Barnett asked to be heard and expressed regret that "the years I had spent in fighting the race's battles had made me financially unable to accept the honor." Unsurprisingly, the Congress added her name to the list of paid delegates.[5]

Wells-Barnett left those meetings to appear with Garvey at an 8:00 P.M. rally in Baltimore on 18 December. Arriving late, she was introduced by Marie Madre Marshall, who reported, "it was tipped off to us that there was going to be sent a spy to report her speech." The crowd roared its approval when Marshall exclaimed, "You know nothing would intimidate Ida B.

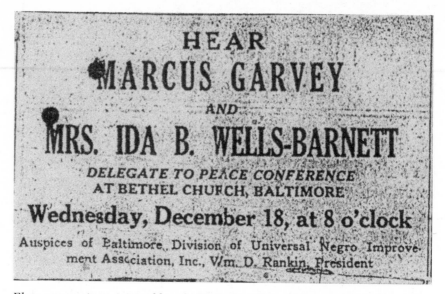

Flyer announcing a joint address by Wells-Barnett and Marcus Garvey, December 1919, from the Military Intelligence Division Files, National Archives.

Wells-Barnett." Expressing fear that the words of "the most fearless and out-spoken speaker or champion that the race has produced" might be used to deny her a passport, Marshall asked the audience to report any spies. Wells-Barnett apparently did temper her words. According to an MID spy (evidently not spotted by the crowd), there was "nothing of interest" in her speech, even though MID agent W. H. Loving asserted she "went to Baltimore for the purpose of delivering one of her favorite addresses."[6]

Loving, a retired army major and full-time MID specialist on "Negro subversion," consistently argued against granting Wells-Barnett a passport. Although Loving sometimes used the threat of subversion to lobby against discrimination, in August 1919 MID Director Marlborough Churchill called him "one of the best types of the 'white man's negro.'" Churchill's memorandum also contained the report of J. E. Cutler, a white MID specialist whose full-time assignment was likewise "Negro subversion." In his report Cutler referred to the revival of the Ku Klux Klan "for the purpose of preventing misconduct on the part of the negroes and misunderstanding as between whites and blacks." With such a mind-set, the government naturally withheld permission to travel to France from African Americans elected by their own people to observe the peace proceedings and lobby for black interests.[7]

Woodrow Wilson, in his quest for self-determination and other idealistic goals outlined in his famous Fourteen Points, could hardly welcome the "Address to the Country and the World" drafted by Wells-Barnett and others. After noting that "every denial or violation of justice, humanity and democracy has become a matter FOR CORRECTION AND ABROGATION ON A WORLD BASIS BY A WORLD COURT," the document further stated that "we must call world attention to the utterly undemocratic conditions under which every person of color is forced to live in this country." As during Malcolm X's attempt in the 1960s to bring the United States before the World Court for violations of human rights, government attempts to repress such movements merely give them attention and credibility. Trotter sneaked across the ocean as a ship's cook and returned as a hero to African Americans.[8]

White America's refusal to apply the tenets of democracy at home disillusioned and angered African Americans who had "closed ranks" during the war. There was a marked reluctance to accept peacefully the continuation of second-class citizenship. In June 1919 a newly established black newspaper, the *Chicago Whip*, pointedly informed whites that "the compromising peace-at-any-price Negro is rapidly passing into the scrap heap of yesterday." Tension in Chicago escalated during the war as jobs lured black southerners, whose mass arrival created severe housing shortages. In the decade between 1910 and 1920, the population of South Side, populated mostly by African Americans, almost tripled. Overcrowding by rural immigrants poorly equipped for urban life created a plethora of social problems, which middle-class black Chicagoans sought to escape—only to be met with hostility as they moved into previously all-white neighborhoods. To repel black newcomers, white Chicagoans organized "protective organizations" and increasingly resorted to violence, including twenty-six bombings from July 1917 to July 1919.[9]

Because of her prior investigations of racial violence, Wells-Barnett became more and more concerned and sought to defuse the situation. In June 1919 she led delegations twice to Mayor William Hale Thompson's office, only to be turned away. The group was told to take their concerns regarding the bombings to the chief of police. In a letter published in the *Chicago Tribune* on 7 July, Wells-Barnett compared the city's racial situation and lack of governmental response to the early situation in East Saint Louis. "In all earnestness," she wrote, "I implore Chicago to set the wheels of justice in motion before it is too late, and Chicago be disgraced by some of the bloody outrages that have disgraced East St. Louis." A little over two

weeks later the *Tribune* deplored the growing racial animosity and acknowledged that "there are a great many intelligent colored men and
women, both in professional and home life, eager to participate in conferences seeking a disposition of the race question." Four days later, on 27
July, the powder keg exploded.[10]

A dispute over a Lake Michigan bathing beach ignited a race war that
lasted thirteen days. Fifteen whites and twenty-three African Americans
died and at least a thousand black families were left homeless. Typical of
the many race riots during the so-called Red Summer of 1919, the Chicago
riot marked the collision of white desire to maintain the racial status quo
and black determination to change it. The local chapter of the NERL
sprang into action at the outbreak, led by its president, N. S. Taylor, and
Wells-Barnett. With local ministers, they established the Protective Association, which met daily during the riot and served as a liaison with the city
government. Eventually, however, Wells-Barnett resigned to protest the
group's support of a proposal to have the state attorney general, Edward J.
Brundage, take charge of an extended investigation of the riot. She was furious when they turned to the man she felt had been derelict in his han-
dling of the East Saint Louis riot two years earlier. Turning in her membership card and leaving to one minister's comment of "good riddance,"
Wells-Barnett walked away with tears streaming down her face. Wells-
Barnett often took personal offense when people disagreed with her. That
tendency, as well as her unwavering conviction that right was always on her
side, led Wells-Barnett into a self-defeating pattern of breaking organizational ties and then bemoaning her isolation.

The Chicago riot was apparently painful for Wells-Barnett, who devoted a mere three and a half pages of her autobiography to the event. She
concluded her discussion of it by noting the report of the Chicago Commission on Race Relations on the riot and noted, "Many recommendations
were made, but few, if any, have been carried out. Chicago has been left
with a heritage of race prejudice which seems to increase rather than decrease." Her words proved true. In testimony before the Commission on
Civil Disorders in 1968, black sociologist Kenneth Clark cited that report
and others, describing them as "the same moving picture re-shown over
and over again, the same analysis, the same recommendations, and the
same inaction."[11]

The willingness of African Americans to fight back alarmed many,
causing wild rumors to be circulated. An MID report in October noted gossip that Wells-Barnett and Oscar DePriest were making bombs and accu-

mulating hand grenades.[12] The increased militancy and resultant hysteria were not limited to northern cities. In Phillips County, Arkansas, where the population was over 75 percent black, some sharecroppers organized a union to combat exploitive practices of white landowners. Late in the night of 30 September 1919, men at a union meeting exchanged gunfire with occupants of a passing car. This triggered four days of violence, known as the Elaine riots, that left five whites and many more African Americans dead. Whites claimed the African Americans were conspiring to kill all the whites and appropriate their land. Many black men were arrested and twelve were sentenced to be executed.[13]

Wells-Barnett immediately mobilized. When the local NERL was too slow in responding, she approached an organization known as the People's Movement (in which her husband was active and Oscar DePriest was a leader). The group sent a petition to the Arkansas governor promising to use its influence to urge African Americans to leave Arkansas if the men were electrocuted. After receiving a letter from one of the imprisoned men, Wells-Barnett journeyed to the Arkansas address given in the letter, meeting with some of the prisoners' wives and mothers. Making herself inconspicuous in order to pass as another relative, she went with them to the jail. According to her account, when the men heard her name whispered to them, "an expression of joy spread over their faces." They agreed to write out full accounts of their experiences, and they sang for her. Before she left, Wells-Barnett told them, "Quit talking about dying; if you believe your God is all powerful, believe he is powerful enough to open these prison doors, and say so. Dying is the last thing you ought to even think about, much less talk about. Pray to live and believe you are going to get out."[14]

As in some previous incidents, Wells-Barnett and the NAACP duplicated efforts. Both she and Walter White investigated the case and published their results—Wells-Barnett in a pamphlet, *The Arkansas Race Riot*. Previously, most white newspapers had been accepting the stories of a black conspiracy. As a result of the increased publicity, the Elaine rioters became a cause célèbre, and all the condemned men were freed by January 1925. Wells-Barnett was gratified when one of the freed men came to her home to express his thanks, but the campaign had exacted its price. Her actions alienated the men of the local NERL and worsened her relations with NAACP leaders, who claimed credit for the men's release and asked Wells-Barnett to turn over any money she had raised for the cause.

Wells-Barnett's feelings of isolation, betrayal, and disappointment also grew out of her increasingly difficult task of keeping the Negro Fellowship

League (NFL) in operation. Until she lost her job as adult probation officer, her salary had supported the group. Fees collected by its employment
bureau could barely meet expenses. Remembering the activism of the
Methodist Episcopal Church in establishing such schools as her alma
mater, Rust College, she turned to Bishop Thomas Nicholson in Chicago
for aid in continuing the NFL and making it a school for social workers. He
referred her request to the district superintendent for the colored churches.
As the superintendent's list of demands grew, Wells-Barnett agreed to turn
the NFL's Sunday services over to the church and to relinquish the presidency to a young male graduate of Garrett Biblical Institute. After acqui-
escing to male leadership, she continued to be annoyed at questions
regarding the lack of support of the NFL by the "leading citizens." Wells-
Barnett was proud that the group's officers included a ragpicker, compar-
ing her supporters to the "fishermen, tax collectors, publicans, and sinners" who followed Jesus. The last straw came when the superintendent
seemed reluctant to trust her with a check to pay off the landlord. She lost
her temper and the arrangement came to an end.[15]

Wells-Barnett was especially defensive about the lack of support she received from the black elite, because it both wounded her personally and diminished her effectiveness. She had been hurt when black leaders talked
Victor F. Lawson into transferring his crucial financial support from the
NFL to the new YMCA. In 1915 another competitor for support arrived in
Chicago when T. Arnold Hill organized a local chapter of the National Urban League. Founded in New York during 1911, the Urban League was an
interracial group dedicated to providing assistance to the hordes of black
migrants entering northern cities. Its conservative stance on labor issues
won the backing of white businesspeople, and its efficiency and profes-
sionalism in providing social services won the allegiance of white progressives and social workers. It also received support among black Chicagoans,
which Wells-Barnett attributed to "the strange way we have of taking hold
of the new to the detriment of the old."[16]

But a number of other factors contributed to the Urban League's receiving greater assistance and the death of the NFL. The Urban League's
well-organized efficiency displaced many other small-scale social aid programs of churches and individuals as well as Wells-Barnett's group. Business support for the Urban League guaranteed it access to more employment opportunities, diminishing the effectiveness of the NFL employment
agency that provided the group's income. In contrast to the Urban
League's staff of full-time social work professionals, the NFL was led by

one woman engaged in numerous other crusades as well as the duties of motherhood. Whereas the federal government saw the NFL's employment activities as "Negro agitation" (in the words of one FBI memorandum), the Department of Labor provided financial assistance to the Urban League's employment bureau.[17]

Wells-Barnett contributed to her own loss of support through her temperament and actions. She tended to see other groups as competitors. For example, she claimed that "it seemed that the Urban League was brought to Chicago to supplant the activities of the Negro Fellowship League." Obviously, she took no role in the Urban League. Her confrontational approach and uncompromising self-righteousness disrupted most of the movements she joined. To herself, Wells-Barnett reluctantly recognized her role in alienating coworkers. An early version of her autobiographical account of one confrontation included the words, "I, as usual, lost what favor I had by becoming furiously angry." However, she struck through those words in her rewrite.[18]

The NFL closed its doors late in 1920. Soon afterward, on 15 December, Wells-Barnett entered the hospital for a gallbladder operation. There were apparently complications; the *Chicago Defender* noted that on Christmas "visitors were allowed for the first time and the Barnett family attended en masse." She remained in the hospital over a month, and her sister Lily came from California to care for her when she returned home. Not until the end of March did the *Broad Ax* announce, "she is now able to be up and around in her lovely home at 3624 Grand Boulevard." In her autobiography, Wells-Barnett claimed it took a full year for her to recuperate, during which she "did more serious thinking from a personal point of view than ever before" and came to the conclusion that she "had nothing to show for all those years of toil and labor."[19]

Her illness seems to have marked a turning point in Wells-Barnett's life. Earlier in 1920, she had not only struggled to keep the NFL in operation but also maintained a hectic schedule of speeches and trips as well as political, civic, and church work. Joining the Metropolitan Community Church soon after its founding by a former pastor of Bethel A.M.E., Wells-Barnett taught an adult Sunday school class and became active in the Metropolitan Center Lyceum that met on Sunday evenings. She also chaired a committee that sought to raise money to win seats for African American women at the Republican National Convention held in Chicago that year.[20]

Trips often took her away from her home in early 1920, and her fre-

In the backyard at 3624 Grand Boulevard; Wells-Barnett and Alfreda standing, Ferdinand seated, and Herman in the window, August 1919 (courtesy of the University of Chicago Library).

quent absences seem to have troubled Wells-Barnett. From a conference in September on Charities and Corrections at Jacksonville, Illinois, she wrote her family of an additional request to speak at a Jacksonville church and explained, "So I won't be home to help my girls celebrate Halloween." The letter contained not only her apology but also a statement of logistical planning that many working mothers can identify with: "Freda is all settled that she goes with Irene & her father or Louise & her father. Ida I hope has seen Essie & the other girls and planned to have them bring her by home from the Y.W.C.A." Later in the letter she makes a telling confession:

> You know all that is in my heart to say to you, so I will not need to say it. Whenever I think of my dear girls, which is all the time, such a feeling of confidence comes over me. I know *my* girls are true to me, to themselves and their God wherever they are, and my heart is content. I have had many troubles and much disappointment in life, but I feel that in you I have abiding joy. I feel that whatever others may do, my girls are now and will be shining examples of noble true womanhood.[21]

The letter reveals her methods of shaping her children and her realization of her family's importance to her. The elaborate arrangements for daughters aged nineteen and sixteen also reflect Wells-Barnett's protectiveness and realization of their impending womanhood.

Possibly as a result of that realization, combined with her poor health and a hospitalization, Wells-Barnett seems to have spent a relatively quiet year at home in 1921. She helped make local arrangements for a national meeting of the NERL, but there were few references to her in the local black papers. One was a notice in the New Year's Eve edition of the *Defender* that "Mrs. Ida B. Wells-Barnett and her daughters, Misses Ida and Alfreda Barnett, will be at home to their gentlemen friends" on New Year's Day. She also became a grandmother in 1921 when Herman's wife gave birth to an eleven-pound boy. According to her daughter, "With time on her hands, and no longer confined to bed, she spent as much time as the nurses would allow fondly hovering over her first grandson." Four years later only Ida remained at home, and the family of three moved from the fourteen-room house on Grand Boulevard to a five-room apartment on East Garfield.[22]

From 1922 to the end of the decade, Wells-Barnett gave speeches, founded short-lived organizations, embarked on solitary crusades, worked for the Republican party, attempted to regain a national leadership role, began her autobiography, and continued to provoke controversy. Although she received honors in her home town, her feelings of alienation and betrayal continued to grow—and they found expression in her emerging autobiography. Indeed, a sense of being overlooked at the national level seems to have been a major spur to Wells-Barnett's writing an account of her life. Once celebrated widely by the black press and seen as the embodiment of the antilynching campaign, she had an international reputation at the turn of the century. In the 1920s her influence had declined. Symbolic of her marginalization in the 1920s was the increasing identification of the antilynching movement with others.

In 1922 Wells-Barnett lobbied both President Warren G. Harding and the Senate for passage of the Dyer bill, which would have imposed heavy penalties on counties where lynchings occurred. However, that bill reached the floor of the Senate largely as the result of the NAACP's movement for federal legislation against lynching. After the failure to get the Dyer bill passed, the NAACP continued the crusade—without any success, but with a lot of publicity. As the group began to be recognized as the premiere advocate of black rights, Wells-Barnett's alienation from it grew. She was not among the participants in the National Conference on Lynching, called by the NAACP in 1919. By 1930 her name had become so divorced from the antilynching movement that she was also absent from the National Antilynching Congress organized by the NERL, which also had lost influence.[23]

Without a voice in the NAACP or the Urban League, Wells-Barnett attempted once again to gain power in the National Association of Colored Women (NACW)—the other powerful national organization for black advancement. She regained the presidency of the Ida B. Wells Club and represented it at the national NACW meeting held at Chicago in August 1924. There she made a run for the presidency but was defeated by Mary McLeod Bethune. The Broad Ax speculated that Wells-Barnett "will not lose any sleep over this defeat," but according to her daughter, she was indeed disappointed.[24]

Although unable to win an office in a national organization, Wells-Barnett remained active in the Ida B. Wells Club, serving as the chair of its civics committee and its program committee after resigning from its presidency. She also continued to found and lead such local women's groups as the Women's Forum in 1926 and the Third Ward Women's Political Club in 1927. Additionally, she participated in Chicago interracial organizations; for example, she was vice president of the multiracial Anthropological Society, which presented programs to foster tolerance and understanding among ethnic groups. Typically, Wells-Barnett strained that tolerance and understanding with a presentation in January 1926 titled "Mixed Marriages." It addressed the strongest taboo in white society—one shared even by many white liberals. She noted that the question, "Do you want your daughter to marry a nigger?" very often "hardened the hearts and stifled the conscience . . . of the nation." Although white men preached racial purity and passed miscegenation laws, at the end of the Civil War their sons and daughters comprised "one-ninth of the so-called black race." Laws, according to Wells-Barnett, were powerless to keep people apart. She claimed that mixed marriages did not lead to degeneracy and "cited such examples as Pushkin, Dumas, Alexander Hamilton, Frederick Douglass and others of mixed blood who had made notable achievements." A participant noted the "tenseness with which the audience had listened," which led the club's president to remind the listeners that they "had no business to join the organization unless they could be tolerant."[25] Apparently, Wells-Barnett shared the militancy of Trotter and Garvey but not their separatist ideology.

The same anger that diminished her effectiveness in organizations fueled her continual crusades. Throughout the decade, Wells-Barnett's outrage over injustice stirred her to protest. For example, in 1927 a Mississippi River flood created mass destruction and devastation. Federal and Red Cross relief efforts were riddled with racism. Reports of black refugees' being denied food and forced to work like slaves on levees and white-owned plantations soon circulated. Wells-Barnett demanded action from Secretary of Commerce Herbert Hoover and urged others to take action. After a "Negro Committee" investigated conditions, she scorned its reports because they minimized the problems, praised the Red Cross, and laid the blame for any discrimination on local committees that had "misinterpreted" Red Cross policies. Urging people to not be "hoodwinked," Wells-Barnett used an analogy to make her point:

> When a doctor visits a patient who has a bullet wound that is infected, he doesn't spend time admiring the part of the body that needs no attention nor draw attention to the symmetry of the patient's limbs. He gets busy at once on the infected wound and cleanses and disinfects the spot which needs it.[26]

In 1928 her crusades included going with a delegation to the Illinois governor to urge an end to the segregation of the state home for girls as well as organizing protests against the police slaying of a sixteen-year-old boy.

The next year she raised her voice in outrage over the stoning of a black Girl Scout outing at Jackson Park beach.[27] Wells-Barnett not only preached eternal vigilance, she practiced it.

A continuing source of disappointment for Wells-Barnett was her inability to play important roles in the Republican party after the franchisement of women. Positions of power seemed to go to her enemies. In 1920 the party named Lethia Fleming as "national director to organize the colored women." Fleming, who was a close ally of Mary Church Terrell and shared Terrell's dislike of Wells-Barnett, continued to have influence and served as director of the Colored Women's Organization's western division in 1928. In the 1924 election, Hallie Q. Brown, another critic of Wells-Barnett, held the post of "national director of the Colored Women's Department." Wells-Barnett's marginal position among black clubwomen on the national level undoubtedly decreased her local influence. Despite her political activism, she had little influence in the 1924 meeting to form the National League of Republican Colored Women, winning no office but merely an appointment to the publicity committee.[28]

Wells-Barnett's limited influence in mainstream Republican politics is illustrated in the elections of 1928 and 1930. During Herbert Hoover's 1928 campaign, a press release that announced the formation of the Colored Voters' Division of the Republican National Committee did not include her name in the list of "outstanding women . . . serving in various key capacities."[29] A private report of a Republican meeting in Chicago a few days later noted:

> You know how Mrs. Barnett would act. She and her cohorts held a meeting of protest last night, against the bringing up here from Kansas City of Myrtle Foster Cook, when she is here, demanded by the Illinois voters, and could do so much better. . . . She has also written a special letter to Mr. Hoover. Thank heaven he may never see it.[30]

Not one to be ignored, she attended the opening of the Division's western headquarters in Chicago that month. Her persistence paid off; she was appointed National Organizer of Illinois Colored Women.[31]

Wells-Barnett quickly ordered calling cards that listed her position and reported to the headquarters office on 10 September, sending out a mass mailing the next day. She also organized a rally and reported having a thousand people present on 20 September. Trouble soon arose, however. The office refused to pay the rental and printing bills for the rally, turned down her request to publish the address she gave, and refused to fill her order for pledge cards and literature for distribution. Wells-Barnett was able to get Oscar DePriest to pay the hall rental, but used her own modest salary to pay for the printing of the flyers that announced the rally and for the publication of her speech under the title, *Why I am for Hoover.* On 8 October she apparently lost her salaried position and financial support for her organizing efforts. "Every mail I get," she complained on 19 October, "begs me to come to the women I have organized and speak, but Roscoe Simmons tells me there is no money to pay expenses."[32]

On 20 October, after returning from a speaking tour of ten counties, Wells-Barnett received a letter from Claude Barnett requesting a statement on "Why I am for Hoover." The indefatigable campaigner sat up until 2:00 A.M. composing a response. Worried about "the apathy of those to whom was confided the duty of combating Democratic propaganda," Wells-Barnett sent another statement detailing numerous Democratic party assaults on black rights. "This time the wolf in sheep's clothing," she wrote, "is spending money like water to lure our folks in the Democratic camp, but very few of them are going to betray our race for 30 pieces of silver or for the prospect of a drink of liquor."[33] She may have felt like an honored insider by Barnett's request, but she was one of dozens he solicited in his role as secretary of publicity for the Republican Colored Voters Division.[34]

The 1930 elections were another disappointment for Wells-Barnett. In the fall of 1929, Ruth Hanna McCormick announced her candidacy for the United States Senate and asked Mary Church Terrell to head her campaign among black women. Wells-Barnett was outraged and organized a protest meeting. The group forwarded resolutions to McCormick; one stated: "We resent the slight thus put upon the Negro women of Illinois, whose vote she solicits, by the employment of an outsider to influence that vote." In her anger, Wells-Barnett evidently referred to a black employee of the candidate as a "spittoon cleaner." In the end all she had accomplished was to create an uproar and hurt her own political ambitions.[35]

Wells-Barnett's political goal was election to the state senate in 1930. In January she unsuccessfully solicited the support of two old political allies—Charles Deneen and Edward Wright—whom she called "still stubborn about helping women" in her diary. Not easily discouraged, on 3 February she ordered the necessary petitions to qualify as a candidate and mailed them to Springfield with more than five hundred names on 12 February. Her campaign, however, received little press coverage aside from what appears to be a paid announcement. People promised support and then did not deliver it. Campaign contributions were scanty—mostly from one woman and Ferdinand Barnett, who contributed both his time and money to open a campaign office and distribute twenty thousand flyers. Wells-Barnett gave speeches wherever she was invited; nevertheless, without the support of either major political faction, she received a mere 585 votes.[36]

The campaign consumed a lot of time between January and April, but it comprised only a portion of the sixty-eight-year-old crusader's activities. In 1930 she served again as president of the Ida B. Wells Club and chaired the Women's Sunday Evening Club. In January 1931, she became a member of the United Clubs Emergency Relief movement, which was formed in response to the worsening economic depression. Continuing the eternal vigilance that she declared the price of liberty, Wells-Barnett wrote articles about such injustices as "rotten conditions in Chicago's public schools" and the nomination of an acknowledged racist to the U.S. Supreme Court. The diary she kept for a few months in 1930 reflected her hectic schedule of meetings. She also appeared often in court and before the board of pardons on behalf of people caught in the criminal justice system.[37]

The year was not only busy but emotionally draining as well. As in her diary from the 1880s, Wells-Barnett recorded her worries about money but continued to attend plays and movies. She was also concerned about "a problem child." Just like his uncle, Jim Wells, her son Herman had a gambling problem and expected Wells-Barnett to "straighten out his tangle." She was heartsick when he disappeared (although he did leave a note on her pillow) and appalled when she found out that her son, a lawyer, had embezzled clients' money to pay for his gambling. Although the rest of her children were successful and respected, she was so tormented by Herman's dilemma that she "read to keep from thinking."[38]

Even though Chicago's black community paid homage to both Barnetts in 1927 with two testimonial dinners, in 1930 Wells-Barnett brooded over the fact that Carter G. Woodson's book on African American history "made no mention of my anti-lynching contribution."[39] For several years she had been working on an autobiography, which she began after a young woman admitted not knowing why Wells-Barnett was important. In the preface she proclaimed, "And so, because our youth are entitled to the facts of race history which only the participant's can give, I am thus led to set forth the facts contained in this volume which I dedicate to them."[40] The words she wrote, however, sometimes seemed more like a brief in her own defense, which gave her side of every dispute she could remember. The manuscript is a record of her public life; very seldom did she discuss her private affairs. Even so, it sometimes sparkles with her spirit—especially in the early chapters. As Wells-Barnett began to tell of the events of 1927 and 1928, the narrative became bogged down in detail. She was still working on the autobiography when she became ill; four days later, on 25 March 1931, she died of uremic poisoning.

Her funeral proved that Wells-Barnett, although controversial, was respected by many. The church was packed and the sidewalks filled with people who "stood outdoors shivering in the biting March wind . . . to get a last look at the woman who has stood as champion in so many causes affecting the welfare of the Race." For almost an hour, mourners, both black and white, passed solemnly by the coffin. "In keeping with the simple lives led by members of the Barnett family," the *Defender* noted that the last rites were held with "the simple dignity and a solemnity befitting the occasion of the passing of a great woman." The minister noted, "She will be missed," the paper continued, "And the throng in the pews, the throng lining the walls, the throng high up in the balcony, the throngs packed in the vestibules, answered with nods of heads, 'She will be missed.'"[41]

Wells-Barnett's sons, stepsons, and nephews were the pallbearers. Her two daughters, two sisters, and two brothers sat in the mourners' seats with Ferdinand Barnett. Lily, George, and Jim had come from California for the funeral. The family decided to forgo the lengthy reading of memorials and telegrams, selecting only one of each. The Ida B. Wells Club, which had hosted her wedding reception over thirty years earlier, presented the only memorial. The telegram was from a personal friend rather than a well-known politician or leader. Ferdinand refused to allow those who had not supported his wife in life to eulogize her in death. The *Defender* described the ceremony as "no fanfare of trumpets, no undue shouting, no flowery oratory—just plain, earnest, sincere words from the mouths of those to whom the grief was real."[42]

A few days after the funeral, Irene McCoy Gaines, a leading black Chicago clubwoman, remembered that Wells-Barnett's last official act was a request made to each city club for books, especially those by African Americans, for a YMCA "book shower." Gaines remarked that the request was in keeping with the deceased's long-standing efforts to foster race pride and noted, "It was her special mission to interpret and express the wrongs and sufferings of an oppressed race." Even those who had disagreed with Wells-Barnett praised her efforts. W. E. B. Du Bois declared, "The passing of Ida Wells Barnett calls for more than an ordinary obituary." He credited

her with beginning "the awakening of the conscience of the nation" and explained that her "work has easily been forgotten because it was taken up on
a much larger scale by the N.A.A.C.P. and carried to greater success."[43]

Never awarded prestigious prizes in life, Wells-Barnett has been showered with honors in death. Recognition came first in Chicago, where a
public housing project was named for her in 1940. Outside of her hometown, however, few remembered her. Alfreda Duster refused to let her
mother's legacy remain unknown. It took incredible persistence—almost
forty years—to get her mother's autobiography published in 1970. By then
Wells-Barnett's uncompromising militancy resonated with a new generation born of the civil rights movement and disillusioned by the slow pace of
change. A new wave of feminists also found inspiration in her life and deplored society's ignorance of her and other women's contributions. Since
then a postage stamp has been issued in her honor, her home has been
made into an historic site, a public television documentary has been produced of her life, and her diaries and writings have become available in
paperback. Dozens of scholars and journalists have written thousands of
words about her. No longer will her name be omitted from history books.
Her story is too important to be ignored.

Few people offer greater insights into the complex issues confronting
African Americans, women, and reformers in general. Wells-Barnett illustrates the inadequacy of ideological labels; she vacillated between integration and separatism, agitation and self-help, nationalism and assimilation.
No theory or cause transcended her desire to "gather my race in my arms
and fly far away with them [to a place safe from harm]." Her destination
sometimes changed but never her desire to protect. Whenever and wherever she encountered injustice, Wells-Barnett sought to make a difference.
She attempted to make the horrors of racism real to a complacent world by
painting pictures with her words, as Martin Luther King, Jr., later used television. Both recognized that evil flourishes in the dark. The gradual demise
of lynching was the result of many factors, but surely the first step had to be
the public's awareness and rejection of the practice.

Wells-Barnett was not wedded to a particular method any more than
she was to an ideology. She recognized the complexity of the problems facing African Americans and sought to use all available tools to improve their
lives. On New Year's Day, less than three months before she died, she wrote
of the passing year's "splendid lessons in life's school." Her list of three began with the success of a local paper's campaign urging people not to shop
where they could not work, which she called "this bloodless battle for

recognition and progress in the economic field." The second lesson was learned when lobbying efforts prevented the confirmation of John J. Parker, a southern segregationist, to the Supreme Court. This victory taught "the strength of our political worth." Finally, Wells-Barnett praised the critically acclaimed performance of black actors in the play, "Green Pastures," which she called a "wonderful testimonial to Negro art and religion."[44] Wells-Barnett visited presidents and scolded newspapers for using the term "darky." Nothing was too big or too small for her to tackle.

Her experiences in politics and reform movements also demonstrate the continuing importance of the concept of race in the United States. It persists in the inability or unwillingness of white reformers to realize how racism taints even their best intentions and sometimes leads them to call naively for color blindness in their movements. Wells-Barnett clearly recognized that for African Americans race was the primary prism through which their lives were viewed and experienced. In determining her life, nothing was more important than her color. Caring deeply about many issues, she often experienced a sense of divided duty but consistently placed race interests first—above political alignments, other causes, ideology, friendships, and sometimes even family.

Few Americans before or after have more consistently refused to compromise with the evil of racial prejudice. Born of rage, her uncompromising militancy limited Wells-Barnett's effectiveness as an organizational leader. Anger constantly got her into trouble but also fueled her continual crusades for justice. Every movement owes its success to a multitude of people and factors; gauging precisely the impact of one individual is impossible. Few people can single-handedly bring change. Some injustices, such as racism, cannot be easily cured but, nonetheless, should not be tolerated. Acquiescence to evil can be complicity by allowing the complacency of ignorance. Ida B. Wells-Barnett reminds the world that society needs its *disturbing elements* "to keep the waters troubled."

NOTES

Chapter 1

1. Alfreda M. Duster, ed., *Crusade for Justice, The Autobiography of Ida B. Wells* (Chicago: University of Chicago Press, 1970), pp. 7–10.

2. See Richard Wade, *Slavery in the Cities: The South, 1820–1860* (New York: Oxford University Press, 1964); Claudia Goldin, *Urban Slavery in the American South, 1820–1860: A Quantitative History* (Chicago: University of Chicago Press, 1976).

3. Duster, *Crusade*, pp. 7–10; A. J. Wells to Alfreda Duster, 9 July 1941, Ida B. Wells Papers, University of Chicago Library.

4. See Leon Litwack, *Been in the Storm So Long: The Aftermath of Slavery* (New York: Alfred A. Knopf, 1979); Herbert Gutman, *The Black Family in Slavery and Freedom, 1750–1925* (New York: Pantheon Books, 1976); Joel Williamson, *After Slavery: The Negro in the South during Reconstruction, 1861–1877* (Chapel Hill: University of North Carolina Press, 1965).

5. Hodding Carter, "A Proud Struggle for Grace, Holly Springs, Mississippi," in Thomas C. Wheeler, ed., *A Vanishing America, The Life and Times of the Small Town* (New York: Holt, Rinehart & Winston, 1964), pp. 56–60.

6. Robert Lowry and Thomas W. Henderson, *A History of Mississippi* (reprint, Spartanburg, SC: The Reprint Co., 1978; orig. pub. 1891), p. 536.

7. Carter, "Proud Struggle," pp. 60–63; William Baskerville Hamilton, "The History of Holly Springs, Mississippi" (M.A. thesis, University of Mississippi, 1931), p. 13.

8. Ruth Watkins, "Reconstruction in Marshall County," *Publications of the Mississippi Historical Society* 12 (1912), p. 208.

9. Edwin C. Bearss, *Decision in Mississippi* (Little Rock: Pioneer Press, 1962), pp. 581–582.

10. John K. Bettersworth, *Confederate Mississippi, The People and Policies of a Cotton State in Wartime* (Philadelphia: Porcupine Press, 1943), pp. 160–163.

11. Ibid.; Carter, "Proud Struggle," p. 64.

12. John Eaton, *Grant, Lincoln and the Freedmen* (New York: Longmans, Green & Co., 1907), p. 2.

13. Hamilton, "History of Holly Springs," pp. 250–263.

14. J. G. Deupree, "The Capture of Holly Springs," *Publications of the Mississippi Historical Society* 4 (1901), pp. 50–60.

15. *The Civil War Diary of Cyrus F. Boyd*, cited in John K. Bettersworth, ed., *Mississippi in the Confederacy, as they saw it* (Baton Rouge: Louisiana State University Press, 1961), pp. 207–208.

16. Duster, *Crusade*, p. 9.

17. M. E. Gill to Edward P. Smith, 30 April 1869, American Missionary Association (AMA) Papers, Amistad Research Center, New Orleans; Duster, *Crusade*, p. 9.

18. Watkins, "Reconstruction," pp. 159, 165, 184–185.

19. Ibid., pp. 189–193.

20. John Hope Franklin, ed., *Reminiscences of an Active Life, The Autobiography of John Roy Lynch* (Chicago: University of Chicago Press, 1970), p. 147.

21. Duster, *Crusade*, p. 9.

22. Watkins, "Reconstruction," pp. 178–179.

23. Ibid., pp. 186–189. Watkins was clearly in sympathy with the Democrats and recounted many negative comments about the Republicans; no incidents of Democratic speakers' being attacked by Republicans were reported.

24. Ibid., p. 172.

25. Duster, *Crusade*, p. 9.

26. Watkins, "Reconstruction," pp. 183, 171–172; Carter, "A Proud Struggle," pp. 68–69; Hamilton, "The History of Holly Springs," pp. 66–67.

27. Duster, *Crusade*, p. 9; Indianapolis *Freeman*, 27 April 1895.

28. Duster, *Crusade*, pp. 9–10, 17–18, 24.

29. "History of Rust College," pamphlet in the Rust College Library, Holly Springs, MS, pp. 4–6.

30. Ibid., p. 7.

31. Ophelia Smith to M. E. Strieby, 5 February 1877, AMA papers.

32. Diary of Ida B. Wells, 12 June 1886, Wells Papers. Information about Combs comes from Miriam DeCosta-Willis, *The Memphis Diary of Ida B. Wells* (Boston: Beacon Press, 1995), p. 77.

33. Diary, 29 December 1885. Although Wells claimed in her autobiography to have quit school as soon as her parents died in 1878, a sketch of her life written by T. Thomas Fortune in 1893 notes she attended Rust for several years between school terms when she was teaching. L. A. Scruggs, *Women of Distinction* (Raleigh, NC: L. A. Scruggs Publisher, 1893), p. 35.

34. Diary, 12 June 1886.

35. Khaled J. Bloom, *The Mississippi Valley's Great Yellow Fever Epidemic of 1878* (Baton Rouge: Louisiana State University Press, 1993), pp. 10, 26–27, 143.

36. Quotes are from the Minute Book, Board of Aldermen, cited in Olga Reed Pruitt, *It Happened Here, True Stories of Holly Springs* (Holly Springs: South Reporter Printing Co., 1950), p. 77; Hamilton, "The History of Holly Springs," p. 81; Carter, "A Proud Struggle," p. 72; Bloom, *Yellow Fever*, pp. 149–151.

37. Duster, *Crusade*, pp. 10–11. The dates of death for Jim and Elizabeth Wells and their son Stanley are from a photocopied, undated clipping of the *Holly Springs Occasional* in the Marshall County Historical Museum, Holly Springs, Mississippi.

38. Duster, *Crusade*, p. 15; "Interview with Alfreda Duster, Black Women Oral History Project, March 8 and 9, 1978," Schlesinger Library, Radcliff College, p. 8.

39. Carter, "Proud Struggle," p. 72; Duster, *Crusade*, p. 12.

40. Duster, *Crusade*, p. 16.

41. Ibid., pp. 12–13, 17.

42. Ibid., p. 17; letter from the U.S. Bureau of the Census to Alfreda Duster, 4 October 1967, Wells Papers.

43. Duster interview, p. 8; Duster, *Crusade*, pp. 17–18.

44. Scruggs, *Women of Distinction*, p. 35; Duster, *Crusade*, p. 18.

Chapter 2

1. Memphis *Daily Avalanche*, 10 May 1866; Robert E. Corlew, *Tennessee, A Short History* (Knoxville: University of Tennessee Press, 1981), p. 149; Armstead L. Robinson, "Plans Dat Comed from God: Institution Building and the Emergence of Black Leadership in Reconstruction Memphis," in Orville Vernon Burton and Robert C. McMath, Jr., eds., *Toward a New South? Studies in Post-Civil War Southern Communities* (Westport, CT: Greenwood Press, 1982), p. 79; John M. Keating, *History of the City of Memphis and Shelby County, Tennessee*, vol. I (Syracuse, NY: D. Mason & Co., 1888), p. 568; Elizabeth A. Merriweather, *Recollections of 92 Years, 1824–1916* (Nashville: Tennessee Historical Commission, 1958), p. 167.

2. Kathleen C. Berkeley, *"Like a Plague of Locusts": From an Antebellum Town to a New South City, Memphis, Tennessee, 1850–1880* (New York: Garland Publishing, 1991), pp. 120–121; Lester C. Lamon, *Blacks in Tennessee, 1791–1970* (Knoxville: University of Tennessee Press, 1981), pp. 29–34; Charles Williams, Jr., "Two Black Communities in Memphis, Tennessee: A Study in Urban Socio-Political Structure" (Ph.D. diss., University of Illinois at Urbana-Champaign, 1982), pp. 30–31; Michael Keith Honey, "Labor and Civil Rights in the South: The Industrial Labor Movement and Black Workers in Memphis, 1929–1945" (Ph.D. diss., Northern Illinois University, 1987), pp. 11–14.

3. U.S. War Department, *Riot at Memphis* (Washington, DC: Government Printing Office, 1866), p. 2.

4. Ibid; *Report of the Select Committee on the Memphis Riots and Massacres* (Washington, DC: Government Printing Office, 1866 [reprint by Johnson Reprint Corporation, New York, 1970]), pp. 1–44; Altina Waller, "Community, Class and Race in the Memphis Riot of 1866," *Journal of Social History* 18 (1984), pp. 233–246; James Gilbert Ryan, "Memphis Riot of 1866: Terror in a Black Community During Reconstruction," *Journal of Negro History* 62 (July 1977), pp. 243–257; Bobby L. Lovett, "Memphis Riots: White Reactions to Blacks in Memphis, May 1865–July 1866," *Tennessee Historical Quarterly* 38 (Spring 1979), pp. 9–33; Jack Holmes, "Underlying Causes of the Memphis Race Riot of 1866," *Tennessee Historical Quarterly* 17 (September 1958), pp. 195–225; Jack Holmes, "The Effects of the Memphis Race Riot of 1866," *West Tennessee Historical Society Papers* 12 (1958), pp. 58–79.

5. *Memphis Argus*, 24 August 1865, cited in Robinson, "Plans," p. 80.

6. Berkeley, *Like a Plague*, p. 122; Robinson, "Plans," p. 81.

7. Robinson, "Plans," pp. 85–88.

8. John McLeod Keating, A *History of the Yellow Fever: The Yellow Fever Epidemic of 1878 in Memphis, Tennessee* (Memphis: Howard Association, 1879), pp. 107, 659; John H. Ellis, "Disease and the Destiny of a City: The 1878 Yellow Fever Epidemic in Memphis," *West Tennessee Historical Society Papers* 28 (1974), pp. 81–82, 87; Rev. D. A. Quinn, *Heroes and Heroines of Memphis* (Providence, RI: E. L. Freeman & Son, 1887), p. 47; John Parham Dromgoole, *Yellow Fever: Heroes, Honors and Horrors* (Louisville: John P. Morton & Co., 1879), p. 64.

9. G. B. Thorton, *The Negro Mortality of Memphis* (Boston: Rockwell & Churchill, 1883), p. 3; William D. Miller, "Rural Ideals in Memphis at the Turn of the Century," *West Tennessee Historical Society Papers* 4 (1958), pp. 41–49, and "Rural Ideals and Urban Progress: Memphis, 1900–1917," *Mississippi Quarterly* 21 (1968), pp. 263–274.

10. Joel M. Roitman, "Race Relations in Memphis, Tennessee: 1880–1905" (M.A. thesis, Memphis State University, 1964), p. 66.

11. Gerald M. Capers, Jr., *The Biography of a River Town, Memphis: Its Heroic Age* (Chapel Hill: University of North Carolina Press, 1939), p. 195.

12. George C. Lee, *Beale Street, Where the Blues Began* (College Park, MD: McGrath Publishing Co., 1969), pp. 13–14; Fred L. Hutchins, "Beale Street As It Was," *West Tennessee Historical Society Papers* 26 (1972), pp. 56–59; Linton Weeks, *Memphis, A Folk History* (Little Rock: Parkhurst, 1982), pp. 109–114; Annette E. Church and Roberta Church, *The Robert R. Churches of Memphis* (Ann Arbor: Edward Bros., 1974), pp. 21–24.

13. Duster, *Crusade*, p. 22.

14. Ibid., p. 31.

15. I. Garland Penn, *The Afro-American Press and Its Editors* (Springfield, MA: Wiley, 1891), p. 409.

16. Ibid., p. 21.

17. Duster, *Crusade*, pp. 21–22.

18. Diary, 29 December 1885, 11 March, 28 November 1886, 11 April 1887, 29 July 1887, Ida B. Wells Papers, University of Chicago Library.

19. Duster, *Crusade*, p. 22; diary, 11 March 1886.

20. Diary, 29 December 1885, 29 July 1887.

21. Holograph copy of early version of Wells's autobiography, Wells Papers.

22. Ibid.; Joseph H. Cartwright, *The Triumph of Jim Crow, Tennessee Race Relations in the 1880s* (Knoxville: University of Tennessee Press, 1976), ch. 3 & 5.

23. Deborah White, *Ar'n't I a Woman?, Female Slaves in the Plantation South* (New York: W. W. Norton, 1985); Evelyn Brooks Higginbotham, "African American Women's History and the Metalanguage of Race," *Signs* 17 (1992), p. 261; Willie Mae Coleman, "Black Women and Segregated Public Transportation: Ninety Years of Resistance," in *Black Women in United States History: The Twentieth Century*, ed. Darlene Clark Hine, vol. 5 (New York: Carlson Publishing Co., 1990), pp. 295–302.

24. William S. McFeely, *Frederick Douglass* (New York: W. W. Norton, 1991), p. 366; Mary Church Terrell, *A Colored Woman in a White World* (Chicago: Ransdell Publishing, 1940), pp. 16–17, 288.

25. Anna Julia Cooper, *A Voice From the South* (1892; New York: Oxford University Press, 1988), pp. 90–91.

26. Duster, *Crusade*, p. 18; *Ida Wells v. Chesapeake, Ohio & Southwestern Railroad Company*, 31 March 1885, manuscript court record, Tennessee State Library and Archives.

27. Memphis *Daily Avalanche*, 28, 29 January 1880, 7 November 1880; Cartwright, *Triumph*, pp. 187–188; Memphis *Avalanche*, 13, 15–16 March 1881; Memphis *Daily Appeal*, 13, 16 March 1881.

28. Memphis *Daily Appeal*, 13 March 1881.

29. Cartwright, *Triumph*, pp. 102–105.

30. Ibid., pp. 184–187.

31. (Washington, D.C.) *People's Advocate*, 18 March 1882.

32. *New York Globe*, 24 May 1884.

33. Duster, *Crusade*, p. 19. Cassells certainly was less than bold in confronting segregation. When the "separate but equal" law had come to a vote in 1881, Cassells had abstained—unlike the other Shelby County representative, Isaac F. Norris, who is recorded as placing one of the two votes against it. Cartwright, *Triumph*, p. 104.

34. Ida B. Wells to Albion Tourgee, 22 February 1893, Albion Tourgee Papers, microfilm edition, University of North Carolina, Chapel Hill.

35. *Ida B. Wells v. Chesapeake, Ohio & Southwestern Railroad Company*, 4 November 1884, manuscript court record, Tennessee State Library and Archives.

36. Ibid.

37. Memphis *Daily Appeal*, 25 December 1884.

38. *New York Globe*, 24 May 1884.

39. Memphis *Daily Appeal*, 25 December 1884; *New York Freeman*, 10 January 1885.

40. Diary, 3, 28 June, 8 July 1886.

41. Duster, *Crusade*, p. 20.

42. Diary, 3 April 1886.

43. Diary, 9 May 1886; *Cleveland Gazette*, 11 December 1886.

44. Brief of Greer and Adams, "Chesapeake, Ohio & Southwestern Railroad Company v. Ida Wells, April 1885," Tennessee State Library and Archives.

45. "Chesapeake, Ohio & Southwestern Railroad Company v. Ida Wells, 5 April 1887," *Tennessee Reports*, 85 (1887), pp. 613–615; Duster, *Crusade*, p. 20.

46. Diary, 3 April 1886.

47. Diary, 11 April 1887.

48. Duster, *Crusade*, p. 21.

Chapter 3

1. Memphis *Daily Appeal*, 2 January 1885.

2. Memphis *Daily Avalanche*, 2 January 1885.

3. Annette E. Church and Roberta Church, *The Robert R. Churches of Memphis* (Ann Arbor: Edward Bros., 1974), p. 33.

4. (Washington, D.C.) *People's Advocate*, 5 January 1884. The case for Wells's authorship of the column is based on several factors. The column was quoted from the *Gate City Press* (Kansas City), which Wells is known to have written for often early in her career. It is also consistent with Wells's style of writing.

5. *Cleveland Gazette*, 14 November 1885.

6. Miriam DeCosta-Willis, ed., *The Memphis Diary of Ida B. Wells* (Boston: Beacon Press, 1995), p. 8.

7. Kathleen Berkeley, "The Politics of Black Education in Memphis, Tennessee, 1868–1881," in Rick Ginsberg and David N. Plank, eds. *Southern Cities, Southern Schools: Public Education in the Urban South* (Westport, CT: Greenwood Press, 1990), p. 215.

8. Alfreda M. Duster, ed., *Crusade for Justice, The Autobiography of Ida B. Wells* (Chicago: University of Chicago Press, 1970), p. 23.

9. Diary, 15 November 1886, 16 May 1887; *Cleveland Gazette*, 4 April 1885. After the group had ceased meeting, Wells led the effort to revive it in 1891. *Indianapolis Freeman*, 2 May 1891.

10. *Cleveland Gazette*, 4 April 1885; Duster, *Crusade*, p. 23.

11. *Cleveland Gazette*, 4 April 1885; diary, 2 May 1887.

12. Diary, 14 February 1886; 29 December 1885; 30 January, 6 May 1886; 1, 11 March 1886.

13. Diary, 24 April, 2, 5 May 1887.

14. Diary, 3 May 1887.

15. Diary, 18 January, 18 September 1887.

16. Diary, 20 February 1887.

17. Diary, 23 May 1886.

18. Diary, 19 May 1886.

19. *Cleveland Gazette*, 31 October, 17 January 1885; diary, 20 February 1887.

20. Diary, 11, 29 April, 6 May 1886.

21. Diary, 29 December 1885.

22. Diary, 12 June 1886.

23. Ibid. DeCosta-Willis identifies Combs in *Memphis Diary*, p. 77.

24. Diary, 13 July, 30 May 1887; DeCosta-Willis, *Memphis Diary*, p. 146; Paul R. Coppock, *Memphis Sketches* (Memphis: Friends of Memphis and Shelby County Libraries, 1976), pp. 68–70.

25. Detroit *Plaindealer*, 15 August 1890; *Nashville Banner*, 27 May 1885; diary, 17 August 1887.

26. Diary, August 12, 17 1887; 8, 13, 20 July 1886.

27. See Ira Berlin, *Slaves Without Masters: The Free Negro in the Antebellum South* (New York: Pantheon Books, 1974); Willard B. Gatewood, *Aristocrats of Color: The Black Elite 1880–1920* (Bloomington: Indiana University Press, 1990); John W. Blassingame, *Black New Orleans, 1860–1880* (Chicago: University of Chicago Press, 1973).

28. Diary, 23 February, 28 November 1886.

29. Diary, 5, 13 January, 1, 15 March 1886; 1 March, 28 September 1887.

30. Cited in Roberta Church and Ronald Walter, *Nineteenth Century Memphis Families of Color, 1850–1900* (Memphis: Murdock, 1987), pp. 127–128.

31. Diary, 29 December 1885, 5 January 1886, 28 March, 12 August 1887. See also 7, 15 November, 11, 14, 25 April 1886.

32. Diary, 11 March, 23 May, 29 April 1886.

33. Diary, 9 May, 28 June, 4 July 1886.

34. Diary, 13, 8 July, 12 September, 2 October 1886.

35. Diary, 13 July 1886.

36. Diary, 13, 20 July 1886.

37. Diary, 20, 29 July 1886.

38. Diary, 29 July 1886.

39. Ibid.

40. Diary 13, 29 July 1886.

41. Diary, 2 August 1886.

42. Miriam DeCosta-Willis, ed., *The Memphis Diary of Ida B. Wells* (Boston: Beacon Press, 1995), p. 94; Duster, *Crusade*, pp. 24–25.

43. Diary, 2 August 1886.

44. Diary, 4 August 1886.

45. Diary, 9 August 1886.

46. Diary, 18, 22, 26 August 1886.

47. Diary, 12 September 1886.

48. Diary, 14 September 1886.

49. Duster, *Crusade*, pp. 25–27.

50. Ibid.; Diary, 2 October 1886.

Chapter 4

1. Diary, 2, 12 October 1886.

2. Duster, *Crusade*, p. 44.

3. *Cleveland Gazette*, 13 December 1884, 28 February 1885; DeCosta-Willis, *Memphis Diary*, p. 28.

4. Diary, 29 December 1884, 23 March, 3 April, 9 May, 4, 26 August, 9, 12 September, 21 December 1886, 14 February 1887; *New York Freeman*, 7 February 1885.

5. DeCosta-Willis, *Memphis Diary*, p. 37; diary, 21, 30 January 1886; *Cleveland Gazette*, 17 January 1885; diary 25, 29 April 1886.

6. *Cleveland Gazette*, 4 July 1885; Green Polonius Hamilton, *Beacon Lights of the Race* (Memphis: F. H. Clark, 1911), pp. 474–485; DeCosta-Willis, *Memphis Diary*, p. 54.

7. Diary, 28 June 1886.

8. See Anne Firor Scott, *The Southern Lady: From Pedestal to Politics, 1830–1930* (Chicago: University of Chicago Press, 1970); Linda K. Kerber, "Separate Spheres, Female Worlds, Woman's Place: The Rhetoric of Women's History," *Journal of American History* 75 (June 1988), pp. 19–39; Barbara Welter, "The Cult of True Womanhood, 1820-1860," *American Quarterly* 18 (Summer 1966), pp. 151–174; Mary P. Ryan, *Womanhood in America: From Colonial Times to the Present* (New York: New Viewpoints, 1975); Mabel Donnelly, *The American Victorian Woman: The Myth and the Reality* (New York: Greenwood Press, 1986).

9. See Deborah Gray White, *Ar'n't I a Woman?: Female Slaves in the Plantation South* (New York: W. W. Norton, 1985); Herbert G. Gutman, *The Black Family in Slavery and Freedom, 1750–1925* (New York: Pantheon, 1976).

10. See James Oliver Horton, "Freedom's Yoke: Gender Conventions Among Antebellum Free Blacks," *Feminist Studies* 12 (1986), pp. 51–76; Shirley J. Carlson, "Black Ideals of Womanhood in the Late Victorian Era," *Journal of Negro History* 77 (Spring 1992), pp. 61–71; Sharon Harley, "For the Good of Family and Race: Gender,

Work and Domestic Roles in the Black Community, 1880–1930," *Signs* 15 (Winter 1990), pp. 336–349; Linda M. Perkins, "The Impact of the 'Cult of True Womanhood' on the Education of Black Women," *Journal of Social Issues* 39 (1983), pp. 17–28.

11. Detroit *Plaindealer*, 15 January 1892; *Washington Grit*, 16 August 1884; Indianapolis *Freeman*, 2 December 1893.

12. *New York Freeman*, 18 February 1888.

13. Diary, 15 June 1886.

14. *Washington Bee*, 5 December 1885; Monroe A. Majors, *Noted Negro Women: Their Triumphs and Activities* (Chicago: Donohue & Henneberry, 1893), p.191; (Kansas City) *American Citizen*, 18 January 1895; diary, 28 June 1886.

15. Diary, 15 June 1886.

16. Diary, 30 January 1886.

17. Diary, 14 February 1886; G. P. Hamilton, *The Bright Side of Memphis* (Memphis: n.p., 1908), p. 263.

18. Diary, 6 May, 3 June 1886. See also 14 February 1886 for an account of another incident between them.

19. Diary, 12, 28 June, 2 August 1886.

20. Diary, 2 , 12, 20 October. Whether he married to help clear the air of rumors, or for spite, or merely on the rebound, Graham divorced after six years but remarried later. *New York Age*, 19 November 1892.

21. Diary, 29 July, 4 August, 1, 4 September 1886. Information about Hackley from Louis Harlan, ed., *The Booker T. Washington Papers*, vol. 5 (Urbana: University of Illinois Press, 1976), p. 427 and Detroit *Plaindealer*, 1 May 1891.

22. Diary, 12 September 1886.

23. *Cleveland Gazette*, 25 December 1886.

24. Diary, 24 August, 1 March 1887.

25. Diary, 21 January 1886.

26. Diary, 28 January 1886.

27. Diary, 8 February 1886.

28. *Washington Bee*, 3 January 1885.

29. Diary, 8, 14 February, 1 March 1886.

30. Diary, 4 July, 11, 28 March, 11, 20 April, 15, 28 June 1886.

31. See Nancy F. Cott, "'Passionlessness': An Interpretation of Victorian Sexual Ideology, 1790-1850," in Nancy F. Cott and Elizabeth Pleck, eds. *A Heritage of Their Own: Toward a New Social History of American Women* (New York: Simon & Schuster, 1979); Carl Vance, ed., *Pleasure and Danger: Exploring Female Sexuality* (New York: Routledge, Kegan & Paul, 1984); John D'Emilio and Estelle B. Freedman, *Intimate Matters: A History of Sexuality in America* (New York: Harper and Row, 1988).

32. I. J. Graham was vice president of the Tennessee Colored Teacher Association in 1896 when that organization petitioned the state legislature regarding unfair appropriations for black and white normal schools. Charles S. Morris went on to graduate from the University of Michigan law school and, after attending Newton Theological Seminary, became an influential and politically active Baptist minister and missionary. Edwin Hackley ran for the Colorado legislature, edited a newspaper, and in 1892 founded a rights organization called the Constitutional Union, which Wells praised in the Memphis *Free Speech* for forcing a county treasurer to keep an African American

clerk. James H. Robinson, "A Social History of the Negro in Memphis and in Shelby County," (Ph.D. diss., Yale University, 1934), pp. 172–173; Harlan, *Washington Papers*, pp. 102, 426; *Topeka Times-Observer*, 20 February 1892.

33. Diary, 2 August, 4 September 1886.

34. Diary, 12 September, 2 October, 28 November 1886. Even as a more mature woman, Wells continued to harbor the romantic illusion of the power of a woman's love to redeem a man as is evidenced in a short story she wrote in 1894. Ida B. Wells, "Two Christmas Days: A Holiday Story," *A.M.E. Zion Church Quarterly* (January 1894), pp. 129–140, reprinted in Mildred I. Thompson, *Ida B. Wells-Barnett, An Exploratory Study of an American Black Woman, 1893–1930* (New York: Carlson Publishing, 1990), pp. 225–234.

35. *Washington Bee*, 9 & 16 May, 6 June 1885.

36. Diary, 28 January, 8 February 1886.

37. *Cleveland Gazette*, 27 September 1884, 28 March 1885; Green Polonius Hamilton, *Booker T. Washington High School: Retrospective, from 1889 to 1927* (Memphis: 1927), unpaginated pamphlet held by the Memphis and Shelby County Public Library.

38. Diary, 23 February 1886.

39. Diary, 21 January, 11 March 1886; Wells, "Two Christmas Days."

40. Diary, 30 January, 18 March 1886.

41. Diary, 18 August 1886.

42. Diary, 12 June 1886.

43. Diary, 21 January 1886.

44. Diary, 13 July 1887.

45. Mary Church Terrell, *A Colored Woman in a White World* (Chicago: Ransdell Publishing, 1940), p. 59.

46. Diary, 1, 14 February 1887.

47. *Cleveland Gazette*, 26 March 1887.

48. Diary, 30 January 1886.

49. Diary, 13 January 1886.

50. Diary, 4 December 1886.

51. Diary, 13 July 1887.

52. Diary, 21 December, 6 May, 1 March, 12 June, 7 September 1886.

53. Diary, 23 February, 20 October, 28 December 1886.

54. Diary, 18 January 1887.

55. Ibid.

56. Diary, 5 May, 17 June, 4 April, 18 September 1887.

57. Diary, 20 March 1887. For information on Stella Butler see DeCosta-Willis, *Memphis Diary*, pp. 118–119.

58. Diary, 14 March, 17 June 1887.

59. Diary, 5 January, 18, 30 March 1886.

60. Diary, 11 April 1886.

61. Diary, 20 March, 6 September 1887.

62. Diary, 29 December 1885, 18 January, 14 February, 1 March 1887.

63. Diary, 28 January 1886.

64. Diary, 11 March 1886.

65. Diary, 30 January 1886. In her 4 July 1886 entry Wells notes, "I took my writ-

ing desk to town to have it filed open & when I returned found my keys where I had hidden them over a week before."

66. Wells's religious affiliation has been the source of much speculation. DeCosta-Willis transcribes Wells's 24 April 1887 allusion to her minister as "Mr. N" and postulates that Wells might have been referring to Taylor Nightingale, which would have made Wells a member of Beale Street Baptist Church. However, Wells notes a letter to the editor by a "Mr. W," who is obviously her pastor as well as a suitor, in her 9 September 1887 diary entry. In the context of that letter, which will be discussed in the next chapter, it seems most likely she was referring to D. R. Wilkins. With this assumption, the letter in the April entry looks more like a W than an N.

67. Sources for the history and theology of the Christian Church include Winfred Ernest Garrison, *An American Religious Movement: A Brief History of the Disciples of Christ* (St. Louis: Christian Board of Publication, 1945); Ronald E. Osborn, *Experiment in Liberty: The Ideal of Freedom in the Experience of the Disciples of Christ* (St. Louis: Bethany Press, 1978); Kenneth Lawrence, ed., *Classic Themes of Disciples Theology* (Fort Worth: Texas Christian University Press, 1986); and Samuel F. Pugh, ed., *Primer for New Disciples* (St. Louis: Bethany Press, 1963).

68. Tucker, *Black Pastors*, p. 7; William Russell Greenfield, "A History of the A.M.E. Church in Tennessee" (B.S. thesis, Tennessee A & I State College, 1942), p. 16.

69. Diary, 3, 18 January 1887.

70. Annette E. Church and Roberta Church, *The Robert R. Churches of Memphis* (Ann Arbor: Edward Bros., 1974), p. 30; Willard B. Gatewood, *Aristocrats of Color: The Black Elite, 1880–1920* (Bloomington: Indiana University Press, 1990), p. 89; Green Polonius Hamilton, *Beacon Lights of the Race* (Memphis: F. H. Clark, 1911), p. 484; diary, 11, 20, 25 April 1886; *Cleveland Gazette*, 24 July 1886; Tucker, *Black Pastors*, pp. 14–15.

71. Quoted in Tucker, *Black Pastors*, p. 18.

72. Quoted in Gatewood, *Aristocrats*, p. 152.

73. Green Polonius Hamilton, *The Bright Side of Memphis* (Memphis: G. P. Hamilton, 1908), pp. 155, 162; *Christian Index*, 9 November 1889.

74. Diary, 28 March, 11 April, 16 July 1887.

75. Diary, 1 March 1886, 11 April 1887.

76. For further discussion of the impact of her faith on Wells see Darryl M. Trimiew, *Voices of the Silenced, The Responsible Self in a Marginalized Community* (Cleveland: Pilgrim Press, 1994), pp. 37–48.

77. David M. Tucker, *Black Pastors and Leaders: Memphis, 1819–1972* (Memphis: Memphis State University Press, 1975), p. 14; *Cleveland Gazette*, 4 April 1885; diary, 11 April, 24 August 1887.

78. Diary, 28 November 1886.

79. Diary, 8 February 1886.

80. Ibid.

81. Wells was not alone in condemning Moody for his segregated southern services. Black newspapers often bemoaned his practices. See St. Paul *Western Appeal*, 13 June 1885, 6 August 1887. See also James F. Findlay, Jr., *Dwight L. Moody: American Evangelist, 1837–1899* (Chicago: University of Chicago Press, 1969), pp. 278–281.

82. Diary, 16 July 1887.

Chapter 5

1. Diary, 20 March 1887, Ida B. Wells Papers, University of Chicago Library; Alfreda M. Duster, ed., *Crusade for Justice, The Autobiography of Ida B. Wells* (Chicago: University of Chicago Press, 1970), p. 31.

2. Diary, 29 December 1885, 30 January, 8 February, 3 June 1886.

3. Diary, 30 May 1887.

4. Diary, 15 June 1886.

5. Ralph Edward Samples, "The Development of Public Education in Tennessee During the Bourbon Era, 1870–1900" (Ed.D. diss., University of Tennessee, 1965), p. 230.

6. Kathleen Berkeley, "The Politics of Black Education in Memphis, Tennessee, 1868–1881," in Rick Ginsberg and David N. Plank, eds. *Southern Cities, Southern Schools: Public Education in the Urban South* (Westport, CT: Greenwood Press, 1990), p. 212; Kathleen C. Berkeley, *"Like a Plague of Locusts": From an Antebellum Town to a New South City, Memphis, Tennessee, 1850–1880* (New York: Garland Publishing, 1991), p. 178.

7. Joel M. Roitman, "Race Relations in Memphis, Tennessee: 1880–1905" (M.A. thesis, Memphis State University, 1964), p. 78.

8. Ibid., pp. 76–77; Berkeley, "Politics," pp. 203, 211–212; Memphis *Daily Appeal*, 13 July 1886.

9. Diary, 2, 20 October 1886.

10. Berkeley, "Politics," p. 212; diary, 2 October 1886.

11. Diary, 20 July, 31 October, 7, 28 November, 4, 21 December 1886. According to a Memphis librarian, Wells also took some course work at LeMoyne. Elaine Mardus to Alfreda Duster, 19 March 1964, Wells Papers.

12. The importance given to education as a means of racial uplift is demonstrated in the fact that African American teachers in Shelby County organized one of the first teachers' institutes in the state of Tennessee before their white counterparts. Robert E. Corlew, "The Negro in Tennessee, 1870–1900" (Ph.D diss., University of Alabama, 1954), p. 335.

13. Diary, 17 June 1887.

14. Duster, *Crusade*, p. 31; diary, 7 November 1887.

15. James H. Robinson, "A Social History of the Negro in Memphis and Shelby County" (Ph.D. diss., Yale University, 1934), pp. 166–168.

16. Quoted in Berkeley, *Like a Plague*, p. 166.

17. David Moss Hillard, "The Development of Public Education in Memphis, Tennessee, 1848–1945" (Ph. D. diss., University of Chicago, 1946), p. 148.

18. Berkeley, *Like a Plague*, pp. 180–184; Hilliard, "Development," pp. 143–144.

19. David M. Tucker, "Black Politics in Memphis, 1865-1875," *West Tennessee Historical Society Papers* 26 (1972), pp. 13–19; Walter P. Adkins, "Beale Street Goes to the Polls" (M.A. thesis, Ohio State University, 1935), pp. 11–12.

20. Lynette B. Wrenn, "School Board Reorganization in Memphis, 1883," *Tennessee Historical Quarterly* 45 (Winter 1986), p. 337.

21. For information on politics in Tennessee and Memphis see Joseph H. Cartwright, *The Triumph of Jim Crow: Tennessee Race Relations in the 1880s* (Knoxville: University of Tennessee Press, 1976); Roger L. Hart, *Redeemers, Bourbons & Populists,*

Tennessee, 1870–1896 (Baton Rouge: Louisiana State University Press, 1975); William D. Miller, *Memphis During the Progressive Era* (Memphis: Memphis State University Press, 1957); Mingo Scott, *The Negro in Tennessee Politics and Governmental Affairs, 1865–1965* (Nashville: Rich, 1964); Joseph Alexander Walker, "The Negro in Tennessee Politics, 1865–1880" (M.A. thesis, Fisk University, 1941).

22. *Cleveland Gazette,* 3 January 1885.

23. Berkeley, "Politics," pp. 215–216; for information on Broughton see Cleveland *Gazette,* 9 January, 25 December 1886; for information on Hamilton, see Roberta Church and Ronald Walter, *Nineteenth Century Memphis Families of Color, 1850–1900* (Memphis: Murdock, 1987), pp. 38–39. Hamilton later published *The Bright Side of Memphis* and *Beacon Lights of the Race.*

24. Diary, 28 June, 21 December 1886; *Cleveland Gazette,* 25 December 1886. Wells used many abbreviations in her diary. DeCosta-Willis identifies "Mrs. B." as Fannie J. Bradshaw, but I believe "Mrs. B." refers to Broughton and "F. J. B." is used when Wells refers to Bradshaw.

25. Diary, 31 October, 28 November 1886. There is some confusion over the circumstances of both Wells's selection as editor of the *Evening Star* and her relationship with the Memphis *Living Way* as a result of Wells's account in her autobiography. She says she was elected to replace "a brilliant man" (Louis M. Brown) who had returned to Washington, but, as he left Memphis in September to go to Kansas City before rejoining the *Washington Bee,* the timing does not appear correct. Wells also says that R. N. Countee asked her to start writing for the *Living Way* after hearing her read the *Evening Star.* This also seems an error because she did not become the editor until after articles she had written in the *Living Way* had been reprinted in other papers numerous times (see, for example, the *New York Freeman,* 4 July and 12 September 1885). Perhaps after Brown left the *Living Way* in January 1885, Wells's role expanded on that paper and that is why she confused the events more than forty years later. Duster, *Crusade,* p. 23; diary, 9 September 1885; *Washington Bee,* 3 January 1885.

26. Diary, 13 January 1886.

27. Diary, 9 September 1887.

28. Diary, 14, 20 March 1887.

29. Diary, 24 April 1887.

30. Diary, 29 July 1887.

31. *Memphis Appeal,* 11 September 1887.

32. *Memphis Avalanche,* 4 September 1887.

33. *Memphis Avalanche,* 25 September 1887.

34. Berkeley, "Politics," pp. 219–220; Wrenn, "School Board," p. 337.

35. Diary, 14 September 1887.

36. I. Garland Penn, *The Afro-American Press and Its Editors* (Springfield, MA: Wiley & Co., 1891); information on the black press in Memphis comes from J. F. Young, *Standard History of Memphis, Tennessee* (Knoxville: H. W. Crew & Co., 1912), p. 460; Vandella Brown, "One-hundred Years of Memphis Black Newspapers, 1880–1980," typescript dated 1981 in the Memphis Public Library; Karen Fitzgerald Brown, "The Black Press of Tennessee 1865–1980," (Ph.D. diss., University of Tennessee, Knoxville, 1982); and Samuel Shannon, "Tennessee," in Henry Lewis Suggs, ed., *The Black Press in the South, 1865–1979* (Westport, CN: Greenwood Press, 1983). For more information on the financial aspects of black journalism see Emma Lou

Thornbrough, "American Negro Newspapers, 1880–1914," *Business History Review* 40 (1966), pp. 467–490.

37. Mrs. N. F. Mossell, *The Work of the Afro-American Woman*, 2d. ed. (Philadelphia: Geo. S. Ferguson, 1908), pp. 98–99, 101. (The first edition appeared in 1894.)

38. *Atchison Blade*, 10 September 1892.

39. Mossell, *Work*, p. 100; Indianapolis *Freeman*, 23 February 1889.

40. *New York Age*, 4 February 1888. For a discussion of the aid male editors provided women journalists see Roger Streitmatter, "African-American Women Journalists and Their Male Editors: A Tradition of Support," *Journalism Quarterly* 70 (Summer 1993), pp. 276–286.

41. *New York Freeman*, 8 May 1886.

42. Information on these women in Penn's book was supplemented by consulting Monroe A. Majors, *Noted Negro Women, Their Triumphs and Activities* (Chicago: Donohue & Henneberry, 1893). For more information see Gloria Wade-Gayles, "Black Women Journalists in the South, 1880–1905," in Darlene Clark Hine, ed., *Black Women in the United States*, vol. 4 (New York: Carlson Publishing Co., 1990), pp. 1409–1423; J. William Snorgrass, "Pioneer Black Women Journalists from the 1850s to the 1950s," *Western Journal of Black Studies* 6 (Fall 1982), pp. 150–158; Alice E. Cunningham, "Early History of Negro Women in Journalism," *Negro History Bulletin* 28 (Summer 1965), pp. 175–179, 193, 197. Brief biographical sketches of eleven leading journalists can be found in Roger Streitmatter, *Raising Her Voice, African-American Women Journalists Who Changed History* (Lexington: University of Kentucky Press, 1994).

43. Emma Lou Thornbrough, *T. Thomas Fortune, Militant Journalist* (Chicago: University of Chicago Press, 1972); Donald E. Drake, "Militancy in Fortune's *New York Age*," *Journal of Negro History* 55 (October 1970), pp. 307–322.

44. *New York Globe*, 24 May 1884; the first two letters from Fortune appeared in the *Memphis Weekly Appeal* on 20 September and 15 November 1882.

45. *New York Freeman*, 10 January, 7 February 1885.

46. Ibid., 7 February 1885.

47. *Cleveland Gazette*, 28 March 1885; *Washington Grit*, 17 May 1884.

48. *Washington Bee*, 9 May 1885; *New York Freeman*, 9 May 1885.

49. *New York Freeman*, 12 December 1885; *Washington Bee*, 5 December 1885.

50. Diary, 28 January 1886.

51. See Chapter 5 for a discussion of this article and others by Wells regarding the role of women.

52. Diary, 29 December 1885, 5 January 1886.

53. *Washington Bee*, 23 January 1886.

54. Ibid.

55. *New York Freeman*, 7 November 1885.

56. Diary, 28 January 1886.

57. David M. Tucker, *Black Pastors and Leaders: Memphis, 1819–1972* (Memphis: Memphis State University Press, 1975), pp. 25–40.

58. Ibid.; Green Polonius Hamilton, *The Bright Side of Memphis* (Memphis: G. P. Hamilton, 1908), pp. 82–83.

59. Memphis *Daily Appeal*, 5, 7 August 1885; Memphis *Daily Avalanche*, 24 January 1886.

60. *New York Freeman*, 12 September 1885.

61. *Cleveland Gazette*, 31 October, 14 November 1885.

62. *Washington Bee*, 5 December 1885.

63. Diary, 1, 11 March 1886.

64. Diary, 1 March 1886.

65. Diary, 11, 18 March 1886.

66. Diary, 15 June, 2, 12 October, 21 December 1886; 3 January, 1 February, 24 April 1887; Duster, *Crusade*, pp. 31–32; Penelope L Bullock, *The Afro-American Periodical Press, 1838–1909* (Baton Rouge: Louisiana State University Press, 1981), pp. 167–168.

67. Duster, *Crusade*, p. 32; Diary, 18 August, 28 November 1886.

68. Diary, 15 June, 4 August 1886; 14 March 1887.

69. Diary, 26 August 1886.

70. Diary, 4 December, 1 September 1886.

71. Diary, 18 February 1887; St. Paul *Western Appeal*, 9 July 1887.

72. Diary, 8 February 1886.

73. *New York Freeman*, 20 August 1887; *Cleveland Gazette*, 27 August 1887; *New Orleans Weekly Pelican*, 13 August 1887.

74. Diary, 12 August 1887.

75. *New Orleans Weekly Pelican*, 13 August 1887.

76. Duster, *Crusade*, p. 32; *Washington Bee*, 20 August 1887.

77. Penn, *Afro-American Press*, p. 380; Indianapolis *Freeman*, 23 February 1889.

78. Penn, *Afro-American Press*, p. 373.

79. *New York Age*, 4 February 1888.

Chapter 6

1. Philip A. Bruce, *The Plantation Negro as Freeman* (New York: G. P. Putnam's Sons, 1889), pp. 12, 20, 268. See also Beverly Guy-Sheftall, *Daughters of Sorrow: Attitudes Toward Black Women, 1880–1920* (New York: Carlson Publishing, 1990) and Patricia Morton, *Disfigured Images: The Historical Assault on African-American Women* (New York: Praeger, 1991).

2. *New York Freeman*, 1 January 1887.

3. *New York Freeman*, 26 December 1885.

4. *New York Freeman*, 18 February 1888.

5. *New York Freeman*, 26 December 1885.

6. Ibid.

7. *Living Way*, 12 September 1885, reprinted in the *New York Freeman*. See chapter 5 for a further discussion of this article.

8. Article in the *Living Way* reprinted in the *New York Freeman*, 12 September 1885; article from the *Free Speech* reprinted in the (Kansas City) *American Citizen*, 11 September 1891.

9. Reprinted in the Detroit *Plaindealer* on 4 July 1890 and in the Indianapolis *Freeman* on 19 July 1890. Although this article was unsigned, it is consistent with the 12 September 1885 column quoted above and signed by Wells. If she did not write it, she at least approved of its publication as editor of the paper.

10. Reprinted in the *New York Freeman*, 15 January 1887.

11. Reprinted in DeCosta-Willis, *Memphis Diary*, pp. 182–184.

12. *New York Freeman*, 8 August 1885.

13. *New York Freeman*, 7 November 1885.

14. Ibid.

15. *Washington Bee*, 5 December 1885.

16. Diary, 28 December 1886; *New York Freeman*, 15 January 1887.

17. *New York Age*, 19 October 1889.

18. *New York Freeman*, 15 January 1887.

19. Diary, 18 March 1886.

20. Diary, 4 September 1886. Accounts of that lynching are found in the *Cleveland Gazette*, 11 September, 16 October 1886.

21. *Washington Bee*, 9 March 1889; *Cleveland Gazette*, 16 March 1889, 21 March 1891; *New York Age*, 28 March 1891.

22. Emma Lou Thornbrough, *T. Thomas Fortune, Militant Journalist* (Chicago: University of Chicago Press, 1972), p. 40; *Trenton Sentinel*, 8 July 1882; *Washington Bee*, 13 March 1897; Indianapolis *Freeman*, 30 July 1889.

23. *Washington Bee*, 4, 18 August 1888.

24. Diary, 11 March 1886; *New York Age*, 11 August 1888; Thornbrough, *Fortune*, pp. 93–94.

25. L. A. Scruggs, *Women of Distinction* (Raleigh, NC: L. A. Scruggs Publisher, 1893), p. 39.

26. Diary, 17, 24 August 1887; Detroit *Plaindealer*, 8 August 1890; I. Garland Penn, *The Afro-American Press and Its Editors* (Springfield, MA: Wiley & Co., 1891), pp. 415–420.

27. Indianapolis *Freeman*, 5 January 1889.

28. *New York Age*, 16 February 1889.

29. *Washington Bee*, 27 March 1886; J. F. Young, *Standard History of Memphis, Tennessee* (Knoxville: H. W. Crew & Co., 1912), p. 460.

30. *Cleveland Gazette*, 4 August 1888; *New Orleans Weekly Pelican*, 19 January 1889.

31. Diary, 17 August 1887; Alfreda M. Duster, ed., *Crusade for Justice, The Autobiography of Ida B. Wells* (Chicago: University of Chicago Press, 1970), p. 35. Wells became part-owner of at least three newspapers during her journalistic career in spite of her persistent financial woes. One reason she was able to buy into these papers was because "even an apparently well-established paper had little monetary value." Emma Lou Thornbrough, "American Negro Newspapers, 1880–1914," *Business History Review* 40 (1966), p. 474.

32. *Cleveland Gazette*, 6 July 1889; Indianapolis *Freeman*, 30 July 1889; *New York Age*, 29 June 1889.

33. As quoted in *New York Age*, 24 August 1889.

34. *Cleveland Gazette*, 24 August 1889; Indianapolis *Freeman*, 24 August 1889.

35. *Washington Bee*, 27 July 1889, 4 October 1890, 18 July, 1 August 1891; 20 February, 21 May 1892.

36. Indianapolis *Freeman*, 19 April 1890; *Cleveland Gazette*, 3 May 1890.

37. Indianapolis *Freeman*, 10 May 1890.

38. Ibid., 7 September 1889, 16 August 1890; Detroit *Plaindealer*, 8 August 1890; Duster, *Crusade*, p. 39.

39. *New York Age,* 22 November 1890.

40. Duster, *Crusade,* pp. 38–39; *New York Age,* 27 June 1891.

41. Duster, *Crusade,* p. 39; Indianapolis *Freeman,* 7 November 1891, 26 March 1892. In one of her letters Wells once again offended the *Freeman* by comments about one of its agents in the area. The 22 August 1891 *Freeman* contained the paper's response: "Some people who would like to shine as journalistic stars would succeed far better if they gave more attention to their own affairs, and kept their nose and fingers out of other people's business."

42. That she was referring to newer teachers was evident in her first handwritten draft of her autobiography, which referred to them as "recruits" and is found in the Wells Papers.

43. Duster, *Crusade,* p. 36.

44. Duster, *Crusade,* pp. 35–37; Indianapolis *Freeman,* 28 February 1891. It is interesting how her termination was reported in the black press. A friendly journal, the *Huntsville Gazette,* reported on 26 September 1891 that she "will resign." The less friendly *Cleveland Gazette* noted on 5 September that she had "been dropped from the list of teachers" without giving any explanation.

45. Duster, *Crusade,* p. 41.

46. (Kansas City) *American Citizen,* 8 May 1891.

47. *New York Freeman,* 27 August, 3 September, 29 October 1887; *Cleveland Gazette,* 17 September 1887, 3 March 1888; *Washington Bee,* 16 August 1890.

48. *Topeka Times-Observer,* 21 November 1891; Detroit *Plaindealer,* 5 February 1892; Indianapolis *Freeman,* 16 January 1892; *Cleveland Gazette,* 6 February 1892.

49. *American Citizen,* 29 January 1892.

50. *New York Freeman,* 28 May 1887.

51. Reprinted in the *New York Freeman,* 9 July 1887.

52. *New York Freeman,* 13 August 1887; *New York Age,* 25 January 1890.

53. *New York Age,* 9 November 1889.

54. Detroit *Plaindealer,* 18 October 1889.

55. *New York Age,* 23 November, 7, 14, 21 December 1889; *American Citizen,* 29 November 1889; Indianapolis *Freeman,* 11 January 1890; *American Citizen,* 17 January 1890; *Washington Bee,* 18 January 1890. See also *New York Freeman,* 17 September 1887; Emma Lou Thornbrough, "The National Afro-American League, 1887–1908," *Journal of Southern History* 27 (February 1961), pp. 494–512.

56. *New York Age,* 23 November 1889, 30 May 1891.

57. *New York Age,* 25 July 1891; *American Citizen,* 7 August 1891; Charles W. Cansler, *Three Generations, The Story of a Colored Family of Eastern Tennessee* (privately printed, 1939), p. 160; *Knoxville Daily Journal* quoted in *New York Age,* 25 July 1891; Detroit *Plaindealer,* 24 July 1891.

58. *New York Age,* 25 July 1891.

59. Detroit *Plaindealer,* 24 July 1891;

60. *Cleveland Gazette,* 1 August 1891.

61. For comments on the editorial see the St. Paul *Appeal,* 8 August 1891 and the *Cleveland Gazette,* 1 August 1891.

62. *New York Age,* 24 October 1991.

63. Duster, *Crusade,* pp. 41–42.

64. See Richard B. Sherman, *The Republican Party and Black America: From McKinley to Hoover, 1896–1933* (Charlottesville: University Press of Virginia, 1973).

65. *New York Age*, 19 November 1892.

66. Indianapolis *Freeman*, 7 June 1890.

67. Detroit *Plaindealer*, 9 May 1890.

68. *American Citizen*, 24 January 1890.

69. *Cleveland Gazette*, 19 July 1890; Indianapolis *Freeman*, 10 May 1890.

70. Ida B. Wells to Booker T. Washington, 30 November 1890, Booker T. Washington Papers, Library of Congress.

71. Duster, *Crusade*, pp. 40–41.

72. *American Citizen*, 11 September 1891; Detroit *Plaindealer*, 4 July 1890.

73. *American Citizen*, 28 August 1891; Indianapolis *Freeman*, 26 September 1891.

74. *Washington Bee*, 13 April 1889; *Cleveland Gazette*, 17 October 1891; Indianapolis *Freeman*, holiday edition, December 1891, 17 May 1890.

75. *New York Age*, 8 August, 12 September 1891. Bruce later became the most vitriolic critic of Wells.

76. Ibid., 13 December 1890; Indianapolis *Freeman*, 21 June 1890, 7 November 1891; *Cleveland Gazette*, 28 March 1892.

77. *Cleveland Gazette*, 21 February 1891; Memphis *Weekly Avalanche*, 13 June 1889.

78. Memphis *Weekly Avalanche*, 6 September 1891. An account of the lynching is found in the *New York Times*, 30 August 1891, and the request by a Jackson, Mississippi, paper that "the people of Memphis should proceed to muzzle the *Free Speech*" is quoted in *New York Age*, 19 September 1891.

79. Memphis *Appeal-Avalanche*, 8 September 1891.

80. Ibid., 10 September 1891. See also David M. Tucker, *Black Pastors and Leaders: Memphis 1819–1972* (Memphis State University Press, 1975), pp. 45–46; Robert E. Corlew, "The Negro in Tennessee, 1870–1900," (Ph.D. diss., University of Alabama, 1954), pp. 381–383.

81. *New York Age*, 6 February 1892.

Chapter 7

1. *Memphis Watchman*, 9 February 1889. Many neighborhoods at that time had both black and white residents. An old-timer recalled, "But we lived in patches. There was no big black belt, no solid black belt anywhere in this city of Memphis." Transcript of oral history interview of Blair T. Hunt by Ronald Walter, 8 September 1976, Memphis Public Library.

2. Because mere rumors were reported in newspapers as fact, there are many versions of the incident and the lynching that followed. This account is a synthesis of earlier accounts, newspaper articles, and Wells's account in her autobiography. Previous accounts include Fred L. Hutchins, *What Happened in Memphis* (Kingsport, TN: Kingsport Press, 1965), pp. 36–41, as well as his letter to Alfreda Duster, 10 July 1963, Wells Papers; David M. Tucker, "Miss Ida B. Wells and Memphis Lynching," *Phylon* 32 (Summer 1971), pp. 112–122; Bettina Aptheker, "The Suppression of the *Free Speech*: Ida B. Wells and the Memphis Lynching, 1892," *San Jose Studies* 3 (1977),

pp. 35–40; and Kenneth W. Goings and Gerald L. Smith, "'Unhidden' Transcripts: Memphis and African American Agency, 1862–1920," *Journal of Urban History* 21 (March 1995), pp. 372–394. Major newspaper sources include all the extant Memphis papers, the *New York Times*, St. Paul *Appeal*, *Cleveland Gazette*, and Detroit *Plaindealer*. Only specific quotes will be cited.

3. Memphis *Appeal-Avalanche*, 11 March 1892.

4. Ibid., 6 March 1892; see 3 March 1892 for an account of the initial fight written before the trouble escalated and stories became confusing.

5. Memphis *Appeal-Avalanche*, 6 March 1892.

6. Ibid., 7 March 1892.

7. *Cleveland Gazette*, 26 March 1892.

8. Memphis *Appeal-Avalanche*, 14 March 1892.

9. Memphis *Commercial*, 10 March 1892.

10. Memphis *Appeal-Avalanche*, 9 March 1892.

11. *New York Times*, 11 March 1892; Memphis *Appeal-Avalanche*, 11 March 1992.

12. Alfreda Duster, ed., *Crusade for Justice, The Autobiography of Ida B. Wells* (Chicago: University of Chicago Press, 1970), pp. 47–48, 55.

13. Ibid., p. 52.

14. Memphis *Appeal-Avalanche*, 22 March 1892.

15. Ibid., 10, 23, 31 March 1892.

16. Detroit *Plaindealer*, 25 March 1892.

17. (Kansas City) *American Citizen*, 11 March 1892; *Langston City Herald*, 26 March 1892.

18. (Coffeyville, Kansas) *Afro-American Advocate*, 18 March 1892; Detroit *Plaindealer*, 6 May 1892; *Huntsville Weekly Gazette*, 28 May 1892; Memphis *Appeal-Avalanche*, 28 March 1992.

19. Indianapolis *Freeman*, 26 March 1892; Memphis *Appeal-Avalanche*, 30, 31 May 1892; Memphis *Weekly Commercial*, 11 May 1892.

20. *Topeka Times-Observer*, 26 March 1892; Detroit *Plaindealer*, 1 April 1892; *American Citizen*, 1 April 1892; *Afro-American Advocate*, 6 May 1992.

21. Indianapolis *Freeman*, 19 March 1892.

22. *New York Age*, 21 September 1889.

23. *Afro-American Advocate*, 25 March 1892; Detroit *Plaindealer*, 11 March 1892; *Langston City Herald*, 16, 23, 30 January, 20, 27 February 1892.

24. *Langston City Herald*, 26 March 1892.

25. *Cleveland Gazette*, 16 April 1892; Duster, *Crusade*, pp. 56–57.

26. Duster, *Crusade*, pp. 57–58.

27. *Langston City Herald*, 16 April 1892.

28. Ibid.

29. Duster, *Crusade*, pp. 54–55; *Cleveland Gazette*, 14 May 1892; Detroit *Plaindealer*, 6 May 1892.

30. Quoted in the *Langston City Herald*, 28 April 1892.

31. Reported in the *Langston City Herald*, 7 May 1892.

32. Duster, *Crusade*, p. 64.

33. W. E. B. Du Bois, "Reconstruction and Its Benefits," *American Historical Review* 15 (July 1910), p. 794. Discussions of the various causes of lynching are found

in W. Fitzhugh Brundage, *Lynchings in the New South, Georgia and Virginia, 1880–1930* (Urbana: University of Illinois Press, 1993); James E. Cutler, *Lynch Law: An Investigation into the History of Lynching in the United States* (New York: Longmans, Green, 1905); Arthur F. Raper, *The Tragedy of Lynching* (Chapel Hill: University of North Carolina Press, 1933); John Dollard, *Caste and Class in a Small Southern Town* (New Haven: Yale University Press, 1937); George C. Wright, *Racial Violence in Kentucky, 1865–1940* (Baton Rouge: Louisiana State University Press, 1990); George C. Rable, *But There Was No Peace: The Role of Violence in the Politics of Reconstruction* (Athens: University of Georgia Press, 1984); Mary Elizabeth Hines, "Death at the Hands of Persons Unknown: The Geography of Lynching in the Deep South, 1882–1910" (Ph.D. diss., Louisiana State University, 1992); Herbert Shapiro, *White Violence and Black Response, From Reconstruction to Montgomery* (Amherst: University of Massachusetts Press, 1988).

34. See Catherine Clinton, "Freedwomen, Sexuality, and Violence During Reconstruction," in Catherine Clinton, ed., *Half Sister of History: Southern Women and the American Past* (Durham, NC: Duke University Press, 1994).

35. For information on honor in the South see Bertram Wyatt-Brown, *Southern Honor: Ethics and Behavior in the Old South* (New York: Oxford University Press, 1982); Steven E. Stowe, *Intimacy and Power in the Old South: Ritual in the Lives of Planters* (Baltimore: Johns Hopkins University Press, 1987); Edward A. Ayers, *Vengeance and Justice: Crime and Punishment in the 19th-Century South* (New York: Oxford University Press, 1984).

36. Sources that discuss the link of rape and lynching include Martha Hodes, "The Sexualization of Reconstruction Politics: White Women and Black Men in the South after the Civil War," *Journal of the History of Sexuality* 3 (January 1993), pp. 402–417; Madelin Joan Olds, "The Rape Complex in the Postbellum South," (D.A. diss., Carnegie Mellon University, 1989); Angela Davis, *Women, Race and Class* (New York: Random House, 1981), pp. 172–201; Gail Bederman, "'Civilization,' the Decline of Middle Class Manliness, and Ida B. Wells's Antilynching Campaign (1892–94)," *Radical History Review* 52 (1992), pp. 4–30; Jacquelyn Dowd Hall, "The Mind that Burns in Each Body: Women, Rape, and Racial Violence," in Sharon Thompson, Anne Snitow, and Christine Stansell, eds., *Powers of Desire: The Politics of Sexuality* (New York: Monthly Review Press, 1983); George M. Fredrickson, *The Black Image in the White Mind* (New York: Harper & Row, 1971); Jonathan M. Wiener, "The 'Black Beast Rapist': White Racial Attitudes in the Postwar South," *Reviews in American History* 13 (June 1985).

37. For a discussion of antebellum rape see Diane Miller Sommerville, "The Rape Myth in the Old South Reconsidered," *Journal of Southern History* (August 1995), pp. 481–518.

38. Quoted in *American Citizen*, 1 July 1892. This version is very close to the one in Wells's *Southern Horrors, Lynch Law in All Its Phases* reprinted in Trudier Harris, comp., *Selected Works of Ida B. Wells-Barnett* (New York: Oxford University Press, 1991), pp. 16–17.

39. Duster, *Crusade*, pp. 58–59.

40. *American Citizen*, 1 July 1892.

41. Harris, *Selected Works*, p. 18.

42. Duster, *Crusade*, pp. 61–62.

43. *American Citizen*, 1 July 1892.

44. Ibid.

45. Duster, *Crusade*, pp. 63–64.

46. Detroit *Plaindealer*, 15, 22 April 1892.

47. Duster, *Crusade*, p. 62.

Chapter 8

1. St. Paul *Appeal*, 10 August 1892; *Detroit Plaindealer*, 15 July 1892.

2. L. A. Scruggs, *Women of Distinction* (Raleigh, NC: L. A. Scruggs Publisher, 1893), p. 38; Indianapolis *Freeman*, 27 April 1895.

3. (Coffeyville, Kansas) *Afro-American Advocate*, 17 June 1892.

4. Ibid.

5. Detroit *Plaindealer*, 17 June 1892; Indianapolis *Freeman*, 30 July 1892.

6. Topeka *Weekly Call*, 25 July 1892; Alfreda M. Duster, ed., *Crusade for Justice, The Autobiography of Ida B. Wells* (Chicago: University of Chicago Press, 1970), p. 67.

7. (Kansas City) *American Citizen*, 3 June 1892; *Langston City Herald*, 4 June 1892.

8. Indianapolis *Freeman*, 16 July 1892.

9. Ibid., 20 August 1892.

10. *American Citizen*, 12 August 1892.

11. *Langston City Herald*, 3 September 1892.

12. Indianapolis *Freeman*, 16 July 1892.

13. David M. Tucker, *Black Pastors and Leaders: Memphis, 1819–1972* (Memphis: Memphis State University Press, 1975), pp. 41–42; *Langston City Herald*, 28 May 1892.

14. Memphis *Appeal-Avalanche*, 8 June 1892.

15. Ibid., 12 June 1892.

16. Ibid., 30 June 1892.

17. Ibid.

18. Detroit *Plaindealer*, 29 July 1892.

19. Ibid., 5 August 1892.

20. *Washington Bee*, 14 July 1894.

21. Detroit *Plaindealer*, 19 August 1892.

22. *American Citizen*, 3 June 1892.

23. Duster, *Crusade*, p. 69.

24. Ibid., p. 63.

25. Wells's articles from the *New York Age* were republished in a pamphlet titled *Southern Horrors, Lynch Law in All Its Phases*, which has been reprinted (with other of her pamphlets) by Oxford University Press. As that printing is more widely available than microfilm of the *Age*, it will serve as the source cited in this discussion of the articles. Trudier Harris, comp., *Selected Works of Ida B. Wells-Barnett* (New York: Oxford University Press, 1991), pp. 16–18.

26. Wells, *Southern Horrors*, p. 18.

27. Ibid.

28. Ibid., p. 19.

29. Ibid.

30. Ibid.

31 Ibid., pp. 20–21.

32. Wells had long noted such cases; in 1891 she wrote of "a clear case of love of a pretty white woman for a 'black, kinky headed Negro.'" *American Citizen*, 9 October 1891.

33. Wells, *Southern Horrors*, pp. 23–26.

34. Ibid., pp. 26–28.

35. Ibid., p. 27.

36. Ibid.

37 Ibid., pp. 28–30.

38. Ibid., pp. 31–34.

39 Ibid.

40 Ibid., pp. 34–36.

41. Ibid.

42. Ibid., pp. 37–39. Colyar's comments were reprinted in several black newspapers; for example, see the *Huntsville Weekly Gazette*, 6 August 1892.

43. Wells, *Southern Horrors*, p. 40.

44. Ibid., p. 41.

45. Ibid., pp. 42.

46. Ibid., pp. 43–45.

47. For further discussion of the issues of manhood and civilization see, Gail Bederman, "'Civilization,' the Decline of Middle-Class Manliness, and Ida B. Wells's Antilynching Campaign (1892–94)," *Radical History Review* 52 (1992), pp. 4–30; Hazel V. Carby, "'On the Threshold of the Woman's Era': Lynching, Empire, and Sexuality in Black Feminist Theory," *Critical Inquiry* 12 (Autumn 1985), pp. 262–277; J. A. Mangan and James Walvin, eds., *Manliness and Morality in Britain and America, 1800–1940* (New York: St. Martin's Press, 1987); Norman Vance, *The Sinews of Spirit: The Ideal of Christian Manliness in Victorian Literature and Religious Thought* (Cambridge, England: Cambridge University Press, 1985).

48. Duster, *Crusade*, p. 70.

49. Duster, *Crusade*, p. 71.

50. Monroe A. Majors, *Noted Negro Women, Their Triumphs and Activities* (Chicago: Donohue & Henneberry, 1893), p. 190; Detroit *Plaindealer*, 24 June 1892.

51. *American Citizen*, 12 August 1892; *New York Times*, 5 April 1892; *American Citizen*, 19, 26 February, 4 March 1892. Taylor called an antilynching article by Douglass "a rehash, in substance clothed in different words of our article which appeared [a] month ago under the Caption 'Is God Dead?'" in the 29 July issue of the *American Citizen*. The New York meeting also raises an interesting conflict in sources. In her autobiography (p. 58) Wells claimed her trip to New York at the time of her exile was her first one to the East. She did not even mention the April meeting in her book. Perhaps she desired to emphasize her role as the originator of the antilynching movement. At the time she wrote her memoirs, she was bitter over the failure of African Americans to acknowledge her contributions and thus maybe downplayed the roles of others both in her mind and her writings.

52. Clipping from the Memphis *Evening Scimitar*, n.d., in Frederick Douglass Papers, Library of Congress; *Huntsville Weekly Gazette*, 21 May 1892; (Coffeyville, Kansas) *Afro-American Advocate*, 3 June 1892; Frederick Douglass, "Lynch Law in the

South," *North American Review*, 155 (July 1892), pp. 17–24. For examples of the attention paid the article in the black press see the *Atchison Blade*, 3 March 1893 and the Indianapolis *Freeman*, 9 July 1892.

Chapter 9

1. *Washington Bee*, 29 October 1892. This speech is noted in the advertisement for another lecture to be held in Washington on 31 October 1892.

2. *Cleveland Gazette*, 15 October 1892; *Washington Bee*, 29 October 1892; Indianapolis *Freeman*, 8 October 1892.

3. *Atchison Blade*, 24 September 1892; Detroit *Plaindealer*, 14 October 1892; Indianapolis *Freeman*, 15 October 1892.

4. Alfreda M. Duster, ed., *Crusade for Justice, The Autobiography of Ida B. Wells* (Chicago: University of Chicago Press, 1970), p. 78.

5. Ibid., p. 79.

6. Ibid.; Detroit *Plaindealer*, 1 October, 16 December 1892.

7. Duster, *Crusade*, pp. 79–80.

8. Ibid., p. 80.

9. Ibid.; holograph manuscript in Ida B. Wells Papers, University of Chicago Library.

10. Duster, *Crusade*, p. 80.

11. (Kansas City) *American Citizen*, 21 October 1892; Mrs. N. F. Mossell, *The Work of the Afro-American Woman*, 2d ed. (Philadelphia: Geo. S. Ferguson, 1908), p. 34; Duster, *Crusade*, p. 80; Detroit *Plaindealer*, 16 December 1892.

12. *Washington Bee*, 29 October 1892; *American Citizen*, 21 October 1892.

13. *Atchison Blade*, 10 December 1892.

14. Ida B. Wells to Frederick Douglass, 17 October 1892, Frederick Douglass Papers, Library of Congress.

15. Ida B. Wells, *Southern Horrors, Lynch Law in All Its Phases*, reprinted in Trudier Harris, comp., *Selected Works of Ida B. Wells-Barnett* (New York: Oxford University Press, 1993), pp. 15–16.

16. Ibid., pp. 14–15; as reported in *Parsons* (Kansas) *Weekly Blade*, 4 February 1893.

17. *Washington Bee*, 29 October 1892; *Cleveland Gazette*, 19 November 1892; Duster, *Crusade*, p. 82.

18. Monroe A. Majors, *Noted Negro Women, Their Triumphs and Activities* (Chicago: Donohue & Henneberry, 1893), p. 193.

19. Duster, *Crusade*, p. 82. At about this time, Wells sent a copy of *Anti-Caste* to a woman in Texas who requested a copy. Mrs. M. R. Rogers Webb to Albion Tourgee, 25 November 1892, Albion Tourgee Papers, microfilm edition, University of North Carolina, Chapel Hill.

20. Memphis *Commercial*, 15 December 1892.

21. Memphis *Commercial*, 15 December 1892; Mossell, *The Work of the Afro-American Woman*, p. 34; Majors, *Noted Negro Women*, p. 193; Indianapolis *Freeman*, 25 February 1893; *American Citizen*, 25 November 1892; *Cleveland Gazette*, 11 February 1893.

22. Duster, *Crusade*, pp. 81–82.

23. Ida B. Wells, "Lynch Law in all Its Phases," *Our Day* (May 1893), pp. 333–

337, reprinted in Mildred I. Thompson, *Ida B. Wells-Barnett: An Exploratory Study of an American Black Woman, 1893–1930* (New York: Carlson Publishing, 1990), p. 171.

24. Ibid., p. 172.

25. Ibid., pp. 172–176.

26. Ibid., pp. 176–177.

27. Ibid., pp. 177–183.

28. Ibid., pp. 183–185.

29. Ibid., pp. 185–187.

30. *American Citizen*, 24 February 1893; Indianapolis *Freeman*, 25 February 1893.

31. *Topeka Weekly Call*, 8 January 1893.

32. Ida B. Wells to Albion Tourgee, 2 July, 3 November 1892, Tourgee Papers.

33. Ida B. Wells to Albion Tourgee, 10, 22 February 1893; Albion Tourgee to Ida B. Wells, undated draft, Tourgee Papers.

34. *Cleveland Gazette*, 26 February 1887; Indianapolis *Freeman*, 22 June 1895.

35. Ferdinand Barnett to Albion Tourgee, 23 February, 4 March 1893, Tourgee Papers.

36. Duster, *Crusade*, p. 83; Mary Church Terrell, "Introducing Ida Wells Barnett—To deliver an Address on Lynching, ca. 1893," holograph manuscript, Mary Church Terrell Papers, Library of Congress.

37. Ibid.; Mary Church Terrell to Lethia Fleming, 19 October 1920, Terrell Papers. For the context of that letter see the letter from Fleming to Terrell, 16 October 1920.

38. Duster, *Crusade*, p. 83.

39. *New York Times*, 2 February 1893.

40. Duster, *Crusade*, pp. 84–85.

41. *Washington Bee*, 28 January 1893; *Christian Banner*, quoted in *American Citizen*, 17 February 1893; *New York Times*, 28 May 1892; *Cleveland Gazette*, 4 June 1892; Ida B. Wells to Frederick Douglass, 14 November 1894, Frederick Douglass Papers.

42. William S. McFeely, *Frederick Douglass* (New York: Norton, 1991), p. 320.

43. Duster, *Crusade*, pp. 72–73.

44. Ibid., p. 72.

45. Ida B. Wells to Frederick Douglass, 20 December 1893, Frederick Douglass Papers.

46. Ida B. Wells to Frederick Douglass, 24 February 1893, Frederick Douglass Papers; Indianapolis *Freeman*, 21 October 1893; *Cleveland Gazette*, 21 October 1893.

47. *Cleveland Gazette*, 26 November 1892; McFeely, *Frederick Douglass*, pp. 366, 370; Indianapolis *Freeman*, 26 November 1892.

48. Duster, *Crusade*, pp. 85–86.

49. Catherine Impey to "My dear Friends," 21 March 1893, Tourgee Papers; Catherine Impey to Mrs. Tourgee, 12 April 1893, Tourgee Papers.

50. Letter published in Topeka *Weekly Call*, 15 April 1893; Duster, *Crusade*, pp. 85–86.

51. Duster, *Crusade*, pp. 85–86. Portions of this pamphlet have been reprinted in Bert James Loewenberg's and Ruth Bogin's, *Black Women in Nineteenth-Century Life* (University Park: Pennsylvania State University Press, 1976), pp. 253–262.

Chapter 10

1. Alfreda M. Duster, ed. *Crusade for Justice, The Autobiography of Ida B. Wells* (Chicago: University of Chicago, 1970), pp. 87–89. Two good sources on both of Wells's British tours are Mary Magdelene Boone Hutton, "The Rhetoric of Ida B. Wells: The Genesis of the Anti-Lynch Movement" (Ph.D. diss., Indiana University, 1975) and copies of two papers by Floyd W. Crawford in the Ida B. Wells Papers, University of Chicago Library.

2. Catherine Impey to Frederick Douglass, 15 February 1883, Frederick Douglass Papers, Library of Congress; *Anti-Caste* 1 (March 1888); ibid. 2 (August 1889); "Catherine Impey," *The Friend* 64 (4 January 1924), p. 19; Louis Harlan, ed., *The Booker T. Washington Papers*, vol. 3 (Urbana: University of Illinois Press, 1973), pp. 33–34.

3. *Anti-Caste* 5 (July 1892), p. 3; ibid. 5 (August 1892), p. 2.

4. James Hunt, "A Friend of Gandhi in Scotland," unpublished manuscript in possession of its author, Shaw University, Raleigh, NC.

5. Duster, *Crusade*, pp. 89–90.

6. "The Present Position of Our Society," *Fraternity* (September 1894), p. 5; Mrs. N. F. Mossell, *The Work of the Afro-American Woman*, 2d ed. (Philadelphia: Geo. S. Ferguson, 1908), pp. 35–36.

7. Duster, *Crusade*, pp. 90–91.

8. *Parsons* (Kansas) *Weekly Blade*, 27 May 1893; (Coffeyville, Kansas) *Afro-American Advocate*, 26 May 1893; Duster, *Crusade*, pp. 92–93.

9. *Edinburgh Evening Gazette*, 1 May 1893.

10. Duster, *Crusade*, p. 103.

11. Ibid., p. 104.

12. Ibid., pp. 104–105.

13. Ibid.; *Fraternity* (September 1893), p. 5.

14. *Edinburgh Evening Gazette*, 1 May 1893; *Scottish Pulpit*, as quoted in Pauline E. Hopkins, "Famous Women of the Negro Race," *Colored American Magazine* 4 (March 1902), p. 280; *Newcastle Leader*, 10 May 1893, as quoted in Duster, *Crusade*, pp. 95–96.

15. *Birmingham Daily Post*, 13 May 1893.

16. Ibid., 16 May 1893.

17. Ibid., 18 May 1893.

18. Ibid.

19. *Birmingham Daily Gazette*, 18 May 1893, photocopy in the Ida B. Wells-Barnett Papers, University of Chicago Library.

20. Ibid.

21. Quoted in the Memphis *Appeal-Avalanche*, 23 May 1893.

22. Ibid.

23. *Washington Post*, 31 May 1893.

24. Indianapolis *Freeman*, 8 June 1893.

25. Duster, *Crusade*, p. 109.

26. Ibid., *Aberdeen Evening Gazette*, 28 June 1893.

27. Duster, *Crusade*, pp. 109–110.

28. Ibid., p. 111.

29. Ibid., p. 113.

30. Detroit *Plaindealer*, 14, 28 April 1893; *Kansas State Ledger*, 28 April 1893; *Cleveland Gazette*, 8 April 1893; *Afro-American Advocate*, 28 April 1893.

31. *Cleveland Gazette*, 3 May 1893; *Atchison Blade*, 10 June 1893; *Parsons Weekly Blade*, 27 May 1893; Indianapolis *Freeman*, 10 June 1893.

32. St. Paul *Appeal* as quoted in *Atchinson Blade*, 24 June 1893.

33. Ibid.; *Cleveland Gazette*, 3 May 1893; *Parsons Weekly Blade*, 8 July 1893; *Huntsville Gazette*, 1 July 1893.

34. Articles by Marian Shaw from the *Fargo Argus* in 1893 reprinted in Marian Shaw, *World's Fair Notes, A Woman Journalist Views Chicago's 1893 Columbian Exposition* (Chicago: Pogo Press, 1992), pp. 25, 56. The physical description of the fair is drawn from Stanley Applebaum, *The Chicago World's Fair of 1893, A Photographic Record* (New York: Dover Publications, 1980). See also Gail Bederman, "'Civilization,' the Decline of Middle-Class Manliness, and Ida B. Wells's Antilynching Campaign (1892–94)," *Radical History Review* 52 (1992), pp. 5–30.

35. Detroit *Plaindealer*, 5 December 1890; *Washington Bee*, 15 November 1890; *New York Age*, 21 February, 14, 28 March 1891; Indianapolis *Freeman*, 22 November 1890, 28 February, 19 December 1891; *Langston City Herald*, 11 June 1892; *Cleveland Gazette*, 25 April 1891; Benjamin C. Truman, *History of the World's Fair* (Philadelphia: Mammoth Publishing, 1893, reprint ed. New York: Arno Press, 1976), p. 167. See also August Meier and Elliott M. Rudwick, "Black Man in the 'White City': Negroes and the Columbian Exposition, 1893," *Phylon* 26 (1965), pp. 354–361; Ann Massa, "Black Women in the 'White City,'" *American Studies* 8 (1974), pp. 319–337; Jeanne Madeline Weimann, *The Fair Women* (Chicago: Academy, 1981) as well as Ferdinand L. Barnett, "The Reason Why," in Ida B. Wells, ed., *The Reason Why the Colored American Is Not in the World's Columbian Exposition* (Chicago, 1893) reprinted in Trudier Harris, comp., *Selected Works of Ida B. Wells-Barnett* (New York: Oxford University Press, 1991), pp. 116–137.

36. *Approved official minutes of the Board of Lady Managers of the World's Columbian Commission, November 19–26* (Chicago, 1891), p. 79; Susan G. Cooke, "To all interested in the colored people," typescript, Logan Family Papers, Library of Congress.

37. Detroit *Plaindealer*, 28 November, 5 December 1890, 24 January, 6 February 1891. The *Plaindealer* solicited opinions on the issue and received a number of replies. See also *Indianapolis Freeman*, 14 February, 29 August 1891; *Cleveland Gazette*, 30 January 1892.

38. *Washington Bee*, 11 June 1892; Detroit *Plaindealer*, 24 March 1893.

39. Frederick Douglass to F. J. Loudin, 6 March 1893, Frederick Douglass Papers.

40. Detroit *Plaindealer*, 17 March 1893; Topeka *Weekly Call*, 26 March, 2 April 1893; Indianapolis *Freeman*, 25 March, 8 April 1893; *Atchison Blade*, 25 March, 22 April 1893; *Cleveland Gazette*, 15, 22 April 1893; *Washington Bee*, 15 April 1893.

41. *Atchison Blade*, 22 April 1893; Indianapolis *Freeman*, 1 April 1893; *Washington Bee*, 15, 29 April 1893.

42. Indianapolis *Freeman*, 5 August 1893.

43. Duster, *Crusade*, pp. 116–117; Topeka *Weekly Call*, 15 July 1893.

44. Topeka *Weekly Call*, 15 July 1893.

45. *Cleveland Gazette*, 15, 22 July 1893; Indianapolis *Freeman*, 26 August 1893.

46. (Kansas City) *American Citizen*, 14 July, 22 September 1893; *Washington Bee*, 15 July 1893; Indianapolis *Freeman*, 12 August 1893; *Cleveland Gazette*, 23 September 1893.

47. *The Reason Why*, Ida B. Wells to Albion Tourgee, 23 February 1893, and inscribed pamphlet, Tourgee Papers.

48. Duster, *Crusade*, pp. 116–117.

49. Indianapolis *Freeman*, 3 March, 15 April 1893; *Atchison Blade*, 15 April 1893; *Cleveland Gazette*, 27 May 1893. Jubilee Day committee chair, Joseph Bannister Adger, believed Wells's opposition was due to the influence of Josephine Ruffin, Adger to Frederick Douglass, 24 February 1893, Douglass Papers.

50. Indianapolis *Freeman*, 4 March 1893.

51. Topeka *Weekly Call*, 15 July 1893. The editorial first appeared in the *New York Age* as part of Wells's "Chicago letter."

52. Duster, *Crusade*, pp. 118–119. Press accounts include Topeka *Weekly Call*, 9 September 1893 and *Cleveland Gazette*, 26 August 1893.

53. Indianapolis *Freeman*, 8 July 1893; Chicago *Inter-Ocean*, 3 September 1893.

Chapter 11

1. Allan H. Spear, *Black Chicago, The Making of a Negro Ghetto, 1890–1920* (Chicago: University of Chicago Press, 1967), pp. 11–19, 4; James R. Grossman, *Land of Hope: Chicago, Black Southerners, and the Great Migration* (Chicago: University of Chicago Press, 1989), pp. 32–33.

2. (Kansas City) *American Citizen*, 15 December 1893.

3. *Washington Bee*, 6 January 1894; *Kansas State Ledger*, 19 January 1894; Indianapolis *Freeman*, 13 January 1894.

4. Ida B. Wells to Frederick Douglass, 20 December 1893; C. H. J. Taylor to Frederick Douglass, 16 April 1894, Frederick Douglass Papers, Library of Congress.

5. Isabelle Mayo to Ida B. Wells, 12 September 1893, Douglass Papers.

6. Ida B. Wells to Frederick Douglass, 6 April 1894, Douglass Papers.

7. *Liverpool Daily Post*, 12 March 1894. Another account of the meeting called Wells "young, well educated, and a capital speaker." "A Sermon on Ibsen—A Colored Woman in the Pulpit," *Christian World* 38 (March 15, 1894), p. 187.

8. Ida B. Wells to Frederick Douglass, 13 March 1894; Douglass to Wells, 27 March 1894; Frederick Douglass to C. F. Aked, Douglass Papers.

9. Ida B. Wells to Frederick Douglass, 6 April 1894, Douglass Papers.

10. Ida B. Wells to Frederick Douglass, 6, 10 May 1894, Douglass Papers; Ida B. Wells to Senator Chandler, 10 May 1894, William B. Chandler Papers, Library of Congress.

11. C. F. Aked to Frederick Douglass, 12 April 1894; Ellen Richardson to Frederick Douglass, 22 April 1894; Frederick Douglass to R. A. Armstrong, 22 May 1894, Douglass Papers; Frederick Douglass to C. F. Aked, 22 May 1894. Wells quoted the letter to Clifford in an article for the *New York Age* that was reprinted in the *Cleveland Gazette*, 18 August 1894.

12. For example, one man gave her "eight address-cards, to introduce you to some of our London friends." Ambrose N. Blatchford to Ida B. Wells, 30 April 1894, Douglass Papers.

13. *New York Voice*, 23 October 1890.

14. Ida B. Wells, in "Symposium—Temperance," *A.M.E. Church Review* 7 (April 1891), p. 380.

15. *Parsons* (Kansas) *Weekly Blade*, 24 December 1892; Topeka *Weekly Call*, 8 January 1893. See H. Walton, Jr., and James Taylor, "Blacks, the Prohibitionists and Disfranchisement," *Quarterly Review of Higher Education* (April 1969), pp. 6–69; Robert Allen, *Reluctant Reformers: Racism and Social Reform Movements in the United States* (Washington, DC: Howard University Press, 1974).

16. Topeka *Weekly Call*, 8 January 1893.

17. Alfreda M. Duster, ed., *Crusade for Justice, The Autobiography of Ida B. Wells* (Chicago: University of Chicago Press, 1970), pp. 111–113.

18. Ibid., pp. 202–203.

19. Isabel Somerset to Frederick Douglass, 22 May 1894, Douglass Papers; *Westminister Gazette*, 20 May 1894. Wells defended herself to Douglass and complained that Willard had been "feted and flattered until she has been made a fool of." Ida B. Wells to Frederick Douglass, 3 June 1894, Douglass Papers.

20. *Westminster Gazette*, 21 May 1894. More information about press coverage of the Wells–Willard dispute can be found in a scrapbook kept by Willard that contains clippings about the fight. Scrapbook 13, reel 32, WCTU series, Temperance and Prohibition Papers, microfilm edition, Duke University.

21. Ruth Bordin, *Frances Willard, A Biography* (Chapel Hill: University of North Carolina Press, 1986), pp. 216, 222, 272. Willard had some justification for her charge of unfairness. According to Wells's 6 May letter to the Chicago *Inter-Ocean*, the two women had talked in early May, and Wells noted that Willard "sees the subject of lynching as she never saw it before, because she, like others, made the mistake of judging the Negro by what his accusers say of him and without hearing his side of the story." Significantly, this letter did not get reproduced in Wells's autobiography like the rest did.

22. See Janet Zollinger Giele, *Two Paths to Women's Equality: Temperance, Suffrage and the Origins of Modern Feminism* (New York: Twayne Publishers, 1995); Barbara Epstein, *The Politics of Domesticity: Women, Evangelism, and Temperance in Nineteenth Century America* (Middleton, CT: Wesleyan University Press, 1981); Paula Baker, "The Domestication of Politics: Women and American Political Society, 1780–1920," *American Historical Review* 89 (June 1984), pp. 620–647. In the continuing battle between Wells and Willard, Wells devoted an entire chapter in her 1895 pamphlet, *A Red Record*, to the subject; Willard raised the issue in her 1895 presidential address to the WCTU. For more on the disputes see Bordin, *Frances Willard*, pp. 216–218, 221–222; Ida B. Wells, *A Red Record, Tabulated Statistics and Alleged Causes of Lynching in the United States, 1892—1893—1894* in Trudier Harris, comp., *Selected Works of Ida B. Wells-Barnett* (New York: Oxford University Press, 1991); Indianapolis *Freeman*, 22 December 1894, 20, 27 April 1895; *Cleveland Gazette*, 11 August 1894, 4 January, 13 July, 29 August 1896; 11, 25 1897.

23. *Christian Commonwealth*, 24 May 1894; Helen P. Bright Clark to Frederick Douglass, 15 June 1894, Douglass Papers; Chicago *Inter-Ocean* as quoted in *Parsons Weekly Blade*, 7 July 1894. Interestingly, Douglass skillfully straddled the fence in the fight between Wells and Willard. See his return letter to Clark on 19 July 1894 and his letter to the editor published in the Indianapolis *Freeman*, 22 December 1894.

24. *New York Times*, 29 April, 2 August 1894. See also 13, 20 May, 1 June 1894.

25. Memphis *Daily Commercial*, 26 May 1894; Memphis *Appeal-Avalanche*, 12 June 1894.

26. *Liverpool Daily Post*, 23 March 1894; letter by Armstrong to the *Christian Register*, 21 March 1894; *London Daily Chronicle*, 28 April 1894; Charles F. Aked, "Lynch Law Rampant—A Deep Disgrace to America—Miss Wells's Crusade," *Christian World* 38 (April 1894), p. 259; Chicago *Inter-Ocean*, 4 August 1984.

27. Memphis *Daily Commercial*, 26 May 1894; *Liverpool Daily Post*, 13 June 1894; Chicago *Inter-Ocean*, 28 May 1894; Wells, *Red Record*, p. 150.

28. *Liverpool Daily Post*, 22 March 1894; *New York Sun*, 30 July 1894; *Manchester Guardian*, 30 March 1894; *Christian Register*, 12 April 1894.

29. *London Sun*, 31 May 1894; *London Chronicle*, 9 June 1894; *Westminister Gazette*, 15 May 1894; Ellen Richardson to Frederick Douglass, 22 April 1894, Douglass Papers. In another letter, dated 29 May 1894, Richardson contrasts Douglass as an "orator" to Wells as an "efficient pleader."

30. *Westminister Gazette*, 12, 15 May 1894. Another "southernized" Englishman wrote the *Manchester Guardian*, "If Ida Wells was fully investigated herself I am afraid she would be found to come from that low, debased African stock who are better dead than alive." *Indianapolis Freeman*, 7 July 1894.

31. Memphis *Commercial*, 26 May 1894; *Cleveland Gazette*, 18 August 1894.

32. *New York Age*, 12 July 1894; *Cleveland Gazette*, 16 June 1894. Fleming insisted he had defended Wells in the past and claimed that Wells "has always been ungrateful for anything this paper has said about her." Indianapolis *Freeman*, 28 July 1894.

33. Indianapolis *Freeman*, 28 April 1894; Leavenworth *Herald*, 7 July 1894; Wichita *People's Friend*, 29 June 1894; *Kansas State Ledger*, 13 July 1894.

34. Indianapolis *Freeman*, 12 May 1894; *Parsons Weekly Blade*, 7, 14 July 1894; *Washington Bee*, 14 July 1894; *Cleveland Gazette*, 9, 16 June 1894; Indianapolis *Freeman*, 7 July 1894. Race leader and former congressman John Mercer Langston learned the costs of criticizing Wells when an Associated Press release quoted him as saying he did not "uphold her views." Black newspapers quickly denounced him, until he insisted he was misquoted and got letters of testimony from other African Americans who had heard the interview. See Indianapolis *Freeman*, 16, 30 June 1894; *Cleveland Gazette*, 7 July 1894; *Huntsville Gazette*, 14 July 1894; Leavenworth *Herald*, 14 July 1894.

35. Duster, *Crusade*, pp. 213–214; "Lynch-Law in America," *Spectator*, 2 June 1894; Memphis *Daily Commercial*, 18 May, 7 August 1894.

36. Memphis *Scimitar*, quoted in *Cleveland Gazette*, 30 June 1894; Memphis *Commercial*, 26 May 1894. The 12 June 1894 Memphis *Appeal-Avalanche* parodied Wells's charges, quipping, "She omitted to say that the mayor of Memphis is a cannibal, and has choice tid-bits of succulent young Africans sent around to his friends."

37. *Westminister Gazette*, 10 May 1894.

38. Ibid. Responding to southern protests, Aked asked, "And why is it a greater offense to charge degraded white women with vice than to charge degraded black men with crime?" Charles F. Aked, "The Race Problem in America," *Contemporary Review* 45 (January–June 1894), p. 826.

39. Indianapolis *Freeman*, 7 July 1894; *Cleveland Gazette*, 14 August 1894.

40. Wichita *People's Friend*, 22 June 1894; Topeka *Weekly Call*, 7 July 1894; *Parsons Weekly Blade*, 23 June 1894; *Cleveland Gazette*, 14 August, 9 June 1894; Memphis *Appeal-Avalanche*, 9 June 1894.

41. *Parsons Weekly Blade*, 30 June 1894; Indianapolis *Freeman*, 9 June 1894; Topeka *Weekly Call*, 4 August 1894.

42. Chicago *Inter-Ocean*, 19 May 1894; Topeka *Weekly Call*, 23 June 1894; Duster, *Crusade*, p. 211; Kansas City *American Citizen*, 13 July 1894. Many of the details of the tour are omitted here as the trip is copiously covered in Wells's autobiography—about one-fourth of the book is devoted to these four months.

43. Duster, *Crusade*, pp. 215–217; (Wichita) *National Baptist World*, 31 August 1894.

44. Quoted in Chicago *Inter-Ocean*, 4 August 1894; Duster, *Crusade*, p. 214; *New York Times*, 27 July 1894.

45. Wichita *People's Friend*, 10 August 1894; Duster, *Crusade*, pp. 218–219; *New York Times* and Memphis *Commercial Appeal*, 30 July 1894.

46. *Cleveland Gazette*, 28 July 1894; Indianapolis *Freeman*, 11, 25 August, 1 September 1894.

47. *Parsons Weekly Blade*, 15 June 1895; Duster, *Crusade*, p. 219.

48. *Kansas State Ledger*, 25 January 1895.

Chapter 12

1. Chicago *Inter-Ocean*, 8 August 1894; (Kansas City) *American Citizen*, 24 August 1894.

2. Alfreda M. Duster, ed. *Crusade for Justice, The Autobiography of Ida B. Wells* (Chicago: University of Chicago Press, 1970), p. 220.

3. *Washington Bee*, 5 January 1895; *American Citizen*, 22 March 1895.

4. Caesar A. A. Taylor was the founder of Wellsford near Jacksonville, Florida. See Indianapolis *Freeman*, 15 December 1894, 9 February 1895.

5. *New York Times*, 4 September 1894; Wichita *People's Friend*, 17 August 1894; *Parsons* (Kansas) *Weekly Blade*, 13 October 1894.

6. Indianapolis *Freeman*, 15 September 1894; *Parsons Weekly Blade*, 22 September 1894.

7. Letter reprinted in *Washington Bee*, 22 September 1894.

8. Topeka *Weekly Call*, 22 September 1894; *National Baptist World*, 28 September 1894; *Huntsville Gazette*, 16 September 1894.

9. *Literary Digest* 9 (September 22, 1894), pp. 1–2; Wichita *People's Friend*, 31 August 1894; *New York Times*, 10 September 1894; *Cleveland Gazette*, 15 September 1894.

10. *New York Times*, 11 September, 23 November 1894; *London Times*, 6 October 1894.

11. *Parsons Weekly Blade*, 29 September 1894. See also 6 October 1894 and 19 January 1895 as well as Indianapolis *Freeman*, 13 October 1894; *Cleveland Gazette*, 18 August, 15 September 1894; Topeka *Weekly Call*, 29 September, 8 December 1894.

12. *Columbus Evening Dispatch*, quoted in *Cleveland Gazette*, 8 September 1894; Indianapolis *Freeman*, 8 September 1894.

13. Both were quoted in Indianapolis *Freeman*, 15 September 1894.

14. *Conservator* quoted in *Washington Bee*, 15 September 1894; letter reprinted in Topeka *Weekly Call*, 26 January 1895; Wichita *People's Friend*, 21 September

1894; *Parsons Weekly Blade*, 22 September 1894; *National Baptist World*, 2 November 1894.

15. Ida B. Wells, *A Red Record, Tabulated Statistics and Alleged Causes of Lynching in the United States, 1892—1893—1894* in Trudier Harris, comp., *Selected Works of Ida B. Wells-Barnett* (New York: Oxford University Press, 1991), pp. 219–220, 147, 213–214.

16. Ibid., pp. 248–249.

17. *New York Times*, 11 September 1894; *Cleveland Gazette*, 5 January 1895; *Parsons Weekly Blade*, 5, 19 January 1895; Topeka *Weekly Call*, 15 September 1894, 19 January 1895; *Congressional Record*, 53rd Congress, 2nd session, XXVI, Pt. 8 (3 August 1894); ibid., 53rd Congress, 3rd session, XXVII, Pt. 1 (9 December 1894).

18. *Woman's Era*, February 1895.

19. Copies of the Boston addresses are found in the Frederick Douglass Papers, Library of Congress. An examination of the articles on lynching listed in the index to the *New York Times* reveals a substantial change in the paper's coverage of the subject.

20. *Parsons Weekly Blade*, 13 April 1895; Duster, *Crusade*, p. 227. Anthony's action in the meeting is also described in Ida Husted Harper, *The Life and Work of Susan B. Anthony*, vol. 2 (Indianapolis: Brown Merrill Co., 1898), pp. 815–816.

21. Duster, *Crusade*, pp. 227–230.

22. Leavenworth *Herald*, 15 May, 5 January 1895; 1 September 1894.

23. *Kansas State Ledger*, 3 May 1895; *Indianapolis Freeman*, 4 August 1894.

24. *American Citizen*, 18 January 1895.

25. Quoted in Leavenworth *Herald*, 3 August 1895. Wells realized the importance of Douglass's support; one of her first destinations on her return to America had been his home, which can be seen in a telegram she sent him on 25 July 1894, Douglass Papers.

26. *Christian Recorder*, 5 July 1894; *Parsons Weekly Blade*, 2 February 1895; Indianapolis *Freeman*, 29 September 1894, 30 March 1895; Leavenworth *Herald*, 13 April, 26 October 1895; Indianapolis *Freeman*, 15 March 1902.

27. Indianapolis *Freeman*, 27 April 1895.

28. Duster, *Crusade*, pp. 221–223.

29. Ibid., pp. 235–238.

30. "Interview with Alfreda Duster," 8 and 9 March 1978, Black Women Oral History Project, Schlesinger Library, Radcliff College, p. 11.

31. Biographical material on Barnett is scarce and contradictory. Sources indicate his birthdate within a range from 1848 to 1859. A long Chicago *Broad Ax* article on 10 November 1906 gives his birthdate as 1859 and says he graduated from law school in 1878, after teaching two years. If so, he was certainly precocious to have accomplished all this by age nineteen. Their daughter, Alfreda Duster, said in a letter to Luther P. Jackson, Jr., on 6 March 1971 (found in the Ida B. Wells Papers in the University of Chicago Library) that her father was fifty-six when she was born (which would make his birthdate about 1849) and that he was eighty-four "or more" when he died (which would have made his birthdate about 1852). Other sources include the 1978 interview of Duster; Albert Nelson Marquis, ed., *The Book of Chicagoans: A Biographical Directory of Leading Living Men and Women of the City of Chicago, 1917* (Chicago, 1917), p. 37; Allan H. Spear, *Black Chicago: The Making of a Negro Ghetto, 1890–1920* (Chicago: University of Chicago Press, 1967), pp. 60–61; Albert Lee Kreiling, "The

Making of Racial Identities in the Black Press: A Cultural Analysis of Race Journalism in Chicago, 1870–1929," (Ph.D. diss., University of Illinois at Urbana-Champaign, 1973), pp. 124–144; Ralph Nelson Davis, "The Negro Newspaper in Chicago," (M.A. thesis, University of Chicago, 1939), pp. 26–28.

32. National Conference of Colored Men of the United States, *Proceedings*, Nashville, Tennessee, 6–9 May 1879 (Washington: Rufus H. Darby, 1879), pp. 83–86.

33. (Washington, DC) *People's Advocate*, 27 August 1881, 25 March 1882; *Trenton Sentinel*, 24 June, 8 July 1882; *Cleveland Gazette*, 24 May 1884; 17 October, 21 November 1885, 26 February, 7 May, 25 June 1887, 25 July 1891.

34. Quoted in the *Trenton Sentinel*, 12 March 1881.

35. All quotes are from Davis, "The Negro Newspaper," pp. 9–25. When Davis was working on his thesis, he interviewed Barnett, who let him see a scrapbook of undated *Conservator* clippings from the early 1880s. Barnett's attitude toward lower-class priorities is also seen in an interview reprinted in the 24 December 1887 *Cleveland Gazette* in which Barnett referred to the "big watch chains and flashy clothing" of many of the masses.

36. (Springfield) *Illinois Record*, 22 October 1898.

37. *Cleveland Gazette*, 22 November 1890; F. L. Barnett to Mrs. Palmer, 20 December 1891, Chicago World's Fair Columbian Exposition Board of Lady Managers, incoming correspondence, Chicago Historical Society; F. L. Barnett to Frederick Douglass, 10 August 1891, Frederick Douglass Papers, Library of Congress; Indianapolis *Freeman*, 22 June 1895; Ferdinand L. Barnett to William E. Chandler, 8 May 1894, William E. Chandler Papers, Library of Congress.

38. Joel A. Rogers to Alfreda Duster, 28 November 1958, Wells Papers; Duster interview, pp. 3, 12–13; Davis, "The Negro Newspaper," p. 27.

39. Stella Reed Garnett, "A Chapter in the Book on The Life of Ida B. Wells," 23 April 1951, enclosed in Stella Reed Garnett to Alfreda Duster, 26 April 1951, Wells Papers; Duster interview, p. 3.

40. *Woman's Era* 7 (July 1895), p. 5; *Richmond Planet*, 6 July 1895; Leavenworth *Herald*, 22 June 1895; *New York Times*, 25 June 1895; *Chicago Tribune*, 28 July 1895; *American Citizen*, 14 June 1895. The *Chicago Tribune* article was headed with the words "Two Notable People Are Married."

41. Indianapolis *Freeman*, 13 April 1895; Leavenworth *Herald*, 20 July, 17 August 1895; (Springfield) *Illinois Record*, 25 February 1899; *Cleveland Gazette*, 7 November 1896, 8 October 1898.

42. *New York Age* article quoted in Duster, *Crusade*, pp. 239–240 and Indianapolis *Freeman*, 6 July 1895; Topeka *Weekly Call*, 6 July 1895.

43. Duster, *Crusade*, p. 241.

44. Ibid., p. 242; Duster interview, pp. 13, 19–20; "Personality," part of a draft of an unpublished biography of Wells-Barnett written by Duster, Wells Papers.

45. Garnett, "A Chapter in the Book." The best sources for information on the history of the *Conservator* are Kreiling, "Making of Racial Identities," and Davis, "The Negro Newspaper." For press comments on Wells-Barnett's assumption of editorship see Indianapolis *Freeman*, 18 July 1895; *Richmond Planet*, 13 July 1895; and Topeka *Weekly Call*, 20 July 1895.

46. (Wichita) *National Reflector*, 21 December 1895; Indianapolis *Freeman*, 7 September 1895; Duster, *Crusade*, pp. 242–243; *Omaha Enterprise*, 11 April 1896;

Omaha Enterprise, 17 August 1895; (Kansas City) *American Citizen,* 29 November 1895.

47. Duster, *Crusade,* pp. 250–251.

48. Ibid., pp. 243–245.

49. Ibid., pp. 248–249.

50. Ibid., pp. 250, 255.

Chapter 13

1. Quoted in (Kansas City) *American Citizen,* 12 July 1895.

2. The best account of the assaults upon black womanhood is Beverly Guy-Sheftall, *Daughters of Sorrow: Attitudes Toward Black Women, 1880–1920* (New York: Carlson, 1990).

3. Ibid., 19 May 1893. Among the best secondary sources on black women's club movement are Elizabeth L. Davis, *Lifting as They Climb: National Association of Colored Women* (Washington, DC: NACW, 1933); Charles Harris Wesley, *The History of the National Association of Colored Women's Clubs, A Legacy of Service* (Washington, DC: NACW, 1984); Dorothy Salem, *To Better Our World: Black Women in Organized Reform* (New York: Carlson, 1990); Gerda Lerner, "Early Community Work of Black Club Women," *Journal of Negro History* 59 (April 1974), pp. 158–167; Kathleen C. Berkeley, " 'Colored Ladies Also Contributed': Black Women's Activities from Benevolence to Social Welfare, 1866–1896," in Walter J. Fraser, Jr., R. Frank Saunders, Jr., and John L. Wakelyn, eds., *The Web of Southern Social Relations: Women, Family, and Education* (Athens: University of Georgia Press, 1985), pp. 181–203; Stephanie J. Shaw, "Black Club Women and the Creation of the National Association of Colored Women," in Darlene Clark Hine, Wilma King, and Linda Reed, eds., *"We Specialize in the Wholly Impossible": A Reader in Black Women's History* (New York: Carlson Publishing, 1995), pp. 433–447; Anne Firor Scott, "Most Invisible of All: Black Women's Voluntary Associations," *Journal of Southern History* 56 (February 1990), pp. 3–22; Wilson Jeremiah Moses, "Domestic Feminism, Conservatism, Sex Roles, and Black Women's Clubs, 1893–1896," *Journal of Social and Behavioral Sciences* 24 (Fall 1978), pp. 166–177; Willie Mae Coleman, "Keeping the Faith and Disturbing the Peace, Black Women: From Anti-Slavery to Women's Suffrage" (Ph.D. diss., University of California, Irvine, 1982); Floris Loretta Barnett Cash, "Womanhood and Protest: The Club Movement Among Black Women, 1892–1922," (Ph.D. diss., State University of New York, Stoneybrook, 1986); Tulia Kay Brown Hamilton, "The National Association of Colored Women, 1896–1920" (Ph.D. diss., Emory University, 1978); Susan Lynn Smith, "The Black Woman's Club Movement: Self-Improvement and Sisterhood" (M.A. thesis, University of Wisconsin, 1986); Emma L. Fields, "The Women's Club Movement in the United States, 1877–1900" (M.A. thesis, Howard University, 1948).

4. Addie Hunton, "Negro Womanhood Defended," *Voice of the Negro* 1 (March 1904), p. 280. These words were in a response to later charges of immorality.

5. Anna Julia Cooper, *A Voice from the South* (Xenia, OH: Aldine Printing House, 1892), p. ii; *American Citizen,* 26 July 1895.

6. Quoted in Guy-Sheftall, *Daughters of Sorrow,* p. 27. A participant's account of the organization of the National Association of Colored Women is found in Davis, *Lifting As They Climb.*

7. *Woman's Era* 1 (August 1894), p. 7; 2 (July 1895), p. 1.

8. *A History of the Convention Movement among the Colored Women of the United States of America as contained in the Minutes of the Conventions, held in Boston, July 29, 30, 31, 1895, and of the National Federation of Afro-American Women, held in Washington, DC., July 20, 21, 22, 1896* (1902), pp. 27, 19. (A copy of this pamphlet is in the Ida B. Wells Papers, University of Chicago Library.)

9. Ibid., p. 12; *Woman's Era* 2 (August 1895), p. 16. The Washington delegation included Anna J. Cooper, Ellen L. Smith, Lucinda Cook, Marion Shadd, and Helen Cook.

10. Coleman, "Keeping the Faith," pp. 74–75.

11. Alfreda M. Duster, ed. *Crusade for Justice, The Autobiography of Ida B. Wells* (Chicago: University of Chicago Press, 1970), p. 243; *A History of the Convention Movement*, pp. 37–61.

12. *Cleveland Gazette*, 8 August 1896; *Woman's Era* 3 (September and August 1896), p. 10; *Washington Bee*, 25 July 1896.

13. Elizabeth Lindsey Davis, *The Story of the Illinois Federation of Colored Women's Clubs* (Chicago, 1922), p. 2; St. Paul *Appeal*, 11 February, 4, 18 March, 15 July 1899; Duster, *Crusade*, pp. 258–259.

14. Duster, *Crusade*, p. 260; Mary Church Terrell, *A Colored Woman in a White World* (Salem, NH: Ayer Co., 1940), pp. 154–155; "Refutation of False Charges," undated document, Mary Church Terrell Papers, Library of Congress; *Chicago Daily News*, 14 August 1899.

15. Duster, *Crusade*, pp. 259–260; Terrell, *Colored Woman*, pp. 153–154; *Minutes of the Second Convention of the National Association of Colored Women: held at Quinn Chapel, 24th Street and Wabash Avenue, Chicago, Ill., August 14th, 15th, and 16th, 1899*, p. 14. (A copy of this pamphlet is available in "American Memory" at the Library of Congress homepage on the Internet.) The *Chicago Times-Herald* noted of Addams's invitation that the "color line was given another good rub."

16. Mollie [Terrell] to Frances [Settle], 5 September 1899; Lethia C. Fleming to Terrell, 16 October 1920; Terrell to Fleming, 19 October 1920; Mary O. Waring to Terrell, 15 November 1922, Terrell Papers.

17. *Washington Bee*, 18 July 1896; Chicago *Broad Ax*, 17 October 1902. See Willard B. Gatewood, *Aristocrats of Color: The Black Elite, 1880–1920* (Bloomington: Indiana University, 1990).

18. Mollie to Fannie, 19 July 1888, Terrell Papers; Karlyn Kohrs Campbell, "Style and Content in the Rhetoric of Early Afro-American Feminists," *Quarterly Journal of Speech* 72 (November 1986), pp. 434–445.

19. Joseph Bannister Adger to Frederick Douglass, 24 February 1893, Frederick Douglass Papers, Library of Congress; Leavenworth *Herald*, 6 July 1895.

20. Anna H. Jones, "The American Colored Woman," *Voice of the Negro* 2 (October 1905), p. 694.

21. *Chicago Times-Herald*, 20 August 1899; Mary Taylor Blauvelt, "The Race Problem as Discussed by Negro Women," *American Journal of Sociology* 6 (March 1901), p. 662; *Buffalo Press*, 12 July 1901, as quoted in the *Washington Bee*, 10 August 1901. The Chicago papers of 1899 were filled with favorable accounts of the NACW meeting.

22. Chicago *Broad Ax*, 3 February 1900; "Club Work as a Factor in the Advance of Colored Women," *Colored American Magazine* 11 (August 1906), p. 83; Mary Church Terrell, "The Duty of the National Association of Colored Women to the

Race," *A.M.E. Church Review* (January 1900), p. 351; "Woman's Part in the Uplift of the Negro Race," *Colored American Magazine* 12 (January 1907), p. 53. For an interesting discussion of the move from protest to self-help see Jack Abramowitz, "Crossroads of Negro Thought, 1890–1895," *Social Education* 18 (March 1954), pp. 117–120.

23. *Washington Colored American*, 2 April 1898; Indianapolis *Freeman*, 3 September 1898; (Springfield) *Illinois Record*, 30 April, 30 August 1898. See also Emma Lou Thornbrough, "The National Afro-American League, 1887–1908," *Journal of Southern History* 27 (February 1961), pp. 494–512 and *T. Thomas Fortune* (Chicago: University of Chicago Press, 1972), pp. 178–207.

24. Duster, *Crusade*, pp. 255–256; *Colored American*, 24 September, 1 October 1898.

25. *Colored American*, 10, 17 December 1898; *Cleveland Gazette*, 24 December 1898; Indianapolis *Freeman*, 1 October, 2 November 1898; 14 January 1899. The Wilmington riot was sparked by an editorial very similar to the ones that caused editors Duke and Wells to be run out of their towns. An editorial in the *Chicago Conservator*, however, noted the underlying reason for the riot was "to carry the elections." Quoted in Chicago *Broad Ax*, 31 December 1898.

26. *Colored American*, 7 January 1899. See also *Cleveland Gazette*, 7 January 1899 and *Boston Transcript*, 3 January 1899.

27. St. Paul *Appeal*, 7 January 1899; *Afro-American Sentinel*, 28 January 1899.

28. *Afro-American Sentinel*, 28 January 1899; *Cleveland Gazette*, 7 January 1899. See also Duster, *Crusade*, pp. 257–258.

29. The best source on Washington remains the two-volume biography by Louis R. Harlan, *The Making of a Black Leader, 1856–1901* (New York: Oxford University Press, 1972) and *The Wizard of Tuskegee, 1901–1915* (New York: Oxford University Press, 1983).

30. Indianapolis *Freeman*, 21 January 1899.

31. *Colored American*, 14 January 1899. Three of the six women on the program reported on the work of the "Women's Auxiliary Association." Wells-Barnett was the only one of the other three women giving a speech. *Official Programme: First Annual Meeting of the Afro-American Council at the Metropolitan Baptist Church, Washington, D. C., Thursday and Friday, December 29 and 30, 1898, Bishop Alexander Walters, president* (1898). (A copy can be found in "American Memory" at the Library of Congress homepage on the Internet.)

32. Ida B. Wells to Booker T. Washington, 30 November 1890, Booker T. Washington Papers, Library of Congress; *Cleveland Gazette*, 18 August 1894; Louis R. Harlan, *The Booker T. Washington Papers*, vol. 5 (Urbana: University of Illinois Press, 1973), pp. 18–19 and vol. 13 (Urbana: University of Illinois Press, 1981), pp. 496–498.

33. *New York Times*, 1 May 1899.

34. Ida B. Wells-Barnett, *Lynch Law in Georgia* (Chicago: Chicago Colored Citizens, 1899).

35. *Parsons* (Kansas) *Weekly Blade*, 17 June 1899; St. Paul *Appeal*, 10 June 1899; *Cleveland Gazette*, 17 June 1899; Chicago *Inter-Ocean*, 5 June 1899; Ida B. Wells-Barnett, *Lynch Law in Georgia*; T. Thomas Fortune to Booker T. Washington, 13 June 1899, Washington Papers; *Birmingham Age-Herald*, 22 June 1899; *New York Times*, 22 June 1899; Harlan, *Making of a Black Leader*, pp. 262–264.

36. T. Thomas Fortune to Booker T. Washington, 25 September 1899, Washington Papers. Fortune referred to the criticism as having "unusual bad grace" after he had "sustained . . . her work from start to finish." Indianapolis *Freeman*, 12 January 1895.

37. *Colored American*, 8, 22 1899; St. Paul *Appeal*, 22 July 1899; Chicago *Broad Ax*, 29 July 1899; *Cleveland Gazette*, 29 July 1899; Duster, *Crusade*, p. 261.

38. Duster, *Crusade*, pp. 261–262; Harlan, *Making of a Black Leader*, pp. 263–265; *Cleveland Gazette*, 26 August, 16 September 1899; St. Paul *Appeal*, 2 September 1899; *Colored American*, 26 August 1899; *Washington Bee*, 16 September 1899; *Chicago Tribune*, 20 August 1899.

39. *Colored American*, 7 October 1899; St. Paul *Appeal*, 21 October 1899.

40. *Cleveland Gazette*, 12, 19 June, 3 July 1897; 22, 29 October 1898; 5, 12 August 1899; Chicago *Inter-Ocean*, 17 July 1897; T. Thomas Fortune to Booker T. Washington, 22 July 1897, Washington Papers; *New York Times*, 15 May 1901.

41. Duster, *Crusade*, pp. 252–253; St. Paul *Appeal*, 5 March 1898; Indianapolis *Freeman*, 5 March 1898; *Colored American*, 16 April 1898; *Cleveland Gazette*, 16 April 1898; *St. Joseph Radical*, quoted in *Parsons Weekly Blade*, 14 May 1898.

42. Baltimore *Afro-American Ledger*, 36 March 1898; *Cleveland Gazette*, 9 April 1898.

43. Duster, *Crusade*, pp. 253–254.

44. St. Paul *Appeal*, 15 October 1898; *Illinois Record*, 29 October, 26 November 1898.

45. Ida B. Wells-Barnett, *Mob Rule in New Orleans* (Chicago, 1900), reprinted in Trudier Harris, comp., *Selected Works of Ida B. Wells-Barnett* (New York: Oxford University Press, 1991), pp. 254–255, 314.

46. Ida B. Wells-Barnett, "Lynch Law in America," *Arena* (January 1900), pp. 15–24.

47. Ida B. Wells-Barnett, "The Negro's Case in Equity," *Independent* (26 April 1900), pp. 1010–1011; Ida B. Wells-Barnett, "Lynching and the Excuse for It" *Independent* (16 May 1901), pp. 1133–1136. On the dispute with Addams see Bettina Aptheker, "Lynching and Rape: An Exchange of Views," *Occasional Paper* 25 (1977):

48. *Chicago Conservator*, 7 July 1900, quoted in Indianapolis *Freeman*, 14 July 1900; Duster, *Crusade*, pp. 264–265; Harlan, *Making of a Black Leader*, pp. 266–268.

49. Duster, *Crusade*, pp. 265–266; Emmett J. Scott to Booker T. Washington, 13 August 1901, Washington Papers; Chicago *Broad Ax*, 31 May 1902; St. Paul *Appeal*, 25 August, 22 September 1900; 9 March, 24 August 1901; 5, 19 July 1902.

50. *Washington Bee*, 26 July 1902; Ida B. Wells-Barnett, "To the members of the Anti-Lynching Bureau," 1 January 1902, copy in "American Memory" at the Library of Congress homepage on the Internet; Indianapolis *Freeman*, 4 April 1903.

51. *Washington Bee*, 26 July 1902; Emmett J. Scott to Booker T. Washington, 17 July 1902, Washington Papers; *Louisville Evening Post*, 3 July 1903; *Louisville Herald*, 4 July 1903; Chicago *Broad Ax*, 11 July 1903.

52. *Washington Bee*, 26 July 1902.

53. Duster, *Crusade*, pp. 280–281; Ida B. Wells-Barnett to W. E. B. Du Bois, 30 May 1903, in Herbert Aptheker, *The Correspondence of W. E. B. Du Bois*, vol. 1 (Amherst: University of Massachusetts, 1973), pp. 55–56.

54. Chicago *Broad Ax*, 20 June, 12, 19 December 1903; E. E. Cooper to Booker T. Washington, 25 November 1903, Washington Papers; Ida B. Wells-Barnett, "Booker

T. Washington and His Critics," *World Today* (April 1904), reprinted in Mildred I. Thompson, *Ida B. Wells-Barnett, An Exploratory Study of an American Black Woman, 1893–1930* (New York: Carlson Publishing, 1990), pp. 255–256.

55. Thompson, *Ida B. Wells-Barnett, An Exploratory Study*, pp. 257–258.

56. Ibid., pp. 258–259.

57. Duster, *Crusade*, p. 283.

Chapter 14

1. Richard Wright, "Introduction," in St. Clair Drake and Horace R. Cayton, *Black Metropolis: A Study of Negro Life in a Northern City* (New York: Harper & Row, 1962), p. xvii. For contemporary comments on Chicago see Indianapolis *Freeman*, 20 August 1890, 25 September 1897; Topeka *Weekly Call*, 7 May 1893, 30 June 1894; *Richmond Planet*, 15 February 1896; St. Paul *Appeal*, 2 October 1897; Richard R. Wright, Jr., "The Negro in Chicago," *Southern Workman* 35 (October 1906), pp. 553–566. The most useful secondary sources include Allan H. Spear, *Black Chicago: The Making of a Negro Ghetto, 1890–1920* (Chicago: University of Chicago Press, 1967); James R. Grossman, *Land of Hope: Chicago, Black Southerners, and the Great Migration* (Chicago: University of Chicago Press, 1989); Harold F. Gosnell, *Negro Politicians: The Rise of Negro Politics in Chicago* (Chicago: University of Chicago Press, 1935); Dempsey J. Travis, *An Autobiography of Black Politics* (Chicago: Urban Research Press, 1987).

2. *Cleveland Gazette*, 8 February 1896; (Wichita) *National Reflector*, 18 January, 11 April 1896; *Richmond Planet*, 25 April 1896; *Cleveland Gazette*, 25 September, 9 January 1897.

3. *Charleston Enquirer* as quoted in Indianapolis *Freeman*, 31 October 1897; *Cleveland Gazette*, 23 October 1897; Indianapolis *Freeman*, 16 October 1897; *Michigan Representative* as quoted in Indianapolis *Freeman*, 16 October 1897.

4. Chicago *Broad Ax*, 18 October 1902; Indianapolis *Freeman*, 24 October 1903.

5. Elizabeth Lindsey Davis, *The Story of the Illinois Federation of Colored Women's Clubs* (Chicago, 1922), pp. 26–27; Alfreda M. Duster, ed., *Crusade for Justice, The Autobiography of Ida B. Wells* (Chicago: University of Chicago Press, 1970), pp. 120–122.

6. Duster, *Crusade*, pp. 249–250; *Omaha Enterprise*, 19 December 1896.

7. Duster, *Crusade*, p. 120; *Cleveland Gazette*, 25 August 1894.

8. Duster, *Crusade*, pp. 247–248.

9. Ray Stannard Baker, *Following the Color Line* (New York: Doubleday, Page & Co., 1908); (Springfield) *Illinois Record*, 18 June 1898; Duster, *Crusade*, pp. 121–122.

10. *New York Age*, 14 September 1905; St. Paul *Appeal*, 10 June 1899; Edward E. Wilson, "Negro Society in Chicago," *Voice of the Negro* 4 (July 1907), pp. 306–309; Chicago *Broad Ax*, 28 June 1902; Cleveland *Gazette*, 17 September 1887; *Indianapolis World*, 24 September 1887; *Atchison Blade*, 7 October 1893. See also Willard B. Gatewood, *Aristocrats of Color: The Black Elite, 1880–1920* (Bloomington: Indiana University Press, 1990), pp. 119–124.

11. *Cleveland Gazette*, 10 October 1896; (Kansas City) *American Citizen*, 11 September 1896; *Washington Bee*, 29 August 1896; *National Reflector*, 20 March 1897; Chicago *Broad Ax*, 10 November 1906, 13 March 1909; Travis, *Autobiography of*

Black Politics, pp. 49–50; Gosnell, *Negro Politicians*, pp. 154–155. Barnett's refusal to pay newspapers for their support of the Republican party was a break with tradition and indicated his political Puritanism. The Democratic editor of *Broad Ax*, Julius Taylor, remarked with amazement that Barnett "did not receive one dollar nor no [sic] consideration" for his efforts for the Republicans at the local, state, and national levels. *Broad Ax*, 21 January 1905.

12. Duster, *Crusade*, pp. 263–264.

13. Emmett J. Scott to Booker T. Washington, 12 July 1904; Booker T. Washington to Charles William Anderson, 16 June 1904; T. Thomas Fortune to Emmett J. Scott, 22 February 1904, Booker T. Washington Papers, Library of Congress; *Washington Bee*, 6 January 1897; *Illinois Record*, 17 September 1898. See also Richard B. Sherman, *The Republican Party and Black America: From McKinley to Hoover, 1896–1933* (Charlottesville: University Press of Virginia, 1973).

14. Booker T. Washington to Charles William Anderson, 16 June 1904, Washington Papers; Chicago *Broad Ax*, 20 August 1904, 11 April, 17 October 1908; Louis Harlan, *The Wizard of Tuskegee, Booker T. Washington, 1901–1915* (New York: Oxford University Press, 1983), pp. 27–28.

15. Duster, *Crusade*, pp. 267–268; St. Paul *Appeal*, 5 April 1902. Yates's reluctance to attend was probably related to an earlier and eventually unsuccessful attempt to prevent the almost-white Fannie Barrier Williams from joining a prominent all-white Chicago woman's club and the refusal to recognize the credentials of Josephine Ruffin at a convention of white women's clubs. See Eleanor Smith, "Historical Relationships between Black and White Women," *Western Journal of Black Studies* 6 (Winter 1980), pp. 251–255 and Nancie Caraway, *Segregated Sisterhood, Racism and the Politics of American Feminism* (Knoxville: University of Tennessee Press, 1991). Further discussion of this issue will follow in a later discussion of the suffrage movement.

16. Duster, *Crusade*, pp. 272–274; Davis, *The Story of the Illinois Federation of Colored Women's Clubs*, p. 27; Emma L. Fields, "The Women's Club Movement in the United States," (M.A. thesis, Howard University, 1948), pp. 24–25, 96–100.

17. Duster, *Crusade*, p. 275.

18. Duster, *Crusade*, pp. 274–278; Spear, *Black Chicago*, pp. 44–45.

19. St. Paul *Appeal*, 10 January 1903; Baltimore *Afro-American Ledger*, 17 January 1903.

20. Duster, *Crusade*, pp. 279–281; Fannie Barrier Williams, "The Frederick Douglass Center," *Voice of the Negro* 1 (December 1904), pp. 601–604.

21. Chicago *Broad Ax*, 16, 23 September, 11 November, 9, 16 December 1905; 20, 27 January, 3, 17 February 1906; Fannie Barrier Williams, "A New Method of Dealing With the Race Problem," *Voice of the Negro* 3 (July 1906), pp. 502–505.

22. Ida B. Wells-Barnett to Charles W. Chestnut, 4 June 1901, Ida B. Wells Papers, University of Chicago; Chicago *Broad Ax*, 8 December 1906, 23 May 1908; *Chicago Defender*, 21 November 1908.

23. Duster, *Crusade*, pp. 289–295; Chicago *Broad Ax*, 5, 12 May 1906; J. B. Wood, *The Negro in Chicago* (Chicago: Chicago Daily News, 1916), p. 15; Gosnell, *Negro Politicians*, pp. 127–128. This is one of several controversial incidents discussed in great detail in Wells-Barnett's autobiography. The extensive attention she gave to some of these indicates her sensitivity about the attacks of her critics as well as making a lengthy treatment of them redundant.

24. Duster, *Crusade*, pp. 282–283; *Broad Ax*, 20 January 1906.

25. Chicago *Broad Ax*, 23, 30 June, 7 July 1906.

26. Duster, *Crusade*, pp. 283–285.

27. Ibid., 285–288.

28. *Chicago Chronicle*, 8 November 1906; Portland *New Age*, 24 November 1906; Chicago *Broad Ax*, 22 August 1903; 3 November 1906.

29. *Chicago Daily News*, 8 November 1906; *Chicago Record-Herald*, 8, 19, 23 November 1906; *Chicago Evening Post*, 8 November 1906; S. Laing Williams to Booker T. Washington, 16 November 1906, Washington Papers; Chicago *Broad Ax*, 30 March 1907; Duster, *Crusade*, p. 294. The 8 December 1906 Portland *New Age* supported Wells-Barnett's charges by blaming his defeat on "the strong and bitter opposition that was made against him at the polls by a large number of prominent colored men."

30. S. Laing Williams to Booker T. Washington, 26 November 1906, Washington Papers; *Boston Guardian*, quoted in Chicago *Broad Ax*, 12 September 1903. See Emma Lou Thornbrough, "The Brownsville Episode and the Negro Vote," *Mississippi Valley Historical Review* 44 (1957–1958), pp. 469–493; James A. Tinsley, "Roosevelt, Foraker, and the Brownsville Affray," *Journal of Negro History* 41 (January 1956), pp. 43–65; August Meier, "Booker T. Washington and the Rise of the NAACP," *Crisis* 59 (February 1954), pp. 69–73, 117–123.

31. Chicago *Broad Ax*, 19 December 1903, 9 April 1904.

32. Stephen R. Fox, *The Guardian of Boston, William Monroe Trotter* (New York: Athenaeum, 1970), p. 82; Elliot Rudwick, "The Niagara Movement," *Journal of Negro History* 42 (October 1957), pp. 183–185.

33. W. E. B. Du Bois, "The Niagara Movement," *Voice of the Negro* 2 (September 1905), p. 621; J. Max Barber, "The Niagara Movement at Harpers Ferry," *Voice of the Negro* 3 (October 1906), pp. 406–408; *Broad Ax*, 7 December 1907. Ironically, one of the victories claimed for the Illinois branch in October 1906 was the election of Barnett as municipal judge, which had not yet been overturned.

34. *St. Louis Post-Dispatch*, 16 August 1906; *Broad Ax*, 22 August 1908. See James L. Crouthamel, "The Springfield Race Riot of 1908," *Journal of Negro History* 45 (July 1960), pp. 164–181.

35. Chicago *Broad Ax*, 31 October 1908; William English Walling, "The Race War in the North," *Independent* 65 (3 September 1908), p. 534; "The Call," quoted in Charles Flint Kellogg, *NAACP: A History of the National Association for the Advancement of Colored People* (Baltimore: Johns Hopkins Press, 1967), p. 298.

36. Mary White Ovington, *The Walls Came Tumbling Down* (New York: Harcourt, Brace, 1947), p. 105; Charles William Anderson to Booker T. Washington, 31 May 1909, Washington Papers.

37. *Proceedings of the National Negro Conference 1909: New York May 31 and June 1* (n.p., n.d.), pp. 174–179.

38. Fox, *Guardian*, p. 127; Kellogg, *NAACP*, p. 21.

39. Oswald Garrison Villard to Francis J. Garrison, 4 June 1909, Oswald Garrison Villard Papers, Harvard University; W. E. B. Du Bois, "The National Committee on the Negro," *Survey* 22 (1909), pp. 408, 401.

40. Oswald Garrison Villard to Francis J. Garrison, 4 June 1909; Mary White Ovington to Oswald Garrison Villard, 2 June 1909, Villard Papers; Mary White Ovington,

"The National Association for the Advancement of Colored People," *Journal of Negro History* 9 (April 1924), p. 111.

41. Duster, *Crusade*, pp. 324–328.

42. Ovington, *Walls*, p. 106; Mary White Ovington, *Black and White Sat Down Together: The Reminiscences of an NAACP Founder*, Ralph E. Luker, ed. (New York: Feminist Press of the City University of New York, 1995), p. 60; W. E. B. Du Bois, *Dusk of Dawn* (New York: Harcourt, Brace, 1940), p. 224; W. E. B. Du Bois, *The Autobiography of W. E. B. Du Bois* (New York: International Publishers, 1968), p. 254.

43. William English Walling to W. E. B. Du Bois, 8 June 1909, in Herbert Aptheker, *The Correspondence of W. E. B. DuBois*, vol. 1 (Amherst: University of Massachusetts, 1973), pp. 147–150; Ovington, *Walls*, p. 106; Duster, *Crusade*, pp. 326–327. See also David Levering Lewis, *W. E. B. DuBois: Biography of a Race, 1868–1919* (New York: Henry Holt, 1993), pp. 386–407.

Chapter 15

1. *Chicago Daily Tribune*, 10–13 November 1909; Alfreda M. Duster, ed. *Crusade for Justice, The Autobiography of Ida B. Wells* (Chicago: University of Chicago Press, 1970), pp. 309–310; Ida B. Wells-Barnett, "How Enfranchisement Stops Lynching," *Original Rights Magazine* (June 1910), pp. 42–53, reprinted in Mildred I. Thompson, *Ida B. Wells-Barnett, An Exploratory Study of an American Black Woman, 1893–1930* (New York: Carlson Publishing, 1990), pp. 271–272.

2. Chicago *Broad Ax*, 25 December 1909; Duster, *Crusade*, pp. 310–312.

3. Duster, *Crusade*, p. 311.

4. Ibid., pp. 315–320; *Chicago Defender*, 1 January 1910; Wells-Barnett, "How Enfranchisement," pp. 272–276.

5. Duster, *Crusade*, pp. 21, 311.

6. Dorothy Salem, *To Better Our World: Black Women in Organized Reform, 1890–1920* (New York: Carlson Publishing, 1990), pp. 105–106; Chicago *Broad Ax*, 30 July 1910; Duster, *Crusade*, pp. 328–329.

7. Minutes, Executive Committee, 25 May 1910, NAACP Papers, Library of Congress.

8. Chicago *Broad Ax*, 24 September 1910; *Chicago Defender*, 24 September 1910; *New York Evening Post*, 15 October 1910; *Crisis* I (November 1914), p. 14.

9. Oswald Garrison Villard to J. E. Spingarn, 19 October 1910, Joel E. Spingarn Papers, Moorland-Spingarn Research Center, Howard University, Washington, DC; *Chicago Defender*, 24 September 1910; *Crisis* I (November 1914), p. 14; Charles Flint Kellogg, *NAACP: A History of the National Association for the Advancement of Colored People* (Baltimore: Johns Hopkins Press, 1967), pp. 62–64; B. Joyce Ross, *J. E. Spingarn and the Rise of the NAACP, 1911–1939* (New York: Atheneum, 1972), pp. 20–21. Ferdinand Barnett's position as assistant state's attorney prevented him from being Green's lawyer, but later he and his wife worked together on similar cases.

10. Ida B. Wells-Barnett to J. E. Spingarn, 21 April 1911, Spingarn Papers. See Christopher Robert Reed, "Organized Racial Reform in Chicago During the Progressive Era: The Chicago NAACP, 1910–1920," *Michigan Historical Review* 14 (Spring 1988), pp. 75–99.

11. *New York Age*, 14 September 1905. For scholarly analyses of the role of the black elite in Chicago and elsewhere see E. Franklin Frazier, "Chicago: A Cross-Section of Negro Life," *Opportunity* 7 (March 1929), pp. 70–73 and *Black Bourgeoisie* (New York: Free Press, 1957); August Meier, "Some Observations on the Negro Middle Class," *Crisis* 64 (October 1957), pp. 461–469, 517; Willard B. Gatewood, *Aristocrats of Color: The Black Elite, 1880–1903* (Bloomington: Indiana University, 1990). Kevin K. Gaines, *Uplifting the Race: Black Leadership, Politics, and Culture in the Twentieth Century* (Chapel Hill: University of North Carolina Press, 1996), provides a more subtle interpretation of the tension between elitist ideas of uplift by class stratification and the more democratic vision of collective social advancement. He argues that Frazier was wrong in his contention that the black elite merely wanted to be white, arguing instead that the goal was also "a positive black identity in a deeply racist society" (p. 3).

12. Booker T. Washington to Emmett Jay Scott, 16 January 1914, Booker T. Washington Papers, Library of Congress; *New York Age*, 13, 20, 27 April 1912, 1 February 1913; *Chicago Defender*, 13, 20 January 1912, 13, 20 April 1912; Mary White Ovington, *The Walls Came Tumbling Down* (New York: Harcourt, Brace, 1947), pp. 124–125. She also noted of black women, "They are ambitious for power, often jealous, very sensitive. But they get things done." For the role of women in the NAACP see Salem, *To Better Our World*, pp. 145–179. See also Rhetaugh Graves Dumas, "Dilemmas of Black Females in Leadership," in La Frances Rodgers-Rose, ed., *The Black Woman* (London: Sage Publications, 1980), pp. 203–215.

13. On the role of women in the black community see Salem, *To Better Our World*; Gerder Lerner, "Early Community Work of Black Club Women," *Journal of Negro History* 59 (April 1914), pp. 158–167; Kathleen C. Berkeley, "'Colored Ladies Also Contributed': Black Women's Activities from Benevolence to Social Welfare, 1866–1896," in Walter J. Fraser, Jr., R. Frank Saunders, Jr., and John L. Wakelyn, eds., *The Web of Southern Social Relations: Women, Family, and Education* (Athens: University of Georgia Press, 1985), pp. 181–203; Cynthia Neverdon-Martin, "Self-Help Programs as Educative Activities of Black Women in the South, 1895–1925: Focus on Four Key Areas," *Journal of Negro Education* 51 (Summer 1982), pp. 207–221; Sharon Harley, "For the Good of Family and Race: Gender, Work, and Domestic Roles in the Black Community, 1880–1930," *Signs* 15 (Winter 1990), pp. 236–349.

14. *Parsons Weekly Blade*, 1 February 1896.

15. For information about the settlement house movement and African Americans see Elisabeth Lasch-Quinn, *Black Neighbors: Race and the Limits of Reform in the American Settlement House Movement, 1890–1945* (Chapel Hill: University of North Carolina Press, 1993); James R. Grossman, *Land of Hope: Chicago, Black Southerners, and the Great Migration* (Chicago: University of Chicago Press, 1989); Steven J. Diner, "Chicago Social Workers and Blacks in the Progressive Era," *Social Science Review* 44 (December 1970), pp. 393–410; Thomas L. Philpott, *The Slum and the Ghetto: Neighborhood Deterioration and Middle-Class Reform, Chicago 1880–1930* (New York: Oxford University Press, 1978); Kathleen McCarthy, *Noblesse Oblige: Charity and Cultural Philanthropy in Chicago, 1849–1929* (Chicago: University of Chicago Press, 1982).

16. Jane Addams, "Has the Emancipation Act Been Nullified by National Indifference," *Survey* 29 (25 January 1913), p. 566.

17. Jane Addams, "Social Control," *Crisis* (January 1911), p. 22.

18. Sophonisba P. Breckinridge, "The Color Line in the Housing Problem," *Survey* 29 (February 1913), pp. 575–576.

19. Louise deKoven Bowen, "The Colored People of Chicago," *Survey* 31 (November 1913), pp. 117–120.

20. Chicago *Inter-Ocean*, 29 July 1900; Bishop A. Grant, "The Institutional Church," *Colored American Magazine* 16 (January 1909), pp. 632–634.

21. St. Paul *Appeal*, 14 July 1900; Chicago *Broad Ax*, 14 March 1908; Duster, *Crusade*, pp. 298–299. This church was founded in 1888 by Moses H. Jackson, who remained its pastor for at least forty years and led the fight to dismantle the Freedmen's board—a separate council for African Americans within the Presbyterian Church. *Chicago Defender*, 23 June 1928.

22. Duster, *Crusade*, pp. 298–301.

23. Ibid., pp. 301–302.

24. Ibid., pp. 302–304; Chicago *Broad Ax*, 7 May 1910. About this time Wells-Barnett had become active in the Ideal Women's Club and served as its president in 1911. As with the Ida B. Wells Club (known by then as the IBW Club), her active participation seems to have waned after she ceased to be president.

25. Duster, *Crusade*, pp. 304–306.

26. Ida B. Wells-Barnett to J. E. Spingarn, 21 April 1911, Spingarn Papers; *Chicago Defender*, 30 April 1910. Both the *Chicago Defender* and the *Broad Ax* carried weekly notices of the meetings.

27. Duster, *Crusade*, pp. 306, 330; *Chicago Defender*, 20 September, 18 October 1913, 26 December 1914; Chicago *Broad Ax*, 24, 31 December 1910, 7 January 1911, 20 December 1913.

28. *Fellowship Herald*, 22 June 1911, copy at the Chicago Historical Society.

29. Chicago *Broad Ax*, 20 May 1911, 16, 30 1912; *Chicago Defender*, 18 April 1914. She apparently used the *Fellowship Herald* to continue her attack on Booker T. Washington. In a 20 April 1912 letter to Emmett J. Scott, Cornelius Bailey Hosmer noted a hostile editorial in it as well as speeches by Wells-Barnett that "bespeak jealousy at the influence of Dr. Washington." Booker T. Washington Papers, Library of Congress.

30. "Interview with Alfreda Duster," 8 and 9 March 1978, Black Women Oral History Project, Schlesinger Library, Radcliff College, pp. 6–7, 17, 21, 28.

31. Ida B. Wells-Barnett, "The Northern Negro Woman's Social and Moral Condition," *Original Rights Magazine* (April 1910), pp. 35–36.

32. Chapter 8, p. 7, typescript manuscript by Alfreda Duster, Ida B. Wells Papers, University of Chicago Library; "Duster Interview," pp. 4–6.

33. Alfreda Duster, "Personality," part of a proposed biography in Wells Papers.

34. Ida B. Wells-Barnett to J. E. Spingarn, 29 July 1913, Joel Spingarn Papers; *Chicago Defender*, 4 December 1915.

35. "Interview with Alfreda Duster," pp. 4–16.

36. Duster, *Crusade*, pp. 330–333.

37. Ida B. Wells-Barnett to Judge Harry Olson, 23 April 1914, Chicago Municipal Court Papers, Chicago Historical Society; *Chicago Defender*, 4 December 1915; Harold F. Gosnell, *Negro Politicians: The Rise of Negro Politics in Chicago* (Chicago: University of Chicago Press, 1935), pp. 50–51, 204.

38. Duster, *Crusade*, p. 333.

39. Ibid., pp. 337–339; letter reprinted in the *Chicago Defender*, 26 June 1915.

40. Duster, *Crusade*, pp. 339–341, provides a detailed account of the case, which also received extensive coverage in the local black papers. See Chicago *Broad Ax*, 17 July 1915, 13 April 1918; *Chicago Defender*, 26 June, 17 July, 21 August, 30 October, 6 November, 4, 25 December 1915, 15 January, 26 February, 11 March 1916, 17 March 1917.

41. Chapter 9, p. 10, typescript by Alfreda Duster, Wells papers; Chicago *Broad Ax*, 11 May 1918, 14 August 1915, 13 October 1917, 27 April 1918; *Chicago Defender*, 16, 23 November, 7 December 1912. Wells-Barnett later expressed disappointment in Jack Johnson for doing little for fellow African Americans, but instead "entertaining the wildest of the underworld of both sexes and especially of the white race." Duster, *Crusade*, pp. 358–359.

42. Chapter 9, pp. 10–11, typescript by Alfreda Duster, Wells Papers.

Chapter 16

1. Ida B. Wells-Barnett, "How Enfranchisement Stops Lynching," *Original Rights Magazine* (June 1910), pp. 42–53, reprinted in Mildred I. Thompson, *Ida B. Wells-Barnett, An Exploratory Study of an American Black Woman, 1893–1930* (New York: Carlson Publishing, 1990), p. 279.

2. Chicago *Broad Ax*, 25 March 1911. For more on racism in popular culture see George Frederickson, *The Black Image in the White Mind: The Debate on Afro-American Character and Destiny, 1817–1914* (Middleton: Wesleyan University Press, 1971); Lawrence J. Friedman, *The White Savage: Racial Fantasies in the Postbellum South* (Englewood Cliffs, NJ: Prentice-Hall, 1970).

3. Quoted in David M. Chalmers, *Hooded Americanism* (New York: New Viewpoints, 1965), p. 26.

4. Alfreda M. Duster, ed., *Crusade for Justice, The Autobiography of Ida B. Wells* (Chicago: University of Chicago Press, 1970), pp. 342–344; *Chicago Defender*, 13 March, 12 June 1915; Chicago *Broad Ax*, 22 May, 19 June 1915.

5. Stephen R. Fox, *The Guardian of Boston: William Monroe Trotter* (New York: Atheneum, 1970), pp. 140–141, 175–176, 179–187; Duster, *Crusade*, pp. 375–377; Chicago *Broad Ax*, 29 November 1913, 9 January 1915; *Chicago Defender*, 21 November 1914, 9 January 1915; *Washington Bee*, 13, 14 June 1914. See also Nancy J. Weiss, "The Negro and the New Freedom: Fighting Wilsonian Segregation," *Political Science Quarterly* 84 (March 1969), pp. 61–79; Christine A. Lunardini, "Standing Firm: William Monroe Trotter's Meetings with Woodrow Wilson, 1913–1914," *Journal of Negro History* 64 (Summer 1979), pp. 244–264; August Meier and Elliott Rudwick, "The Rise of Segregation in the Federal Bureaucracy, 1900–1930," *Phylon* 28 (Summer 1967), pp. 178–184.

6. For example, in 1915 she wrote two letters to the renowned black author Charles W. Chestnutt on NFL letterhead asking him to speak to the NERL.

7. *Chicago Defender*, 29 March, 19 April 1913.

8. Chicago *Broad Ax*, 22 February 1913, 16, 23 January, 27 February 1915, 17 August 1918; *Chicago Defender*, 9, 16 January, 27 February, 17 April 1915, 16 September 1916, 29 September 1917. At the 1917 meeting in New York, Wells-Barnett stayed with

Madam C. J. Walker, whose phenomenal success in the cosmetics business she celebrated in her autobiography. Duster, *Crusade*, pp. 378–379.

9. *Chicago Defender*, 9 April 1910. For Chicago politics see Harold F. Gosnell, *Negro Politicians: The Rise of Negro Politics in Chicago* (Chicago: University of Chicago Press, 1935); Dempsey J. Travis, *An Autobiography of Black Politics* (Chicago: Urban Research Press, 1989); Allan H. Spear, *Black Chicago: The Making of a Negro Ghetto, 1890–1920* (Chicago: University of Chicago Press, 1967). On African Americans in Illinois, see also Donald F. Tingley, *The Structuring of a State: The History of Illinois, 1899–1928* (Chicago: University of Chicago Press, 1980), pp. 281–319.

10. On the suffrage campaign in Illinois see *The Transformation of the Woman Suffrage Movement: The Case of Illinois, 1850–1920* (New Brunswick, NJ: Rutgers University Press, 1986). See also Wanda A. Hendricks, "Ida B. Wells-Barnett and the Alpha Suffrage Club of Chicago," in Marjorie Spruill Wheeler, ed., *One Woman, One Vote: Rediscovering the Woman Suffrage Movement* (Troutdale, OR: New Sage Press, 1995), pp. 263–275.

11. *Chicago Daily Tribune*, 4 March 1913.

12. Chicago *Broad Ax*, 29 March 1913; *Chicago Defender*, 8 March 1913.

13. There have been many excellent studies of the suffrage movement, its attitudes toward race, and the role of black women. Among the ones found most useful for this study are Rosalyn Marian Terborg-Penn, "Afro-Americans in the Struggle for Woman Suffrage," (Ph.D. diss., Howard University, 1977) and "Discontented Black Feminists: Prelude and Postscript to the Passage of the Nineteenth Amendment," in Darlene Clark Hine, Wilma King, Linda Reed, eds., *"We Specialize in the Wholly Impossible": A Reader in Black Women's History* (New York: Carlson, 1995); Aileen S. Kraditor, *The Ideas of the Woman Suffrage Movement, 1890–1920* (New York: Columbia University Press, 1965); Eleanor Flexner, *Century of Struggle: The Woman's Rights Movement in the United States* (Cambridge: Harvard University Press, 1975); Wanda Ann Hendricks, "The Politics of Race: Black Women in Illinois, 1890–1920," (Ph.D. diss., Purdue University, 1990); Steven M. Buechler, *Women's Movements in the United States: Woman Suffrage, Equal Rights, and Beyond* (New Brunswick, NJ: Rutgers University Press, 1990); Willie Mae Coleman, "Keeping the Faith and Disturbing the Peace. Black Women: From Anti-Slavery to Women's Suffrage," (Ph.D. diss., University of California, Irvine, 1982). On issues of race and class in the feminist movement also see bell hooks, *Ain't I a Woman, black women and feminism* (Boston: South End Press, 1981); Angela Y. Davis, *Women, Race, & Class* (New York: Random House, 1983); Nancie Caraway, *Segregated Sisterhood, Racism and the Politics of American Feminism* (Knoxville: University of Tennessee Press, 1991); Barbara Hilkert Andolsen, *"Daughters of Jefferson, Daughters of Bootblacks": Racism in American Feminism* (Macon, GA: Mercer University Press, 1986).

14. Duster, *Crusade*, p. 230.

15. Ida Husted Harper to Mary Church Terrell, 18 March 1919, Mary Church Terrell Papers, Library of Congress.

16. *Chicago Defender*, 5 July 1913, 15 April, 9 May 1914.

17. Ibid., 30 March 1912; John D. Buenker, "The Urban Political Machine and Woman Suffrage: A Study in Political Adaptability," *Historian* 33 (February 1971), pp. 267–268.

18. "The Suffrage Conquest of Illinois," *Literary Digest* 46 (28 June 1913), pp. 1409–1411; *Chicago Defender*, 19 July 1913.

19. "Suffrage Conquest," p. 1410; *Chicago Defender*, 23 August 1913; Chicago *Broad Ax*, 14 June 1913.

20. Duster, *Crusade*, p. 346; *Chicago Defender*, 29 November 1913, 18 April 1914; Jean Fagan Yellin, "DuBois' *Crisis* and Woman's Suffrage," *Massachusetts Review* 14 (Spring 1973), pp. 365–375; Bettina Aptheker, "W. E. B. Du Bois & the Struggle for Women's Rights: 1910–1920," *San Jose Studies* 1 (May 1975), pp. 7–16.

21. *Chicago Defender*, 7 February 1914; Chicago *Broad Ax*, 7 February 1914.

22. Duster, *Crusade*, pp. 346–347; Katherine E. Williams, "The Alpha Suffrage Club," *Half-Century Magazine* (September 1916), p. 12.

23. *Chicago Defender*, 12 September, 3, 10, 17, 31 October 1914; Chicago *Broad Ax*, 22 November 1913; 27 June, 12 September, 3, 10, 17, 24, 31 October, 7 November 1914.

24. Chicago *Broad Ax*, 6 February 1915; *Alpha Suffrage Record*, 18 March 1915 (misdated 18 March 1914), copy in the Ida B. Wells Papers, University of Chicago; *Chicago Defender*, 2 January, 6, 13 February 1915; Oscar DePriest, "Chicago and Woman's Suffrage," *Crisis* 10 (August 1915), p. 179.

25. Duster, *Crusade*, pp. 348–352.

26. Ibid., p. 352; Gosnell, *Negro Politicians*, pp. 40–41, 50.

27. Duster, *Crusade*, pp. 348, 351–353.

28. *Chicago Defender*, 14 October 1916.

29. *Chicago Defender*, 27 January 1917, 9 March 1918; for the multiplicity of ASC activities see both the *Chicago Defender* and the Chicago *Broad Ax*, which carried announcements of ASC meetings on a regular basis.

30. *Chicago Defender*, 6 August 1913; Chicago *Broad Ax*, 8, 15 February 1913; George Washington Ellis to Ida B. Wells-Barnett, 13 February 1913, George Washington Ellis Papers in the Irene McCoy Gaines Papers, Chicago Historical Society. Both major black papers in Chicago chronicled her many activities.

31. *Chicago Defender*, 19 March 1910, 25 July, 17 October 1914. The *Chicago Tribune* letter was quoted in the *Chicago Defender*, 9 May 1914.

32. See Elliott M. Rudwick, *Race Riot at East St. Louis, July 2, 1917* (Carbondale: Southern Illinois University Press, 1964). Contemporary accounts include: "The Illinois Race War and Its Brutal Aftermath," *Current Opinion* (August 1917), pp. 75–77; *St. Louis Post-Dispatch*, 3 July 1917; *Chicago Defender*, 2 June, 7 July 1917; "East St. Louis Race Riots," *Literary Digest* (14 July 1917), pp. 10–11.

33. There are two extensive accounts of Wells-Barnett's actions: Chapter 43 of *Crusade for Justice* and Ida B. Wells-Barnett, *The East St. Louis Massacre, The Greatest Outrage of the Century*, a pamphlet published by the NFL in 1917. (A copy can be found in the Military Intelligence Division Papers, National Archives.) Among the most useful of the numerous newspaper reports of her efforts are *Chicago Herald*, 6 July 1917, and Chicago *Broad Ax*, 28 July 1917.

34. *St. Louis Post-Dispatch*, 3 July 1917.

35. Chicago *Broad Ax*, 27 October 1917.

36. *Chicago Defender*, 2 March 1918.

37. Ibid., 13, 20, 27 October, 1 December 1917, 19 January, 16 February 1918.

38. Some of the cases in which they became involved included winning reprieves from death sentences for David Shanks, J. K. Smith, and John Cloures; blocking extradition of Lee Chamber and Emile Nixon; defending Marcus Garvey in a civil suit in Chicago; and seeking a fair trial for the renowned black boxer, Jack Johnson, who was

famous outside of the ring for his relationships with white women. *Chicago Defender*, 23 November 1912, 15 September, 6 October 1917, 4 May, 22 June 1918, 16 February 1929.

39. Duster, *Crusade*, pp. 388, 392–395; *Chicago Defender*, 13 November 1917, 17 August 1918.

40. Hinton G. Claybaugh to A. Bruce Bielaski, 5 July 1917, Bureau File OG37586, Record Group 65, National Archives; Wells-Barnett, *East St. Louis*, p. 23; Ralph A. Hayes to Inspector General, 24 November 1917, Military Intelligence Division (MID) File 10218-60, Record Group 165, National Archives.

41. The best source is C. M. D. Ellis, "'Negro Subversion': The Investigation of Black Unrest and Radicalism by Agencies of the United States Government, 1917–1920" (Ph.D. diss., University of Aberdeen, 1984). The MID files comprise six rolls of microfilm on "Negro Subversion," but the Bureau files on black activity are largely intermixed with others in what is known as the Old German Files.

42. Memorandum for Lieut. Col. Pakenham, 21 December 1918, MID File 10213-61.

43. Bulletin No. 33, enclosed in W. H. Loving to Chief, Military Intelligence Branch, 16 April 1918, MID File 10218-120. On the Houston riot, see Robert V. Haynes, *A Night of Violence: The Houston Riot of 1919* (Baton Rouge: Louisiana State University Press, 1976).

44. A succinct account of the grievances of African Americans regarding the executions can be found in Mary Church Terrell to Newton D. Baker, undated copy of a letter found in the Mary Church Terrell Papers, Library of Congress. MID files contain many references to the events, including a report of the visit to a victim's mother in W. H. Loving to Chief, Military Intelligence Branch, 5 February 1918, MID File 10218-102.

45. Duster, *Crusade*, pp. 367–370.

46. W. H. Loving to Director of Military Intelligence, 20 December 1918, MID File 10218-302; "British Secret Report on Unrest Among the Negroes," 7 October 1919, MID File 10218-378.

47. See Jane L Scheiber and Henry N. Scheiber, "The Wilson Administration and the Wartime Mobilization of Black Americans, 1917–18," *Labor History* 10 (Summer 1969), pp. 433–458; William J. Breen, "Black Women and the Great War: Mobilization and Reform in the South," *Journal of Southern History* 44 (August 1978),   pp. 421–440.

48. Chicago *Broad Ax*, 22 December 1917, 5 October, 21 December 1918.

Chapter 17

1. W. H. Loving to Director, Military Intelligence, 23 December 1918, Military Intelligence Division File 12218-274, Record Group 165, National Archives.

2. Marcus Garvey, "West Indies in the Mirror of Truth," *Champion Magazine* 1 (January 1917), pp. 167–168, reprinted in Cary D. Wintz, *African American Political Thought, 1890–1930, Washington, DuBois, Garvey, and Randolph* (London: M. E. Sharpe, 1996), p. 186. Alfreda M. Duster, ed., *Crusade for Justice, The Autobiography of Ida B. Wells* (Chicago: University of Chicago Press, 1970), p. 380; *Chicago Defender*, 18 November 1916; On Garvey see Judith Stein, *The World of Marcus Garvey*,

Race and Class in Modern Society (Baton Rouge: Louisiana State University Press, 1986); Tony Martin, *Race First: The Ideological and Organizational Struggles of Marcus Garvey and the Universal Negro Improvement Association* (Dover, MA: Majority Press, 1976); E. David Cronon, *Black Moses: The Story of Marcus Garvey and the Universal Negro Improvement League* (Madison: University of Wisconsin Press, 1955).

3. Report of D. Davidson to Special Agent Finch, 5 December 1918, MID File 10218-261.

4. Duster, *Crusade*, pp. 380–382; Chicago *Broad Ax*, 4 October, 15 November 1919; *Chicago Defender*, 21 January 1922. Garvey and Wells-Barnett saw each other as victims of the jealousy of Du Bois. An editorial in the UNIA paper claimed that Du Bois had stolen Wells-Barnett's antilynching crusade and failed to give her credit. *Negro World*, 1 October 1921.

5. W. H. Loving to Director of Military Intelligence, 20 December 1918, MID File 10218-302; Duster, *Crusade*, pp. 379–380. Chicago *Broad Ax*, 21 December 1918; Also see Stephen R. Fox, *The Guardian of Boston: William Monroe Trotter* (New York: Atheneum, 1970), pp. 221–225.

6. W. H. Loving to Director of Military Intelligence, 20 December 1918, MID File 10218-261.

7. M. Churchill to Chief of Staff, 20 August 1919, MID File 10218-361; J. E. Cutler to Director of Military Intelligence, 18 August 1919, enclosed in MID File 10218-361; Wrisley Brown to Lieut. Col. Pakeham, 21 December 1918, MID file 10218-261; W. H. Loving to Director of Military Intelligence, 20 December 1918, MID File 10218-302.

8. Chicago *Broad Ax*, 4 January 1919; *Washington Bee*, 2 August 1919. MID agent Loving lamented that Trotter's influence had been waning until the manner in which he tricked the government "revived his former influence." W. H. Loving to Director of Military Intelligence, 6 August 1919, enclosed in MID File 10218-361. A year later the *Broad Ax* was still gloating over how "Mr. Trotter beat President Wilson with both hands down" in its 14 August 1920 edition.

9. *Chicago Whip*, 28 June 1919. On the conditions in Chicago see William M. Tuttle, Jr., "Contested Neighborhoods and Racial Violence: Prelude to the Chicago Riot of 1919," *Journal of Negro History* 55 (October 1970), pp. 266–288 and *Race Riot: Chicago in the Red Summer of 1919* (New York: Atheneum, 1970). Sources on the riot include Chicago Commission on Race Relations, *The Negro in Chicago* (Chicago: University of Chicago Press, 1922).

10. *Chicago Tribune*, 7, 23 July 1919; Chicago *Broad Ax*, 7 June 1919.

11. Duster, *Crusade*, pp. 405–408; *Report of the National Advisory Commission on Civil Disorders* (New York: Bantam Books, 1968), p. 29; "Interview with Alfreda Duster, March 8 and 9, 1978," Black Women Oral History Project, Schlesinger Library, Radcliff College, p. 36. Wells-Barnett's autobiographical treatment of the Chicago riot seems not only brief but also rather disjointed and unfocused.

12. Thomas B. Crockett to Director of Military Intelligence, 20 October 1919, MID File 10218-377.

13. See Ida B. Wells-Barnett, *The Arkansas Race Riot* (Chicago, 1919); Walter White, "The Race Conflict in Arkansas," *Survey* 43 (13 December 1919), pp. 233–234; O. A. Rogers, "The Elaine Race Riots of 1919," *Arkansas Historical Quarterly* 19 (Summer 1960), pp. 142–150.

14. Duster, *Crusade*, pp. 397–403. Another account of her speech to the prisoners is found on page 5 of her pamphlet about the riot (see note 13).

15. Duster, *Crusade*, pp. 355–358.

16. Ibid., p. 373; Dorothy Salem, *To Better Our World: Black Women in Organized Reform* (New York: Carlson, 1990), pp. 185–189. On the National Urban League, see Nancy J. Weiss, *The National Urban League, 1910–1940* (New York: Oxford University Press, 1974); Arvah E. Strickland, *History of the Chicago Urban League* (Urbana: University of Illinois Press, 1966); and Guichard Parris and Lester Brooks, *Blacks in the City: A History of the National Urban League* (Boston: Little, Brown, 1971).

17. "Negro Agitation," 25 August 1919, Bureau File OG3057, Record Group 65, National Archives; Allan H. Spear, *Black Chicago: The Making of a Negro Ghetto, 1890–1920* (Chicago: University of Chicago Press, 1967), pp. 169–174. Some of the activities that lost Wells-Barnett business and government support included an investigation of discrimination by the Council of Defense in registering workers for employment in the munitions factory and a scheme with Trotter to recruit black workers for employment in France. *Chicago Defender*, 22, 29 June 1918; "To the Young Men Who Want to Go to France," flyer in Ida B. Wells Papers, University of Chicago Library.

18. Duster, *Crusade*, p. 372; Chapter LXV, p. 4, typewritten manuscript, Wells Papers.

19. *Chicago Defender*, 1 January 1921; Chicago *Broad Ax*, 26 March 1921; Duster, *Crusade*, p. 414; *Chicago Defender*, 22 January, 5 February 1921.

20. Duster, *Crusade*, p. xxx; *Chicago Defender*, 8 April, 19 June 1920; Chicago *Broad Ax*, 13, 20 November 1920; Mother to My Dear Folks, letter dated 30 October 1920, Wells Papers.

21. Mother to My Dear Folks, letter dated 30 October 1920, Wells Papers.

22. *Chicago Defender*, 31 December 1921; Chapter 8, p. 7, typescript by Alfreda Duster in Wells Papers; Duster, *Crusade*, p. xxx. Alfreda Duster indicated the move in the preface to the autobiography, but the personal information given at the beginning of Wells-Barnett's 1930 diary gives her address as being the old one at 3624 Grand—then it changed to S. Parkway. Perhaps the Barnetts rented out the larger house for awhile and then returned.

23. *Chicago Defender*, 23 September 1922, 6 December 1930; *The Signers of the National Conference on Lynching* (New York, 1919). For more on the antilynching crusade, see Robert L. Zangrando, *The NAACP Crusade Against Lynching, 1909–1950* (Philadelphia: Temple University Press, 1980); Donald L. Grant, "The Development of the Anti-Lynching Reform Movement in the United States: 1883–1932," (Ph.D. diss., University of Missouri, Columbia, 1972).

24. Chicago *Broad Ax*, 19 January, 23 August 1924; Duster, *Crusade*, p. xxvii; "Duster Interview," p. 34.

25. Quotes are from the *Chicago Defender*, 9 January 1926. *Chicago Broad Ax*, 14 January 1925, 30 January 1926; *Chicago Defender*, 5 February, 5 March, 10 December 1927, 16 February 1929.

26. *Chicago Defender*, 9 July 1927; see also 11 June and 16 July 1927.

27. *Chicago Defender*, 7 April, 22 December 1928, 10 August 1929.

28. Chicago *Broad Ax*, 9 October 1920, 18 October 1924; Lethia Fleming to

Claude A. Barnett, 23 October 1928, Box 333, Claude Barnett Papers, Chicago Historical Society; Minutes of the National League of Republican Colored Women, 9 August
1924, Nannie Helen Burroughs papers, Library of Congress.

29. Press release for 2 August, Box 334, Barnett Papers.

30. P. L. Prattis to Claude Barnett, 8 August 1928, Box 333, Barnett papers.

31. "Republican National Headquarters Opened in Chicago," unidentified newspaper clipping, Box 338 and Lethia Fleming to Claude A. Barnett, 23 October 1928,
Box 333, Barnett Papers.

32. Calling card, Wells Papers; Ida B. Wells-Barnett to Claude Barnett, 19 Octo-
ber 1928; Ida B. Wells-Barnett, *Why I am for Hoover* (1920), Ida B. Wells-Barnett
Folder, Chicago Historical Society; "Veteran Woman Politician Addresses Club
Women," unidentified clipping, Box 338, Barnett Papers. A month after Simmons told
Wells-Barnett that he had no money for her, a newspaper published a long list of indi-
viduals receiving weekly payments ranging from $50 to $125. *Chicago Defender*, 10
November 1928.

33. Ida B. Wells-Barnett to Claude Barnett, undated but probably 21 October
1928, Box 333, Barnett Papers; Ida B. Wells-Barnett to Claude Barnett, 21 October
1928, Wells Folder, Chicago Historical Society.

34. No relation to Ferdinand, Claude Barnett was the founder of a black press service—the Associated Negro Press. See Lawrence D. Hogan, *A Black National News
Service: The Associated Negro Press and Claude Barnett, 1919–1945* (Cranbury, NJ: Associated University Presses, 1984).

35. *Chicago Defender*, 5, 12, 19 October 1929.

36. Ida B. Wells-Barnett's 1930 diary, 24, 27 January; 3, 12 February, 19 May,
Wells Papers; *Chicago Defender*, 8 March, 10 April 1930; State of Illinois, *Tabulated
Statements of Canvass of Returns, Cook County*, 8 April 1930.

37. *Chicago Defender*, 1 March, 3 May, 26 April, 10 May, 27 September 1930, 3
January 1931; 1930 diary, 6 January, 19 May 1930.

38. 1930 diary, 7, 9 January, 19 May 1930.

39. *Chicago Defender*, 23, 30 April, 7, 14 May 1930; 1930 diary, 13 January. Two
hundred of the city's elite turned out for the banquet jointly honoring them in May.

40. Duster, *Crusade*, pp. 3–5.

41. *Chicago Defender*, 4 April 1931.

42. Ibid. According to Lucy B. Miller, a friend and neighbor of the Barnetts, Ferdinand refused to let any of the other Chicago clubwomen participate in the funeral because of how they had treated his wife while she was alive. Interview, Lucy B. Miller, 19
February 1941, quoted in Eunice Rivers Walker, "Ida B. Wells-Barnett, Her Contribution to the Field of Social Welfare" (MSW thesis, Loyola University, 1941), p. 78. Ferdinand Barnett moved in with his youngest daughter, Alfreda Duster, soon after his
wife's death and remained there for the last five years of his life. Alfreda M. Duster to
Dr. Luther P. Jackson, Jr., 3 March 1971, Wells Papers.

43. Irene McCoy Gaines, "Mother of Clubs," 30 March 1931, Irene McCoy
Gaines Papers, Chicago Historical Society; W. E. B. Du Bois, "Postscript," *Crisis* (June
1931), p. 207.

44. Ida B. Wells-Barnett, "The New Year," 1 January 1931, typescript in Ida B.
Wells Papers.

WRITINGS ABOUT
IDA B. WELLS-BARNETT

Adams, Samuel L. "Ida B. Wells: A Founder Who Knew Her Place." *Crisis* 101 (January 1994): pp. 43–44.

Aptheker, Bettina. "Lynching and Rape: An Exchange of Views," *Occasional Paper* 25 (1977).

——. "The Suppression of the *Free Speech*: Ida B. Wells and the Memphis Lynching, 1892." *San Jose Studies* 3 (1977): pp. 34–40.

Boyd, Joyce. "Review Essay: Canon Configuration for Ida B. Wells-Barnett." *Black Scholar* 24 (Winter 1991): pp. 8–20.

Braxton, Joanne M. *Black Women Writing Autobiography: A Tradition Within a Tradition.* Philadelphia: Temple University Press, 1989.

Campbell, Karlyn Kohrs. "Style and Content in the Rhetoric of Early Afro-American Feminists." *Quarterly Journal of Speech* 72 (1986): pp. 434–445.

Carby, Hazel V. "'On the Threshold of the Woman's Era': Lynching, Empire, and Sexuality in Black Feminist Theory." *Critical Inquiry* 12 (Autumn 1985): pp. 262–277.

Davis, Simone W. "The 'Weak Race' and the Winchester: Political Voices in Pamphlets of Ida B. Wells-Barnett." *Legacy* 12 (1995): pp. 77–89.

DeCosta-Willis, Miriam. *The Memphis Diary of Ida B. Wells.* Boston: Beacon Press, 1995.

DeMott, John. "Ida B. Wells, Journalist." *Grassroots Editor* 30 (Fall 1989): pp. 20–32.

Duster, Alfreda M., ed. *Crusade for Justice, The Autobiography of Ida B. Wells.* Chicago: University of Chicago Press, 1970.

Franklin, V. P. *Living Our Stories, Telling Our Truths: Autobiography and the Making of the African American Intellectual Tradition.* New York: Scribner, 1995.

Giddings, Paula. *When and Where I Enter: The Impact of Black Women on Race and Sex in America.* New York: William Morrow, 1984.

——. "Ida Wells-Barnett." In *Portraits of American Women from the Civil War to the Present,* edited by G. J. Barker-Benfield and Catherine Clinton. New York: St. Martin's Press, 1991.

Harris, Trudier, comp. *Selected Works of Ida B. Wells-Barnett.* New York: Oxford University Press, 1991.

Hendricks, Wanda A. "Ida B. Wells-Barnett and the Alpha Suffrage Club of Chicago." In *One Woman, One Vote: Rediscovering the Woman Suffrage Movement,* edited by Marjorie Spruill Wheeler. Troutdale, OR: New Sage Press, 1995.

——. "The Politics of Race: Black Women in Illinois, 1890–1920." Ph.D. diss., Purdue University, 1990.

Holt, Thomas. "The Lonely Warrior: Ida B. Wells-Barnett and the Struggle for Black Leadership." In *Black Leaders of the Twentieth Century,* edited by John Hope Franklin and August Meier. Chicago: University of Chicago Press, 1982.

Humrich, Shauna L. "Ida B. Wells-Barnett: The Making of a Public Reputation." *Purview Southeast* (1989): pp. 1–20.

Hutton, Mary Magdelene Boone. "The Rhetoric of Ida B. Wells: The Genesis of the Anti-Lynch Movement." Ph.D. diss., Indiana University, 1975.

"Interview with Alfred Duster, 8 and 9 March 1978," Black Women Oral History Project. Schlesinger Library, Radcliff College.

Logan, Shirley W. "Rhetorical Strategies in Ida B. Wells's *Southern Horrors: Lynch Law in All Its Phases.*" *Sage* 8 (Summer 1991): pp. 3–9.

Loewenberg, Bert James, and Bogin, Ruth. *Black Women in Nineteenth-Century Life.* University Park: Pennsylvania State University Press, 1976.

Majors, Monroe A. *Noted Negro Women: Their Triumphs and Activities.* Chicago: Donohue & Henneberry, 1893.

Mossell, Mrs. N. F. *The Work of the Afro-American Woman,* 2d. ed. Philadelphia: Geo. S. Ferguson, 1908.

Northrop, Henry Davenport. *The College of Life; or Practical Self-Educator: A Manual of Self-Improvement of the Colored Race.* Chicago: Publication & Lithograph, 1895.

Ochiai, Akiko. "Ida B. Wells and Her Crusade for Justice: An African American Woman's Testimonial Autobiography." *Soundings* 75 (Summer/Fall 1992): pp. 365–382.

Peebles-Wilkins, Wilma, and Aracelis, Fran. "Two Outstanding Women in Social Welfare History: Mary Church Terrell and Ida B. Wells-Barnett." *Affilia* 5 (Winter 1990): pp. 87–95.

Penn, I. Garland. *The Afro-American Press and Its Editors.* Springfield, MA: Wiley & Co., 1891.

Royster, Jacqueline Jones. *Southern Horrors and Other Writings: The Anti-Lynching Campaign of Ida B. Wells, 1892–1900.* Boston: Bedford Books, 1997.

Schechter, Patricia Ann. "'To Tell the Truth Freely': Ida B. Wells and the Politics of Race, Gender, and Reform in America, 1880–1913." Ph.D. diss., Princeton University, 1993.

Scruggs, L. A. *Women of Distinction.* Raleigh, NC: L. A. Scruggs Publisher, 1893.

Sterling, Dorothy. *Black Foremothers: Three Lives.* New York: Feminist Press, 1988.

————. *We Are Your Sisters: Black Women in the Nineteenth Century.* New York: W. W. Norton, 1984.

Streitmatter, Roger. *Raising Her Voice, African-American Women Journalists Who Changed History.* Lexington: University of Kentucky Press, 1994.

Thompson, Mildred I. *Ida B. Wells-Barnett, An Exploratory Study of an American Black Woman, 1893–1930.* New York: Carlson Publishing, 1990.

Townes, Emilie Maureen. "The Social and Moral Perspectives of Ida B. Wells-Barnett as Resources for a Contemporary Afro-American Christian Social Ethic." Ph.D. diss., Northwestern University, 1989.

————. *Womanist Justice, Womanist Hope.* Atlanta: Scholars Press, 1993.

Trimiew, Darryl M. *Voices of the Silenced, The Responsible Self in a Marginalized Community.* Cleveland: Pilgrim Press, 1994.

Tucker, David M. "Miss Ida B. Wells and Memphis Lynching," *Phylon* 32 (Summer 1971): pp. 112–122.

Wade-Gayles, Gloria. "Black Women Journalists in the South, 1880–1905." In *Black Women in the United States,* edited by Darlene Clark Hine. Vol. 4. New York: Carlson Publishing Co., 1990.

Walker, Eunice Rivers. "Ida B. Wells-Barnett, Her Contribution to the Field of Social Welfare." MSW thesis, Loyola University, 1941.

Wood, Norman B. *The White Side of a Black Subject.* Chicago: American Publishing House, 1897.

INDEX